ENTREPRENEURSHIP
STRATEGY

To Peter, Dylan, and Austin,
for your love and support in life's entrepreneurial journey, and to
my parents, Helga and Hal, for showing me the world and being my guiding light.
—*Lisa*

To my father, Ralph Richard, and mother, Angela Richard.
For their relentless pursuit of their own dreams—thank
you both for showing me early on your entrepreneurial spirit and passion.
—*Jill*

ENTREPRENEURSHIP
STRATEGY

Changing Patterns in New Venture Creation, Growth, and Reinvention

LISA K. GUNDRY
DePaul University

JILL R. KICKUL
Miami University

SAGE Publications
Thousand Oaks ■ London ■ New Delhi

For information:

Sage Publications, Inc.
2455 Teller Road
Thousand Oaks, California 91320
E-mail: order@sagepub.com

Sage Publications Ltd.
1 Oliver's Yard
55 City Road
London EC1Y 1SP
United Kingdom

Sage Publications India Pvt. Ltd.
B-42, Panchsheel Enclave
Post Box 4109
New Delhi 110 017 India

Printed in the United States of America.

Library of Congress Cataloging-in-Publication Data

Gundry, Lisa K.
Entrepreneurship strategy: changing patterns in new venture creation, growth, and reinvention / Lisa K. Gundry, Jill R. Kickul.
    p. cm.
Includes bibliographical references and index.
ISBN 1-4129-1656-9, 978-1-4129-1656-1 (cloth)
   1. Strategic planning. 2. Entrepreneurship. 3. Small business—Management.
I. Kickul, Jill R. II. Title.
HD30.28.G8359 2007
658.4′21—dc22

                                        2006003793

This book is printed on acid-free paper.

06   07   08   09   10   10   9   8   7   6   5   4   3   2   1

Acquisitions Editor:	Al Bruckner
Editorial Assistant:	MaryAnn Vail
Project Editor:	Tracy Alpern
Associate Editors:	Katja Werlich Fried
	Deya Saoud
Copy Editor:	Jacqueline Tasch
Typesetter:	C&M Digitals (P) Ltd.
Proofreader:	Joyce Li
Indexer:	David Luljak
Cover Designer:	Edgar Abarca

Contents

Foreword

For me, entrepreneurship is a religion, a way of life, a passion. I think I have always been an entrepreneur at heart, even before I knew what it really meant or had heard the word used in business. In my corporate life, many of my bosses probably thought I was just a pain, the squeaky wheel who was always trying to break, bend, or change the rules. In retrospect, I now realize those are the very same qualities that have helped me succeed as an entrepreneur: the scrappiness, resourcefulness, healthy dose of skepticism, ability to question authority without backing down, persistence, sense of humor, and humility. It takes some of each, I think, to see the world differently, discover new ways to solve old dilemmas, or redefine problems and solutions altogether.

What makes these entrepreneurs tick? Why do they keep picking themselves up when they get knocked down? What causes them to try again? In *Entrepreneurship Strategy: Changing Patterns in New Venture Creation, Growth, and Reinvention,* you will get to see a range of entrepreneurs in action. Each has a unique style, his or her own journey but there are many traits that are shared. Some entrepreneurs started their companies when another door closed; others had a burning idea that needed a home; all set out to change the world in some important way.

I took one entrepreneurial management class in business school, and we reviewed case studies of entrepreneurs in all shapes and sizes. There was no textbook for the class, only their personal journeys and stories of their successes and failures from which to draw lessons. Some entrepreneurs were self-trained; others had degrees; all were passionate about what they were doing. Whether you are an entrepreneur yourself, have one in your family, or just wondered what all the hype was about, it is reassuring to see that there is some science behind the art of entrepreneurship. Although it may seem very "seat of the pants" at times, there are stages and common themes most entrepreneurs address as they are taking their vision from concept to reality. Drs. Gundry and Kickul's book shows many entrepreneurial paths, starting from very different places. There is no single way to be an entrepreneur; lots of roads can get you there.

Each entrepreneur had to validate his or her idea with the target audience, whether through formal market research or not. All had a defining moment when they knew their business was "real" or had to course-correct to survive. Once the market is validated, competitors start to pay attention so entrepreneurs have to stay relevant and ahead of the pack to have a competitive offer. An entrepreneur never sleeps long enough. The wheels are always turning, but that is what makes it so fun and exciting; entrepreneurs never get bored.

Entrepreneurship is part art, part science, always intoxicating. Once you get bitten, it is hard to go back to a desk job. Corporate America has its perks, but entrepreneurs tend to upset the apple cart in most corporations—unless they started the company as did Richard Branson, Donald Trump, Oprah Winfrey, the list goes on. What makes people successful, inspiring, and magnetic entrepreneurs also makes them tough to manage and direct as employees. At some point in their careers, entrepreneurs put their money where their mouth is and do it their way. Whether they are motivated by fear, guilt, greed, or passion, they are indeed motivated to succeed, and the real ones don't stop until they do.

From the very first chapter of this book, you will find an underlying model to help budding entrepreneurs add to their skills by using the Innovator's Toolkit exercises. Understanding the book's Strategic Reflection Points and completing the Strategy in Action checklist help to increase the probability of the new venture becoming a success. These things take time, however, and Drs. Gundry and Kickul's book gives you the framework, tools, pitfalls, and success stories to help navigate and demystify the process. Entrepreneurship is a journey that lasts a lifetime for many of us who were bitten by the bug. I have never met an overnight sensation, but I know plenty of entrepreneurs who perfect their craft over and over again. It permeates every aspect of their lives in most cases. The motivation must come from within to be authentic. In my experience, if you don't have it on the inside, you cannot make it on the outside.

Every person spotlighted in this book had days, weeks, months, or in some cases years when no one else saw the potential in the opportunity they could envision. Sometimes, all it takes is reconnecting the dots in a different way to show others the path. Having a road map to get those creative juices flowing can be just the thought-starter to get the engine fired up again. Drs. Gundry and Kickul's book may just be that kick in the pants needed for your entrepreneurial wheels to turn faster or in a different direction. You'll be inspired by the entrepreneurs showcased, and if you pay attention, you can learn from their mistakes so that you can make other higher quality ones along your entrepreneurial journey.

So join the conversation, grab a seat at the table, and let your mind wander with all the possibilities among us to leave the world better than we found it with our unique mark. I truly believe entrepreneurship could solve many of the world's biggest problems. People who are excited to get up in the morning and think about new products or services or innovative techniques to deliver them to new audiences will have more energy, healthier habits, sharper minds, and more optimistic outlooks, I think. They will create opportunities for others and constantly challenge the status quo so that inertia will not kick in. So my recommendation: Take two books, read one, pass along the other to someone you care about, and call me in the morning!

—*Paige Arnof-Fenn*
Founder and CEO, Mavens & Moguls, www.mavensandmoguls.com

Acknowledgments

The writing of this text was in itself an entrepreneurial journey, and without the key support we received from many people professionally and personally, this work would never have come to life.

First, we owe a debt of gratitude to our gifted editorial team at Sage Publications. Al Bruckner, Senior Acquisitions Editor, gave us the encouragement to write a textbook founded on the spirit of innovation and creativity that drives entrepreneurship around the world. Al's leadership of this project was outstanding, and we thank him for all his efforts along the way. In addition, Katja Fried and Deya Saoud, our Associate Editors, and MaryAnn Vail, Senior Editorial Assistant, guided a smooth review and revision process that helped us create a much-improved final manuscript for which future students will surely be grateful. We feel much appreciation for the anonymous reviewers who provided extensive feedback on each chapter. Their perspectives, drawn from years of classroom and research experience, were of great value in shaping this book for multiple audiences and cultures. Tracy Alpern, our Project Editor, and Jacqueline Tasch, Copy Editor, came on board, and we are grateful for their efforts to take this book from paper to press, and we extend our heartfelt thanks for all the hard work that our publication team exerted on our behalf.

Many of the theories and practices that unfold in this book grow out of the work of our academic colleagues and entrepreneur-practitioners we have come to know. Our work has been influenced by entrepreneurship and management scholars who deserve recognition: Professors Jerry Katz (Saint Louis University), Teresa Nelson (Simmons School of Management), and Norris Krueger (TEAMS/Entrepreneurship Northwest). Special thanks to Professors Vipin Gupta and Cynthia Ingols (Simmons School of Management) and to Professor Laurence Weinstein (Sacred Heart University) for permitting us to reprint their cases. Special thanks to DePaul Professors Scott Young, Harold Welsch, Gerhard Plaschka, Patrick Murphy, Raman Chadha, and Br. Leo V. Ryan, C.S.V., Professor Emeritus, for creating and sustaining an environment in which entrepreneurship thrives—inside and outside the classroom. Thank you to the entrepreneurial leadership at Simmons College, including Dean Deborah Merrill-Sands and Professor Fiona Wilson.

Many entrepreneurs gave generously of their time and knowledge and deserve special recognition. Paige Arnof-Fenn, who kindly contributed the Foreword and allowed us to reprint one of her columns from *Entrepreneur* magazine, lent her expertise to this book to enhance its relevancy to the complex and dynamic world of the entrepreneur. Other entrepreneurs graciously allowed us to enter inside the world of their businesses and to interview them for cases and vignettes. They include: Lisa Santos, Southport Grocery and Café; Jacqueline Corbett Cyr, Corbett Cyr Consulting; Matthew Hinson, Wakeworks Staffing; Andy Szatko, Grassroots Landscaping; Adam Makos, Ghost Wings; Joseph Keeley, College Nannies & Tutors; Julie E. LeMoine, U C How Technologies; Gretchen Fox, FOX Relocation Management; Joyce Amaral, Yomega Corporation; Laura McCann, Zweave; Annette Ricci, Reel-EZ Display; Charles (Chuck) Stack and Prasad Kodukula, Constant Compliance (2Ci); Carolyn Sanchez Crozier, CS&C-Julex Learning; and Addie Swartz, B*tween Productions, Inc. Special thanks to Kathleen Elliott, Angel Investor; Andrew J. Sherman, Partner, Dickstein Shapiro Morin & Oshinsky LLP; and Marianne Hudson, Kauffman Foundation, for use of materials, and to Sharon Bower (Saint Louis University), who put us in contact with the winners of the Global Student Entrepreneur™ Award Winners interviewed for this book.

Laurel Ofstein, Assistant Director of the Leo V. Ryan Center for Creativity and Innovation at DePaul University, contributed to the formation of this book in extraordinary ways. Her impeccable assistance in interviewing some of the entrepreneurs profiled and in writing the JetBlue and Netflix cases clearly shows in this book, and she did much of the work while she was completing her MBA at DePaul. She served ever patiently as our third set of eyes as we prepared the final manuscript. Thank you, Laurel, from the bottom of our hearts. Thank you to the following students at DePaul University: Bodee Kittikamron, for help organizing permissions needed and passing them on to Laurel and us; and Andres Ayala, Arby Gonzalez, Maria Mendoza, and Anastasiya Oliyar, who allowed us to include the strategic plan they wrote for a course in this book, confirming our belief that students learn much from other students. We are grateful to Raman Chadha, Executive Director of the Coleman Center at DePaul University, for allowing us to reprint entrepreneurial stories from the *Coleman Center Newsletter* as vignettes. At Simmons School of Management, we are grateful for our aspiring women entrepreneurs and for the many insights and perspectives of the Coleman Foundation and John Hancock Financial Fellows, namely Laney Whitcanack and Maureen Vasquez, as well as graduate assistants, Mandy Osborne and Sandra Pomerantz. Finally, a special thanks to Stephen and Carolyn McCandless who in memory of Stephen's sister, Elizabeth J. McCandless, have dedicated and provided continual support to the Simmons entrepreneurship program.

The process of writing, with its continual "visions and revisions," had a way of consuming the hours of our days. Heartfelt thanks, much gratitude, and big hugs go out to our families and dear friends, whose support pushed us, lifted us, and enabled us to create this work: Peter, my sons, Dylan and Austin, and Helga and Hal (for Lisa), and Ralph and Angela Richard (for Jill).

To all those mentioned here and to the many others whose presence has touched our lives and our classrooms, including former and present students, colleagues, mentors, and friends:

Thank you. We remember you always. . . .

Introduction

The entrepreneurship journey is one of the most exciting ones on which you will ever embark. In our combined years of experience teaching students in the United States and several other countries, working with entrepreneurs inside and outside our classrooms and starting and running our own businesses, we have observed that the entrepreneurship start-up and growth process is dynamic and evolutionary. Strategies that have worked in the pre-start-up stage and during the launch of the business will not be satisfactory as the business encounters the challenges of growth or the need for reinvention. We write this book out of the perspective and belief that entrepreneurial strategies evolve and change just as the businesses for which they have been designed grow and change. We also want this book to be a companion for you as you consider entrepreneurship as a career. The first sentence of this Introduction contains the word *exciting*, and, yes, a book on entrepreneurship can—and should—be as exciting and interesting as the process it purports to teach. So, why should you read this book as part of your entrepreneurial studies?

This book presents a framework for strategy in entrepreneurial organizations, a framework that incorporates new venture emergence, early growth, and reinvention and innovation in established ventures. The focus of the text is on *entrepreneurial* strategies that can be crafted and implemented within small and medium-size organizations as these firms proceed through the stages of development. You will not find it helpful to read about strategies deployed in large organizations and then try to "size the strategy down" to fit your small company. In this book, you will learn strategies that fit your business as it starts and grows.

The unique approach of this book is its segmentation of entrepreneurship strategies *across the life cycle* of business growth. Most books on strategy present content that is segmented by the type or level of strategy (e.g., marketing, human resources, production strategies) rather than the changing pattern of strategic needs faced by the new venture.

The book is written from the point of view of you, the founder, and the entrepreneurial team. Increasingly, entrepreneurs are relying on the expertise and input of key stakeholders as they launch and develop their businesses. Whether these stakeholders are outside the firm in the role of advisers or inside in the roles of investors and employees, the entrepreneur's ability to create a powerful and agile team capable of breakthrough thinking shapes the new venture's potential success and growth.

All businesses start with an idea. Ideas grow out of creative inspiration coupled with sound and rigorous analysis. A unique feature of this book is its emphasis on the key strategic roles of creativity, opportunity identification, opportunity evaluation, and innovation in the emergence and growth of entrepreneurial firms. It's not just about creativity in the early days of business start-up; rather, this book will help you maintain the innovative edge throughout the life of the business. Today, this is not just a way to differentiate your business; it's a way to ensure your very survival.

Each chapter contains the following features to enhance learning and application so that you can take the material and use it easily. Here is what you will find in each chapter:

- **Contemporary Cases**—Include several Global Student Entrepreneurs of the Year award winners who launched businesses as college students, cases that are especially relevant for college students.
- **The Innovator's Toolkit**—Designed to enable students to learn and use innovative techniques as they design and implement strategic decisions in organizations.
- **Strategic Reflection Points**—Exercises and discussion points that give students the opportunity to reflect on the material presented and to engage in meaningful discussion with other students or teams.
- **Strategy in Action**—Theme-based vignettes in each chapter that emphasize topical areas and showcase entrepreneurs around the world doing what it is you have just read about.
- **Speaking of Strategy**—Brief interviews and stories of entrepreneurs across industries and stages of growth related to some aspect of the chapter topic.
- **Failures and Foibles**—A box in each chapter that describes mistakes, faulty assumptions, and misperceptions of entrepreneurs related to the chapter theme and highlights the learning that grew out of the failure. We all want to learn from others' experiences.
- **Research in Practice**—A summary of recent research on the chapter topic, stimulating interest in the material and providing linkages to scholarship for the assignment of research papers and topical reviews.

The book is organized into three distinct sections reflective of the entrepreneur's needs and the entrepreneurial firm's stages of development.

Part I: Entrepreneurial Strategies for the Emerging Venture

- **Entrepreneurship and Strategy: A Framework for New Venture Formation**—You will be introduced to the strategic roles of creativity, opportunity identification, opportunity evaluation, and innovation in the emergence and growth of entrepreneurial firms. This strategic approach examines three distinct stages of the entrepreneurship process and provides you with strategies you can use to launch, grow, and revitalize your new venture.

- **Strategies for Opportunity Identification: The Creative Process**—Creative thinking and behavior are vitally important to discovering and refining entrepreneurial opportunities. Becoming more "idea prone," learning how to conduct an effective opportunity SEARCH (a process described in this chapter), and designing an environment for your venture that supports creativity will help you launch and sustain an innovative organization.

- **Strategies for Evaluating Opportunities: The Assessment Process**—Evaluating opportunities and undertaking a feasibility analysis help entrepreneurs determine the new venture's chance to succeed. Several areas for assessment are provided, and you will learn methods to evaluate the initial idea as well as later innovative ideas for the business.

- **Developing New Venture Strategy: Preparation and Launch**—Strategic planning should be an ongoing activity in the new venture. Your strategic vision for the new venture enables you to launch a business with a purpose, and it helps you prepare for crises that can occur in the early stages of new venture development. The vision, and ultimately the strategic plan, should include strategies to manage ethical behavior, of increasing importance today. This leads to several positive outcomes, including building employee and customer loyalty, reducing hiring costs, driving sales, maintaining loyal vendor relationships, and lessening the risks of loss of suppliers and unexpected cost increases. Learn how to construct a code of ethics that supports the business' strategic vision.

- **Market Entry: Positioning the Firm for Strategic Advantage**—Determining your new venture's value solution is an important strategy that will help you keep track of the key drivers in your industry that drive buyer behaviors. You should also construct a perceptual map for your venture that helps you position your products and services competitively within your industry. You will also learn how to develop your go-to-market strategy, which delivers your value solution to your target market in the most creative and effective way possible.

Part II: Entrepreneurial Strategies for the Growing Venture

- **Financial Resource Capabilities**—It's critical to the success of the venture for the entrepreneur to understand financing needs for all stages of the life cycle and to make effective choices regarding debt and equity financing. Venture capital and angel investors have different needs and requirements that should be well understood in order to form appropriate financial partnerships. This involves learning how to conduct a due diligence analysis for your venture.

- **The Evolving Management Team: Capabilities for Nurturing Growth**—Building an effective management team requires entrepreneurial leadership skills that fit the needs of your growing venture. These include the ability to select and retain team members and employees, identify an appropriate set of advisers and directors, and choose the right legal structure for the growing business.

- **Building Networks and Strategic Alliances**—Developing strategic alliances of good "fit" helps you facilitate your business's initiatives, capabilities, and resources. Social capital, acquired through personal and professional networks, is an especially valuable type of resource; it includes ideas, knowledge, information, opportunities, contacts, and referrals.

Part III: Entrepreneurial Strategies for Sustaining Growth in the Established Venture

- **Innovative Strategies for Entrepreneurial Growth**—Keeping the established business on the innovative edge involves consideration of the strategic scope and capabilities of the venture, avoiding common innovation mistakes, developing a portfolio of initiatives, and creating an environment that supports innovation and change.
- **Strategies for the Growing Venture: Mergers, Acquisitions, Franchising, and Exit Strategies**—Navigating the decisions that come with growth can include the choices of mergers, acquisitions, and franchising. It is also important to carefully evaluate the range of exit strategies available to you as part of the planning for growth.
- **Beyond the Strategic Entrepreneurial Model: Learning From Failure**—Entrepreneurs who have experienced failure often describe it as the downside of rapid growth. Gaining a perspective on failure through research, along with valuable lessons from those who have failed, increases your chance of entrepreneurial success.

It is our intent that as you work through the start-up and growth process, you will be able to integrate theory with the practical experiences of all the entrepreneurs and firms profiled, greatly increasing the likelihood of success in your entrepreneurial career. So fasten your seat belt, and let the journey begin. . . .

PART I

Entrepreneurial Strategies for the Emerging Venture

Entrepreneurship and Strategy

A Framework for New Venture Development

A lot of people have ideas, but there are few who decide to do something about them now. Not tomorrow. Not next week. But today. The true entrepreneur is a doer, not a dreamer.

—Nolan Bushnell, founder
of Atari and Chuck E. Cheese's

Objectives:

1. Understand the key role of strategy in the discovery and exploitation of opportunities as entrepreneurial firms form and grow

2. Learn about contemporary trends and patterns in entrepreneurship, including its role in the global economy and the increase in social entrepreneurship

3. Understand the significance of entrepreneurial firms to innovation in the economy

4. Become aware of the key traits and behaviors associated with successful entrepreneurship

5. Learn how a well-established model of strategy (7S model) can be used to develop strategy for emerging organizations

6. Use the Creative Tool: Diagnostics for Entrepreneurial Systems to learn about needs, problems, and changes for an industry in which you are interested

WANTED: Entrepreneur

Immediate opening. **Exciting, exhausting, high-risk position.**

Must have the ability to discover new business opportunities, discern market needs, and match with appropriate solutions before they become obvious. Applicant must be willing to invest hard work and create effort before others recognize the merit of their ideas. Ability to work with financial institutions, investors, and venture capitalists to attract financial backing will be essential for upward mobility in the position. Pay will be very poor for failure and very good for success.

SOURCE: Russell S. Sobel, West Virginia University Entrepreneurship Center. Used with permission.

A s you begin your entrepreneurship experience, you are embarking on a journey that is undertaken daily by millions of people around the world. Each step of this journey is one that involves the discovery, evaluation, and exploitation of opportunities in order to bring new goods, services, and processes to the marketplace (Shane, 2003; Venkataraman, 1997). Entrepreneurship can be defined as *the identification and exploitation of previously unexploited opportunities* (Hitt, Ireland, Camp, & Sexton, 2001). As you can see, the recognition of opportunities that lead to the creation of new business ventures is the heart of entrepreneurship today. Throughout this book, the following questions will guide our examination of the entrepreneurship process (Shane & Venkataraman, 2000, p. 18):

1. Why, when, and how do opportunities for the creation of goods and services come into existence?

2. Why, when, and how do some people and not others discover and exploit these opportunities?

3. Why, when, and how are different modes of strategic action used to exploit entrepreneurial opportunities?

What is the relationship between entrepreneurship and strategy? Both entrepreneurship and strategic management focus on the ways in which businesses create change by exploiting opportunities they discover within the uncertain environments in which they operate (Ireland, Hitt, & Sirmon, 2003). Entrepreneurs are able to create wealth by identifying opportunities and then developing competitive advantages to exploit them (Hitt & Ireland, 2002; Hitt et al., 2001; Ireland, Hitt, Camp, & Sexton, 2001). Thus, *strategic entrepreneurship* is the integration of entrepreneurship and strategic management knowledge (Ireland et al., 2003). Successful entrepreneurs are able to notice the possibilities that many other people seem to miss, and, more important, they are then able to find the means to turn these possibilities into action: to bring to the market something novel and useful.

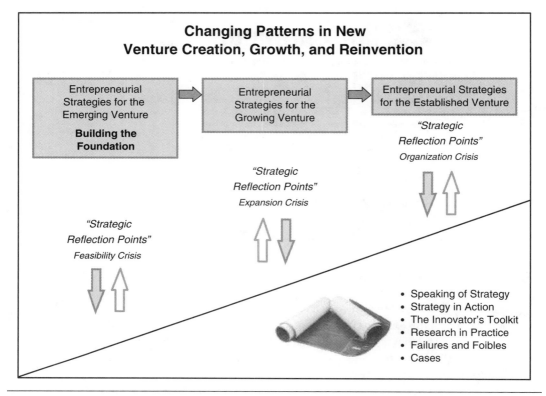

Figure 1.1   Framework for the Book

This textbook presents a framework for strategy in entrepreneurial organizations that incorporates new venture emergence, early growth, and reinvention and innovation in established ventures. The focus of the text is on *entrepreneurial strategies* that can be crafted and implemented within small and medium-size organizations as these firms proceed through the stages of development. The unique approach of this book is its segmentation of entrepreneurship strategies *across the life cycle* of business growth. Most strategy texts present content that is segmented by the type or level of strategy (e.g., marketing, human resources, production strategies) rather than the changing pattern of strategic needs faced by the new venture. Finally, the textbook includes opportunities to examine and assess multiple themes and crisis points (labeled Strategic Reflection Points) that can determine the sustainability and growth of the emerging enterprise (see Figure 1.1).

Our book is written from the point of view of the founder or the entrepreneurial team. Increasingly, entrepreneurs are relying on the expertise and input of key stakeholders as they launch and develop their businesses. Whether these stakeholders are outside the firm in the role of advisers or inside in the roles of investors and employees, the entrepreneur's ability to create a powerful team capable of breakthrough thinking shapes the new venture's potential success and growth. This book strongly emphasizes the key strategic roles of *creativity, opportunity identification, opportunity evaluation and implementation,* and *continual innovation* in the emergence and growth of entrepreneurial firms. Table 1.1 displays these strategic roles,

Table 1.1   Entrepreneurial Stages: Changing Patterns, Strategies, and Entrepreneurial Roles

	Stage I: Entrepreneurial Strategies for the Emerging Venture	*Stage II: Entrepreneurial Strategies for the Growing Venture*	*Stage III: Entrepreneurial Strategies for the Established Venture*
Changing patterns of strategic needs of entrepreneurial firms	Strategic framework for new venture formation Creativity and opportunity identification (the discovery process) Evaluating and exploiting opportunities (the assessment process) Market entry	Financial resource capabilities The evolving management team: capabilities for nurturing growth by building networks and strategic alliances	Creativity and innovation strategies for breakthrough thinking: reinvention and change to sustain growth Tapping new markets and opportunities: franchising, mergers & acquisitions
	The strategic plan: vision and values, the internal and external environment, and organizational strategies for the entrepreneurial team	The strategic plan for the growing venture	Building an entrepreneurial model: Learning from failure and serial entrepreneurship
Strategic roles	Creativity, opportunity identification, and evaluation	Opportunity implementation and firm growth	Continual innovation and reinvention

along with the changing patterns and needs of the entrepreneurial firm and the overall strategy and planning initiatives needed to take the firm to the next stage of growth.

Contemporary Entrepreneurship: Trends and Patterns

Emerging businesses are significant players in the world's economy today. In the United States, they produce about half of the economy's output, employ half of the private-sector workforce, fill niche markets, innovate, increase competition, and give people in all circumstances a chance to succeed. Across industries, new ventures are confronted by a variety of business conditions, and they tackle them with unique solutions using diverse resources (Small Business Office of Advocacy, 2004).

Entrepreneurial firms can be found in all sizes and in all stages of the life cycle. Over the last decade, small firms have provided 60 to 80 percent of the net new jobs in the economy, and according to the U.S. Bureau of the Census, most of these net new jobs come from start-ups within the first two years of operation (Acs & Armington, 2003). Most of the new employment in the economy continues to be an outgrowth of innovation, the engine that spurs job growth. Schumpeter (1942), one of the first economic scholars to focus on entrepreneurial activities, coined the term *creative destruction* to describe the phenomenon in which new firms innovate to enter the market and compete with already established businesses, and as a result, some of these older counterparts close due to lower productivity, which has put them at a competitive disadvantage.

Consider the following trends and patterns in recent entrepreneurial activity in the United States (Small Business Office of Advocacy, 2005):

- In 2004, there were about 5.8 million employer firms (nonfarm). From 1995–2003, self-employment increased by 8.2 percent, to a total of 15 million self-employed people. Women represented half of this increase; their share of self-employment was up from 33.1 percent to 34.2 percent.
- Following population trends, self-employment among individuals of Hispanic and Asian/Native American heritage has significantly increased between 1995 and 2003, 65.8 percent and 38.4 percent, respectively. African American self-employment also rose by 20.3 percent during this period.
- In 2004, small business fared well. The number of new employers exceeded those closing their businesses, and the number of self-employed increased.
- Entrepreneurial firms benefited from the continued recovery in the economy in 2004, along with the abundant supply of credit. Small business borrowing increased slightly. Equity investment for later-stage financing was easier to attract than early-stage financing. However, angel investors continued to be important for providing funding to early-stage entrepreneurs in 2004.
- In fiscal year 2004, the federal government granted $69.2 billion, or 23 percent of $299.9 billion in federal prime contracts to small businesses.

Around the world, entrepreneurial activity is thriving. The following findings emerged in the *Global Entrepreneurship Monitor's* research analysis of 34 countries (Acs, Arenius, Hay, & Minniti, 2005).

- A large number of people are engaged in entrepreneurial endeavors around the globe. About 73 million adults are either starting a new business or managing a young business of which they are also an owner. The average level of activity was 9.3 percent, representing 1 out of every 11 adults around the world.
- Three out of every five people involved in entrepreneurship around the world are opportunity entrepreneurs, defined as participating in entrepreneurial activities to exploit a perceived business opportunity. Opportunity entrepreneurs are more likely to be found in high-income countries.
- Two in five people are necessity entrepreneurs, who pursue entrepreneurship because all other employment options are either absent or unsatisfactory. Necessity entrepreneurs are more likely to be found in low-income countries.
- Young people between the ages of 25 and 34 tend to be involved in entrepreneurial activity in every country studied, more than people of any other age groups. This tended to vary by income levels, and low-income countries saw more activity across all age groups.
- In high-income countries, 57 percent of entrepreneurs have a postsecondary degree, compared to 38 percent in middle-income countries and 23 percent in low-income countries.

In summary, these patterns suggest very strongly that entrepreneurship is alive and vibrant around the globe. Economists agree that entrepreneurship is responsible for much of the competition and innovation in the business world. The innovations introduced by entrepreneurs challenge and make obsolete the technologies, products, and services of existing industries (Acs et al., 2005).

Innovation as the primary driver of entrepreneurial behavior is the focus of this book. One type of innovation that is gaining much attention today is social innovation, a mission of some entrepreneurs who are seeking not only to create new value in the form of products but also to create change in the very communities in which they reside.

Entrepreneurship That Matters: Social Value Creation

The literature widely assumes economic motives as the sole, or primary, purpose of new organization creation (Kirzner, 1983; Schumpeter, 1934). These themes pervade current literature, which sees the entrepreneurial process as one based on recognizing the value of resources and "exploiting" them for economic success (Shane & Venkataraman, 2000). "Entrepreneurship can be explained by considering the nexus of enterprising individuals and valuable opportunities" (Shane, 2003, p. 9)

At the same time, some evidence suggests that economic gain may not be the only, or key, motive for all entrepreneurs. For example, a review of literature (Newbert, 2003) found that economic motives such as wealth creation were generally not the prominent motive of entrepreneurs, who appear to have both economic and ethical motivations for their actions. Moreover, Wiklund, Davidsson, and Delmar (2003) suggest that "noneconomic" concerns may be more important than anticipated financial gain to small business managers when they consider expanding their firms. Specifically, concern about employee well-being was seen to be important; it may be viewed as a motivation for the "positive atmosphere" of the small venture. However, on a broader scale, consider the following remarks by UN Secretary-General Kofi Annan (1999):

> Let us choose to unite the power of markets with the strength of universal ideals. Let us choose to reconcile the creative forces of private entrepreneurship with the needs of the disadvantaged and the requirements of future generations.

Why does recognizing the full picture matter when it comes to entrepreneurial motives? Secretary-General Annan's rallying cry seems immensely timely. In recent times, corporate scandal has eroded trust and belief in the value of business and in its ability to create both economic *and* social progress. At the same time, significant inequalities and challenges exist in both developed and developing nations. Mr. Annan hopes that private enterprise that concerns itself with *both* economic and social value creation can be a powerful solution to world issues.

This idea of social value creation is rooted within the social entrepreneurship literature and has more recently received attention among academic and clinical entrepreneurship researchers. Underlying social entrepreneurship are the multiple benefits and rewards that are exhibited by a heightened sense of accountability to the constituencies served, as well as the outcomes that are created. Social entrepreneurs seek to provide social improvements and enhancements to their communities, including attractive (both social and financial) return to their key stakeholders. Social entrepreneurs assess their impact and influence in terms of the social outcomes, not simply in terms of size, growth, or processes. However, much of the social entrepreneurship field is concerned with the creation of nonprofit ventures. Although the creation of new and innovative nonprofits is critical, there is also a substantial need for educating future entrepreneurs about how for-profit venture creation can integrate both social and financial outcomes. A critical starting point is to understand the diverse "for whom and for what" motives and beliefs of our future aspiring entrepreneurs, so that both women and men act as the change agents for themselves and their communities, thereby allowing them to invent new profitable and sustainable approaches that create solutions to change society for the better.

Strategy in Action

Social Entrepreneurs—Doing Business With a Conscience

There are many breeds of entrepreneurs. Some are out to revolutionize the software industry, some to start a family restaurant, while another might set out to provide employment in poverty-stricken areas or to bring medicine to the sick. It's still a business, but with different objectives. It is not to say that other entrepreneurs don't have a social conscience, but some make a career out of it. For them, the motivation is the drive to create social change. They see problems around them that they feel need to be addressed, yet aren't. They see kids with insufficient education, parents without jobs or the opportunity of employment, or sick countrymen without access to the proper health care.

Pushpika Freitas is a good example. A native of India and based in Chicago, IL, Freitas is a graduate of DePaul University. She was one of the founders of Marketplace India, a non-profit organization that employs Indian women in the poorer neighborhoods of Mumbai as artisans, designing and creating clothing lines that are sold in India and the United States.

"The primary goal is empowering the women through employment," said Freitas. "If women cannot put food on the table, you cannot talk about dignity, you cannot talk about them making changes in their lives and the lives of their families."

Marketplace India is currently extending its reach. It has been vital to the livelihoods of the nearly 500 women that the organization employs as artisans, and for many, this work constitutes one of the few, if any, options that these women have for employment. Religions, cultural and economic constraints play their role. Yet families have the same goals for their children as they do in the U.S. "It's not young women who just finished school who would be working with Marketplace, it's their mothers who would be," says Freitas.

With Marketplace they have that opportunity, and with it comes larger implications. "That is the next step, bringing about social change," said Freitas, "But having it come from grassroots as opposed to a middle-class Indian social worker coming in and saying, "this is what I think things should be."

Freitas, who benefited from a good education and a progressive idealism instilled in her by her parents, was moved by the plight of a small group of Indian women she began working with over 20 years ago.

"Marketplace originated because it was very close to my heart . . . I got involved working with a couple of women and realized that they had very little control over their lives or over the money that they earned. It was at that point that I realized that I'm in the minority here, which is why I started Marketplace."

Since then, the organization has grown to employ 480 artisans mostly in and around Mumbai. Much of the focus now is on getting more people involved in Marketplace.

"We want to expand the program," said Freitas, "So at the moment we're talking about 480 artisans, but tomorrow can we be at 1,000, can we be at 1,500?"

Social entrepreneurship has been given consistently more attention in recent years. It has had a long history in Chicago. Jane Addams formed the Hull House Settlement in Chicago with friend Ellen g. Starr in 1889, after visiting a similar settlement in Toynbee Hall, in London's East End. She was moved and intrigued by poverty and its roots, one of the many causes she took up in her lifetime. Hull House was situated in the middle of one of the poorest neighborhoods in Chicago at the time (on the near west side) and was intended to be a place of education, culture and a safe haven for the area residents. She was not running a charity or overseeing a highly profitable corporation. The mission of Hull House was to empower the residents, to improve conditions, to give people help in the pulling themselves up by their bootstraps, who might not otherwise be allowed the opportunity.

Addams said, "Social advance depends as much upon the process through which it is secured as upon the result itself." Her Hull House, which was host to around 2,000 people a week just a few years after its inception, helped countless immigrant families and neighborhood residents in her lifetime and beyond. In 1931, Jane Addams became the first American woman to be awarded the Nobel Peace Prize.

Others throughout history who have had a substantial impact through their social work can also be considered social entrepreneurs. Clara Barton, creator of the American Red Cross, James Grant, who helped to temporarily stop a war in El Salvador so the nation's children could be immunized, and Bill Drayton–who also coined the term "social entrepreneur" over twenty years ago, who founded Ashoka, an organization that invests in social entrepreneurs throughout the world.

Social entrepreneurship is a relatively new name, but the idea has been around for many years. From Jane Addams to Pushpika Freitas, the driving force is the same: to empower people to better lives by providing them with the means to get that life, whether it be education, employment or even simple entertainment. They go into these new ventures with a mission not based on profits, but on social change. But at the same time, these organizations can be successful, self-sustaining businesses.

"I think that one of the things that Marketplace has demonstrated is that you can have a social goal and be involved in an economic venture," notes Pushpika Freitas. "And I think more of this can be done."

SOURCE: Reprinted from *Epicentre*, Newsletter of the Coleman Entrepreneurship Center at DePaul University, Winter, 2005. Used with permission.

Strategic Reflection Point

Exploring a Social Entrepreneurship Mission

Find an organization that you believe has a social entrepreneurship mission (explore a couple of the social entrepreneurship Web sites including: www.changemakers.net or www.ashoka.org).

1. What do you see as being entrepreneurial (and not entrepreneurial)?

2. What is the relationship between the organization's mission and its actual activities and planned initiatives?

3. Do you have any suggestions about how the organization could improve its social entrepreneurship mission, strategy, and messaging to the community?

The Role of Innovation in Entrepreneurship Strategy

One of this book's distinctive features is the emphasis on the role of innovation in the entrepreneurship start-up and growth process. Entrepreneurial firms are vital to the development of new ideas, technologies, and actions across industries today. While small entrepreneurial companies are not as common in capital-intensive industries such as auto manufacturing, aerospace, and oil research, they play major roles in the development of newer technology industries, including biotechnology, medical electronics, medical equipment, and telecommunications. Large companies are often dependent on small firms' discoveries and inventions (Small Business Office of Advocacy, 2004).

Research in Practice: **Small Firms and Innovation**

Consider the following findings that are derived from research using a database of 1,270 innovative companies, conducted by the Small Business Administration's Office of Advocacy (2004).

- Between 2000 and 2002, the number of actively innovative firms (defined as firms with more than 15 patents during the previous five years) increased. Whereas 104 firms were dropped from the database, 318 firms were added to it.
- Small firms are having a powerful influence on technology. They represented 40 percent of the highly innovative firms in 2002, up from 33 percent in 2000.
- Large firms in biotechnology, medical electronics, semiconductor, and telecommunications industries have a higher than anticipated number of citations of small firm patents.

In conclusion, small firms are integral to the innovation process, even when they are not responsible for the final or breakthrough technology.

Throughout this book, students of entrepreneurship will find creative tools you can use to develop and implement strategies for the emergence, growth, and renewal of the entrepreneurial organization. Here is the first.

The Innovator's Toolkit: Are You Right for Entrepreneurship?

Allis (2003) has developed a set of commonly noted traits of entrepreneurs. Being an entrepreneur is not for everyone. Not everyone can handle the risks and responsibilities of having dozens or hundreds of people's lives depending on your choices or the stress of reporting to a board of directors or panel of investors. An analysis of the traits commonly found among successful entrepreneurs may assist in deciding if you are right to be an entrepreneur.

Here is a list of commonly noted traits of entrepreneurs. Put a check next to each one you believe you have:

_____ Initiative	_____ Ability to prioritize
_____ Bias toward action	_____ Drive toward efficiency
_____ Vision	_____ Ability to take feedback
_____ Determination	_____ Tolerance for stress
_____ Courage	_____ Decisiveness
_____ Creativity	_____ Ability to deal with failure
_____ Perseverance and persistence	_____ Ability to learn from mistakes
_____ Drive to achieve	_____ Ability to delay gratification
_____ Orientation toward opportunity	_____ Ability to plan
_____ Ability to deal with the abstract and ambiguity	_____ Ability to build a team
	_____ Ability to inspire and lead people

Do you have these attributes? If you checked more than half, you may have what it takes to become a successful entrepreneur.

As part of a series of interviews conducted with six successful entrepreneurs in the North Carolina region, Allis (2003) asked the question, What traits are most important for an aspiring entrepreneur to have? He gave the entrepreneurs 15 options and asked them to number their choices 1 through 15 in order of importance. The results were very interesting. The most important trait for aspiring entrepreneurs to have, according to these successful entrepreneurs, was "being able to build a solid team." The second and third most important skills were "leadership & the ability to inspire" and "persistence." The least important attribute of all, No. 15, was "a college degree." Here are the full results in order of importance:

1. Being able to build a solid team	5. Integrity
2. Leadership & the ability to inspire	6. Ability to communicate effectively
3. Persistence	7. Confidence
4. Motivation & ambition	8. Being able to execute

9. Having a bias toward action
10. Having a good idea or plan
11. Knowledge of marketing
12. Good networking skills

13. Having the right advisers
14. Knowledge of accounting & finance
15. A college degree

Would you work 70- hour plus weeks for months on end, sleep at the office when you get backed up, and put your own money on the line when payroll is due and the bank has yet to approve a loan? Would you be the janitor, the receptionist, the custom support representative, and the bookkeeper, as well as the president? Could you get up and present in front of a room of investors, after already being turned down by 105 other banks, angel investors, and venture capital firms? If you think so, then you just might have what it takes to become a successful entrepreneur.

SOURCE: From Allis, R., *Zero to One Million.* Virante, Inc., www.zeromillion.com, copyright © 2003. Reprinted with permission.

No successful entrepreneur would say it is easy or that no risk is involved. If it were easy, if there was no risk, and if it did not take years of dedication and persistence, everyone might be an entrepreneur. Unfortunately, the market does not have compassion or feelings. It doesn't pull for the person who works the hardest or has the best idea. It pulls for the person who works the most intelligently, sells what the market demands, puts together the needed resources, and executes. Let's take a look at the best and worst things about being an entrepreneur.

Failures and Foibles

The Next Time I Start a New Venture . . .

Although many entrepreneurs make their share of mistakes, the seasoned entrepreneur is able to turn those mistakes into ideas and plans of what NOT to do the second, third time around. Consider the following statements from entrepreneurs who comment on the next time they start a new venture:

- I will make sure I have sufficient start-up and back-up capital. Nothing is as sure to kill a new venture as running out of money early in the game. If your plan says you need a certain amount of capital, get it—and a little more, for back-up.
- I will be certain there is a market for my "great idea" before I run with it. I'll never be caught with a "solution in search of a problem" again!
- I will spend more time and care managing the business. I don't like to deal with details, but somebody has to or the business will suffer. Next time I'll hire a manager to do right what I was doing ineffectively.
- I'll know something about the business I plan to start. Nothing is as sure a sign of impending trouble than an entrepreneur who asks, "how hard can it be?" when he or she has

never before done whatever "it" is. I'll stick to a business I know, or I'll make darn sure I learn about it before I start.

- I'll have "It's the cash flow, Stupid!" tattooed on my forehead. Cash-flow problems are easy to understand. If your suppliers give you 30 days to pay, and you give your customers 60 days to pay, the cash will flow out before it can flow in. Duh.
- I will have a lawyer draw up my partnership agreements. I will not let my partners become "former friends."
- I will know my competition as well as or better than my competition knows me, and I will look for competitors where I least expect to find them.
- I will stay on top of new developments. I will never stop learning about my business and my customers.
- I will plan for success and growth. Too much success is a bad thing if you're not prepared for it.
- I will maintain a balance in my life between work and family. I will not let my success go to my head.
- I will learn how to count up to ten. I will not try to make two and two equal five, just because I'm so sure things will turn out better than I have any good reason to expect they will.

SOURCE: List from Canadian Foundation for Economic Education. www.cfee.org. Reprinted with permission.

Review Questions

1. How do you think most entrepreneurs view failure? (Consider the implicit assumptions and weigh the positive and negative consequences of failure.)

2. How much do you think the severity of the failure matters in influencing the entrepreneur to launch another business?

3. How do other countries view failure and its association with entrepreneurial start-up (e.g., choose Germany, Sweden, China, Brazil)? Does it hinder the rate of start-up activity in that country?

Beyond Traits: Scripting Our Own Entrepreneurial Strategies

Entrepreneurs may not differ significantly in personality, and they may agree on the most common mistakes they have made over their entrepreneurial career; however, they may perceive and act upon new opportunities in different ways. These differences may be due to how they think and process information they receive on a daily basis. Researchers have commented that one way to increase an individual's effectiveness in the new venture creation process is to better understand the role of entrepreneurial cognition. As defined by Mitchell et al. (2002), "entrepreneurial cognitions are the knowledge structures that people use to make assessments, judgments, or decisions involving opportunity evaluation, venture creation, and growth" (p. 97). Researchers have postulated that cognition has the potential to make a significant contribution to the study of entrepreneurship (e.g., Allinson, Chell, & Hayes, 2000; Allinson & Hayes, 1996; Baron, 1998; Busenitz & Barney, 1997; Mitchell et al., 2002) and that understanding entrepreneurial cognition is imperative to comprehend what creates the notion of "entrepreneurial alertness" (Kirzner, 1979) and how it can be developed to encourage entrepreneurial behaviors and strategic action for the firm.

To better comprehend entrepreneurial cognition, researchers have developed a cognitive style model with multiple dimensions (e.g., Allinson & Hayes, 1996; Leonard, Scholl, & Kowalski, 1999). Early on, Ornstein (1977) referred to two modes of awareness, reflecting the rational and intuitive sides of an individual. Other scholars have noted that nearly all cognitive styles are "subordinate to, and reflect, a broad super-ordinate stylistic difference" (Miller, 1987, p. 253), and this represents a long-established distinction between contrasting modes of thought (Sadler-Smith & Allinson, 2000). According to Nickerson, Perkins, and Smith (1985):

> The view that there are two qualitatively different types of thinking is widely shared. Among the terms used to describe one type are analytic, deductive, rigorous, constrained, convergent, formal and critical. Representative of the terms used to describe the other type are synthetic, inductive, expansive, unconstrained, divergent, informal, diffuse and creative. No doubt the partitioning of thinking into two types involves something of an oversimplification but possibly a useful one. (p. 50)

This superordinate dimension of cognitive style is identified as intuition analysis (Allinson et al., 2000). Drawing on the work of a number of theorists and empirical researchers who have argued that the dimensions of cognitive style can be ordered within a unitary framework, Allinson and Hayes (1996) reported the development and validation of a new instrument, the Cognitive Style Index (CSI). Thus, an individual's cognitive style may influence their preference for different types of learning, knowledge gathering, information processing, and decision making, which constitute many of the critical stages and related tasks an entrepreneur is confronted with in developing a business. Kickul, Gundry, and Whitcanack (in press) developed a model (see Figure 1.2) that describes several of the relevant tasks associated with the intention to launch a new venture and its initiation.

The Kickul et al. (in press) study reveals the influence of cognitive style on entrepreneurial self-efficacy and shows that styles can predict how students perceive their own self-efficacy regarding different stages of the entrepreneurial intentions model. The results disclosed that an individual's cognitive style mattered greatly in directing attention to specific tasks of the new venture development process that fit most closely with his or her preferred style and away from other tasks that rely on the thinking style that is less preferred. For example, Kickul et al. found that individuals who prefer the intuitive style of information processing were comfortable with the opportunity identification or searching tasks (e.g., discovery and refinement of new ideas and

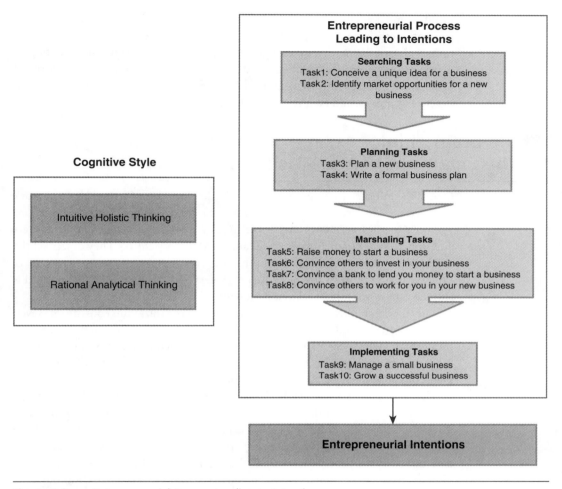

Figure 1.2   Entrepreneurial Process Leading to Intentions

opportunities) of the new venture development process and then wanted to proceed directly to implementing their ideas. The problem with this approach is that necessary stages of the venture development process are skipped entirely, or at best given very short shrift, in this group's rush to get to the implementation tasks. Similarly, individuals with the analytic preferred mode of thinking skip the search for opportunities and begin the venture development process with the planning tasks. Thus, they pay little attention to the need for divergent thinking to refine and improve an idea or opportunity, preferring to get right to the work of building the business.

These findings facilitate our understanding of why, for example, some entrepreneurs discover gaps in the plan or infrastructure of their new ventures that may have been the result of such cognitive "skipping over" the key tasks in the business creation process. Furthermore, the research may indicate the important role of pedagogical approaches and new methodologies in entrepreneurship education. The pedagogical goal is to effectively stimulate student development in both the intuitive and analytic cognitive areas so that students are able to fully participate in all stages of the new venture creation cycle and deepen their entrepreneurial intentions. Many of the new methodologies and approaches to learning about entrepreneurship are within this textbook and in the following chapters in the form of Speaking of Strategy interviews and stories, Strategic Reflection Points, Research in Practice examples, and Failures and Foibles.

Whole Brain Thinking: An Introduction to Strategy for the Emerging Venture Using the 7-S Model

One of the initial steps in firm creation is the development of a strategic framework in which new opportunities and innovations can be quickly positioned within your venture. One such framework is the McKinsey 7-S Model (developed by Tom Peters and Robert Waterman, former consultants at McKinsey & Co). They described the 7-S Model in their article "Structure Is Not Organization" (Waterman, Peters, & Phillips, 1980) and *In Search of Excellence* (Peters & Waterman, 1982). The model is still relevant to venture development today.

The model builds on the premise that an organization consists of seven elements, divided into what the authors called the hard S's and the soft S's (Waterman et al., 1980). The hard S's (Strategy, Structure, and Systems) are fairly easy to identify. They can be found in companies' strategy statements, corporate plans, organizational charts, and other documentations.

The four soft S's (Style, Staff, Skills, and Shared Values/Superordinate Goals), however, are more embedded in the organization and more challenging to locate. They are difficult to describe because capabilities, values, and dimensions of the company culture are continuously developing and changing. The soft S's are highly determined by the people who work in the organization. Therefore, it is much more difficult to plan or to influence the characteristics of the soft elements. Although the soft factors are below the surface, they strongly influence the Structures, Strategies, and Systems of the organization. Table 1.2 presents the 7-S Model adapted from Waterman et al. (1980), applied to entrepreneurial firms.

Effective entrepreneurial organizations achieve a fit between these seven elements. If one element changes, it affects all the others. For example, integrating new technology into the business influences Staff and Skills, in that employees must learn new ways of doing things. In turn, their performance expectations are likely to change. The interaction with customers may also be different than it was at start-up.

As small firms grow and change in response to markets and other demands of their environment, many entrepreneurs focus their efforts on the hard S's—Strategy, Structure and Systems—because these are much easier to observe and change. However, it is just as vital to the survival of the business that entrepreneurs pay attention to the soft S's: Skills, Staff, Style, and Shared Values. We know from the landmark book, *In Search of Excellence* (Peters & Waterman, 1982), that most successful businesses work hard at and excel at these soft S's. In fact, the soft factors can make or break a company because new structures and strategies are difficult to build if they rely on entrepreneurial styles and values that are a poor fit with the needs of a changing company. These problems often are visible in the dissatisfying

Table 1.2   Description of the 7-S Model: Applications to Entrepreneurial Firms

The Hard S's	Description
Strategy	Actions a company plans to launch its venture and enter the marketplace, in response to or anticipation of changes in its external environment: the competitive advantage offered by the firm.
Structure	Basis for specialization and coordination influenced primarily by strategy, firm size, and diversity. The configuration of tasks and individuals/teams required to achieve desired performance.
Systems	Formal and informal processes and procedures that support the strategy and structure of the firm through launch and growth, enabling the firm to operate as a well-oiled machine.
The Soft S's	
Style / Culture	The culture of the organization, consisting of two components: • Organizational Culture: the dominant values, beliefs, and norms that evolve over time and become relatively enduring features of organizational life. The founder and start-up team establish these values and reward desired performance, leading to shared expectations. • Management Style: The behavior of managers: what they expect and reinforce. What does the founder and management team focus on? What matters to them and how do they carry out the mission and values of the company?
Staff	The people in the company and the processes used to develop managers and employees. How are newcomers introduced to the company's way of doing things (socialization)? Career development opportunities in the company.
Skills	The distinctive competences—what the company does best, ways of expanding or shifting competences as the firm moves from start-up to early growth, maturation, and reinvention.
Shared Values/ Superordinate Goals	Guiding concepts: what is important to the founders. The principles guiding the business to meet its stated goals. As the firm grows, values and goals are shared and understood.

SOURCE: Adapted from R. H. Waterman, Jr., T. J. Peters, and J. R. Phillips, "Structure Is Not Organization," *Business Horizons* 23, no. 3(1980): 14–26.

results of spectacular mega-mergers. The lack of success and synergies in such mergers often results from a clash of completely different cultures, values, and styles, which makes it difficult to establish effective common systems and structures. Although many entrepreneurial firms are never involved in mega-mergers, it is never too early in the firm's life cycle to pay close attention to the soft S's and build the new organization in a mindful way.

Strategic Reflection Point

The 7-S's and Entrepreneurship

- Why do some entrepreneurs pay less attention to the so-called soft S's in the model above? In your experience, have you known entrepreneurs or managers who neglected these elements? Why is this a pitfall for new venture development and business growth?
- Do you think that in the present business climate, customers, employees, suppliers, and other stakeholders of a venture are increasingly aware of the importance of the Skills, Staff, Style, and Shared Values?
- How have ethical values and expectations changed with regard to entrepreneurial activities?

The 7-S Model is also a valuable tool to initiate entrepreneurial change processes and to give you direction. A helpful application is to determine the current state of each element and to compare this with the ideal state. Based on your findings, you can develop action plans to achieve the intended state.

One of the many ways that you can make use of many of these elements to your advantage is to consider the following tool, which allows you to view how each element may relate to and intersect with others in building your own entrepreneurial organization.

The Innovator's Toolkit: Diagnostics for Entrepreneurial Systems Throughout the Venture's Life Cycle

One of the first steps in developing an understanding of entrepreneurship is to begin the research process by interviewing entrepreneurs. This provides the would-be entrepreneur with much useful information that can be used to begin to diagnose whether an idea is workable and how to transform it into a new venture (adapted from French & Bell, 1978).

Step 1: In the space below list the five or six most important questions you would ask the entrepreneur about his or her organization:

Step 2: In the following list, circle those variables that your five or six questions would address. Add any variables not listed that your questions would address.

1. Formal authority structure

2. Work-process technology

3. Informal teams and groupings

4. Relation of system to external factors: government and markets

5. Formal reward system

6. Informal reward system

7. Selection of employees

8. Employee and management training and development

9. Organizational culture: norms and values

10. Financial performance: equity, assets, profitability

11. Employee and management turnover

12. Employee satisfaction with roles/positions

13. Employee performance evaluations

14. Performance evaluation and appraisal of organizational units

15. Satisfaction of members with interpersonal relationships

16. Strategy and mission of organization

17. Resource limitations

18. Communication and information channels

19. Informal leadership

20. Control systems (including operating and accounting systems)

21. _____

22. _____

23. _____

24. _____

25. _____

26. _____

27. _____

Step 3: Arrange the variables you have checked into categories. Look over the items you have checked to determine whether they fall into groupings. In the spaces provided here, list the items that belong together, describe their common theme, and give each grouping a descriptive name.

Category name:
  (Variables)
  Briefly describe why items fall in this group.

Category name:
  (Variables)
  Briefly describe why items fall in this group.

Category name:
  (Variables)
  Briefly describe why items fall in this group.

Category name:
  (Variables)
  Briefly describe why items fall in this group.

Category name:
  (Variables)
  Briefly describe why items fall in this group.

Category name:
  (Variables)
  Briefly describe why items fall in this group.

Step 4: This next section is designed to help you understand the relationships among the categories you have just created. First, list each category in the appropriate space in the left-hand column of the following table. Then imagine that the elements of Category 1 underwent major change (which is quite likely within the life span of an organization). Assign each of the other categories (write in the category number) to one of the three spaces to the right of Category 1 to indicate what you feel would be the likely effects. Do the same for all the remaining categories you have listed (use category numbers below).

Categorical Diagnostics

		Likely to show a great deal of change	Likely to show moderate change	Likely to show no change
Category 1				
Category 2				
Category 3				
Category 4				
Category 5				
Category 6				
Category 7				
Category 8				

You can now depict your own entrepreneurial organization graphically by drawing a picture of the causal relationships between the categories. For each category, draw a circle and write the name of the category in the circle. Then draw arrows between the various circles to represent the direction of influence between them. For example, if Category 1 is likely to cause change in Category 2, it might appear as follows:

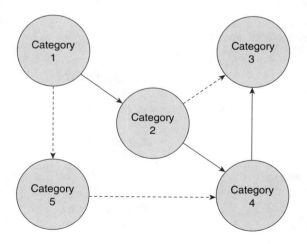

If only moderate change is likely to occur, draw a dotted line between categories. Now arrange all the circles and arrows in a way that most clearly depicts the relationships. Which categories seem to have the strongest ties or relationships with others? Is one category more central or essential in influencing other categories? As your firm grows, consider which categories you have the most and least control over. As an entrepreneur, how can you mitigate and positively change the influence that one category has on another?

Summary of Chapter Objectives

1. Understand the key role of strategy in the discovery and exploitation of opportunities as entrepreneurial firms form and grow.
    *   This book strongly emphasizes the key strategic roles of creativity, opportunity identification, opportunity evaluation, and innovation in the emergence and growth of entrepreneurial firms.
    *   This strategic approach examines three distinct stages of the entrepreneurship process, and provides you with strategies you can use to launch, grow, and revitalize the firm.

2. Learn about contemporary trends and patterns in entrepreneurship, including its role in the global economy and the increase in social entrepreneurship.
    *   Entrepreneurships are formed by 1 out of every 11 adults around the world today. In the United States, entrepreneurships produce about half the economic output, employ half of the private sector workforce, and give people in all circumstances a chance to succeed.
    *   The number and percentage of people of color and women who start companies are increasing significantly.
    *   Entrepreneurships are continuing to benefit from the economic recovery. Credit is more abundant, and while equity investment is still difficult to attract for early-stage financing, angel investments are available.
    *   Social entrepreneurs are driven to empower people by providing the means to better their lives; the mission of these self-sustaining firms is social change.

3. Understand the significance of entrepreneurial firms to innovation in the economy.
    *   Entrepreneurial firms account for a significant percentage of patents and innovations.
    *   Large firms rely on smaller firms, especially in newer technologies such as biotechnology, medical electronics, and telecommunications.
    *   As you will see throughout this book, innovation can be a highly successful competitive strategy for the survival and growth of firms.

4. Become aware of the key traits and behaviors associated with successful entrepreneurship
   - There are many traits and behaviors of successful entrepreneurs. Some of these can certainly be learned and reinforced to better prepare you for the journey to entrepreneurship.
   - Beyond traits and behavior, entrepreneurial cognition can have a significant influence on how you consider and evaluate the different tasks in the new venture creation process.

5. Learn how a well-established model of strategy (7-S Model) can be used to develop strategy for emerging organizations
   - These seven elements are distinguished in so-called hard S's and soft S's. The hard elements are simpler to identify. They are the Structures, Strategies, and Systems of the firm. They can be found in strategy statements, corporate plans, organizational charts, and other documentations.
   - The four soft S's, however, are difficult to describe because capabilities, values, and elements of corporate culture are continuously developing and changing. These elements are the Skills, Staff, Style, and Shared Values found in the organization. They are highly determined by the people who work in the organization. Therefore, it is much more difficult to plan or to influence the characteristics of the soft elements. Although the soft factors are below the surface, they can have a great impact of the hard Structures, Strategies, and Systems of the organization.

6. Use the creative tool, Diagnostics for Entrepreneurial Systems, to learn about needs, problems, and changes for a firm and industry in which you are interested.
   - Begin the information-gathering process by interviewing entrepreneurs in the industry in which you are interested.
   - The diagnostics tool will help you become attuned to the needed changes in the industry and market and help you become more idea prone.

CASE 1.1   Floral Design Business in Full Bloom

Call it stubbornness, call it ingenuity, call it what you want; but entrepreneurs follow their own path. "I was the classic artisan entrepreneur," said Casey Cooper, owner of Botanicals Inc., "I hated being told what to do and I was going to do my own flowers." She did just that. Starting out doing flowers for a friend's wedding ten years ago, arranging the flowers on her washing machine, she has built up Botanicals Inc. to be one of the most well-known and respected floral design businesses in Chicago.

Cooper, a DePaul University graduate, has been in the floral industry for nearly twenty years, working at various flower shops and freelancing with others. After graduating from DePaul, she went into theatre and helped to found a theatre company in Chicago, where she worked for two years as Artistic Director. But after doing the flowers for her friend's wedding, one reference led to another and orders slowly started coming in. She decided to make a business out of it.

Her previous experience in the business was crucial in her own venture, especially in the floral industry, although running her own business proved to be a bit different. "It is a tough business because you're dealing with perishable products which are expensive, and you're dealing with expensive staffing, because you need people that are skilled," said Cooper, "And you're dealing with really subjective clients, because color and design is very subjective."

Within a couple of years, the basement operation was outgrown and the business was moved to an old Wicker Park mansion. Not long after, more space was needed, so another move was made, followed by an expansion, and then a final move to the location that Botanicals is housed in now, a 6,500 square foot studio near Lincoln Park that has housed the business since 2002.

Setting the Standard

During her years in the flower industry, Cooper developed a sense of how she wanted her work to look like. "For a long time there was this very tortured-looking, high-style shlocky stuff out there that people do, and still do. We veered away from that," said Cooper. "Everything we do is extremely organic, whether it is modern and [chic], it still has a very organic feeling and root to it. Our product quality is something that we protect beyond anything."

With a vision in mind, she continued to expand the client base and ended up getting the attention of local magazines and media, which featured her business in several pieces. As time went on, Botanicals went from doing weddings to large-scale corporate and social events, even doing work for the Field Museum events, as well as being featured on Oprah's 50th birthday show earlier in 2004. "To expand and push beyond our limits, I think is something we've become very well known for," said Cooper. Not long ago the services offered by Botanicals were expanded as clients asked for more than flower arrangements. Botanicals Inc. now does complete designs for special events, including table settings, lighting, props, linens, and so on.

Getting Better With Age

The rise in business that Botanicals has seen in the past couple years has not made Cooper's job any more difficult. If anything, she seems more comfortable now than she did years ago, "The more growth we experience now, the better the infrastructure is really. It feels better, and it runs more smoothly," said Cooper. "It's been such a natural evolution that it doesn't feel like there's any additional pressure on." It seems the most irritation she will face on any given day is a touchy smoke alarm, which goes off whenever someone uses the toaster in the break room.

She has got plenty of help with her, too. Since hiring the first full-time employee back in 1997, she has since grown the business to the point where it employs 35 people, full-time and part-time included. The new design studio on Elston

Avenue is state of the art, with 6,500 square feet of space to accommodate the level of business they handle.

It has been over a decade since she started setting up flower arrangements on her washing machine, and yet time seems to fly by when it comes to the business. "It's always been fast, and it still feels fast," she said, "It feels like there's this train that started and we're always running behind it trying to get on."

A Look Back

Without a doubt, the experience she had working in the floral industry before going into business for herself was essential, but that experience was mostly limited to the creative, design-oriented part of the business. "Just because I was good at doing flowers didn't mean that I was cut out to run this huge business," she said. She did have a good sense of design and how to pick up new business along the way, but never really sought out consulting help until recently.

"I did not build this business to support the life that I wanted to have. I just kept building the business, and all of the sudden it was like, 'This is not the life I want.' So there was a lot of back-tracking and trying to figure out how we can set this up to support the life we want," she said. Cooper credits the business consulting she received with helping to sort some of that out.

Now, with things running smoothly, she is taking time to focus on some other aspects of her business. Staring in January, she will be teaching design classes, and she is also currently working on a book project. For the first time in quite a while, she is taking a step back, "This is probably the first time in 10 years that I feel like I can actually catch my breath."

SOURCE: Reprinted from *Epicentre,* Newsletter of the Coleman Entrepreneurship Center at DePaul University, Winter, 2005. Used with permission.

Discussion Questions

1. What were some of the key decisions Casey Cooper had to make as Botanicals, Inc. grew?

2. What entrepreneurial skills were needed as the business launched? Did these needs change over time?

3. What do you recommend Cooper do now? Are there opportunities she could pursue?

CASE 1.2   Speaking of Strategy: Southport Grocery and Café

Southport Grocery and Café is a specialty food store and café located in the middle of the burgeoning shopping and dining destination that is the Southport Avenue corridor on the north side of Chicago, Illinois. The neighborhood is known as Lakeview, and Southport Grocery & Café captures the quality-focused, yet down-to-earth nature of its neighbors. This same balance occurs in the café's kitchen, with dishes that are at once modern and new, yet accessible and comforting.

Owner/chef Lisa Santos has combined an exciting array of specialty food groceries and a charming café serving modern comfort food. Founded in 2003, Lisa Santos discovered a way to combine her love of food with her business acumen and experience. She describes her strategy as, "We're a learning environment for food." Eighteen months after its opening, Southport Grocery and Café has 4 full-time employees and 9 part-time employees. The story, however, starts much earlier.

The Passion for Food Begins

Lisa Santos' passion for food began at an early age. "I still have my first cookbook from when I was 5 years old. Some of my fondest childhood memories are of sleepovers at my grandma's house where we'd just hang out in the kitchen and bake." After spending more than ten years in Financial Services at CNA Insurance Company, Lisa decided to follow her passion for food and enrolled in the Cooking & Hospitality Institute of Chicago (CHIC).

"From the very beginning, even before cooking school, I had thought of starting my own food business. When I travel, I love digging around in fine food groceries just as much as I like dining at new restaurants. Southport Grocery and Café is a great blend of both of these interests–interests that I think many Chicagoans share. I like doing things that aren't already done," says Lisa, "And this combination of fine food groceries and a café meets the needs of people who love to cook as well as those who just love to eat!" While many specialty grocers have an international focus, Southport Grocery & Café fills an unusual niche by first concentrating on domestic foodstuffs. "It's such an interesting time in American food production. It's very possible now to find high-quality specialty products and artisan-produced foodstuffs right here in the U.S." And Lisa admits that finding a passionate producer or artisan is almost as important as the product itself.

"I really enjoy the hunt of finding things that are good AND domestic. The best part of that search is finding a company where the owners are just as excited about being found as you are about [tasting] their product. That energy and momentum really carries through to our enthusiasm in the store." The café menu changes seasonally to reflect the best products available. The revenue split is approximately 35% grocery to 65% café, although in some months the split is even. Annual revenue in 2004 was $450,000.00. The growth rate has been 11% in its first year. The grocery business tends to increase around the holidays. Lisa explains that at start-up,

"We had both the grocery and the café. But then we didn't know whether the concept was going to take off. Are people going to get these groceries? These are higher end, fine food groceries. And I'm happy to say although we've had to tweak some things we carry, people get it. And I think it's why people want to come to us–because it's a little different. It's not just a café and it's not just a fine food grocery. And we use a lot in our menu. We say right on our menu 'featuring the products of the grocery store' because we really try to cross-market the two sides of our store.

"When you open you go with a lot of 'gut'– you know what you think will work, you go by intuition, whatever. Over time you tweak it as you listen to the customer. It's amazing how valuable that is. But then, over time, you have information. A great example of how you've got to go with your gut sometimes, but you've also got to look at your information happened last January. I went to the Fancy Food Show–it's one of the big trade shows. Before we went, I knew what products I like, what I'm looking for, what packaging sells, that kind of thing. I thought I'd better get some information on what the top selling product groups in my store are. I just ran a report in ten seconds. My gut was *completely* wrong. I thought our best sellers were pastas, sauces–you know, easy to make dinner-type stuff. Those *are* good selling items. But it was by far candy. And it's not like candy was first and pastas and sauces were a close second–it was third!

"That tells me our customers are here to enjoy and treat themselves. Not too long ago, vendors were coming to us with low-carb bread, and we tasted it and thought, this is horrible! I'm not going to serve this. So we didn't do anything. So for a short period of time we had people doing things like ordering the burger without the bun, you know what I mean? But, now that's all over with, at least for our customers. So that was very eye-opening–to look at what moves, what doesn't move, and then marry what my gut says to the numbers.

"I concern myself with looking for high-quality, artesian product–we're talking grocery-side now. I also concern myself with learning about what specialty foods the large grocers are beginning to offer. I have it pretty easy with the big grocer near me, because they put these foods in little kiosks that kind of bump out on the aisle so I can preview what they're doing. And a lot of times it keeps me on my toes. It doesn't really bother me because I've got lots of products that are out there that don't go through the big distributors. It really keeps me focused on differentiating ourselves.

"There are two distinct markets in the grocery side of my business. There are the people that are big cooks, home chefs, and they're looking for a certain kind of oil or whatever and they come in looking for it. And then there are other people who like to cook, they like food, they like to do interesting things, they're having people over, but they're busy. They don't have time to figure it out. They just want something to serve their friends. And the other thing that's really starting to happen, the thing I see more and more, is people using the two sides of our business, because the store is not literally split. When you see the store from the street you can tell that there's a café and there's a grocery—it's not one behind the other. I wanted people to be able to see and react, 'Wow there's a lot going on in there. I want to go in there.' It's great to see people waiting for their food and they'll pop up and start looking at the groceries and they start stock-piling stuff, or they finish eating and they say, 'That vinaigrette you make for the fruit is really good. Do you sell it?' It's nice to see that people experience both sides of it.

"Also, my market is neighborhood and it is destination. When we first opened, I would have thought we would have been a neighborhood place. I mean we are, but there are a lot of people who hear about us and come from other areas. It's a lot bigger percentage than I thought when we first opened. And I think it's that differentiation. For the neighborhood people, there's nothing else like us on the street, even from a food perspective. There's a lot of bar food and a lot of things with the TVs on the walls and all that. And that gets to be kind of old. Especially

if you have kids you don't necessarily want to be eating all the time with the television on."

What is the competitive environment for Southport Grocery and Café? There is no direct competition in the area; there are places that sell prepared food to take out and have a couple of little tables for customers to sit down and eat, but nobody with an actual café. "Nobody has the specific model we have. And that's what I think is a little risky, because you don't know if it will work, but it differentiates us from everybody. I've noticed I get a lot of calls from realtors, building owners, who love the concept. They think their neighborhood needs one. It's quite a compliment. I'm just not ready yet, even from an investment standpoint. There are two ways to go with this business. One is to open more, but another is to take certain aspects of the business and get expertise at them. We wholesale out our baked goods now to five locations. I never dreamed that I would be wholesaling out our baked goods, but we bake our own things and people love them.

"Now is the time . . . I have a year-and-a-half of data, so I can really sit down and say OK, how much can the store really make? Where do I take it from here? Is it better to open another location? Is it better to take baking, move it somewhere else with cheap rent, and market everything out of wholesaling, and then maybe do that with our prepared food? To me, just from a personal perspective, that's a lot more interesting than just opening another location—I think it's the control problem I have because if there's more than one location, there's only one of me. And letting the customer see my face, people like to see the owner. On weekends, my husband's there and the customers know him. They like to know that we're there. It makes them feel like they're coming to my house. There's a lot of legwork that would need to be done figuring out what fork in the road we take. I have some great employees.

"Maybe there's a way you build a business so that the customer contact for my wholesale customers and then for my retail customers are very different people. The wholesale people are other business people. But maybe there's a way to build a business where you have one key contact point for your retail customers, the in, the out, the 200 people per day, and then you build the back end dealing with the business customers."

Southport Grocery and Café developed a relationship with Intelligentsia Coffee, a Chicago-based purveyor of fine roasted coffees that has two retail stores in the city. Intelligentsia now carries Southport's cupcakes, a product that has garnered much attention in the food news. Lisa explains how this strategic relationship developed:

"Intelligentsia is the coffee that I wanted to carry to use in the café. So we had a relationship because of that. I've been very blessed with the press, I mean the press loves the store. Every time I turn around, someone was writing an article. I don't have a publicist, I cannot afford one. Those are all priceless things. I mean, we can't afford that kind of advertising. And, as a matter of fact, I think because of that, I don't really advertise all that much. Something's always going on where we're going to be mentioned in some publication. Advertising is hard. It's expensive.

"People latched onto those cupcakes. My husband and I thought for sure it would be the chocolate-chip toffee scones that were going to be the top thing. I think the cupcakes make people feel like they're at home–they're very comforting.

"I worked a little directly with Doug Zell, the co-founder of Intelligentsia Coffee, and then with Marcus Bonnie who heads up the two retail locations. Marcus comes in since he lives in the neighborhood. They love our baked goods. They're going back to their stores wanting more from the baked goods they had been offering their customers. They were buying biscotti frozen in a box from somewhere out west. Then they tried ours and said, 'These are so good!' And so it just was born.

"Then the next thing I know, the Book Cellar in Lincoln Square, she needs food . . . We got hooked up through the Women's Business Development Center of the SBA. . . .

"And it's basically just word of mouth. It's amazing. The small business community,

especially with food, we all know each other. I think for the most part, you all want to help each other. We want each other to succeed. And now Olivia's Market, the new urban grocery store in Bucktown, wants our soups and our baked goods. Starting Monday we're going to be in Millennium Park where people turn in their bikes. I mean, I'm at a point where I can't take any more business.

"And it's not a breaking point from a space issue. I can have people baking in the middle of the night. But it's from a staffing issue. I need to do some analysis around . . . have sort of a step-stone, 'if I hired another baker, what would that level be?' In a way it's all scary because anything you need to do is another investment, but it's a fun business problem to figure out."

Lisa Santos heeds the often advised "listen to your customers" very seriously. "My former boss at CNA taught me something very important. He said 'you tend to always think you know the way to get it done, and you probably do, but the businesses [our internal customers] want to feel some give-and-take.' And I looked at him and said, 'you know Myron, you are right. I know I go in thinking I've cleaned up a thousand messes, just get out of my way!' And he said, 'but you've got to learn to listen.'

"And I look at how Southport Grocery and Café looks today versus how we looked when we opened, even the menu. The evolution is incredible in a year-and-a-half. It's based on customer response. I have a gut check. If I hear it once from a customer, I listen and file it away in my head. If I hear it twice I'm think, 'hmmm, I've heard that twice now.' If I hear it three times from three customers on three different occasions, we have to try it. I read the book, *Crowning the Customer* (by Feargal Quinn), that addresses the balance between doing market research and just testing things out. Without listening, I don't think we would be where we are today, without listening and reacting.

"I would think it's like this in any business, but especially in the kitchen environment. Many people, especially with the prep cooks and the dishwashers, have seen a thousand kitchens. We treat them as valued employees because they know stuff, tricks, that I would never know because I'm not immersed in that. So it goes both ways. And the one thing, knock on wood, I've had a lot of turnover in my business—and that's just how the business is, you get a lot of summer help, what have you. But with all the turnover, the turnover in the key positions is a lot less than what is expected. I have two gentlemen in the kitchen now, one who's just been here a year, and one who will be here a year in July. That's unheard of for people who are dishwashers. They've even told me, they've worked at places where the chef or the owner didn't even know their name.

"There was one Sunday where the service in the kitchen was horrible. I was so upset and I thought how do I explain to these guys the fact that they have a variable part of their compensation—they get tips because the kitchen gets tips and retail—they each get part of the pot. And that how they get the food out and how quickly they wash the dishes impacts that. And so, of course being the true business person that I am, balanced scorecard is screaming in my head. So I took a piece of paper while they were cleaning the kitchen and I divided it into four and I had a picture of them on the bottom, then I had a picture of them doing dishes and a picture of the customer and a money bag on the top. It was funny because I'm explaining it to one guy who doesn't speak any English so I have a translator. So here I am, trying to explain to this very diverse workgroup how this is all connected, why it's important. And I kind of felt good. They got it. I try to treat the employees as a critical part of the business. Sometimes they just want me to tell them what they need to do. I don't think it stifles them though because I still get people coming up and saying, 'you know, I used to do it this way somewhere else.' And I welcome that.

"I explain things to them. When they see me going to Restaurant Depot to buy something, they might say, 'oh, we could use some more ramekins.' I say, 'OK guys this is how much ramekins cost, do we really need them?' They're like, (gasp) it costs that much? And I say, yes. And they know where the business is financially. They know there are months when we still struggle. It's funny how you define if that team is built. It's so different now than when we first opened. When we first opened it was just basic things like, are the coolers stocked and can we open the door? As complex as a small business is, but it's all about time, service and quality and as much cross-training as you can do because if one person's sick, you're in the tank sometimes if you haven't trained someone else. When you go to market, I think it's unrealistic to think that everything is going to be in a row the day you open those doors. But I think that all those things need to be there in your head so you can start moving toward them."

What will Santos be testing out in the near future?

"This is the year of the deli case. My analysis in January very clearly showed me that the prepared food that we have in our open-air cooler, we do very well in. So we bought a deli case. It will be filled by next week. Basically it's a little bit more work in the kitchen but it's got a good margin and I think it's what the customers want—prepared salads, antipasto-type foods. And this is a good time of year to test that out as well. It's also the year to put on-line shopping on our website. You know when you go on our website you can see the names of some of our items. You can go to the Grocery section and it lists all the things, but we don't have [an online] shopping cart. It's amazing how many requests I get for that. People ask, 'So are you set up for shipping yet?' We get calls from people based on our website asking, 'can you ship this out?' And my gut is, if they could just click and send . . . I mean if people are taking the time to call . . .

"My web developer has already done a really good job. If you type in any grocery product that we carry, we show up before the manufacturer's website! We're first! I'm not a technical person. I know there's some sort of name-calling convention, so the infrastructure is there. I'm taking a little bit of a gamble like if I got 20,000 orders the first day, but we've got a big basement downstairs. We could react. My next analytical step is I want to analyze how much can this 2,000 square foot space get us? That would be model number one. Model number two would be what it would take to be open Mondays, because when I'm there on Mondays there are a lot of people out on the street.

"A lot of people don't work 9–5 Monday through Friday. It's a whole new world out there—I thought everybody worked 9–5!

"I think the third model will be, and this one I shouldn't show my true colors because I think my gut is right, but I've been proven wrong before. We're open from 8 in the morning until 7 at night. We were open until 9 at night when we first opened and people do not perceive us as a nighttime place. I don't know if it's the name with 'grocery & café.' And I'm not really excited about being open 8 in the morning until 11 at night. But I think I need to do that analysis. I think part of that analysis is an extremely expensive, or some sort of a marketing campaign because it didn't happen naturally . . . I would rather invest in we'll say the fourth model that I will do that says, what will it take to really expand wholesale baking? We like to do business with people like us: small business owners that are excited that they are carrying our stuff."

Santos has even turned down business that didn't feel right:

"There was a restaurant that's more cafeteria-style. They wanted our cookies, had never tasted them. So right then I was like, I want you [to] want my stuff because you are addicted to it! They found us through one of our distributors. My distributor heard them talking and said, 'I know someone who does wonderful baking.' So first of all, red flag, she's never had the stuff. Can they really want it? Number two, it's a national franchise. Number three they're a cafeteria-style so they were going to wrap them in saran wrap by the checkout. It just didn't feel right. The money is good but my gut just said this isn't right. I know

all the other business owners that I sell to. We talk to each other. . . And we've been blessed with being able to use our down-time for the most part, and it pays well more than half my rent."

Santos considers whether her company should focus on the wholesale side of the business in the future.

"Do we take that as our business model, spin off things that we've become experts at—quality driven at—and make it its own business. We could rent some cheap space on Ravenswood, bake out of there, ship to our own store and to whomever else."

Reflecting on the past eighteen months in which she has turned her culinary passion into a thriving business, Lisa Santos says,

"It's been amazing. And trust me there have been nights where I have felt that I've made the biggest mistake of my life. I'm very lucky that I have a very supportive family and husband and friends. And my father is my informal advisor. We're heading in the right direction. The numbers look good for where we're supposed to be, and maybe a little ahead of the curve in terms of a new business. But worst case, what if this doesn't work? I've had the best time of my life trying to make it work! You have a chance to try and test out all of these things you've learned. It doesn't matter what happens, it's worth it."

SOURCE: Interview with Lisa Santos by Lisa Gundry. Reprinted with permission.

Discussion Questions

1. What are some of the key factors that led to Southport Grocery and Café's success?

2. What are the key challenges and opportunities facing Southport Grocery and Café?

3. What differentiates the business from its competition?

4. What would you advise Lisa Santos to do to grow her business in the future?

References

Acs, Z. J., Arenius, P., Hay, M., & Minniti, M. (2005). *Global entrepreneurship monitor: Executive report* (Babson College and London Business School). Retrieved February 9, 2006, from http://www.gemconsortium.org/document.asp?id=444

Acs, Z. J., & Armington, C. (2003). *Endogenous growth and entrepreneurial activity in cities* (Working paper). Washington, DC: U.S. Department of Commerce, Bureau of the Census, Center for Economic Studies.

Allinson, C. W., Chell, E., & Hayes, J. (2000). Intuition and entrepreneurial behavior. *European Journal of Work and Organizational Psychology, 9*(1), 31–43.

Allinson, C. W., & Hayes, J. (1996). The cognitive style index: A measure of intuition-analysis for organizational research. *Journal of Management Studies, 33*(1), 119–135.

Allis, R. P. M. (2003). *Zero to one million: How to build a company to one million dollars in sales.* Chapel Hill, NC: Virante, Inc.

Annan, K. (1999). Speech to the World Economic Forum. Retrieved December 12, 2005, from http://worldbenefit.case.edu/inquiry/feature_un.cfm

Baron, R. A. (1998). Cognitive mechanisms in entrepreneurship: Why and when entrepreneurs think differently than other people. *Journal of Business Venturing, 13*(4), 275–294.

Busenitz, L. W., & Barney, J. B. (1997). Differences between entrepreneurs and managers in large organizations: Biases and heuristics in strategic decision-making. *Journal of Business Venturing, 12*(1), 9–30.

French, W. L., & Bell, C. H. (1978). *Organization development.* Englewood Cliffs, NJ: Prentice Hall.

Hitt, M. A., & Ireland, R. D. (2002). The essence of strategic leadership: Managing human and social capital. *Journal of Leadership and Organization Studies, 9*(1), 3–14.

Hitt, M. A., Ireland, R. D., Camp, S. M., & Sexton, D. L. (2001). Strategic entrepreneurship: Entrepreneurial strategies for wealth creation. *Strategic Management Journal, 22,* 479–491.

Ireland, R. D., Hitt, D. M., Camp, S. M., & Sexton, D. L. (2001). Integrating entrepreneurship and strategic management action to create firm wealth. *Academy of Management Executive, 15*(1), 49–63.

Ireland, R. D., Hitt, M. A., & Sirmon, D. G. (2003). A model of strategic entrepreneurship: The construct and its dimensions. *Journal of Management, 29*(6), 963–989.

Kickul, J., Gundry, L. K., & Whitcanack. L. (in press). Intuition *versus* analysis? Testing differential models of cognitive style on entrepreneurial self-efficacy and intentionality. *Entrepreneurship: Theory and Practice.*

Kirzner, I. (1979). *Perception, opportunity, and profit.* Chicago: University of Chicago Press.

Kirzner, I. (1983). *Discovery and the capitalist process.* Chicago: University of Chicago Press.

Leonard, H. H., Scholl, R. W., & Kowalski, K. B. (1999). Information processing style and decision making. *Journal of Organizational Behavior, 20,* 407–420.

Miller, A. (1987). Cognitive styles: An integrated model. *Educational Psychology, 7*(4), 251–268.

Mitchell, R., Busenitz, L., Lant, T., McDougall, P., Morse, E., & Smith, B. (2002). Toward a theory of entrepreneurial cognition: Rethinking the people side of entrepreneurship research. *Entrepreneurship Theory & Practice, 27*(2), 93–104.

Newbert, S. L. (2003) Realizing the spirit and impact of Adam Smith's capitalism through entrepreneurship. *Journal of Business Ethics, 46,* 251–261.

Nickerson, R., Perkins, D., & Smith, E. (1985). *The teaching of thinking.* Hillsdale, NJ: Lawrence Erlbaum.

Ornstein, R. E. (1977). *The psychology of consciousness.* New York: Harcourt Brace.

Peters, T. J., & Waterman, R. H., Jr. (1982). *In search of excellence.* New York: Harper & Row.

Sadler-Smith, E., & Allinson, C. W. (2000). Learning preferences and cognitive style: Some implications for continuing professional development. *Management Learning, 31*(2), 239–256.

Schumpeter, J. A. (1934). *The theory of economic development.* Cambridge, MA: Harvard University Press.

Schumpeter, J. A. (1942). *Capitalism, socialism, and democracy.* New York: Harper & Row.

Shane, S. (2003). *A general theory of entrepreneurship: The individual-opportunity nexus.* Cheltenham, UK: Edward Elgar.

Shane, S., & Venkataraman, S. (2000). The promise of entrepreneurship as a field of research. *Academy of Management Review, 25*(1), 217–226.

Small Business Office of Advocacy. (2004). *Small firms and technology: Acquisitions, inventor movement, and technology transfer.* Washington, DC: Author.

Small Business Office of Advocacy. (2005). *The small business economy: A report to the president.* Washington, DC: Government Printing Office.

Venkataraman, S. (1997). The distinctive domain of entrepreneurship research: An editor's perspective. In J. Katz & J. Brockhaus (Eds.), *Advances in entrepreneurship, firm emergence, and growth* (Vol. 3, pp. 119–138). Greenwich, CT: JAI Press.

Waterman, R. H., Jr., Peters, T. J., & Phillips, J. R. (1980). Structure is not organization. *Business Horizons 23*(3), 14–26.

Wiklund, J., Davidsson, P., & Delmar, F. (2003). What do they think & feel about growth? An expectancy-value approach to small business managers' attitudes towards growth. *Entrepreneurship Theory & Practice, 27*(3), 247–270.

CHAPTER 2

Strategies for Opportunity Identification

The Creative Process

Some people only see what is. They never see what can be.

—Albert Einstein

I never think about why something hasn't been done already. I think about why nobody has done it right yet.[1]

—Marcia Kilgore,
founder of Bliss Spa, New York and London

Objectives:

1. Understand the role of creative thinking and behavior as entrepreneurs discover and refine entrepreneurial opportunities

2. Know the three strategies for innovation available to entrepreneurs

3. Enhance the entrepreneurial mind-set necessary to recognize opportunities

4. Use the model of opportunity identification, including scanning the environment; discovering needs, problems, and opportunities in the industry and marketplace; and generating ideas for new products, services, technologies, and processes

5. Learn the sources of ideas and opportunities for new ventures

6. Learn and conduct the Opportunity SEARCH process for idea generation

7. Build an entrepreneurial culture that supports creativity and innovation

Strategy in Action

Creating the Blissful Salon Experience

Marcia Kilgore is the founder and creative director of Bliss, a spa that began in New York and has grown to open new locations including London. Kilgore began her career as a personal trainer in Manhattan. She grew up in Saskatchewan, where there was not much else to do besides playing hockey and working out. After three years of training people in weightlifting, she focused on what was a very personal experience:

"I had bad skin for a long time, and I never really knew how to take care of it. Everything I tried didn't work, and every morning I would wake up and want to cry when I looked in the mirror. So I decided to take a skin care course, just for myself. I figured it might be fun to give skin treatments to my friends too, but once they found out I knew how to do them they wanted facials, and their friends began calling me, too. So I started to charge people" (Lieber, 1998, p. 25). Thus, her idea grew out of personal frustration, and when she found she had a skill others demanded, the opportunity emerged. At the time she opened her spa, there was not much competition, and the environment of the salons that she went to made her feel bad about her skin. She was criticized and did not have a positive experience.

With her firsthand experience, Kilgore knew what was missing in the industry: a warm, comforting, fun atmosphere, without criticism or intimidation. The overall environment should be relaxed: nice lighting, soft music, wine. Kilgore had both a niche and the talent and experience to support it; she was ready to begin business.

Kilgore's first spa was called "Let's Face It." Soon the name was changed because she felt it projected the wrong image: when clients come for a skin treatment, they shouldn't have to "face" anything. She recalls thinking about the experience people were having, and how one could describe the best feeling—happiness or elation. She named her spa Bliss, and launched it in 1996 with an experienced group of technicians that came along from Let's Face It. The creative possibilities of the new name soon emerged. Kilgore developed a mail order catalog called "Bliss Out" and a press kit known as "Pub-Bliss-ity." In 2001, BlissLondon was launched, and later QuickBliss spa service station at Bloomingdale's 59th Street in New York City was opened. As of 2005 Bliss has five U.S. spa locations including three in New York City, one in Chicago and one in San Francisco.

Kilgore notes that, "The great advantage of being young is that you're not jaded. I'm always hearing from fashion editors and others about how I'm so positive, that I think anything can happen. Why not? Be smart, find your niche, make it happen. I never think about why something hasn't been done already. I think about why nobody has done it right yet" (Lieber, 1998, p. 19).

SOURCE: R. Lieber, *Upstart Start-ups* (New York: Broadway Books, 1998); *About Bliss: Meet Our Founder*, retrieved from www.blissworld.com/about/marcia.

Creativity and Entrepreneurship: Turning Ideas Into New Venture Opportunities

All successful businesses have one experience in common: They all began with the foundation of a good idea. The idea may first have been just a glimmer, an unorganized series of thoughts or intuitions that are then refined and put to the test to determine if they can be formed into a viable new venture opportunity. However the idea was generated and the opportunity identified, new entrants to an industry are likely to be the ones who question tradition and challenge "the way things are done around here."

In a study of firm innovation, 500 CEOs were asked which firms took best advantage of change in their industry during the past 10 years: Newcomers, traditional competitors, or their own companies? Overwhelmingly, the answer was newcomers. They were also asked whether those newcomers were successful because they executed better or because they changed the rules of the game. Two thirds of the CEOs answered that it was by changing the rules. Yet, a myth prevails among founders and managers that what is needed is better execution and that strategy is the easy part (Hamel, 1998)!

Entrepreneurships are built on the generation of novel and useful ideas. An idea, opportunity, or solution is creative if it is novel and useful (Amabile, 1998). Creativity, part of the entrepreneurial mind-set, is one of the most fundamental dimensions of strategic entrepreneurship. Consider all the ways entrepreneurs need to use creativity:

- Generating ideas for new (or improved) products, services, technologies, and processes
- Finding an identifiable market to which the products and services will appeal
- Identifying a problem that calls out for an innovative solution
- Determining how to implement the opportunities they identify
- Persuading others of the value of the idea, so that they invest in, buy from, or form alliances with the new venture (For more on the broad application of creativity to entrepreneurial problem solving, see Ward, 2004)
- Retaining the entrepreneurial spirit as the firm grows, reinventing and renewing the organization so that it stays on the innovative edge

Innovation is the outcome of creativity: the solution to a problem or the way to embrace an opportunity. Innovation is the product, service, technology, or process that emerges from creative thinking along with an application that results in new venture formation or reinvention in an existing firm. There are three innovative strategies entrepreneurs can select (Dunden, 2002; Gaglio & Katz, 2001).

- Imitative innovation strategies involve taking an idea that somebody else has already discovered and building a new venture around that idea.
- Evolutionary innovation strategies involve taking an idea and offering a way to do something better (or quicker, cheaper, or with more choices) than it is done presently.
- Revolutionary innovation strategies reject existing ideas and present a way to do things radically different from the way they are done now.

Review Question

1. Why is creativity important in starting a new entrepreneurial venture?

Ideas Into Opportunities

The process through which entrepreneurs search, capture, and refine new ideas that lead to business opportunities is called *opportunity recognition*. While many entrepreneurs describe having a "Eureka!" moment, the likelihood that a viable opportunity or "great idea" simply popped into mind is slim. Rather, ideas are the result of scanning and interpreting the environment around us. You may recall seeing a new product or service in a store—or perhaps, listening to or reading an advertisement in media such as television, radio, newspapers, magazines, or the Internet—and thinking, "Why didn't *I* think of that?" Individuals and teams that are *idea prone* have learned to be aware of the cues that surround them and to actively search for and make connections between environmental stimuli and market need. Researchers believe opportunity recognition is one of the most fundamental and important behaviors of entrepreneurs (Gaglio, 1997). Entrepreneurship as a field of study is increasingly being defined as the nexus, or the connecting link, between enterprising individuals and valuable opportunities (Venkataraman, 1997).

Entrepreneurial opportunities are characterized by the introduction of new goods, services, raw materials, markets, and methods of organizing through the formation of new relationships (Shane & Venkataraman, 2000). Entrepreneurial opportunities can be differentiated from other types of opportunities in that they involve the creation or identification of new ends and means unnoticed by other market participants (Eckhardt & Shane, 2003; Gaglio & Katz, 2001). Successful entrepreneurs are able to identify the right opportunities to pursue because they have developed the ability to notice them.

Entrepreneurial alertness is a phrase that is used to describe this ability. It means that entrepreneurs have a special set of observational and cognitive skills that help them identify good opportunities. It can seem to be a flash of insight. Some scholars have suggested that entrepreneurs are able to notice things that have been overlooked without actually launching a formal search for opportunities (Kirzner, 1973, 1979, 1985). However, it is also important to consider why entrepreneurs search for new ideas (Gaglio & Katz, 2001). For example, if the owner of a clothing store notices that clients ask for particular brands or sizes not offered in the store, she might contact her manufacturers or designers to inquire about purchasing these to keep customers satisfied and coming back, and this additional stock could possibly attract new customers.

Alertness is part of what makes up the *entrepreneurial mind-set*, and such a mind-set is needed if individuals and management teams intend to become strategic entrepreneurs (Ireland, Hitt, & Sirmon, 2003). Having an entrepreneurial mind-set means that you think about business in such a way that uncertainty is viewed as a benefit (McGrath & MacMillan, 2000). How can uncertainty—or not being able to predict future events with any probability—possibly be a positive way to look at business?

Among some of the most common characteristics successful entrepreneurs share is the ability to embrace risk and cope with ambiguity in the face of uncertainty and change. In fact, organizations that can successfully cope with uncertainty are likely to perform better than those that cannot deal with not knowing all the information or the results of decisions (Brorstrom, 2002). Therefore, having

Table 2.1 The Entrepreneurial Mind-Set

Growth-oriented
Willingness to take calculated risks
Tolerance for ambiguity
Learning from failure
Promotes flexibility, creativity, innovation, and renewal

an entrepreneurial mind-set can become part of a firm's competitive advantage. Table 2.1 presents the attributes of this mind-set.

Review Questions

1. Which of the attributes of the entrepreneurial mind-set do you feel are most important to the success of the entrepreneurial venture?

2. Have you observed or worked for entrepreneurs who displayed some of these attributes?

3. In what ways did these influence the business?

The next section presents a creative process for the entrepreneurial opportunity search, including the most common sources of ideas for new ventures as well as improvements to existing business products, services, technologies, and business processes. Figure 2.1 illustrates the Opportunity Identification Process, which begins with the assessment of the external environment. This assessment leads to the discovery of a need, problem, or challenge. You will learn the SEARCH process that can help you identify the likelihood of developing a business opportunity from your analysis of the need, problem, or challenge. First, we will look at some of the most common sources of ideas for new ventures.

Sources of Ideas for New Ventures

Work Experience

More than half of all ideas for new ventures emerge from the experiences entrepreneurs have working in the industry for employers. The idea may grow out of observing what customers complain about or what is not yet available to them through the employer's firm or in the industry. In your own work experience, you may recall thinking that there might be a different way of doing the work, selling the product, or performing the service. Phyllis Apelbaum, president and CEO of Arrow Messenger Service in Chicago, Illinois, a messenger and delivery service

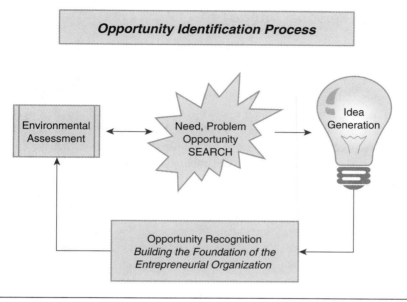

Figure 2.1   Opportunity Identification Process

business with more than $8 million in revenues per year, founded her business after working for a firm in the same industry for several years. The firm had changed ownership and, subsequently, the culture changed to one that was not as warm and inclusive as it had been before. Apelbaum first considered moving to another organization in the industry, and a friend suggested to her, "Imagine if you're worth that much to them, what you could be worth to yourself?" While Apelbaum wasn't sure she was ready to start her own venture, her old boss (the original owner of the firm) told her, "If you could do it for me, you can do it for yourself."[2]

A Similar Business

Even if you don't have years of work experience in an industry or market, you might see a business in an area that intrigues you because you like certain products or you learn that there is a growing market for this business and you think of a way to expand on the opportunity. Howard Schultz got the idea for offering gourmet coffee in coffee shops after noticing the neighborhood coffee bars on every corner in Italy. He bought Starbucks, a tiny Seattle roastery, in 1987, and today, Starbucks has 8,500 stores and 90,000 employees from Alaska to Bangkok (Lustgarten, 2004). Schultz developed his opportunity by challenging the belief that people would not willing to spend more than $1 on a cup of coffee.

Similarly, Herb Kelleher of Southwest Airlines challenged the prevailing assumption at airlines that passengers wanted reserved seats on the plane. Southwest does not have reserved seating, only reserved sections. Assignment to section is based on a first-come, first-served policy. Interestingly, passengers don't seem to complain, and many even relish the chance to get in line early to pick any seat they choose in section A!

Hobby or Personal Interest

Many people find a way to turn their hobbies into successful new ventures, seeing an opportunity to transfer their passion to others with similar interests. Brian Maxwell was a top-ranked runner competing in the London marathon. He was leading by one minute when he developed a stomach cramp. He finished in seventh place. When he returned home, he met up with Jennifer Biddulph, also a runner, who was a nutrition food science student at University of California, Berkeley. Maxwell realized that stomach cramp problems were common to athletes in many sports, and he and Biddulph set about mixing hundreds of combinations of raw ingredients trying to find a snack bar that would digest easily and provide quick energy. They finally attained the right combination of fructose, oat bran, and milk protein. They called it the PowerBar®, and today, these energy bars are available in many flavors with different ingredients and are sold in 30 countries. The company has grown into an $82 million business owned by Nestlé (Thompson, 2005).

Chance Happening, or Serendipity

"Name the greatest of all the inventors. Accident"

—Mark Twain (Notebook)

Earlier, it was noted that successful entrepreneurs are alert and pay attention to things most people miss. This increases the likelihood that a good idea or opportunity will not go unnoticed, even if it is a chance happening. Learning to be observant to cues around them has led many entrepreneurs to discover products and services that arise out of the unexpected. In the 1950s, researchers at 3M were working with fluorochemicals to be used on airplanes. One day, some spilled on a researcher's tennis shoe, and she found the chemical was impossible to remove. Over time, she noticed that the spot where the fluorochemical had spilled was still clean. While it was not the laboratory's goal, Scotchgard—the brand name of the fabric protector—today is used to keep carpets, furniture, clothing, car upholstery, and many other things stain-free (Jones, 1991).

In 1930, a woman named Ruth Wakefield was the owner of the Toll House Inn, located on the toll road between Boston and New Bedford, Massachusetts. While mixing a batch of cookies, she discovered she was out of baker's chocolate. She substituted some semi-sweetened chocolate, which she broke into small pieces and added to the dough. She expected the chocolate pieces to melt and become absorbed by the dough, creating chocolate cookies. When she removed the pan from the oven, to her surprise, she saw that in fact the chocolate had not melted into the dough, and her cookies were not chocolate cookies. Purely by accident, Wakefield had invented the chocolate chip cookie. She named them Toll House® cookies, after her inn. Today, with the recipe owned and distributed by Nestlé, they still are the most popular cookie in America, with more than seven billion consumed annually; half of the cookies baked in American homes are some variation of this recipe (Jones, 1991).

Family and Friends

Ideas can come to you through your conversations with your family and friends, and if you are open to these suggestions, a great business opportunity can result. Joan Eckert, founder of F. H. Clothing Co. (a.k.a. Fat Hat Company), wanted to build her dream house in Norwich, Vermont, a picturesque town just across the river from Dartmouth College. She contacted a friend who was a carpenter to help her build the home, but he said he would only come to Vermont if she provided him with a warm and wonderful hat. This was in 1980, and Eckert did make him a hat—a "floppy, drapeable, shapeable" hat, and as people in the town saw it, they wanted one. The Fat Hat Factory was launched, and later Eckert determined that if she could make shapeable hats, she could also design shapeable and comfortable clothing for all body types. The company (www.fathat.com/Storycont.html) is situated in a rambling old barn in Quechee, Vermont; it offers a wide range of floppy, shapeable clothing (www.fathat.com).

Education and Expertise

Entrepreneurs are able to identify ideas for new businesses by tapping their own expertise and experiences and offer products and services that others (either consumers or other businesses) are willing to buy. Another way to use your expertise is to consider what you *know* rather than what you *do* as a source of business opportunities. Andrew Koven studying at Syracuse University in New York state, where he ran a profitable business moving college students in and out of storage each semester. Helping him reach his target were effective marketing methods: campus sales reps, event sponsorships, and advertising. Companies that wanted to reach the same market—college students—contacted him for his assistance. They viewed Andrew as someone who could successfully sell things to college students. What Andrew *did* was "sell storage." What Andrew *knew* was "how to market to college students," and it was this knowledge that led to the emergence of the college marketing company, now known as University Sales and Marketing. Koven's first client was Jones Soda, a gourmet soda company that was looking for college students to help sell its product to stores near campuses (Lieber, 1998).

Research in Practice: Which Came First—the Idea or the Ownership Decision?

In the nationwide Panel Study of Entrepreneurial Dynamics,[3] 480 entrepreneurs were asked whether the business idea or the decision to start some kind of business came first. Here are the responses:

The business idea came first	35%
The decision to start a business came first	44%
The idea and the decision occurred simultaneously	20%

(Continued)

(Continued)

The entrepreneurs were also asked, "What led to your business idea?" The following table presents the answers to this question. Work experience in a particular industry or market was the most frequently mentioned source of ideas, followed by discussion with family and friends. The implication from this data is that there are multiple reasons for the new venture journey, and you can choose the reason that works for you.

What Led to Your Business Idea?

It developed from another idea I was considering	24%
My experience in a particular industry or market	57%
Thinking about solving a particular problem	30%
Discussions with my family and friends	45%
Discussions with potential or existing customers	30%
Discussions with existing suppliers or distributors	13%
Discussions with potential or existing investors/lenders	8%
Knowledge or expertise with technology	28%

SOURCE: Adapted from G. E. Hills and R. P. Singh, "Opportunity Recognition," in *Handbook of Entrepreneurial Dynamics: The Process of Business Creation,* edited by W. B. Gartner, K. G. Shaver, N. M. Carter, and P. D. Reynolds (Thousand Oaks, CA: Sage, 2004), Table 24.4, p. 268.

Review Questions

1. Discuss ways in which entrepreneurs get their business ideas.

2. What expertise and skills do you have?

3. How could you start a business with those skills?

The Opportunity SEARCH

The pathway to entrepreneurial opportunities can be described as a creative process that includes six distinct phases. This approach is designed to help you learn how to more creatively develop and identify ideas that lead to viable new ventures. The process uses the acronym SEARCH, which will help you remember the necessary steps through which you should proceed. This process, shown in Table 2.2, can be applied to ideas that are invented by entrepreneurs, are adapted from other businesses or processes, or that emerge from an analysis of market needs or problems.

Table 2.2   The Opportunity SEARCH: A Creative Approach to New Venture
Idea Generation

S = Scan the environment

E = Expand on the idea

A = Adapt the idea to the circumstances

R = Revise and reconnect the idea's
components

C = Create the opportunity

H = Harvest the idea and develop the vision

Scan the Environment

Ideas for new ventures, or for new products, services, technologies, or business
processes around which an entrepreneurial venture is built, emerge from a careful
assessment of the external environment. This assessment includes several components, along with some useful tools to help you ask the right questions and probe
for the unexpected solutions, needs, problems, and opportunities in the environment. *What trends, needs, or problems can be identified in the environment?*
In Chapter 4, you will be introduced to the strategic management tool, TOWS
(Threats, Opportunities, Weaknesses, and Strengths), which provides a different
perspective from a traditional SWOT (Strengths, Weaknesses, Opportunities, and
Threats) analysis, allowing the entrepreneur to design strategic solutions to the
information discovered through the SWOT analysis. As you immerse yourself in the
environment of your new venture, be careful to notice the threats and opportunities presented by social, economic, political, legal, and other forces that influence
what your new venture will be able to do.

As you try to learn what there is to know about an industry and market that
interest you, begin by collecting secondary information, using the Internet, industry research, trade associations, magazines, newsletters, and many other sources.
This is an excellent way to hone your observational skills, so that you can become a
better trend-spotter, keeping your "finger on the pulse" of the industry and marketplace. Thus, scanning the environment is based on effective intuition and analysis. This is a very important point because if entrepreneurs used only the results of
market analysis, or relied only on "what they already know (or think they know!),"
many great ideas would remain untapped.

Why didn't Ford produce the first minivan? The idea for the minivan originated at
Ford Motor Company with Lee Iacocca and his engineer colleague, Hal Sperlich.
The idea was rejected by Henry Ford II because he believed it would not be a market success. Remember, this was the Ford that had just produced the enormously
successful Mustang, and the image of a sports car did not fit with a new "boxy" car
designed for a family. Iacocca and Sperlich left Ford after this dispute and went to

Chrysler. It's not an exaggeration to say that the Chrysler minivan was responsible for the company's survival during the downturn of the early 1980s.

Why wasn't Barnes & Noble the first to see the potential for on-line book retailing? Jeff Bezos, founder of Amazon.com, saw the opportunity to provide books using technology that capitalized on the method of book distribution. While Barnes & Noble developed an on-line presence, its core business focus at that time was its stores. Furthermore, Amazon did not compete on price because other on-line booksellers, such as Barnes & Noble, offered prices comparable to (or even less than) Amazon's. What Amazon excels at is building and sustaining a relationship with customers. When customers return to Amazon's site, they are greeted and offered recommendations based on their preferences. The experience it has created is akin to walking into the bookstore and having your own salesperson greet you and make suggestions about what you might like.

The Innovator's Toolkit: Just Ask!

To really learn about the problems, needs, and opportunities of the marketplace, you have to ask the right questions. Use these questions as a guide to understanding much more about the environment in which your business operates.

1. *What frustrates customers or users of this industry?* Some of the best ideas come from looking at things that bug you, including not having enough options or selection, not getting the product or service quickly enough, and experiencing poor quality.

2. *What should businesses be making, providing, selling in this industry that many are not yet doing?* What do you believe customers will want three to six months from now? One year from now?

3. *What have you experienced as a consumer of this industry or as an employee in this industry?* How would you do business differently? What would you change based on what you experienced?

4. *What does everybody think "won't work" in this industry or in a previous organization for which you have worked?* Asking questions about what others have thought impossible is a great way to get new ideas. John Seely Brown, who served for years as the head of Xerox Corporation's Palo Alto Research Center, was known for questioning the orthodoxies of his industry and organization. He recounted a time when Xerox wanted to figure out how to make copiers that produce less noise. However, Brown felt this wasn't an interesting problem. He reframed it and said that if they were asked to make a machine that makes *no* noise, that would be far more interesting. He was told that was impossible. Brown challenged them to think about how they could make a machine that had no moving parts. This led to a radical shift in architecture that reflected new ways of thinking about copiers, printers, and mechanical systems.

Make a list of all the questions you have about the industry and market: about trends, customers, suppliers, and competitors, and then find out the answers through your own research and observation. Ask people in the industry, ask customers, even ask competitors. Some of the most valuable strategic alliances are formed by members of the same industry who cooperate by exchanging information and knowledge to benefit all parties.

Expand on the Idea

After you have collected information about the environment, you now know much more about the needs and problems encountered in the industry. This will help you build onto your original idea so that it is a better fit to the needs of the environment. Using the method of *divergent thinking*, entrepreneurs amplify and elaborate on an idea, identifying what is good about it and enhancing these qualities. To expand on your idea creatively, consider the following challenges:

What need or problem can this idea resolve?

What attributes would make this idea very attractive to the market?

Are there any new market segments to which this idea might appeal?

What experience can this idea create for customers? What is its potential value?

Sometimes the original idea can expand to include additional, perhaps even unexpected solutions for customers. Pierre Omidyar launched a company called Auction Web in September, 1995, because his girlfriend wanted to trade PEZ dispensers and interact with other collectors on the Internet. The result was the development of "Anti-commercial" software, and Omidyar expanded on the idea by empowering users to develop their own solutions. The site was soon renamed eBay. At the end of 2005, eBay had more than 100 million registered users and reported consolidated net revenues of $4.552 billion for 2005, representing a 39 percent increase over 2004 ("eBay Inc.," 2006). The key to eBay's success has been to expand the original software idea into a vision of the business as a loyal community of users.

Adapt the Idea to the Circumstances

Many new ventures are founded on the concept of adaptation: taking an idea that exists in some other form, or in some other industry or market, and applying it in a new way. Adaptation is evolutionary in its approach, and entrepreneurs have successfully launched firms, or even discovered an entirely new application for something that already exists. Finding a new use for something that might seem quite ordinary can, in fact, lead to an extraordinary outcome.

Consider the case of Rangaswamy Srinivasan. He was employed by IBM in the early 1980s, working with lasers and cutting organic plastics. He recalled sitting at his Thanksgiving dinner table and staring at the turkey. Suddenly, he wondered how a laser would cut organic matter like a turkey—or a person. Srinivasan stashed a turkey leg and took it to his office the next day. With no one around, he used the laser to slice through the turkey leg and then looked at the results under a microscope. He observed that the laser cut right through and removed small bits of material without causing heat burns to the tissue. Srinivasan's work was instrumental in the development of laser eye surgery, an idea that came to him by adapting a technology—lasers—to a new problem—cutting human tissue. He was inducted into the Inventors Hall of Fame in 2002 (Kurlantzick, 2003).

Adaptation comes from asking how ideas can be fitted to a new situation. This relies on a creative process of generating alternative uses and applications. These alternatives can take many forms:

- *What other uses are there for a product, service, or technology?* Scott Paper Company, a large distributor of bathroom tissue, received a shipment of paper that was too heavy and wrinkled. Arthur Scott did not send the paper back to the manufacturer. Instead, he perforated the tissue so that it could be dispensed in single sheets, named them Sani Towels, and sold them to railroad stations, hotels, schools, and businesses. Today, they are available in designer colors and textures. Paper towels were created by putting something to a new use.

- *What has been successfully implemented in one field that could be adapted to another?* Consider Global Positioning Systems (GPS) to track geographical locations; could they be used to track people, including children, to ensure safety?

- *How can knowledge from an unrelated field be applied to the idea?* A rug manufacturer, for example, can get many ideas for colors and textures of fabrics by reading about the work of cosmetologists.

- *How can a product or service be adapted for an entirely different market?* Could you adapt it from a business market to a residential or personal market? From children to teens or seniors? From experts to novices (or vice versa)?

Revise and Reconnect the Idea's Components

When an idea is expanded and adapted, it takes on a new form. The idea has been shaped and changed through the SEARCH process so far, and this next step involves revising it so that it contains greater potential value.

George Zimmer, founder of The Men's Wearhouse, a chain of men's clothing stores that is growing rapidly, took an idea of providing value in men's clothing at reasonable prices and combined it with good, fast services in the store, such as alterations. This revision made the idea a little bit better, and The Men's Wearhouse did that little bit extraordinarily well. This is an example of an evolutionary innovation strategy: incremental changes to already existing ideas that refine them to make them better.

Vance Patterson, CEO of Patterson Fan Company, a manufacturer of industrial fans, discovered two of his employees cooking hamburgers for lunch in the parking lot. They were using an odd-looking grill that they had built out of spare parts. They found that the unusual shape of the flared fan parts was able to keep the unit cooler than other grills and allowed the air to circulate more freely. Patterson patented the grill in the names of the employee inventors and the Patterson Company and eventually formed a new company named Down South, Inc., to make and sell the Town and Country Grill.

Revising and reconnecting parts of the idea is about experimentation and trial and error. Some parts of the original idea may not work; others can be enhanced and refined. By submitting the idea to this process, entrepreneurs can prevent some of what is called idea infatuation, a pitfall of the opportunity identification process in which entrepreneurs mistakenly believe the idea is flawless and has inherent market value without subjecting it to any further analysis. Most new products and services are not commercial successes until the second or even third revision. By building such revision into the opportunity search process, entrepreneurs can anticipate and correct some of the weaknesses in the idea. It is far less costly to do this early than to learn of these flaws after market entry.

Create the Opportunity

Not all good ideas are viable business opportunities. After the idea has been expanded, adapted to the need or problem, and revised, the next step in the process is to build the business opportunity. This involves obtaining an accurate under-standing of how the intended market will use the idea to fill its need or solve its problem. Gaining acceptance of the idea is a necessary step in developing the opportunity.

- *Understand your audience:* What are the needs of your potential investors, customers, and employees? Many new ventures include these constituents in the opportunity identification process so their unique perspectives can be learned. You may look at your opportunity as a way to solve your constituents' problems. What do they want? What frustrates them? How can your idea resolve these? By framing your idea as a solution to a group's or organization's problem, you can create a potentially successful new venture opportunity.

- *Gain the support of your stakeholders:* Entrepreneurs are the experts on their ideas. Realize that others may not have the in-depth expertise and knowledge of the entrepreneur or the team, so it is important to explain the idea as fully as possible in terms your stakeholders can understand. If there is resistance, learn the sources. If you have fully explored the weaknesses or potential flaws of your idea, these can be addressed by acknowledging them and stating how they will be remedied. Without support or sponsorship, good ideas will never be formed into new venture opportunities.

- *Evaluate the idea's feasibility:* Chapter 3 presents models and methods to help you assess the potential value of the idea.

Harvest: Develop the Vision for Implementation

Many entrepreneurs are anxious to move from the idea generation stage to con-ducting financial and growth projections. While such projections are necessary to a sound analysis, making the leap at this juncture leads to a major gap in the build-ing of your organization. Harvesting the opportunity involves *creating the vision* for its evaluation and potential implementation. It means considering what will hap-pen if the idea is put into action. Here are some key questions that should be asked as entrepreneurs complete the SEARCH process.

- What is the problem or need this opportunity intends to resolve or fill?
- What still needs improvement? As you will see in Chapter 3, evaluation of the opportunity should be designed to provide the information needed for improvement.
- What obstacles does the entrepreneur anticipate?
- What does the entrepreneur want to become known for?
- If the opportunity is harvested, what difference can the new venture make for its intended market?

Review Question

1. What are the six phases of the creative process for finding entrepreneurial opportunities?

Strategic Reflection Point

Applying the SEARCH Process to Your Own Idea

Each December, *Entrepreneur* publishes the hottest trends and best ideas for the coming year. Here are some of the more recent best business ideas that have been presented. Select one or two, and individually or in teams, put the idea through the SEARCH process to see what opportunities emerge.

Identity theft prevention and recovery: Identity theft is becoming a clear danger as millions of people have been affected. Companies that offer services that alert consumers of suspicious activities are much in demand, and the market remains largely untapped (Torres, 2005).

Functional food: adding nutrients such as calcium and soy protein to enhance products, and on-line specialty foods, ranging from gourmet cheese and fine wines to gluten-free and diabetic-friendly products (Torres, 2004b). Chocolate is also a very hot food, with the opening of new cafés dedicated to chocolate.

Financial planning: About 77 million baby boomers will need to deal with financial planning and asset management to live comfortably. Consider breaking this large demographic into niches by profession or asset level (Torres, 2004a).

Travel with a purpose: People yearn to get away, but not just on any old vacation. Trips that enable people to explore, learn, and experience something new or even exotic are in great demand. These can include extreme adventures such as rappelling or white water rafting, but also sailing and bird watching. Sizzling markets are women (culinary tours and spa getaways) and adults who want to learn a new skill, sport, or hobby. More than 30 million adults took an educational trip in the last three years, according to the Travel Industry Association of America (Pennington, 2005).

Hispanic marketing: The purchasing power of this market is expected to hit $1.2 trillion in 2010 (Torres, 2004c). Consider the possibilities of teaching companies how to communicate in Hispanic-oriented media and how to be sensitive to this market when mass marketing.

Technology security consulting: With spam, security breaches, software patches, viruses, worms, and hackers abounding, individuals and companies are in need of security consultants.

Data backup is also important, with companies relying on data storage for Sarbanes-Oxley compliance (Kooser, 2004b).

Niche health and fitness: Potential customers might be looking for a place to go when their dogs are stressed out, or their families need exercise, or they are tired of a gym with fit-and-trim model types. Pregnant women are attracted to a fusion of Pilates and Yoga called PiYo, and small firms are catering to the needs of this special group (Kooser, 2004a).

Senior clothing and products: helping seniors maintain dignity and alleviate pain in dressing (Spaeder, 2004). Also, retrofitting homes for senior living is becoming a hot area. The National Association of Home Builders in Washington, D.C., estimates that the aging-in-place remodeling market will be up to $25 billion of the more than $214 billion remodeling market in the near future (Prather, 2005).

Social entrepreneurship: As Chapter 1 discussed, social responsibility is a driving force in the founding of new businesses. Gap Inc. recently severed its ties to 70 overseas factories because of code of conduct violations related to child labor (Cooper, 2005c).

Building Green: In the aftermath of Hurricane Katrina in 2005, it became clear how dependent the United States is on natural resources. Gas prices shot up dramatically; companies that are thinking about the future are building and operating Green through the use of environmentally friendly materials, alternative energy sources, and simple changes such as using motion sensors to save electricity when the office is empty (Cooper, 2005b).

Teen grooming products: Teens—and not just girls—are looking for much more than acne cream. Teenage boys are also demanding products in this industry that includes hair care, cosmetics, skin care, and ethnic health and beauty items (Pennington, 2004).

Education and tutoring services: According to educational market research firm Eduventures, tutoring is a $4 billion market that is likely to grow 15 percent in the coming years. This is influenced, in part, by the No Child Left Behind Act, which requires schools to provide tutoring services to students in schools that do not meet performance standards (Spaeder, 2005).

Aftermarket accessories: Products that go with iPods and cell phones (think of the color possibilities) are wildly popular as consumers desire ways to customize their personal tech gear (Cooper, 2005a).

Other trends or ideas: What have you noticed around you?

Failures and Foibles

Caviar, Anyone?

Can entrepreneurs or managers be too quick to jump on opportunities? Is it possible to become "idea infatuated" and insist that the business try something that perhaps it should reject? Consider the story of Howard Lester, chairman of Williams-Sonoma. He is honest in his admission that the company's growth is not attributable to his own taste in mixers and pasta spoons. He believes his success is based on honestly owning up to what he doesn't know, including leaving the buying to the experts.

(Continued)

(Continued)

When he joined Williams-Sonoma, he was eager to go on a buying trip with the company founder, Chuck Williams. He thought it would be fun to go to Europe on a buying trip, so he went to the Williams-Sonoma store in Beverly Hills, California, and told the employees, "I'm going with Chuck to Europe, so tell me what things you need and I'll be sure to get them for you" (Bonamici, 2004, p. 200). At the top of the list they gave Lester was a caviar server, a tray or dish that holds vodka cups around the edge and the caviar in the middle. Chuck Williams didn't say much to Lester on the way to Europe. After two or three days of shopping in Florence and Paris, Williams still hadn't mentioned the caviar server. They found a seller with a room full of more than 100 caviar servers, and Williams told Lester to pick the one he wanted. Lester recalled,

So we bought 24. They didn't sell. We probably sold one. I bought two myself. It's a great lesson learned that we talk about a lot around here: It's as important what we don't sell as what we do sell—Chuck really taught me that. (Bonamici, 2004, p. 200)

Strategic Reflection Point

The Proactive Personality

Do successful entrepreneurs possess the ability to search for and find opportunities more readily than other people? There is a construct known as *the proactive personality,* defined as the capability of acting in such a way as to influence change in the environment. According to Bateman and Crant (1993), proactive personalities "scan for opportunities, show initiative, take action and persevere until they reach closure by bringing about change" (p. 105). How might this personality affect the business? More specifically, does it have an impact on the search for opportunities and on innovation?

Research has shown the link between a proactive personality, strategic orientation of the new venture, and the innovations these firms produce (Bateman & Crant, 1993; Kickul & Gundry, 2002). In a study of 107 small business owners, proactive personality was connected to a strategic orientation for the business, an orientation that enabled flexibility and change in response to the surrounding business conditions. Proactive owners tended to employ a prospector strategy (Miles & Snow, 1978), in which they search the marketplace for new products, services, and technologies. They are the *creators of change* in their industries, relying on environmental scanning and long-range forecasting to help them identify new opportunities critical to their success (Miles & Snow, 1978).

The authors found that proactive entrepreneurs are opportunistic, and by using a prospector strategy, they were able to engage in *innovative targeting* (e.g., new or improved products, venturing into new markets, using new channels of distribution), developing *innovative systems* for their organizations (e.g., new ways of organizing or managing), and creating *innovative boundary supports* (new methods of financing, integrating new information technology) (Kickul & Gundry, 2002). Figure 2.2 illustrates the model developed in this study.

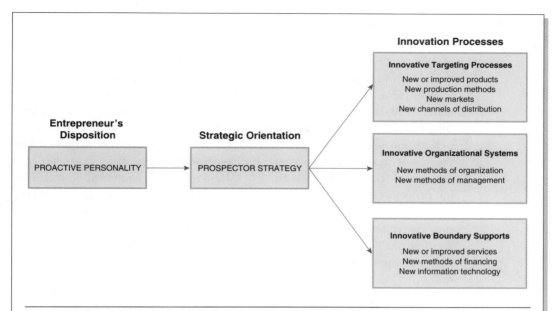

Figure 2.2   The Proactive Entrepreneur Personality, Prospector Strategy, and Innovations

Use the following scale to assess your own degree of proactivity.

	Strongly Agree						Strongly Disagree
	1	2	3	4	5	6	7
I enjoy facing and overcoming obstacles to my ideas.							
Nothing is more exciting than seeing my ideas turn into reality.							
I excel at identifying opportunities.							
I love to challenge the status quo.							
I can spot a good opportunity long before others can.							

SOURCE: T. S. Bateman & J. M. Crant, "The Proactive Component of Organizational Behavior: A Measure and Correlates." *Journal of Organizational Behavior* 14 (1993): 103–118. Reprinted with permission.

Review Question

1. Explain the importance of the proactive personality and prospector strategy in supporting innovative activities in new ventures.

Building the Entrepreneurial Culture to Support Creativity and Innovation

An innovative organization does not automatically develop out of an innovative business idea or opportunity. Entrepreneurs have to model creative leadership, deliberately set expectations, and reinforce them to the stakeholders of the new venture. David Thomson, a national brand manager at Unilever who led the relaunch of the Salon Selectives line of hair products, believes that recognition is fuel—it fans the fires of creativity and helps your business reach potential that it may never have anticipated (Gundry & LaMantia, 2001). New ventures are founded on creativity, but many lose their creative edge as the firm continues. It is important to found the firm on core values that support innovative behavior. To build a new venture culture that embraces creative thinking and behavior, entrepreneurs must institute a set of norms that reinforce curiosity, experimentation, and learning. Table 2.3 presents a comparison of some of the key cultural values and norms that prohibit and those that encourage creativity and innovation. A *prohibitive* culture is one that keeps ideas and opportunities from emerging and being put into practice. An *inquisitive* culture is one that seeks to discover what's right about new ideas and concepts (Prather & Gundry, 1995).

The creative process described in this chapter enables entrepreneurs to generate ideas that can be turned into viable business opportunities and to build their new venture cultures to support ongoing creative thinking and innovation. In the next

Table 2.3   Prohibitive Versus Inquisitive Culture

Prohibitive Culture	Inquisitive Culture
Allow only formal meetings and interactions: Ideas are shared at scheduled times	Encourage informal meetings and conversations: Ideas are shared anywhere, anytime
Expect and reward only success	Recognize and reward "nice tries"
Encourage your team or your employees to hold knowledge closely	Encourage your team or employees to share knowledge freely
Frown on risk taking	Value risk taking and experimentation
Reinforce behaviors that uphold tradition: "We've always done it this way"	Reinforce behaviors that question tradition: "Why do we always do it that way?"
Closely monitor the work and time of others: Don't trust them, they will slack off	Allow others to perform their work the way they believe is best: Trust in their expertise
Encourage interaction with insiders only	Encourage interaction with customers and others outside your organization
Focus on internal processes and short-term performance	Focus on external changes and long-term performance

chapter, we examine methods to evaluate opportunities to ensure strategic success in the marketplace.

Review Questions

1. Why is it important to found a company on values that support innovation?

2. List three characteristics of a prohibitive culture that you have observed through your work or research experience, and how they differ from an inquisitive culture.

Summary of Chapter Objectives

1. Understand the role of creative thinking and behavior as entrepreneurs discover and refine entrepreneurial opportunities
   - Creativity is the generation of novel and useful ideas. Entrepreneurs use creativity to generate ideas for new products and services, to identify markets for them, to determine how to implement the ideas, to persuade investors and other stakeholders of the value of the ideas, and to retain the entrepreneurial culture necessary for innovation as the firm grows.
   - Opportunity recognition is one of the most basic entrepreneurial behaviors.

2. Know the three strategies for innovation available to entrepreneurs
   - Imitative strategies take an idea that somebody else has already discovered and build a business around that idea.
   - Evolutionary strategies take an idea and offer a way to do something slightly different than it is done now.
   - Revolutionary innovation strategies reject existing ideas and present a way to do things that is radically different.

3. Enhance the entrepreneurial mind-set necessary to recognize opportunities
   - Entrepreneurial alertness means that entrepreneurs have a special set of observational and thinking skills that help them identify good opportunities.
   - Among some of the most common characteristics successful entrepreneurs share is the ability to embrace risk and cope with ambiguity in the face of uncertainty and change.

4. Use the model of opportunity identification, including scanning the environment; discovering needs, problems, and opportunities in the industry and marketplace; and generating ideas for new products, services, technologies, and processes.
   - Begin by scanning the environment, leading to the emergence of needs, problems, and opportunities. Generate ideas that can solve problems or capitalize on opportunities.

5. Learn the sources of ideas and opportunities for new ventures
   - Ideas for new business come from a variety of sources, including work experience (the most common source), observation of a similar business, hobbies or personal interests, a chance happening, discussions with family and friends, and sales education and experience.
   - A majority of entrepreneurs who have been included in studies knew they wanted to start a business and were highly motivated to find business ideas.

6. Learn and conduct the Opportunity SEARCH process for idea generation.
   - Scan the environment: What trends, needs, or problems can you observe and learn about?
   - Expand on the idea: Use divergent thinking to ask how your idea could be built upon, appeal to a new market segment, or add value in new ways.
   - Adapt the idea to the circumstances: What alternate uses or applications of your idea are possible? How can it be fitted to new situations?
   - Revise and reconnect the idea's components: Use experimentation and trial-and-error to refine your idea and make it better.
   - Create the opportunity: How will your stakeholders use the idea? Can it be turned into an opportunity to solve their problems and fill their needs? Do you have support?
   - Harvest the idea and develop the vision: Build the vision for implementing the opportunity. What still needs improvement? What obstacles do you anticipate? What do you hope to learn through evaluation of the opportunity and early testing of its feasibility?

7. Build an entrepreneurial culture that supports creativity and innovation
   - Entrepreneurs set the culture of their organization and determine whether it embraces change, experimentation, and creativity. A *prohibitive* culture is one that keeps ideas and opportunities from emerging and being put into practice. An *inquisitive* culture is one that seeks to discover what's right about new ideas and concepts.

CASE 2.1   Speaking of Strategy: Jacquelyn Corbett Cyr—Innovation by Design

Jacquelyn Corbett Cyr was still a student at Dalhousie University in Halifax, Nova Scotia, Canada, when she started her new media communications business in January 2000. Her background in design and her interest in finding a way to provide presentation and training tools for companies, tools that would be engaging to both consumers and employees, helped her envision the idea for her business. Corbett Cyr Consulting is the name of the company, and Jacquelyn and her husband, Dave, who has a background in industrial design, work with companies and organizations both large and small to create dynamic advertising, training, and presentation tools. In 2003, Jacquelyn won the prestigious Global Student Entrepreneur Award for her region.

"Both Dave and I worked as independent contractors before starting this business. I was a designer, and he was an animator. We had done that for a while, and we decided to start a company together. We saw a market for this particular service, but we weren't sure if the timing was right. Our first big contract was with an engineering firm in the [United] States, where we completed a large industrial visualization project. We photographed their plants and obtained blueprints and other materials so we could build the entire factory and use animation to convey its inner processes. We created a training module that the company could use to teach its employees. When they get new employees they can run this module and talk to the employees about it, rather than trying to give them tours of the complicated factories and try to explain things with only words. It was after completing this project that we became convinced that industrial visualization was an untapped market. There simply weren't many companies doing anything like it at that point, and it was a useful and efficient tool. It saved companies so much in terms of training dollars."

Once Jacquelyn and Dave accomplished that, they thought about other ways to apply their work in an industrial setting. Corbett Cyr Consulting's clients realized that traditional training materials are often bland and boring and don't teach employees what they need to know in a way that is memorable or effective. Jacquelyn is always on the lookout for new ways to use her technology and new markets that might be interested in using visual forms of communication. Like many successful business owners, Jacquelyn and Dave have found opportunities in some unexpected places.

Jacquelyn explains, "Dave actually met one of our best clients in the airport. They started talking, and it turns out this gentleman worked in construction and had invented a new technology for builders. We found a way to work together creating presentations for trade shows so people could understand his product and how it worked." Jacquelyn underscores, "People need to realize that when looking for business opportunities you don't just do it at your desk. It can happen anywhere, anytime."

How does Jacquelyn know if an idea is worth pursuing? She advises, "Talk to people in the industry. It's a big thing. My dad is an engineer. My sister is an architectural engineering technician. I want to know what things are valuable in their industries. My dad was particularly excited about our idea; he could see the applications for it. He referred us to different companies so we could talk to them to see if our concept would be a valuable tool. I did a small-scale initial feasibility study first just by talking to people in the industry. After we saw positive results with that, we did a full feasibility study and concluded that this was something worth pursuing."

How does Jacquelyn find out about her target market? "I'm finishing my science degree. So I understand the background of what's going on, and the sort of problems these clients run into trying to get any sort of visualization work done. Other consultants may not understand where they're coming from. It's important to have the sort of background where you can know your customers' market as well as your own. You can zero in on their issues and know how to solve them. You don't have to take a month researching their industry—you understand it going in."

Does Jacquelyn find it a challenge to innovate? She says, "I think the pressure is constantly on. Unless you're a business with major market share, you have to fight for your part of the sector. To do that, you have to put yourself in a position where you're willing to constantly challenge yourself to try to find new ideas and better, more efficient ways of doing things. You have to stay on top of every part of that market you're trying to service. Because if you let it slide for even two weeks, you know someone else that has stayed on top of it can come in there and take your place.

"I think the constant assessment and awareness of your plan—your whole strategy from the beginning—and keeping those goals in sight is probably the hardest thing to do. It's especially difficult when things start going well, and you have so much day-to-day stuff to keep up with. It is imperative that you keep that strategy at the top of your mind with every step you take."

So how can business owners become more adept at spotting opportunities? Jacquelyn suggests, "Do research, read trade publications, talk to professionals in the field you're targeting, find out what problems they've run into, consider what they're missing. A lot of the time, people see a problem and just walk by, expecting that somebody will eventually figure it out. If you can see a problem and work to identify an appropriate and efficient solution, that's your idea—that's your opportunity."

How can you tell if an idea is the wrong one for you? Jacquelyn advises, "You have to know if it's not going to work. If you're trying to sell an idea, whether it's a good or a service, and no one is buying into it, that's a sign that it might not work—or it might simply be the wrong time for that concept. In entrepreneurship, everyone thinks their idea is the greatest. But if you're honest with yourself and don't allow any place for attachment to concepts until they've been analyzed for effectiveness in the marketplace, you'll know when it's not the greatest anymore. I've owned a couple of businesses, and there are reasons I stopped running with those ventures. I had a magazine that I sold to a publishing company, and I was so glad when I did. I no longer felt the confidence I had when I first started. I'd seen it grow, but I saw an end that was closer than I'd expected when I began that project's business plan. Exit strategies and a willingness to move on are necessities in successful entrepreneurs. And, as much as you strategize, they're both pretty much intuitive.

"Another way to tell if an idea is worth investing in is what I call the Love Money Rule. Suppose you need $20,000 for start-up. Ask yourself if you would take the money in the form of a loan from your mother or your best friend. If you find yourself hesitant because you're not confident that you could pay them back, then this is probably not the business for you."

Finally, Jacquelyn says that if you consistently assess yourself and your company, you should have a pretty good awareness of where you are and where you're headed. If you push yourself to critically evaluate every idea you bring to the market as if it belonged to someone else, you'll put yourself in a position to legitimately judge your concepts. And that is innovation truly by design.

SOURCE: The interview with Jacquelyn Corbett Cyr, a winner of the Global Student Entrepreneur of the Year Award, Canada, 2003, was conducted by Lisa Gundry. Reprinted with permission.

Discussion Questions

1. From what source(s) did the idea for Corbett Cyr Consulting emerge?

2. What steps of the Opportunity SEARCH process did Jacquelyn Corbett Cyr and her husband undertake as they identified the opportunity for the new venture?

3. What does this case inspire you to do?

CASE 2.2   Matthew Hinson: Changing the World of Student Employment

Wake Works Staffing, Inc., is located in Winston Salem, North Carolina, at Wake Forest University. It has 167 employees and provides staffing services—for example, servers, bartenders, and valet parkers—to a variety of major hotels and conference centers in the local market. Matthew's entrepreneurial career began earlier than most:

"I'm more or less a serial entrepreneur. I've been doing it since I was six. I had a company in high school that did emerging technology consulting for senators and a lot of Capitol Hill businesses—I grew up in [Washington] D.C. So in that situation, I employed six individuals who were roughly my father's age, and they moonlighted for me. So it's an entrepreneurial bug, if you will."

The Opportunity

Matthew "got the idea for Wake Works because I paid a portion of my tuition. I was working as a waiter at a hotel downtown, and I saw the absolutely horrendous level of staffing that they had. Workers would come in drunk, and they were sometimes belligerent. So I went to the hotel general manager and said, 'What if I could provide you with well-spoken and more importantly, well-trained, employees?' He was very excited about the concept; not having to keep a very large permanent staff was appealing to him."

The idea behind Wake Works grew out of Matthew's experience at the restaurant, but how did he know it was a good opportunity? How can an entrepreneur evaluate the viability of what seems to be a good business idea?

"Winston-Salem is home to the second-largest conference center in the state so they do a large economy of scale there. I put together a business plan and ran it past three entrepreneurs I had come in contact with in the area, mostly in high tech fields. Honestly, the capital to start it up was so minimal that I figured if I could put $5,000 away and give it a shot, I might as well.

"So we started doing a massive flyer campaign and ended up having 300 people come out to the initial informational meeting. As soon as I started talking about drug tests and background checks for employees, the crowd dwindled instantly, but at the same time, we got a great 50 to 70 students out of our first-run cast in a matter of weeks."

What advice does Matthew give to entrepreneurs who are wondering whether their idea is a good new venture opportunity?

"I guess the biggest tip that I would have would be to ask for help. There are a lot of resources out there—especially if you're a student entrepreneur and you're coming through this process. Any large university has access to a large number of resources, whether it's the students who have graduated and have gone on to accomplish great things entrepreneurially, professors, what have you. So I took advantage of a lot of resources on Wake's campus.

"Wake's the kind of place where eventually most students are going to go off and do great things, but right now they're poor. So if you need computer programs written, I've got three or four computer science majors to put together some custom software that we now sell to restaurants to help train their employees. I needed artwork, and I got an art major to do all of our logo and creative design stuff. I hired MBA students to do our marketing. So the resources are there, you just need to ask the right questions and ask the right people. Any major university has those resources."

Entrepreneurship on Campus: Influencing Business Start-Ups

At the time Matthew was starting his business, he found no formal organization of any kind to support entrepreneurship. When he arrived, he started the Center for Undergraduate

Entrepreneurship. He serves as the program administrator for the initiative.

"Essentially it's an idea incubator, as opposed to a business incubator, because business incubators carry a lot of legal liability with them. We just got a $5 million grant from the Kaufmann Foundation to keep this incubator going indefinitely and also to buy a Chair, essentially, within the business school to provide additional resources in the form of a professor. We bring a lot of local businesspeople in to talk in the incubator and to pool a resource guide of people in the area and organizations in the area that can help out with this kind of thing."

Matthew had to convince the university that the business name, *Wake Works,* and its logo and colors were legal and that his company was not infringing on the university's trademark or copyright.

"Once they saw the success and once they saw the impact we were having on the community, they became very helpful and were very welcoming. But it took proving that a student-run company could work and could be productive in order to get that resolved."

Up and Running: Launching *Wake Works*

Matthew describes the path he took to establishing his business: "We wrote a business plan. I got a small business loan from a bank, purchased a little bit of hardware—not a whole lot. I was able to launch with resources I already had. The beauty of the company is that it really does require very little infrastructure to run. And because of the custom software that we developed to do all the company administration tasks, essentially from a dorm room, it was established by three people full time. We could really run a staff of 167. There wasn't a whole lot of ramping up in terms of infrastructure. We have offices now, but it's only because we're making a fair profit. So I [worked out of] a dorm room for a considerable amount of time."

To create market awareness, *Wake Works* advertised on educational Web sites and ran a lot of ads in educational magazines in the area.

"We tried on campus—did a few Internet ads here and there. Mostly, it's word of mouth now. We've never had a problem raising a labor pool. I've got 60 applications on my desk right now that I can't put in the system because we've capped off the company. We evaluate each individual after every single job using an on-line statistical analysis tool, and the bottom 10 percent of the scores every single semester are let go and we bring in usually 20 or 30 more individuals."

Innovating Through a Modified Business Model

Wake Works' revenue model is based on taking 9 percent of the gross of every student's paycheck and charging a per head fee to the client. Matthew explains,

"We found that we were really taking too much money from the students, and so we raised our rates with the client by 30 percent, and because our margins of quality are so drastically different from anyone else in our market, we were able to charge the client a significant amount more and to charge the students a lot less. Our business model is sound. Our software is sound. So we're essentially selling our industry experience more than anything and selling the know-how. But at the same time, this business is about keeping your employees happy and, more than anything, treating them as they should be treated. We're also expanding to a great deal of private party work and strategic partnerships with catering. We will be opening up franchises, or licensees, hopefully at Princeton and Vanderbilt. So it's grown a lot in two years.

How does *Wake Works* investigate how clients' staffing needs are changing? Does the company rely on feedback from clients, or does Matthew do additional research?

"There's a company based out of Zurich, Switzerland, called Quask. They do a lot of statistical analysis and a lot of on-line survey tools for the Fortune 500. I contacted them and offered the idea of being a testimonial for them and shouting their name to the heavens if they'll give me their software at a significantly reduced rate because I can't afford it. We eventually struck a deal, and I got their $2,000 piece of software for $200. It runs some really sophisticated on-line surveys for us. It measures employee satisfaction with their jobs, with their employers, and with the clients. And also from our clients, what can we do better? It's anonymous so they can get on there and blast us if they like, and they can tell it to us straight. It's brought a lot of small changes in how we manage, how we train our managers, that kind of thing, and how we do day-to-day business operations."

Rewards of Entrepreneurship: Beyond the Dollar

"Making [one] dollar is like making one hundred. If I'm serving as a consultant for someone else, I try to charge them as much as I can, and the money becomes its own reward. However, when working for yourself, I would say that the actual amount of money you're making is not irrelevant, but it becomes less important. I could have probably made more working at McDonald's, flipping burgers 40 hours a week, than I have actually [made] from my work because of the sheer number of hours it's taken to put this thing together. There's a great deal of satisfaction that the idea I came up with is not only going to survive my lifetime in college but should also go on in perpetuity, at least on this campus, if not elsewhere.

"We start pay at $10 an hour and go up to $20. We are very, very flexible in terms of employment. You only have to work for us twice a semester to stay an employee, and we just send you e-mail once a week asking, do you want to work? If yes, hit the yes button. It no, hit the no button, and it goes back to the database. We've very flexible, very scalable. We allow employees, and students especially, to have a high quality of living while in college. They are not tied down to working at a restaurant or working for the bookstore."

What advice does Matthew have for student entrepreneurs?

"Take a risk. Take a jump. You're 21, you're 20, you're 22. You really have no other responsibilities in the world. You always hear, college is a time to be adventurous. Be adventurous in this. All you can do is fail. And that's not necessarily a bad thing.

"I would say that there is a lot of wariness among the business community. If you walk into a meeting—I've had the experience where I've walked into meetings and had people say 'So when's your boss showing up?' Because I'm a kid in a suit. And that's just sort of the nature of the beast. So I would say age discrimination on some level is always going to be a concern. But at the same time, people are very excited to see that spark in young people. All of our accounting services and all of our legal services are actually provided pro bono by three or four different accounting and law firms that have said, wow—this is a really great idea, we're willing to give you 15 hours a month in order to help you move along. So the age can also have its advantages as well. It's problematic in that yes, you're still young, and you're still naive. But that's also your greatest resource. You don't have a whole lot to lose—typically, no spouse and kids at that point—so honestly if you fall on your face a few times, if you've learned a good lesson, you can move forward. I've had several failed different concepts as well and they've all taught me lots of positive information."

SOURCE: This case was prepared with the assistance of Laurel Ofstein, who conducted the interview with Matthew Hinson, a winner of the Global Student Entrepreneur of the Year Award, 2003. Reprinted with permission.

Discussion Questions

1. How did Matthew discover the idea for Wake Works?

2. Does Matthew demonstrate some of the characteristics of the entrepreneurial mind-set?

3. In what ways did Matthew use creative processes to launch his venture?

4. Was there any opportunity in this industry to create a different kind of company? What values did Matthew build into Wake Works?

Notes

1. The quotation is in Lieber, 1998.
2. Interview with Phyllis Apelbaum was conducted by Laurel Ofstein.
3. Adapted from G. E. Hills and R. P. Singh, "Opportunity Recognition," in *Handbook of Entrepreneurial Dynamics: The Process of Business Creation,* edited by W. B. Gartner, K. G. Shaver, N. M. Carter, and P. D. Reynolds (Thousand Oaks, CA: Sage, 2004), Table 24.1, p. 266.

References

Amabile, T. (1998, September–October). How to kill creativity. *Harvard Business Review,* pp. 77–87.

Bateman, T. S., & Crant, J. M. (1993). The proactive component of organizational behavior: A measure and correlates. *Journal of Organizational Behavior, 14,* 103–118.

Bonamici, K. (2004, November 15). You do the dishes, I'll mind the store. *Fortune,* p. 200.

Brorstrom, B. (2002). The world's richest municipality: The importance of institutions for municipal development. *Journal of Economic Issues, 36*(4), 55–78.

Cooper, S. (2005a). Aftermarket accessories. *Entrepreneur, 33*(12), 95.

Cooper, S. (2005b). Building green. *Entrepreneur, 33*(12), 94–95.

Cooper, S. (2005c). Social entrepreneurship *Entrepreneur, 33*(12), 94.

Dunden, E. (2002). *The seeds of innovation.* New York: Amacom.

ebay Inc. announces fourth quarter and full year 2005 financial results. (2006, January 18). Retrieved February 12, 2006, from http://investor.ebay.com/financial.cfm?Financial ReleaseYear=2006

Eckhardt, J. T., & Shane, S. A. (2003). Opportunities and entrepreneurship. *Journal of Management, 29*(3), 333–349.

Gaglio, C. M. (1997). Opportunity identification: Review, critique, and suggested research directions. In J. A. Katz (Ed.), *Advances in entrepreneurship, firm emergence, and growth* (Vol. 3, pp. 139–202). Greenwich, CT: JAI Press.

Gaglio, C. M., & Katz, J. A. (2001). The psychological basis of opportunity identification: Entrepreneurial alertness. *Small Business Economics, 16,* 95–11

Gundry, L. K., & LaMantia, M. (2001). *Breakthrough teams for breakneck times: Unlocking the genius of creative collaboration.* New York: Dearborn Books.

Hamel, G. (1998). The challenge today: Changing the rules of the game. *Business Strategy Review, 9*(2), 19–26.

Ireland, R. D., Hitt, M. A., & Sirmon, D. G. (2003). A model of strategic entrepreneurship: The construct and its dimensions. *Journal of Management, 29*(6), 963–989.

Jones, C. F. (1991). *Mistakes that worked.* New York: Doubleday.

Kickul, J., & Gundry, L. K. (2002). Prospecting for strategic advantage: The proactive entrepreneurial personality and small firm innovation. *Journal of Small Business Management, 40*(2), 85–97.

Kirzner, I. (1973). *Competition and entrepreneurship.* Chicago: University of Chicago Press.

Kirzner, I. (1979). *Perception, opportunity, and profit.* Chicago: University of Chicago Press.

Kirzner, I. (1985). *Discovery and the capitalist process.* Chicago: University of Chicago Press.

Kooser, A. C. (2004a). Niche health and fitness. *Entrepreneur, 32*(12), 89.

Kooser, A. C. (2004b). Technology security consulting. *Entrepreneur, 32*(12), 86–87.

Kurlantzick, J. (2003, May). The innovation toolkit. *Entrepreneur* (May). Retrieved January 27, 2006, from http://www.entrepreneur.com/article/0,4621,307944,00.html

Lieber, R. (1998). *Upstart start-ups.* New York: Broadway Books.

Lustgarten, A. (2004, November 15). A hot, steaming cup of customer awareness. *Fortune,* p. 192.

McGrath, R. M., & MacMillan, I. C. (2000). *The entrepreneurial mindset.* Boston: Harvard Business School Press.

Miles, R. E., & Snow, C. C. (1978). *Organizational strategy, structure, and process.* New York: McGraw-Hill.

Pennington, A.Y. (2004). Hot teen businesses. *Entrepreneur, 32*(12), 84.

Pennington, A.Y. (2005). Travel with a purpose. *Entrepreneur, 33*(12), 102.

Prather, C. W., & Gundry, L. K. (1995). *Blueprints for innovation.* New York: American Management Association.

Prather, M. (2005). Senior retrofitting. *Entrepreneur, 33*(12), 96.

Shane, S., & Venkataraman, S. (2000). The promise of entrepreneurship as a field of research. *Academy of Management Review, 26*(1), 217–226.

Spaeder, K. E. (2004). Hot seniors businesses. *Entrepreneur, 32*(12), 86–87.

Spaeder, K. E. (2005). Education and tutoring products and services. *Entrepreneur, 33*(12), 100.

Thompson, S. (2005, March 21). Nestlé makes nutrition its No. 1 priority in U.S. *Advertising Age,* p. 36.

Torres, N. L. (2004a). Financial planning. *Entrepreneur, 32*(12), 83.

Torres, N. L. (2004b). Functional food. *Entrepreneur, 32*(12), 80–83.

Torres, N. L. (2004c). Hispanic marketing. *Entrepreneur, 32*(12), 85.

Torres, N. L. (2005). Identify theft prevention and recovery. *Entrepreneur 33*(12): 93.

Venkataraman, S. (1997). The distinctive domain of entrepreneurship research: An editor's perspective. In J. Katz & R. Brockhaus (Eds.), *Advances in entrepreneurship, firm emergence, and growth* (Vol. 3, pp. 119–138). Greenwich, CT: JAI Press.

Ward, T. (2004). Cognition, creativity, and entrepreneurship. *Journal of Business Venturing, 19,* 173–188.

CHAPTER 3

Strategies for Evaluating Opportunities

The Assessment Process

Being an entrepreneur doesn't mean jump off a ledge and make a parachute on the way down.

—Fred Smith, founder of FedEx

Be wary of the man who urges an action in which he himself incurs no risk.

—Joaquín Setanti, circa 1614, Catalán, Spain

Objectives:

1. Understand the role of opportunity evaluation in the entrepreneurship process

2. Learn methods of evaluation that can be used for the initial idea and subsequent opportunities in the life cycle of the new venture

3. Prepare the Opportunity Organizational Proposal (OOPs), which is based on a comprehensive analysis of the feasibility of the venture idea

4. Undertake the feasibility analysis by completing the five sections of the OOPs

Strategy in Action

Scott Cook, Founder of Intuit

Scott Cook is the founder of Intuit, the company that developed Quicken and Quickbooks, the personal and business financial tools. He has been Intuit's CEO for more than 22 years, building the company into a $1.7 billion enterprise. While most people are familiar with Intuit's progress and are likely to have used one of its products to help manage their personal or business finances, Cook's entrepreneurial journey is not widely known.

In 1983, when he launched Intuit, Cook already had significant corporate experience. He held an MBA from Harvard and had worked at Procter & Gamble as a brand manager and at Bain as a consultant. Cook's founding principle was, "Listen to your customers." His strategy was in place before the publication of *In Search of Excellence,* by Tom Peters and Bob Waterman, the book that made paying attention to your customers a core business value of excellent companies. Consider this Cook program, which emerged during the early days of Intuit, called Follow Me Home.

Intuit employees were assigned to stay in the local computer store until someone bought Quicken off the shelf (this was back when people did that sort of thing). The employees would then ask the buyers to take them home so they could see how difficult the product was to install. By observing customers at home, Intuit employees could gain valuable insights from every action, from how easily the shrink-wrap came off to which lines of the directions caused frustration. Cook insists, "If there were problems, the fault was Intuit's, not the customer's. Every pause, every source of frustration, [was] evidence of something Intuit needed to fix." Cook believes in radical simplification. He always knew that Intuit had to do more than just make Quicken better and easier than every other software program; it needed to make Quicken better and easier than the pen and paper check-writing process that Quicken aimed to replace. Cook knew that if he and his company were alert and creative and open-minded enough, then accomplishing this was possible: Their customers would tell them how.

Cook's assumption proved to be true. During Intuit's second decade, "customers invented our mid-market business before we even saw the possibility." Entrepreneurs had begun using Quicken to run the finances of their companies, modifying the program to suit their needs. The launch of Quickbooks came in 1992, and it allowed small businesses to manage their money in ways that had not been possible. By the end of its first full month on the market, Quickbooks became the best-selling accounting software. Cook claims this happened because of the fundamental innovation in Quickbooks. "It didn't come out of any big fancy R&D lab. It came out of us being closer to understanding the customer and the prospect than anyone else."

One of the key pieces of advice Cook shared for budding entrepreneurs is especially appropriate during the phase of the life cycle when the opportunity is being assessed and the entrepreneur wants to find out whether or not the concept will work. What does Cook advise?

"Behave humbly. Be humble about your importance, about how many answers you know, and about how much you don't know (which is always more than you think), humble about the need to engage with and learn from people around you, humble about customers, humble about learning. Please understand that I'm saying *behave* humbly; I don't think you can actually will yourself to *be* humble, but you can behave humbly. Which means saying, often, 'I was wrong.'

(Continued)

(Continued)

Which you'll discover is the moment when the real insights and breakthroughs occur. And when it's hard to behave humbly because you're afraid people won't value you, just remember: People already know, they can see through you. They know what you're good at and what you're not, so don't pretend. Instead, try being true. Be human and vulnerable, the way you really are. And you'll find that by admitting you're not good at stuff, you build a bridge to people. You give them room to contribute."

Cook says, "Realize that to a scary degree a company grows to reflect its founder. Unlike with your kids, there are no unalterable genetics to blame, it's all nurture. You get to start the code. So be customer-driven. My biggest surprise was discovering how customers will invent your business for you. And commit to the right values—be straight, tell the truth. Especially the bad news. You'll discover that people always get over it, and even admire the effort you make trying to fix things. Short-term losses become long-term gains."

SOURCE: M. Hopkins, "25 Entrepreneurs We Love," *INC,* April 1, 2004. Retrieved February 13, 2006, from http://www.inc.com/magazine/20040401/25cook.html; C. Tkaczyk, "The Best Ideas Come From the Front Line," *Fortune,* Nov. 15, 2004, p. 193.

Opportunity Evaluation: Will the Idea for the New Venture Work?

Once entrepreneurs have developed the idea(s) for the new ventures, they must begin the process of assessing whether or not the idea is in fact a viable business opportunity. Many new ventures have been launched around bad business ideas. An idea can seem sound in theory but in reality have poor marketplace potential. While failures can also be attributed to poor execution of the idea, it is important to assess feasibility as early as possible to avoid the much costlier effects of failed implementation. So how do entrepreneurs determine if an idea is an appropriate investment for their resources?

The U.S. Patent Office has granted some unusual patents in its history. Consider, for example, whether necessity really drove these inventions (Jones, 1991).

- A propeller-driven rocking chair
- An automatic spaghetti-spinning fork
- A power-operated pool cue stick
- A baby-patting machine
- An electronic snore depressor
- A parakeet diaper
- An alarm clock that squirts the sleeper's face

As you can see from these amusing examples, assessing an idea's potential to become a good business opportunity is absolutely necessary to avoid the allocation

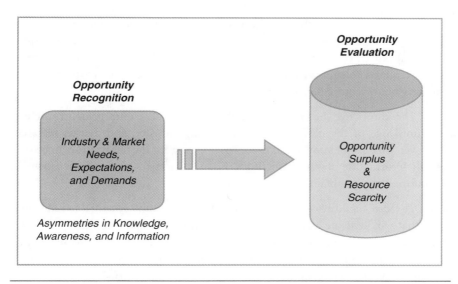

Figure 3.1   Opportunity Recognition to Opportunity Evaluation: The Assessment Process

of scarce resources, including the entrepreneur's time and effort. As we have seen in Chapter 2's discussion of opportunity identification, the process begins by determining the unique needs of the industry and marketplace, including what customers expect and demand that the new venture can provide. Many ideas and opportunities exist; however, resources are scarce, and this means that you must be very careful in your evaluation of business opportunities to be sure they can be supported by the knowledge and information you possess or can obtain fairly easily. Figure 3.1 illustrates the movement from opportunity identification to opportunity evaluation.

The evaluation process begins with some fundamental questions to help entrepreneurs assess the potential for the new venture to succeed. Evaluation of business opportunities should be conducted not just by the entrepreneur but also by as many stakeholders in the new venture as possible: potential customers or clients, employees, advisers, investors, and suppliers.

Four Primary Areas for Assessment

There are many questions to ask during opportunity evaluation, and they can be classified according to four primary areas for exploration:

1. *The people* behind the idea: the background, talents, and experience of the entrepreneur and the management team, employees, and advisers. Even a great idea with high market potential requires an entrepreneur or team behind it that can effectively (and passionately) support and grow the idea. It is then much more likely to be successful. An entrepreneur's skills and talents might have led to the discovery of the idea, but does the entrepreneur have the competence to turn the idea into a business?

2. *The resources* available to the entrepreneur and the management team, including the equity and debt sources of capital that are available and accessible, additional assistance from people with expertise needed by the firm, and the technology required to support the idea. What relationships can the entrepreneur or team rely on to acquire the necessary resources?

3. *The knowledge and information* possessed by the entrepreneur, including knowledge of the new venture concept, the industry, and market research. Moreover, what is not known that needs to be known for the new venture to be successful? Information about competitors? About customers' preferences? How will this information be obtained?

4. *The idea's ability to generate revenue.* How great is the potential to sell something that will generate actual revenues? One of the mistakes would-be entrepreneurs make is to assume that everyone will love the idea and that people will be standing in line to buy it, once the business opens. To what degree can the entrepreneur manage and contain the costs while maximizing returns?

These questions form the basis for the opportunity evaluation, and their answers will help the entrepreneur move forward to create strategies that ultimately support the viable business model.

Review Questions

1. How do the four questions for assessing a business opportunity help entrepreneurs evaluate whether their business idea is viable?

2. Do you think entrepreneurs should proceed with an idea that has inherent weaknesses in any of these areas?

The Innovator's Toolkit: **Business Evaluation Scoring Technique (BEST)**

The Business Evaluation Scoring Technique (BEST) was developed to help entrepreneurs evaluate a group of ideas before deciding which ones to pursue. The tool considers the various "windows of opportunity" related to new ventures. Answer the following questions by scoring them on a 1–5 scale: 1 = low and 5 = high.

1. Is the business really differentiated from other similar businesses?

2. Does the business have growth potential?

3. Will the business require capital? (Note: A low dollar requirement receives a higher score, while a high dollar requirement should receive a low score)

4. Can financing be secured?

5. Does the business suit the individual's entrepreneurial profile (e.g., mind-set, experience)?

Total Score	Description	Action
20–25	Excellent prospects	Must try
15–19	Very good prospects	Should try
11–14	Reasonable prospects	Try if nothing else is available
10 and under	Poor prospects	Avoid this loser

SOURCE: Edward Williams, http://www.entrepreneurialprocess.com/new_site/best_technique.htm. Reprinted with permission.

Assessing the Feasibility of the New Venture Idea

Evaluating a new venture idea involves testing its *feasibility*, the extent to which the idea is a viable and realistic business opportunity. One of the first steps required in assessing the feasibility of an idea is to become aware of forces and factors in the internal and external environment that directly influence the new venture opportunity.

Factors internal to the venture include:

- *The knowledge, skills, and abilities* of the entrepreneur, the management team members, employees, and advisers

- *The resources available* to the entrepreneur, including people, financial resources, and technologies that can be acquired for the launch and growth of the opportunity

Factors external to the new venture include:

- *The industry:* competitors, structure of the industry, barriers to entry, and trends that affect businesses in the sector in which the new venture intends to locate

- *The market:* knowledge of the preferences, values, and buying behavior of the target market, including demographic and psychographic information necessary to appropriately position, promote, and price the products and services

- *Social norms, values, and trends* surrounding the new venture idea. Is it a fad? Is there an increasing need for or awareness of the product or service? Are there ethical concerns about the product, service, or its effects? Realize that a product or service (and any of its components) may be legal but unethical. The social environment of a new venture often involves the perceptions—not necessarily the reality—of the opportunity in the minds of customers and citizens.

- *Legal and regulatory forces* that could affect the business operations, including laws, policies, procedures, and regulations pertinent to the industry or municipality in which the new venture is located

Conducting an environmental feasibility analysis will help the entrepreneur prepare a strategic plan—the topic of Chapter 4.

In the next section, we examine the major questions to ask that will help you determine the feasibility of your business opportunity. A model that can guide the entrepreneur through the opportunity evaluation process is presented.

Fourteen Questions to Ask Every Time

To evaluate opportunities, Allis (2003) has developed a set of questions for entrepreneurs.[1] The answers are helpful as entrepreneurs prepare to conduct a comprehensive feasibility analysis and to develop subsequent strategies for the emerging venture.

1. What is the need you fill or problem you solve? (value solution)
2. To whom are you selling? (target market)
3. How could you make money? (revenue model)
4. How will you differentiate your company from what is already out there? (unique selling proposition)
5. What are the barriers to entry?
6. How many competitors do you have and of what quality are they? (competitive analysis)
7. How big is your market in dollars? (market size)
8. How fast is the market growing or shrinking? (market growth)
9. What percent of the market do you believe you could gain? (market share)
10. What type of company would this be? (lifestyle or high growth potential, sole proprietorship or corporation)
11. How much would it cost to get started? (start-up costs)
12. Do you plan to use debt capital or raise investment? If so, how much and what type? (investment needs)
13. Do you plan to sell your company or go public (list the company on the stock markets) one day? (exit strategy)
14. If you take on investment, how much money do you think your investors will get back in return? (return on investment)

Strategic Reflection Point

ALUO to Evaluate the New Venture Idea

ALUO (Advantages, Limitations, Uniqueness, and Opportunity) is a useful tool that enables the entrepreneur to examine the advantages and limitations of an idea. Most entrepreneurs do this, but ALUO is helpful because it also asks you to consider what is unique about the idea and what opportunity emerges from the advantages, limitations, and uniqueness of the idea (Gundry & LaMantia, 2001).

A: What are the advantages of the idea? How does it build on or extend what is already available in the market?

L: What are the limitations of the product or service? This may be hard for the entrepreneur to assess realistically (watch out for idea infatuation!). You may want to ask others for their opinions on this. What elements of your idea might not work as well as predicted? What flaws might exist?

U: What is unique about the idea? What can't be substituted by something already available in the marketplace? Is your idea easily imitated by others? How can the entrepreneur make it difficult for others to copy? If the product or service is not unique, are there ancillary products or services that could be packaged to maintain uniqueness?

O: What opportunities emerge from the unique features and advantages (or even the limitations, as you consider ways these could be minimized)?

The Feasibility Analysis: Beginning the Evaluation Process

The KIC: Knowledge of Industry Checklist

While it may be tempting to take the leap into writing a business plan as soon as you develop and refine your business idea or opportunity, this can prove to be a serious mistake. Many would-be entrepreneurs underestimate their competitors (both in number and in capability) and therefore develop entrepreneurship strategies that have no likelihood of success. Don't fall into that trap—idea infatuation is one of the strongest predictors of business failure because infatuated entrepreneurs ignore or discount objective industry and market data that even slightly questions their idea. To increase the odds of success and help you identify potential flaws and areas for improvement a priori, start with the KIC: Knowledge of Industry Checklist. A complete industrial analysis usually includes a review of an industry's recent performance, its current status, and the outlook for the future. Many analyses include a combination of text and statistical data. Some of the points entrepreneurs consider in this analysis are given below.

Current Industry Analysis

- Describe the industry as specifically as possible. Some business ideas fall into more than one industrial classification.
- What are the current trends in the industry?
- What is the current size of the industry? Is it dominated by large players? Are there a significant number of small to medium-size enterprises in the industry?
- Where is the industry located? Is it local, regional, national, or global?
- What is the average sales and profitability for this industry?

The Innovator's Toolkit: **Give Me Five**

When you have gathered preliminary information about your industry, try this challenge to push thinking forward with respect to this industry. Your responses to this exercise will help you formulate your competitive strategy for successful industry entry and growth (Gundry & LaMantia, 2001).

- *Give Me Five* things you have observed as a consumer or employee of this industry.
- *Give Me Five* things businesses in this industry should be thinking about right now.
- *Give Me Five* things customers of this industry would tell you if you asked them.
- *Give Me Five* actions or behaviors businesses in this industry should take within the next six months to two years to remain competitive.
- *Give Me Five* ideas that businesses in this industry haven't even thought about yet.

Competitor Analysis

- Obtain basic information on the competitors you have identified. Who are the direct competitors of the new venture?
- Where are the competitors located? Be careful not to assume that a competitor located across the country—or the world—is not a direct competitor. Many firms conduct business on-line, and a remote competitor may prove to be a formidable one if it has a strong on-line presence.
- What are the advantages and disadvantages of the competitors?
- What features of their products or services are similar to yours?
- How are your products or services distinctive from those of your competitors? This is a key part of the competitive analysis.

The following worksheet will help you gather data about your competitors. Use additional worksheets to identify more competitors. You will use the information in this worksheet, Table 3.1, to help you develop your competitive strategy in Chapter 4.

Sources of Information for the Industry and Competitor Analysis

There are many sources of industry analysis: investment firms, business and trade periodicals, trade associations, and government agencies. To conduct a thorough industry analysis, include a variety of sources. Appendix 3.1 contains some recommended sources for your research, including Internet and print sources. As you conduct your research, don't neglect to record your own personal observations: Visit competitors in a nondisruptive manner. What do you notice? What could be improved? How is the product or service used? Create the experience of being a customer of this business and industry.

Table 3.1   Worksheet for Competitor Analysis

Competitor Identification	Business Name _____	Business Name _____	Business Name _____	Business Name _____
Key product or service				
Location(s)				
Local, regional, national or global?				
Primary features of product or service				
Advantages of product or service				
Disadvantages of product or service				
Target market				
Market share				
Pricing				

(Continued)

Table 3.1 (Continued)

Competitor Identification	*Business Name* ______	*Business Name* ______	*Business Name* ______	*Business Name* ______
Promotional activities				
Knowledge, skills, and abilities of key staff				
Resources				
Image				
Culture of the business (norms and values)				
Financial condition				
How is your venture distinctive from this competitor?				

Failures and Foibles

Knowing What's *Not* a Good Opportunity

In 2005, for the fourth year in a row, Stew Leonard's, a family-owned fresh food store with locations in Norwalk and Danbury, Connecticut, and Yonkers, New York, has been named to *Fortune* magazine's "100 Best Companies to Work For" list. The company placed 29 on the 2005 list, when for the first time, companies were also listed by their size—large, mid-size, and small.

Stew Leonard's, a small company with less than 2,000 employees, is ranked 15 when compared to other small companies that also made the list. Stew Leonard's was dubbed the "Disneyland of Dairy Stores" by the *New York Times* because of it had its own milk processing plant and costumed characters, scheduled entertainment, a petting zoo, and animatronics were in its stores. The company has received worldwide acclaim for excellence in customer service and quality and is featured in two of management expert Tom Peters's books: *A Passion for Excellence* and *Thriving on Chaos.* In 1992, Stew Leonard's earned an entry into *The Guinness Book of World Records* for having "the greatest sales per unit area of any single food store in the United States."

Tom Leonard, son of the founder, was walking around the store one day when he was approached by a man who asked if the store carried shaving cream. Tom replied that it did not. The man went on to explain that shaving cream was one of the hottest items in grocery stores, and Stew Leonard's ought to get some. Tom admitted that was an interesting fact and took out his day-timer to made a note of it. The customer interrupted and said, "Tom, today is your lucky day. I sell shaving cream." Tom got excited and placed the order right there. "And the first week," he notes, the shaving cream "sold very well."

However, sales slid, and within a few weeks, Tom learned that the shaving cream was not moving, and the stores were stuck with trailer loads of the product. Tom realized that shaving cream was unlike most of the products sold at Stew Leonard's Dairy: It was not perishable. Customers had purchased the shaving cream during the first week or two, but then they were set for a few months and didn't need any more.

But Tom was not discouraged: "When we have a situation such as this, we know what to do." So he had the advertising department draw up a sign that said, "Shaving Cream: 99 cents a can. Buy 1, get 2 free." Tom recalls that he then learned the biggest marketing lesson of his life:

"If the customers don't want one, they surely don't want THREE! It took us months to get rid of the stuff."

Tom's story is an important one because it reminds entrepreneurs that what might appear to be a great opportunity just might not be a good fit with your business.

SOURCE: http://www.stewleonards.com

From KIC to OOPs:
The Opportunity Organizational Proposal

In the first section of this chapter, we examined the key factors that are part of the opportunity assessment. A comprehensive feasibility study is conducted to help the entrepreneur determine whether the opportunity can lead to the emergence and growth of a successful organization. The Opportunity Organizational Proposal is composed of five major sections. You can use the detailed outline below as you analyze the potential of a business opportunity and decide whether or not to move ahead and create the new organization. The worksheets you will need for investigating financial feasibility are found in Appendix 3.1 at the end of this chapter.

Outline for the Opportunity Organizational Proposal: Feasibility Analysis

Description of Your Business

What business are you really *in?* Describe your product or service in the most concise way you can, and think beyond the characteristics of the product or service to the *experience* that you hope the customer receives from buying the product or service.

The Product or Service

• *Describe what you are selling and how it will benefit your customers.* Explain how your product or service is different from the competition. Answer the question, "Why will people buy from me?" (your product/service concept, benefits, and customer profile). It is important that you can concisely and accurately describe your product or service in terms that are relevant to your customer and that the customer can understand. The ability to describe your product or service will be a critical factor in the success of your marketing and advertising. What are the things about your product or service that are important to your customer? What words immediately create an image of your business?

• *What are the unique characteristics of your product or service?* What are the unique features of the product or service? How do these features meet your customers' needs or preferences? What are the benefits of this product or service compared to the competition? Describe your product or service very simply, and use photos or drawings to illustrate how it works.

• *What are the specific shortcomings of the product or service?* Can it become obsolete soon? Is it perishable, is it difficult to use or install, or are there legal restrictions? An honest assessment of your product or service is extremely important during this analysis. Entrepreneurs do themselves no favor by being in denial or failing to see the disadvantages *before* going into business. Noting them now will help you prepare solutions or ways to minimize these issues.

• *What is your product's stage of development?* Is the product still in the idea stage, or is there a model or working prototype available? Have any samples been manufactured? If it is still in the idea or prototype stage, what is the time frame for getting it ready for production.

• *Research any legal restrictions and rights.* List any patents, copyrights, trademarks, or licenses that apply to your product or service. If you are entering into a franchise agreement, partnerships, distributorships, and so on, these should be discussed in this section. Seek the assistance of patent attorneys or intellectual copyright specialists for assistance. Also, list the government regulations with which you must comply, including any government approvals required, and research zoning restrictions carefully. If you will be home based and your clients will be coming to your house, will your neighborhood's zoning restrictions be an issue?

- *What are the insurance requirements?* Research the liability of your product or service, and consult an insurance specialist to be sure you are protected adequately. This will depend on the nature of your business. A landscape design firm is in a different liability situation than a children's gymnastics and fitness center, for example. If you have employees, you will need insurance to protect them from harm also, along with any insurance benefits you want to provide your staff.

- *Estimate production or service delivery costs.* Will you be producing or subcontracting out the manufacturing or delivery of your product or service? List all the costs, including labor, supplies, shipping, repairs, and so on.

The Industry and Market

- *Describe the current industry.* Determine the trends present in the industry, the size of the industry, the location, and the average sales and profitability of the industry. Use the KIC (Knowledge of Industry Checklist) presented earlier in the chapter for this section of the feasibility analysis.

- *What is the market potential for your idea?* Describe the market for your product or service as specifically as possible. Is the industry in a period of growth, stability, or decline? Can you predict the demand for your product or service over the next six months to two years? Would-be entrepreneurs should interview business owners, managers, or other insiders in the industry to learn about trends and market potential for the industry.

- *What is the impact of technology on the industry and market?* What is the level of technology in use in the industry today? How available or accessible is that technology to the entrepreneur? How can you remain up-to-date with technological changes in this industry? What resources will be required to access the technology at start-up? During the growth stage several months ahead?

- *What economic and legal/regulatory factors affect this industry?* Are there global businesses in this industry and market? How will these impact your operations or customers? What laws and regulations govern the industry, and what information do you need to be sure you operate within legal guidelines?

- *What ethical values are associated with this industry?* Are there any ethical guidelines for the industry? How can you be proactive and develop a set of ethical norms and behaviors in this business? Are there concerns perceived by customers or others in the industry about ethical behavior?

- *Who are the primary competitors?* Where are they located, and what are the unique features of their products or services? What are the advantages and disadvantages of these competitors, and how can your business be distinctive? Use the information from your competitor analysis worksheet presented earlier in this chapter.

- *Who are your customers or clients?* You will need demographic information, including statistics on where they live, income, educational level, number of children, and so on—whatever factors are relevant to your business opportunity. Searching by zip code through library databases (see the earlier section on sources in this chapter) will be helpful.

You will also need psychographic information, including your customers' preferences, values, attitudes, buying behavior, and so on. You can also use primary research, such as conducting surveys and interviews with potential customers to find out what they think about your ideas and whether or not they would buy the product or service.

Use creative approaches to learn all you can about your potential customers. Don't just listen to their words (or written responses on a survey). Try to observe their behavior—it often tells you much more about what they really think about your product or service. For example, if you are developing a new food, observe how much people eat (or drink) of the samples—not just what they say about them. If you are going to be offering a new consulting service, ask a small sample of potential clients to use the service (or a component of the service) and find out what problems the service solved (or didn't solve) for them. Remember Scott Cook's employees at Intuit who observed how the customers used Quicken as they were developing the product.

• *How will you accomplish market penetration?* How will you reach your target customers? What forms of distribution, advertising, and promotion will you use? How will your potential customers become aware of your business?

The Management

• *What is your management and technical experience?* Briefly describe your management/technical skills related to this product or service. Who will you also have on your management team? Will you develop a board of advisers, including industry experts, accountants, or lawyers?

• *Consider the three crucial areas of experience and expertise:*
  1. Marketing strategies: This means knowing what kind of product or service to sell, how to target and reach your customers, and how to sell your product or service at a price that maximizes your profits.
  2. Technical ability: You must be able to get the work done and done right, so you will have satisfied customers.
  3. Financial knowledge: While you do not necessarily have to be a financial wizard, you do need to know how to plan and control your business's cash flow, how to raise or borrow the money you will need to start your business, and how to get through tight periods without being caught short of cash. A certain amount of financial sophistication is becoming more and more important in today's increasingly complex financial world, even for the small business owner. Being able to focus on the bottom line and pay attention to the numbers is as essential as the ability to price your products and services, manage your cash flow, and make sure you collect payment for the work you do.

The Financing: Estimating the Necessary Funds to Launch the New Venture

• *How much seed money do you need?* Entrepreneurs must estimate the costs of the new venture for at least the first several months. Every business is different and has its own specific cash needs at different stages of development, so there is no universal method for estimating your start-up costs. Some businesses can be started on a shoestring budget whereas others may require considerable investment in inventory or equipment. It is vitally important to know that you will have enough money to launch your business venture.

- *What expenses will you have during the start-up phase?* Some of these expenses will be one-time costs such as the fee for incorporating your business or the price of a sign for your building. Some will be ongoing, such as the cost of utilities, inventory, insurance, and so on. While identifying these costs, decide whether they are essential or optional. A realistic start-up budget should include only those things that are necessary to start the business. These essential expenses can then be divided into two separate categories: fixed and variable. Fixed expenses include rent, utilities, administrative costs, and insurance costs. Variable expenses include inventory, shipping and packaging costs, sales commissions, and other costs associated with the direct sale of a product or service.

- *Allow for surprise expenses.* Even with the best of research, opening a new business has a way of costing more than you anticipate. There are two ways to make allowances for such expenses. The first is to add a little padding to each item in the budget. The problem with that approach, however, is that it destroys the accuracy of your carefully wrought plan. The second approach is to add a separate line item, which we call contingencies, to account for the unforeseeable.

Talk to others who have started similar businesses to get a good idea of how much to allow for contingencies. If you cannot get good information, we recommend that contingencies should equal at least 20 percent of the total of all other start-up expenses.

- *Use a worksheet that lists all the various categories of costs.* Appendix 3.2 at the end of this chapter contains a worksheet you can use to estimate your initial expenses (both one-time and ongoing). When listing your start-up costs, be sure to explain your research and how you arrived at your forecasts of expenses. Give sources, amounts, and terms of proposed loans. Also explain in detail how much will be contributed by each investor and what percent ownership each will have. All this information can then be included within your business plan and presentation to your investors and lenders.

Review Question

1. Discuss the risks an entrepreneur faces if he or she does not complete a feasibility analysis.

Next Steps: Strategic Planning for the Emerging Venture

When the entrepreneur has completed the feasibility analysis, the next steps into business involve strategic planning for the new venture. In Chapter 4, we will examine how to develop a strategic plan and strategies for the launch of the business.

The results of a feasibility analysis can provide entrepreneurs with a much better understanding of the capabilities of the new venture. In the Panel Study of Entrepreneurial Dynamics,[2] 480 entrepreneurs reported how certain they were, on a scale of 1 (very low certainty) to 5 (very high certainty) that the new venture would be able to accomplish the following tasks and activities. The average response is given below:

Obtain raw materials:	1.4
Attract employees	2.3
Obtain start-up capital	2.6
Obtain working capital	2.8
Deal with distributors	2.9
Attract customers	4.0
Compete with other firms	3.5
Comply with regulators	4.0
Keep up with technological advances	3.3
Obtain a bank's help	2.2
Obtain venture capitalists' help	1.7

Review Questions

1. Why do you think the entrepreneurs were fairly confident they would be able to attract customers (4.0) and comply with regulators (4.0)?

2. Why do you suppose they tended to be less certain they would be able to obtain a bank's help (2.2), venture capitalists' assistance (1.7), or raw materials (1.4)?

3. Does this suggest to you what entrepreneurs need to focus on as they prepare for the launch of the new venture?

Summary of Chapter Objectives

1. Understand the role of opportunity evaluation in the entrepreneurship process
   • The evaluation process begins with some fundamental questions to help entrepreneurs assess the potential for the new venture to succeed.

- Four primary areas for assessment are: the *people* behind the idea (the entrepreneur and the management team); the *resources* available to carry out the idea; *knowledge and information* about the industry and market, including barriers to entry, location, competitors, social and economic trends, regulatory factors, target market, and market penetration; and the *ability to generate revenue.*

2. Learn methods for evaluation that can be used for the initial idea and subsequent opportunities in the life cycle of the new venture
   - Creative tools such as ALUO (Advantages, Limitations, Uniqueness, and Opportunity) can help entrepreneurs identify the key strategic points and differences surrounding their ideas for the business.
   - The KIC (Knowledge of Industry Checklist), including a comprehensive competitor analysis, is a useful guide for collecting and interpreting information about the industry.
   - "Give Me Five" is a creative tool that is helpful to understanding the experience that the product or service should provide to customers. It asks you to take the perspective of significant constituents to your business.

3. Prepare the Opportunity Organizational Proposal (OOPs), which is based on a comprehensive analysis of the feasibility of the venture idea
   - The OOPs will help the entrepreneur evaluate the ability of the business idea to effectively solve the problem or fill the need for which it was intended, as well as the degree to which the idea can generate sufficient revenues to warrant the resources needed to bring the opportunity into action.

4. Undertake the feasibility analysis by completing the five sections of the OOPs
   - Section I: Description of the Business, asks what business are your really in, and what experience does your product or service bring to the customer?
   - Section II: The Product or Service, asks you to delineate as specifically as possible the benefits of what you are selling to the customer. What are the unique features of the product or service? What are the shortcomings? What stage of development is the product or service in presently? Are there any legal restrictions, insurance requirements, or product delivery costs that are involved?
   - Section III: The Industry and Market, contains an analysis of current trends in the industry, and the complete KIC (with competitor analysis); the market potential for the opportunity, the impact of technology on the industry and market, economic and regulatory factors, ethical values associated with the industry, information on the customers, and market penetration.
   - Section IV: The Management, including the managerial and technical experience of the entrepreneur and any team members, including marketing, technical skills, and financial knowledge.
   - Section V: The Financing, in which you estimate your start-up costs, the expected annual sales forecast, cost of goods sold, operating expenses, gross profit, pricing and break-even points, and sources of start-up capital.

CASE 3.1 Speaking of Strategy: Kate Spade

Kate and Andy Spade are the owners of a $125 million business that designs fragrances, china, and other accessories. The business started in 1993 as a handbag company, when Kate—then an editor at *Mademoiselle* magazine, could not find the particular type of handbag she was looking for. Kate grew up in Kansas City, Missouri, and her fresh sense of style and singular personality reflect a keen sense of wit, propriety, and a no-nonsense approach to life. Kate has spent most of her professional career in the accessories business. In 1986, after she graduated college, she took a job at *Mademoiselle* magazine and was Senior Fashion Editor/Head of Accessories until she left in 1991. During her time at the magazine, Kate believed that the market lacked stylish, practical handbags. Not one to simply complain or settle for something less than what she desired, she began designing her own. Together with her partner and husband, Andy Spade, Kate identified a void in the market, combined their talents, took a risk, and designed six simple shapes that emphasized utility, color, and fabric. These six original designs continue to be the company's signature styles.

Kate did some sketches, investigated production costs, and created a line of classically shaped bags in satin-finished nylon, as well as interesting colors and fabrics. With their fingers crossed, Kate and Andy launched Kate Spade Handbags in January 1993.

In the early days of the company's growth, Kate and Andy realized they would need help to build the business. In late 1993, Pamela Bell joined Kate Spade to help locate sources of materials and produce the handbags. The following year, Elyce Arons, an old friend of Kate and Andy's from their college days at Arizona State University, came on board and was initially responsible for sales and public relations. Within a short period of time, a partnership was formed with Kate, Andy, Pamela,

and Elyce each contributing unique experience and strengths to the equation. Taking a modest, creative approach to design and marketing rather than risk being a flash in the fashion pan, the four partners, together with a collaborative team of people, continue to build a company based on vision, graciousness, and old-fashioned hard work.

In 1996, Kate was recognized by the Council of Fashion Designers of America (CFDA) for being America's new fashion talent in accessories, and in 1998, this organization once again honored her as best accessory designer of the year. In 1999, Kate was honored when her handbags were exhibited at the Cooper Hewitt Museum for the first national design triennial, celebrating American design excellence. That same year, she was recognized for her new home collection.

Kate Spade opened its first shop in 1996 in the Soho neighborhood of New York City. It quickly outgrew the space and moved around the corner in the fall of 1997. The store became a laboratory for different categories, from paper to travel. In 1998, Kate Spade opened in Boston; in 2000, in Chicago and San Francisco; and by 2004, in Atlanta, Houston, Charlotte, Dallas, and Boca Raton. Most recently, the company has expanded to locations in Las Vegas and Palo Alto, California, and outside the United States to Japan (four stores), Hong Kong (three stores), and the Philippines.

Appealing to a diverse group of women, the company's growth continues. "Kate Spade paper and social stationery" was introduced in 1998 and includes such items as personal organizers, address books, journals, illustrated note cards, and classic pencils and erasers. In November of 1999, Kate Spade introduced a much anticipated shoe collection incorporating her unique sense of style and sophisticated use of color. "Kate Spade glasses" was introduced in the spring of

2001, providing yet another natural extension of the refreshing and sophisticated Kate Spade aesthetic. The eye glasses collection features clean shapes, classic proportions and, naturally, an element of surprise. The line includes both sunglasses and ophthalmic frames exemplifying Kate's personal style. Kate Spade and Estée Lauder launched "Kate Spade beauty" with great success in the spring of 2002, with a signature fragrance based on the scent of a white floral bouquet. The most recent addition to the world of Kate Spade, "Kate Spade at home," was introduced in 2004. The home collection includes bedding, bath items, china, wallpaper, textiles, and other vibrant accessories for home.

As Kate Spade grows and evolves, a great deal of product development continues to occur within the company. Based on Kate's love of textiles, pattern, and strong geometric shapes, the company developed a signature, iconic design element inspired by the op art movement of the 1960s; this element has proved multifaceted and naturally developed into a new company mark and graphic art pattern. Various interpretations of the design were incorporated into the handbag, luggage, shoe, glasses, and paper collections and introduced as the "noel weave" collection in the fall of 2001. The company plans to incorporate this signature mark into its identity system and product collections going forward as a complement to the enduring "Kate Spade New York" logo.

In 2004, Kate was presented with three prestigious design awards: *House Beautiful's* Giants of Design award for tastemaker, *Bon Appetit's* American food and entertaining award for designer of the year, and *elle decor's* elle decor international design award for bedding. The first Kate Spade music CD was issues recently: "the eight songs," written and recorded exclusively for Kate Spade by Beaumont, a modern pop band from the United Kingdom. It is a tribute to 1960s cocktail music with a jolt of modern glamour. Beaumont captures the sparkle and kick of Kate Spade in an unexpected and vibrant style.

The history and success of Kate Spade rests on the ability of Kate and Andy to identify and evaluate the right opportunities for their business. Their advice for entrepreneurs evaluating new opportunities is to ask if they really understand the opportunity and if it fits in with what they do extraordinarily well in the business. Even if the idea seems glamorous or is interesting, it may not be a feasible business opportunity. Andy explains, "If we do something interesting that doesn't sell, we don't perceive that as a success. We don't go back and tell people that the customers 'just didn't get it.'"

SOURCES: J. Creswell, "You Can't Say the Customer Doesn't Get It," *Fortune,* November 15, 2004, p. 196; R. Lieber, *Upstart Start-ups* (New York: Broadway Books, 1998); www.KateSpade.com.

Discussion Questions

1. How did Kate Spade determine if her idea was in fact a good business opportunity?

2. What criteria do you think Kate and Andy Spade use to decide whether or not to expand their accessories into other product lines and markets?

3. Why do you think Kate Spade has been so successful and distinctive in the extremely competitive fashion industry?

CASE 3.2   Andy Szatko: A Grassroots Approach to Entrepreneurship

Grassroots Landscaping, Inc.

During his freshman year at the University of Nebraska-Lincoln in the spring of 2000, Andy Szatko, who was majoring in horticulture, founded *Grassroots Landscaping* (now *Premier Landscape Construction*). When he told people that he wanted to start a landscaping business, the reaction was that starting a business at 19 years old is a bad idea, and at the very least, he should wait until he finished college. Andy Szatko did not listen to that advice. He started the business with a 1989 Ford truck and a few hand tools. His first jobs came from family and friends, and while he worked on these jobs, neighbors would stop by to see the kind of work he was doing. He told them about himself and his ambitions to create a successful landscaping company. Through word of mouth, his business grew quickly, and two years later, he purchased a new truck, which enables him to haul and carry more material. He also hired one full-time employee to help him stay organized. Andy contracted with his father, a carpenter, to do woodwork and build arbors for clients.

Grassroots Landscaping incorporated in late 2003. Andy notes, "We are now legally *Grassroots Landscaping, Inc.* That was pretty exciting stuff . . . moving more into a formal company. I did that because, in the past year, the company has been just me, I've been doing the work. A lot of the stuff comes from my head. In order to make it its own separate identity, I went ahead and incorporated it. That was a great first step."

"I hire two full-time people during the season. I've been doing general landscape contracting, planting plants, and retaining walls. In the past couple of years, I've put a lot of effort into lawn maintenance such as mowing, fertilizing, and clean-up during the spring and fall. Just this past year—I didn't really advertise it this year, but it's going to be a big push for me during this next year—we started to offer custom carpentry work. The reason I'm doing that . . . my dad is retiring from the Corps of Engineers and throughout his life, he's always built custom carpentry.

In my parent's home, growing up, [my dad] always built every single piece of furniture in our house. He has built everything, so I asked him if he wanted to join ranks with me and start offering custom carpentry. We're going to be building bridges, arbors, Adirondack chairs, benches, . . . pretty much anything that a client wants made of wood, we would incorporate into the landscaping. It's really exciting. I'm finding right now that there's quite a bit of demand for that out there. So we're really excited about pushing that service this upcoming year. [My dad] knows everything about it. He does quality work."

In the world of landscaping, much of what Andy sells is the ability to create a design or image a client tells him about: "For one of the jobs we did this past year, a client of mine came to me and said: 'I have this picture of an arbor from a Web site. I really like it, but I don't have any dimensions or anything. Could you build it for me, or something like it?' I gave the picture to my dad, and from just a picture from the Internet, he was able to come up with the measurements and the style of wood, exactly as the picture showed it. The clients were ecstatic about it. It turned out to be a really good project. So we can take anything from pictures, to just a rough sketch, and be able to transform it into what the people want for their landscape."

Andy reports that he hadn't actually thought about starting his own company. When he was 16 years old, he worked at a local nursery, actually part of a regional nursery and landscape center. He worked in the nursery selling plants, unloading trucks, and doing general labor at the store. He was there for about two-and-a-half years and left to attend college.

He began to enjoy working outside, working with plants, and seeing different plants. Andy explains, "I got a kick out of it, but I never thought of doing anything with it. My whole life, ever since I was seven years old, I wanted to go into meteorology. I love thunderstorms. I love going outside during thunderstorms and watching lightning. I've even gone to chase a few tornadoes, but I never was too successful in actually seeing one.

"When I got to college, I started off studying meteorology. During my freshman year, I started looking at the program and some of the requirements. The classes that were required really weren't interesting to me. Without having an actual degree, you can still be a storm spotter, meaning if a storm's coming, you get activated and you report in as far as storm spotting, or chasing, and that's more or less what I like to do—to be outside working. So I came to the conclusion shortly after school started that I didn't want to be behind a radar screen in an office.

Working at the nursery, I really liked landscaping and plants in general. So I switched over to the horticulture and landscaping degree, figuring I could do the weather thing kind of as a hobby and concentrate on landscaping. And having worked for a landscaping company before, I kind of saw how things should be run and how they could be better.

During the spring semester of my freshman year, I started thinking maybe I can start talking to family and friends—just small-scale side projects. So I went and got some hand tools, and I got a new truck so I could haul around materials, and that spring, I went out and started doing it more or less as a side project while still working at the nursery. But I found out that I could invest a lot more time into the company and make more money and do more things I like to do. So it kind of just evolved slowly and then my freshman year, it just kind of kicked into gear and went from there."

How did Andy evaluate whether his idea to start the landscaping company was in fact a good business opportunity?

Andy recalls, "Omaha is the largest city in Nebraska. When I would drive around and look at all the new housing developments that were starting, in the back of my mind, I was thinking about the possibilities. I also saw a lot of older landscapes that were overrun. Also, having worked at the nursery, I saw all the people that would come in and buy these plants and have questions about what plants they should choose. So I didn't do any formal research, but I still would think in the back of my head that the industry was very large and growing. I thought there's got to be a way I could make it work. So, without formal research, I just jumped into it. But I was just thinking along the way, it's a big industry, and there's always work: Grass always needs to be cut, trees need to be trimmed, plants need to be replaced . . . it's an ongoing industry. There's never really an end to it."

Building the Business: From the Idea to Formal System Development

"I knew I would need something to start billing customers with and a way to track what was going on. I came up with a really rough Excel spreadsheet where I laid out materials, labor, a description of what the job was, and an estimate of the price. So, I started off getting the forms all ready to go. Having never taken a business course in my life, I was winging it—thinking about what should go in there. Those were pretty good for the first year since we did mostly small-scale landscaping jobs.

"I also had to go out and purchase tools and equipment. I didn't need a whole lot of tools to start out with because they were smaller jobs. So I just went out and got a several hand tools, and purchased a 1989 Ford F150—found a good deal and talked my parents into purchasing it for me. My car at the time was a Honda Accord. I convinced them that the Accord wouldn't last a lot longer . . . I finally convinced them to help me out to get the truck, and that was the biggest feat right there—to be able to get the truck.

Because my dad builds all kinds of things, he had a lot of tools and equipment that I would borrow . . . So those are the initial things I did to set up the company. As far as finding jobs, they really came pretty evenly because family members would give me the chance to do a little something to their house. Then, often people in the neighborhood would ask me who I was."

Word of mouth helped Andy create awareness of Grassroots Landscaping. He admits he never did any advertising for the first three years of the company. It was all word of mouth. And as he read stories about entrepreneurs in magazines, he learned how important referrals from satisfied clients can be.

Did his age affect customers' perceptions? Andy replies, "Being young and trying to run your own company is pretty hard. A lot of people get the idea that young kids aren't reliable and try to do things the easy way. So when I was first starting out, I had people who would literally sit down and talk to me about how impressed they were that I was so young and was actually taking the effort and the time to put together a company and do the sales and estimating and all the work that went with it. By virtue of my age, I landed a couple of jobs in the first couple years . . . just because I was young and ambitious."

On Being an Entrepreneur and a Student

"Starting a business when you're a student is really hard. For me, I think I made it harder on myself. Having to pay the bills, I ended up staying away from home. Actually, the school (Nebraska) is in Lincoln, which is about an hour away from Omaha where I based the company. So I'm doing work in Omaha, my family's up in Omaha, my tools are up in Omaha, and my fiancee's up in Omaha, and I'm in Lincoln trying to sell and put things together and trying to go to school at the same time.

"When I first started, after that freshman year, since things went pretty good that summer,

I decided to go to school in Omaha at night at [the University of Nebraska, Omaha]. So I took a year and went to school here in Omaha so I could work on the business and develop it up here. The horticulture program has a two-year program at Omaha and then you have to go down to Lincoln to finish up the degree. So I took that second year in Omaha and worked on the company and was able to be closer to everything I was doing. That really helped to give me an even better start to the company. I was able to spend more time because I wasn't driving back and forth from Omaha to Lincoln.

"But, starting a company is really hard. You have to separate your time from your work. You can't expect not to put time into a company if you really want to build it up. The nice thing is that this was during my busy season, so this was time when I wasn't in school. In the winter, people are always asking, are you doing snow removal? What are you doing? And I would just say: 'No, I'm focusing on school.'

"When I was at Omaha, my horticulture professor helped me tremendously just because he was a great guy to talk with and get some ideas from. [My professor] also hired me and one other guy who was in my class—he also runs his own landscaping company and was starting it at the same time as I was. So we were talking to him about retaining walls, and it turns out he needed a large series of retaining walls at his home. So he gave us the opportunity to build all those walls—estimate it and do the work. It was an amazing opportunity to develop a relationship with someone well-known in the field and to do such a large project."

Andy advises would-be student entrepreneurs to be sure to take advantage of any resources available to students in their colleges and universities, especially if there is an entrepreneurship department or center. Andy notes that these academic resources offer a tremendous opportunity to learn and teach yourself—and they have people to help you to build the company you want to build.

"After I went to the Entrepreneurship Center, they were offering to look over my business plan and give me tips and suggestions about what to do. Just being able to talk to someone about payroll is helpful," Andy says.

Greatest Challenge of Entrepreneurship

Andy reports that the biggest challenge for him was in saying no. "That was my biggest thing—I wanted to please everyone who called me, that I was working for, and so I would bend over backward for a client and try to do everything I could for them. When I did that, eventually in the second or third year I was working, I found that doing that overextended what I was capable of doing. Then I started to see flaws, or to think of things I could have done better if I hadn't been so stretched for time. So, I've learned a really valuable lesson in the fact that you're not going to please everybody. You're not going to be able to take on all the work that comes your way. You have to be able to control the growth so that your quality doesn't dip, but you're still able to grow the company at a good rate.

"I've made quite a few little mistakes involving clients. Just this past year, I didn't have a contract that really spelled everything out for a client. I had talked to them about the design and showed them all the different types of plants. . . . Everything was listed on there. We got the go-ahead, went in, and started doing the work. We had planted a few of the trees that were in the design. [The client] came home that day and said, 'What are these trees doing here? We talked about not having them there.' I said, 'I don't have anywhere in my notes about this.' He was sure that we had talked about it and that we weren't going to put those trees in. Because of that, I had to go back and dig up the trees I had just planted, take them, and eat the cost for those because I get most of my materials from a wholesale dealer, and I couldn't just take them back after they'd been planted.

"So, I've learned that you need to have everything spelled out, you need to have that final check . . . Communication is key. That was a big mistake, but it was really a small one in the overall business. Because of it, I'm drafting new contracts and learned to do new things.

"Probably my biggest mistake—when I was growing, I didn't say no, and I took on a lot of work, which, like I said, overextended me. I was doing too much just by myself, and it stressed the quality of my work at the time."

Grassroots Landscaping: Future Plans and Innovative Strategies

Andy plans to expand to include carpentry work. Despite the fact that a lot of his clients ask about snow removal services, he does not really care to do that. He would rather spend his time during the winter concentrating on sales, doing design work, talking with other companies, and giving contracts out. His ideas for expansion of the business include Christmas lighting design and installation. He has observed a demand for these types of services. How does Andy innovate in his business?

"As for innovation . . . right now I'm starting my own plant/landscaping database where, after I do a design for someone, I will print off pictures or descriptions of each plant that I installed on their landscape. I'm putting this all together by myself, so I'm going to have my own plant encyclopedia, I guess you could say. I give each client a binder so that they always have it, and they know what to do with the plants as they go along. I've never heard of anyone doing that. I think it's a really neat idea because it shows that I'm putting that extra step, extra effort into my work—my designs—that people will appreciate." It is clear that Andy provides his clients with much more than landscaping—he shares information with them and teaches them about the products in which they have invested.

This strategy is paying off for the business because Andy gets referrals from satisfied clients who call him up and say, "Here's an opportunity for you, what do you think?" It's a position other entrepreneurs may envy, having opportunities given to you by your clients.

"It's fun to take my wife or friends past jobs that I've done and get their reaction or their input. They say, you should think about doing this, or they'll give me new ideas that I had never thought of. It's really fun to take people by and talk about, hey—I just did that. It's a real sense of pride that I get."

What advice does Andy Szatko have for college students considering entrepreneurship?

"The first thing I would say to them is that they need to test themselves and see if it's for them. Entrepreneurship isn't for everybody. I questioned myself at first—trying to build a business and everything depends on you. It can be really stressful. Being able to test yourself to see if you're willing to put in the hours, to be able to take the stress. It's a lot of hard work, especially if you want to go that extra mile to create the really successful company that most entrepreneurs want to develop.

"Also, when you're starting out and building your business, go to trade shows, go to conferences, get involved in organizations related to your industry—even not associated with your industry. Just having that visibility is priceless. I ended up getting involved with the local chamber of commerce, and I recently joined the Nebraska Nursery and Landscaping Association. Meeting these new people has just been great. They give you tips on what you should do. People give each other business. If you're starting out and trying to build your business, go to trade shows, conferences, and any other organization with which you can get involved. Talk to other companies—see what they're doing. Get

out there and talk to those people who are willing to help you. There are all kinds of sources I know of through [the University of Nebraska, Lincoln's] Alumni Association, such as talking to people who have agreed to be mentors for me. It's a great way to be able to talk to people and get advice, and develop your business from there. You want to get a broad range of advice and opinions.

"Finally, don't get discouraged. It's really easy to get discouraged—especially if things don't take off right away. I've been discouraged a couple times—because you don't have a good day or you don't land a contract that you really wanted. But, that's the name of the game—you just have to keep going and be confident in your abilities to build a successful company."

Discussion Questions

1. How did Andy Szatko evaluate the idea for Grassroots Landscaping?

2. Despite unfavorable reactions to his idea, Andy persisted in creating the business. How can entrepreneurs ascertain whether to go ahead in the face of negative feedback?

3. Andy describes one of his mistakes as the inability to say no. How can entrepreneurs guard against the temptation to expand too early or to take on business that may not be in the best interests of the company's growth?

SOURCE: Case prepared with the assistance of Laurel Ofstein, who conducted the interview with Andy Szatko, winner of the Global Student Entrepreneur of the Year Award, Northern Plains Region, 2003. Printed with permission.

Notes

1. From Allis, R., *Zero to One Million.* Virante, Inc., www.zeromillion.com, copyright © 2003. Reprinted with permission.
2. Adapted from C. H. Matthews and S. E. Human, "The Economic and Community Context for Entrepreneurship," in *Handbook of Entrepreneurial Dynamics: The Process of Business Creation,* edited by W. B. Gartner, K. G. Shaver, N. M. Carter, and P. D. Reynolds (Thousand Oaks, CA: Sage, 2004), Table 36.14, p. 424.

References

Allis, R. (2003). *Zero to one million.* Virante, Inc. Retrieved January 31, 2006, from http:// www.zeromillion.com/entrepreneurship/business-idea-evaluation.html

Gundry, L. K., & LaMantia, M. (2001). *Breakthrough teams for breakneck times: Unlocking the genius of creative collaboration.* New York: Dearborn Books.

Jones, C. F. (1991). *Mistakes that worked.* New York: Doubleday.

Lieber, R. (1998). *Upstart start-ups.* New York: Broadway Books.

Appendix 3.1
Sources for Industry and Market Research

Industry and Market Resources

Standard Industry Classification (SIC) and North American Industry Classification System (NAICS) manuals for your industry's classification. You need your SIC code to use certain references, such as the industry norms and business ratios reference books. Where to find a SIC/NAICS Code:

http://www.census.gov/epcd/www/naicstab.htm

Databases*

ABI Inform Global: ABI/INFORM Global is a business and management article database. ABI/INFORM provides in-depth coverage of business and economic conditions and a wide variety of other topics from more than 1,800 business and management publications. The *Wall Street Journal* is available full text within this database.

Business & Industry Database: Contains facts, figures, and key events for international public and private companies, industries, products, and markets for manufacturing and service industries. It covers all the primary business information sources from leading trade magazines, newsletters, and the general business press to international business dailies.

Business Source Premier: Business Source Premier is a business periodical database that includes both scholarly journals and business periodicals. Topics covered in this database include the following: management, economics, finance, international business, and much more.

General Business File: Use General Business File to find company profiles and Investext analyst reports. Use this database to analyze company performance, company activity, industry events, and industry trends. General Business File contains broker research reports, trade publications, journals, and company directory listings.

*The database descriptions were provided by Kathleen Berger and Linda Wolf, Simmons School of Management Librarians.

Industry Surveys from Standard & Poor's NetAdVantage: Use this database to find industry ratios. This database provides comprehensive coverage of 51 major U.S. industries. Each survey contains an industry profile, key ratios and statistics, and a comparative company analysis.

LexisNexis Academic: LexisNexis Academic provides access to full-text information from national and regional newspapers, international news sources, business news journals, industry and market news sources, Securities and Exchange Commission filings, legal news sources, and much more.

MarketLine: MarketLine provides profiles of 10,000 companies and contains information on 2,000 industry profiles. MarketLine also contains 50 country profiles that give quick access to country data points, trends, and analysis.

PROMT (Predicasts Overview of Markets and Technology): Use this database to research companies, the products and technologies they produce, and the markets in which they compete. Includes summaries and full text from nearly 1,000 business and trade journals, industry newsletters, newspapers, market research studies, news releases, and investment and brokerage firm reports.

TableBase: Use TableBase to obtain statistical information. TableBase is the database that specializes exclusively in tabular data on companies, industries, products, and demographics. International in scope, it covers more than 90 industries.

Additional Databases: Reuters Business Insights, Plunketts Industry Almanacs, available in Business Source Premier.

Print Sources

Encyclopedia of American Industries
Encyclopedia of Emerging Industries

Internet Resources

Small Business Administration, www.sbaonline.sba.gov

http://www.lib.duke.edu/reference/subjects/business/isi: For emerging market reports, see also ISI Emerging Markets

Hoover's, an online resource for up-to-date, comprehensive company, industry, and market information: http://www.hoovers.com/free/ind/dir.xhtml

Internet Intelligence Index, http://www.fuld.com/Tindex/I3.html: Created by the Fuld & Company Library, this site provides "links to nearly 600 intelligence-related Internet sites, covering everything from macro-economic data to individual patent and stock quote information." Notice the sections on "Industry-Specific Internet Resources" and "International Internet Resources" further down the page. Fuld & Company offers management consulting in competitive intelligence.

Business.com: Covers more than 28 industries, from accounting to utilities. Business.com provides a directory of industry Web sites.

Other References

Value Line Reports by Industry

Dun & Bradstreet's Industry Norms and Key Business Ratios: 10Ks, annual reports, prospectuses and other public company reports filed with the Securities and Exchange Commission. 10Ks are annual reports that include description of the industry in which the business is located, company performance, financial condition, product or service focus, strategy, and information about the company's management.

Thomas' Register of American Manufacturers

American Wholesalers and Distributors Directory

Wholesale & Retail Trade USA

Trade Associations and Research:

Encyclopedia of Associations

Associations (Yahoo)—http://dir.yahoo.com/Business_and_Economy/
   Organizations/Trade_Associations/

The Internet Public Library—Retail Trade—http://www.ipl.org/div/aon/browse/
   bus41.72.00/

Trade Shows: www.expoguide.com, www.tsnn.com, and www.tscentral.com.

Associations Online and Associations Database: Links to associations with Web
   sites. Two sites that are useful: www.asaenet.org/gateway/GatewayHP.html and
   www.trainingforum.com/assoc.html

Chambers of Commerce

Competitors' Web sites, brochures, ads, etc.

Statistics/Demographics

Overview of U.S. Bureau of Labor Statistics by industry: http://www.bls.gov/bls/
   industry.htm

American Factfinder: http://factfinder.census.gov/

State & County Quick Facts: http://quickfacts.census.gov

The Sourcebook of Zip Code Demographics

Generation X: Americans Born 1965 to 1976 (Ithaca, New York: The New
   Strategist Editors, 2004)

Entrepreneurship organizations, such as the National Organization for Women
   Business Owners, National Federation of Independent Businesses, and others

Conduct surveys of potential customers and employees, or see if such surveys
   already exist in any of the above sources

Business Plans

U.S. Small Business Administration Business Plan Basics, http://www.sba.gov/
   starting_business/planning/basic.html

Company and Industry Resources—Financial Information

Databases (in addition to the ones previously described)

Bloomberg Terminal: The Bloomberg Terminal provides minute-by-minute financial, economic, and government information covering all market sectors. Data available from Bloomberg includes stock prices and financial summaries for every public company traded anywhere in the world; currency exchange rates; economic statistics such as GDP, GNP, CPI, and much more. The Bloomberg Terminal is stand-alone terminal and is available in the library only.

Print Sources

Annual Statement Studies: comparative historical data and other sources of composite financial data by industry.

Industry Norms and Key Business Ratios: provides statistics on more than 800 lines of business.

> *Entrepreneur*
> *Fast Company*
> *Forbes*
> *Fortune*
> *INC.*
> *Wall Street Journal*

Web Sites

Company Web sites: Company Web sites are a good source of financial information. Annual reports can be found on company Web sites, usually located under the investor relations section. Company Web sites also contain press releases that provide financial information. Example: http://investor.colgate.com/

EDGAR SEC Filings: The SEC Electronic Data Gathering, Analysis, and Retrieval system contains forms filed by companies and others that are required by law. In this database, you can search for company filings such as the Form 10-K. http://www.sec.gov/edgar.shtml

Forbes.com: The Forbes.com Web site provides access to business and financial news as well as company information and rankings. http://www.forbes.com/

Fortune.com: The Fortune.com Web site provides access to business and financial news as well as company information and rankings. http://www.fortune.com/fortune/

Yahoo! Finance: This Web site provides company stock information as well as company profiles, company news, key statistics, listings of competitors and industry information. http://finance.yahoo.com/

Appendix 3.2
Estimating Start-Up Expenses

Start-Up Expenses
Enter your company name here

Notes on Preparation

EXPENSES—Begin by estimating expenses. What will it cost you to get your business up and running? The key to accuracy here is attention to detail. For each category of expense, draw up a list of everything you will need to purchase. This will include both tangible assets (for example, equipment, inventory) and services (for example, remodeling, insurance). Then determine where you might purchase these goods or services. Research more than one vendor, that is, comparison shop. Do not look at price alone; terms of payment, delivery, reliability, and service are also important.

CONTINGENCIES—Add a reserve for contingencies. Be sure to explain in your narrative how you decided on the amount you are putting into this reserve.

WORKING CAPITAL—You cannot open with an empty bank account. You need a cash cushion to meet expenses while the business gets going. Eventually you should do a 12-month cash flow projection. This is where you will work out your estimate of working capital needs. For now, either leave this line blank or put in your best rough guess. After you have done your cash flow, you can come back and enter the carefully researched figure.

SOURCES—Now that you have estimated how much capital will be needed to start, you should turn your attention to the top part of this worksheet. Enter the amounts you will put in yourself, how much will be injected by partners or investors, and how much will be supplied by borrowing.

COLLATERAL—If you will be using this plan to support a bank loan request, use the section near the bottom to show what assets are offered as collateral to secure the loan, and give your estimate of the value of these items. Be prepared to offer some proof of your estimates of collateral values.

Sources of Capital

Owners' Investment (name and percent ownership)

Your name and percent ownership $
Other investor
Other investor
Other investor

Total Investment   **$**

Bank Loans

Bank 1 $
Bank 2
Bank 3
Bank 4

Total Bank Loans   **$**

Other Loans

Source 1 $
Source 2

Total Other Loans   **$**

Start-Up Expenses

Buildings/Real Estate

Purchase $
Construction
Remodeling
Other

Total Buildings/Real Estate   **$**

Leasehold Improvements

Item 1 $
Item 2
Item 3
Item 4

Total Leasehold Improvements   **$**

Capital Equipment List

Furniture $
Equipment
Fixtures
Machinery
Other

Total Capital Equipment   **$**

Location and Administative Expenses

Rental	$
Utility deposits	
Legal and accounting fees	
Prepaid insurance	
Preopening salaries	
Other	

Total Location and Administrative Expenses $

Opening Inventory

Category 1	$
Category 2	
Category 3	
Category 4	
Category 5	

Total Inventory $

Advertising and Promotional Expenses

Advertising	$
Signage	
Printing	
Travel/entertainment	
Other/additional categories	

Total Advertising/Promotional Expenses $

Other Expenses

Other expense 1	$
Other expense 2	

Total Other Expenses $

Reserve for Contingencies $

Working Capital $

Summary Statement

Sources of Capital

Owners' and other investments	$
Bank loans	
Other loans	

Total Source of Funds $

Start-Up Expenses

Buildings/real estate	$
Leasehold improvements	
Capital equipment	
Location/administration expenses	

Opening inventory
Advertising/promotional expenses
Other expenses
Contingency fund
Working capital

Total Start-Up Expenses   **$**

Security and Collateral for Loan Proposal

Collateral for Loans	Value	Description
Real estate		
Other collateral		
Other collateral		
Other collateral		

Owners
Your name here
Other owner
Other owner

Loan Guarantors (other than owners)
Loan guarantor 1
Loan guarantor 2
Loan guarantor 3

Glossary of Terms Used in Determining Start-Up Expenses

The following terms are explained; some may apply to particular businesses and not to others.

Legal, accounting, and professional services: Professional fees are associated with registering your legal form of business, reviewing contracts and agreements, and preparing financial information for your business plan. This area also includes consultants and other professionals.

Advertising and promotions: This includes all promotional costs associated with opening your business.

Deposits for utilities: Advance payments required to obtain electric, gas, telephone, water, and sewer.

Licenses and permits: Fees for licenses, permits, and other requirements related to starting your business and making its operations legal.

Prepaid insurance: Advance payments required to obtain business insurance that protects the contents of your business against fire, theft, and other losses.

Salary and wages: Base pay plus overtime and bonuses, includes owner's draw on this line item. For purposes of estimating net profit, it is important that all costs, including owner's draw, be part of the projection.

Payroll taxes: Includes paid vacations, sick leave, health insurance, unemployment insurance, Medicare, and social security taxes. (Note: Usually 10 to 15 percent of gross payroll)

Taxes, licenses, and permits: Excise tax, inventory tax, real estate tax, sales tax, other nonpayroll taxes, and license or permit fees as applicable.

Truck and vehicle: Includes mileage, parking, tolls, and so on prior to opening the business.

Travel: Includes conference, hotel, meal, and transportation charges related to securing prospective distributors, suppliers, and customers.

Tools and supplies: Services, supplies, and tools purchased prior to opening, for use in the business.

Machines and equipment: Acquisition cost plus installation expense. If you plan to pay by installments, enter your down payment.

Building improvements: Includes costs of structural changes, repairs, painting, and decorating.

Land and buildings: Includes the down payment for lease, rent, or purchase and deposits required.

Depreciation: If property you acquire to use in your business has a useful life of more than one year, you generally cannot deduct the entire cost as a business expense in the year you acquire it. You must spread the cost over more than one tax year and deduct part of it each year.

Starting inventory: Includes acquisition cost plus transportation.

Cash (working capital): Amount of money you will need to maintain your business until the business generates enough sales to cover normal operating expenses.

Other costs (specify): Includes those start-up costs that may be unique to your business and do not have an account listed on the worksheet.

The Expected Annual Revenue (Sales) Forecast for the First Year

To help determine this, estimate:

a. How many different customers do you anticipate serving in a 12-month period?

b. How many times in a 12-month period will the average customer return to purchase something?

c. How much will the average customer spend on each visit to your business?

d. Multiply (a) × (b) × (c) = Estimated annual revenue (sales)

   1. Estimating your annual revenue (sales) will help you set a sales goal for your business and provide you with tools to manage your day-to-day operations.

By monitoring each of these factors on a daily, weekly, and monthly basis, you will know if your business is on target to meet its sales goal or if adjustments must be made to increase sales or decrease expenses.

Estimated Sales and Earnings (First and Second Year)

Forecasting sales and earnings is important for your financial success. It may take several years before your business begins to generate satisfactory profits, but your sales goal should be to break even (match sales with expenses) by the end of the first year and show modest profits. Do not include start-up expenses.

How many products and services do you expect to sell? What will your gross revenues be? What percentage of market share do you think you will reach in one year?

Cost of Goods Sold

Estimate the cost of sales for the sales found under revenue (sales). Include the cost of the labor used to produce the product or service (direct labor), materials used in the final product or service (direct material), and their transportation and handling costs. If you plan to manufacture goods, consider the cost of raw materials, labor, and delivery of goods. If you plan to sell retail or wholesale goods and services, consider markup, inventory costs, and freight. Refer to the Risk Management Association's studies for more information to help you compute these costs. See www.rmahq.org.

Total Revenue (Sales) minus Total Cost of Goods Sold = Gross Profit

GROSS PROFIT – TOTAL EXPENSES = NET PROFIT

- Pricing Your Product or Service

  Calculate your sales breakeven point: $_____

  Sales Breakeven Point = Total Fixed Expenses / Gross Profit

  Gross Profit = Difference between the selling price of a product or service and its variable cost/unit.

Example: Total fixed expenses of $35,000 divided by gross profit of $15 (assume that the selling price is $100 and variable cost/unit is $85). Your sales breakeven point would then be $233,333 (the sale of 2,333 units).

The *Sales Breakeven Point* tells you the amount of sales that must be made to cover all the expenses identified. Once you've figured your breakeven point, you can begin making plans to achieve your sales goal. The "Total Revenue" that you will need to breakeven at the end of the year is equal to your "Total Fixed Expenses" divided by your "Gross Profit"

- *An alternative way to determine if you can meet your business's financial obligations:*
    a. Project your average total monthly revenue (sales): $_____
    b. Project your average total monthly expenses: $_____

Divide total revenue and total expenses by 12 to obtain a monthly average for each. Subtract the monthly expenses from the monthly revenue (sales) figure to obtain the monthly net profit or loss. This number will help you determine if your monthly revenue (sales) forecast is realistic in relationship to your monthly expenses.

- *Where will you find money to start your business?*

There are many sources of debt and equity available to entrepreneurs for start-up capital. Some of the most commonly used ones are listed below. There are many other sources you can research that may apply to your state, the ownership status (minority, women-owned, etc.), or the industry in which your business is classified.

Personal savings	$ _____
Family and friends	$ _____
Bank loan	$ _____
Retirement account	$ _____
Investor(s)	$ _____
Partners	$ _____
Credit cards	$ _____
Other	$ _____

SOURCE: Adapted from SCORE Locator: Copyright © 1997 Geographic Services Corporation, P.O. Box 1450, Norwich, VT 05055.

CHAPTER 4

Developing New Venture Strategy

Preparation and Launch

You've taken care of a company . . . wouldn't it be more fun to build one?[1]

— David Neeleman, founder and CEO of JetBlue Airways

Avoid the mistakes of the dot-bomb era. Those folks mistook an exit strategy for a business plan. Go into it with the idea of running a business for the long term.

— James Goodnight, founder of SAS

Objectives:

1. Understand the importance of planning as an ongoing activity central to entrepreneurship, the four reasons why entrepreneurs and managers of new ventures should plan, and the strategic entrepreneurship perspective

2. Know how to create a strategic vision for the new venture; learn how each component of the vision contributes to the development of the strategic plan

3. Understand the important benefits of managing company values and ethics

4. Learn how to create a code of ethics to guide firm behavior in support of the overall business strategy

Speaking of Strategy

Red Hat—Bringing New Value and New Values to the Marketplace

Red Hat, Inc., is the world's leading open source and Linux provider. Founded in 1993, Red Hat is headquartered in Raleigh, North Carolina, with satellite offices worldwide. Red Hat is leading Linux and open source solutions into the mainstream by making high-quality, low-cost technology accessible. Red Hat provides operating system platforms along with middleware, applications, and management solutions, as well as support, training, and consulting services to customers worldwide and through top-tier partnerships. Red Hat's open source strategy offers customers a long-term plan for building infrastructures that are based on and leverage open source technologies with a focus on security and ease of management. Red Hat's mission is "to be the defining technology company of the 21st century." They describe what they do: "We serve global enterprises through technology and services made possible by the open source model. Solutions include Red Hat Enterprise Linux operating platforms, sold through a subscription model, and a broad range of services: consulting, 24x7 support, Red Hat Network. Red Hat's global training program operates in more than 60 locations worldwide and features RHCE, the global standard Linux certification."

How does open source technology work? Here is how Red Hat describes the process: "All software is written with source code. With open source software, the code is protected by a special license that ensures everyone has access to that code. That means no one company can fully own it. Freedom means choice. Choice means power."

Open source enables the customer, not the software provider, to have control over the technology used. "Customers can see the code, change it, and learn from it. Bugs are more quickly found and fixed. And when customers don't like how one vendor is serving them, they can choose another without overhauling their infrastructure. No more technology lock-in."

How does Red Hat make a difference? "We believe open source simply creates better software. It multiplies one company's development capacity many times over. Everyone collaborates, and the best software wins. Not just within one company, but among an Internet-connected, worldwide community. It's no coincidence that the rise of open source closely followed the rise of the Internet. The perfect breeding ground for collaboration, the Internet moves ideas and code around the world in an instant." Red Hat points out that "the concept behind open source is not new. For centuries, universities and research communities have shared their work. Monks copied books by hand. Scientists publish new discoveries in journals. Mathematical formulas are distributed, improved, redistributed. Imagine if all of this past knowledge was kept hidden or its use was restricted to only those who are willing to pay for it. Yet this is the mentality behind the proprietary software model. In the same way shared knowledge propels the whole of society forward, open technology development can drive innovation for an entire industry." The culture of Red Hat is closely connected to its mission and values. Red Hat has been described as the biggest small company in the world.

"With more than 800 Red Hatters across 26 offices worldwide, we rarely think of ourselves as a small company. Until you consider our competition. We stand among giants—competing and partnering with companies many times our size. This is a challenge we've always welcomed. Despite our relative size, our continued success is proof of the power of the open source model. We pride ourselves on collaboration, openness, and the exponential value that comes from joining people of different perspectives to find the best way." According to Red Hat, "Open source forms the foundation of our company's culture because open source is changing the world. In our industry, it returns the balance of power to the customer. In our society, it allows people to be exposed to technology who might not otherwise have the opportunity. No matter how large we grow, we hold these ideals close. Red Hat may be small compared to the company we keep—but don't underestimate the power of more than 800 people who've found a cause worth being passionate about."

According to Jennifer Lamb, enterprise sales engineer, working at Red Hat is a different experience from working at other organizations: "Red Hat is a very open, innovative company with very few political or procedural barriers. It's one of the few companies I know of that allows its employees to directly effect change at all levels and across departments. The people who work here are well rounded, motivated, open-minded, and committed to constantly growing intellectually, professionally, and culturally on an individual and team basis." Her feelings are echoed by software engineer, Todd Warner: When asked to describe the best part about working at Red Hat, he responded: "Three things: the people, the code, and the cause."

SOURCE: http://www.redhat.com. Printed with permission.

Discussion Questions

1. What do you think is the vision of Red Hat, Inc.?

2. What elements of the strategic visioning process can you identify in the Red Hat vignette?

3. In what ways does Red Hat align its vision with its practices? How has it managed to become so successful?

4. What lessons can be adapted by entrepreneurs in other industries from the Red Hat story?

Strategic Planning and Entrepreneurship

When the idea and the opportunity for the new venture have been formulated, it may seem that the next step is to launch the business. This can prove to be a fatal mistake, no matter how much potential the opportunity has. Many entrepreneurs and managers of ventures neglect to take the time to plan strategically for their businesses. Systematic planning is a formal process that is well worth the investment of time and effort. It provides the road map for the new venture. History's greatest person of ideas, Leonardo da Vinci, once said, "He who loves practice without theory is like the sailor who boards a ship without a rudder and compass and never knows where he may cast."

Strategic planning requires taking a long-range view of the venture and developing the vision to guide operations. It involves identifying opportunities and threats in the external environment and assessing how the venture's internal and external strengths and weaknesses can be leveraged to take advantage of the opportunities and minimize the threats. Although a feasibility analysis or comprehensive business plan may be written, these do not take the place of strategic planning—an activity that should be ongoing throughout the life cycle of the new venture.

New ventures that have a strategy and plan accordingly outperform those firms that do not (Miller & Cardinal, 1994). There are four major reasons why entrepreneurs and managers of new ventures should embrace planning (Cascio, 1998):

1. The probability for business success increases.

2. Managerial leaders can more effectively adapt to change.

3. Planning helps provide a meaningful context and direction for employee work.

4. Planning helps align controls to key objectives.

Historically, entrepreneurs have tended to avoid strategic planning, thinking it was only for "big" companies and that it was a rigid, formalized process that took up valuable time and resources. Today, the roles of strategy and strategic planning in new venture formation are considered prerequisites of success, and entrepreneurs are likely to be proactive in their approaches, ensuring the survival and longevity of their ventures. Planning helps founders to make decisions, to balance resource supply and demand, and to turn abstract goals into concrete operational steps, reducing the likelihood of that ventures disband and enhancing product development and venture organizing activity (Delmar & Shane, 2003).

Entrepreneurship and Strategic Management: The Creation of Wealth and Value

Entrepreneurship, as we have described earlier, is the discovery and exploitation of profitable opportunities. *Strategic management* involves the development of a *sustainable competitive advantage* and the ability of the firm to create wealth through these efforts (De Carolis, 2003; Rouse & Daellenbach, 1999). Management scholars have shown that favorable market positions (Porter, 1985) and acquisition of resources that are valuable, rare, and difficult to imitate (Barney, 2001) are the most common ways to achieve sustainable competitive advantage.

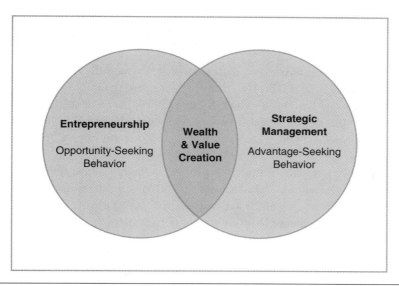

Figure 4.1   The Strategic Entrepreneurship Perspective

The integration of entrepreneurship and strategic management leads to an emergent framework for new venture formation and growth:

> Entrepreneurship and strategic management both focus on how firms create change (adapt or proact) by exploiting opportunities resulting from uncertainty in their external environment (Hitt et al., 2001; Ireland et al., 2001). Firms create wealth by identifying opportunities in their external environments and then developing competitive advantages to exploit them (Hitt et al., 2001; Ireland et al., 2001). Based on this work, we conclude that *strategic entrepreneurship* results from the integration of entrepreneurship and strategic management knowledge. (Ireland, Hitt, & Sirmon, 2003, p. 966)

Figure 4.1 illustrates the strategic entrepreneurship perspective, in which wealth and value are created by integrating knowledge from the two fields. Strategic entrepreneurship does not pertain only to small firms. Enterprises of all sizes need to continually search for opportunities and create and sustain competitive advantages in order to survive. In this chapter, we examine the role and process of strategic visioning, as well as the importance of the strategic plan.

Creating the Strategic Vision: Articulating Need and Purpose

Searching for the idea and developing the business opportunity involve creativity and rigorous research. This work should lead to the creation of the *strategic vision:* an articulation of what the new venture is about and the need that it fills. Each person involved in the venture needs to know why it exists. Although this seems obvious to the entrepreneur, other key players such as employees, management team members, suppliers, lenders, investors, and so on do not necessarily understand it.

The identification of the new venture's purpose reveals the real values that the organization will impart. This is a critical step in ensuring that the venture is on its way to success and that it can persist through difficult times. If the founding team has not done this step, it is likely to exhibit symptoms of passivity (the "whatever" attitude), nonengagement ("I don't know"), and disconnection ("that's not my problem").

Creating the strategic vision is a process of *merging and combining*, then *deciding and eliminating*. Take the time to bring out all the possibilities and individual visions of each of the key players (diverge), give them careful thought, combine them, and merge (converge) perspectives before deciding to eliminate any one.

Divergence and convergence are two modes of thinking that are necessary for a decision to be made, yet it is important to recognize the difference between the two modes of thought. Typically, when people get together to make a decision or to solve a problem, as soon as a few ideas are suggested, people begin evaluating and judging them. Common reactions include phrases such as, "Yes, but . . ." "That's not in the budget," or "We already thought of that and here's why it won't work. . . ." This premature convergence shuts down the flow of creative thinking, suppressing new ideas and potentially innovative solutions and decisions.

Divergence involves generating ideas and thoughts, building on them, and allowing all the ideas to remain on the table for a period of time. When there is a sufficient quantity of ideas (more than one or even five!), convergence, or judging and evaluating the ideas, can be introduced. This is the time for the ALUO (Advantages, Limitations, Uniqueness, and Opportunity) tool introduced in Chapter 3, a very helpful tool for developing (or refining) your vision. Individuals in the new venture bring different perspectives and have value to contribute. Co-creating the strategic vision is the first step toward establishing respect among the venture's key constituents. It is the first real symbolic event that helps set the stage for an innovative business environment and operation (Gundry & LaMantia, 2001).

Some entrepreneurs avoid formal strategic planning because they believe they must strictly adhere to the plan in the future. That is, they view the vision as something that is set in stone, immutable, and static. This is a misconception of the planning process. Having a vision enables the venture to launch with a purpose, and it helps it keep going under circumstances that are unanticipated, including crises that threaten the firm's survival. The vision that the entrepreneur and management team creates at start-up will probably look different one year or five years later because it will evolve to reflect changes internal or external to the organization (Gundry & LaMantia, 2001).

The Innovator's Toolkit: Strategic Visioning

The following questions are posed by the entrepreneur to each of the key players involved in the new venture (including the entrepreneur), who will answer them individually. When the group comes together, responses are shared.

1. What is the opportunity or problem that led to the launch of the new venture?
2. What obstacles do you perceive for yourself and the team?
3. What stands in the way of your progress?
4. How will you know if you are on the right track?
5. For what do you desire to be known?
6. What difference do you want the venture to make?
7. What are you passionate about?
8. What talents/abilities do you personally want to contribute?
9. What kind of organization do you wish to build?

Individual answers to the above questions are shared, and the information in the table below is constructed from the pooled responses. This helps the entrepreneur and the team create the strategic vision that will guide the venture through start-up and early growth.

Table 4.1   Strategic Visioning

Question/Area of Inquiry	Component of Strategic Vision
What opportunity or problem led to venture launch?	Purpose: What we are attempting to do
What obstacles confront the venture team?	Potential pitfalls to overcome
What blocks progress?	Resources needed
How will we know we are on the right track?	Data to be gathered
For what do we desire to be known?	Values we will formulate and actions we will take
What difference do we wish to make?	Customer and market needs
What is each key player passionate about?	Personally meaningful goals
What talents and abilities do the venture members wish to contribute?	Who we can be as a team
What kind of organization do we wish to build?	New venture culture: shared values and behaviors

┌─ **Strategic Reflection Point** ──────────────────────────────────

Communicating the Vision

An interesting way to be sure you can articulate the vision for your business in an effective manner is to try the elevator test (Moore, 2002). It helps you think about how you would tell someone about the product or service you provide (what it is you do) in the time it takes to get to your floor in an elevator. Your statement should communicate quickly and clearly the purpose of your product/service in the following form:

  For . . . (the target customer)

  Who wants . . . (the key need)?

  The . . . (name of your product/service)

  That . . . (what do you in fact provide)

  Unlike . . . (competitive product and key benefit)

  Our product . . . (competitive advantage)

Once you have articulated the strategic vision for your business, the next step is to begin the strategic planning that will enable you to carry out the vision in the operations of the company. Communicating and operationalizing strategy are two of the most critical components of the strategic planning process. A company's vision is only as strong as the actual entrepreneurial behaviors support.

Values Creation: Developing
Strategy in Good Company

Business ethics and values are the subject of increasingly great attention today in light of the numerous scandals involving unethical and unlawful actions on the part of managers. In 2002, the Sarbanes-Oxley Act was passed, requiring every publicly held company to annually disclose the code of ethics espoused by the company's CEO and senior financial officers. Compliance is one reason for founders and managers to consider values and ethical behavior; however, there are several practical and rewarding aspects to the process of actively managing ethics in entrepreneurial organizations, including conducting business on a higher level of trust among the stakeholders (Alford, 2005).

Ethics is behavior that conforms to moral principles and values, and business ethics is the discipline of developing and practicing business relationships that conform to these moral principles (Alford, 2005). Many businesses design formal ethics programs, including creating a code of ethics. Many businesses have had what is called a code of conduct, a corporate code of ethics, or values-based management since the beginning of the 20th century (Newberg, 2004). One interesting result of the Sarbanes-Oxley Act is that the ethical commitments embodied in the codes act as a signal to potential investors, employees, and customers that these are good firms with which to do business (Alford, 2005; Newberg, 2004). Research has identified key strategic benefits to businesses that have ethics programs (Devero, 2003):

- Build employee loyalty, reducing hiring and training costs
- Reduce theft and other anticompany activity
- Drive sales and build customer loyalty
- Create community goodwill that can lend support for tax advantages and strategic alliances
- Attract quality applicants with minimum investment in recruitment
- Maintain loyal vendor relationships, reducing loss of suppliers and unexpected cost increases

All of the above activities and outcomes are important components of the new venture formation process. In summary, research shows that firms can gain competitive advantage through the appropriate management of business ethics, or managing company values as it is sometimes called (Alford, 2005).

Research in Practice:	A Comparative Study on the Ethics of Entrepreneurs and Managers

Researchers have examined the stakeholder-agency theory as a foundation for the comparison of ethical attitudes and standards of entrepreneurs and managers. Stakeholder-agency theory proposes that managers (who are "agents" or nonowner stakeholders in the organization) could take advantage of the company unless it had effective mechanisms of corporate governance (Hasnas, 1998; Hill & Jones, 1992). The theory of property (Becker, 1977; Bucar & Hisrich, 2001) is a supplement to stakeholder-agency theory in that it maintains that the owner-stakeholders are not subjected to the same ethical considerations as nonowner stakeholders.

Recently, 165 entrepreneurs and 128 managers completed a survey that asked them to respond to questions and scenarios (Bucar & Hisrich, 2001). In the sample, managers tended to have a higher educational level than entrepreneurs, with 72 percent and 29 percent of the managers having postgraduate or bachelor level education, respectively, compared to 35 percent and 29 percent of the entrepreneurs sampled. The average age of entrepreneurs was 44; for managers it was 38. About 78 percent of the entrepreneurs, and 70 percent of the managers, were male.

The findings, presented in Table 4.2, show that in general, entrepreneurs and managers differed only slightly in their views regarding the ethics of various activities. However, there were some significant differences that indicated that entrepreneurs are more prone to hold ethical attitudes (Bucar & Hisrich, 2001).

Table 4.2   Ethical Perceptions Regarding Activities

Activities	Entrepreneurs Yes – Ethical	Entrepreneurs No – Not Ethical	Managers Yes – Ethical	Managers No – Not Ethical	X^2
Use company services for personal use	30 (18.5%)	132 (81.5%)	35 (28.2%)	89 (71.8%)	3.77[2]
Remove company supplies for personal use	11 (6.7%)	154 (93.3%)	18 (14.1%)	110 (85.9%)	4.42[2]
Overstate expense accounts by more than 10%	2 (1.2%)	163 (98.8%)	7 (5.5%)	121 (94.5%)	4.39[2]
Overstate expense accounts by less than 10%	12 (7.3%)	153 (92.9%)	17 (13.9%)	110 (86.6%)	3.00[3]
Use company time for non-company benefits	31 (19.3%)	130 (80.7%)	37 (29.6%)	88 (70.4%)	4.16[2]
Give gifts/favors for preferential treatment	25 (15.2%)	139 (84.8%)	15 (11.7%)	113 (88.3%)	0.76
Accept gifts/favors for preferential treatment	12 (7.3%)	153 (92.7%)	14 (11.0%)	113 (89.0%)	1.25
Blame for errors an innocent co-worker	2 (1.2%)	163 (98.8%)	5 (3.9%)	123 (96.1%)	2.24
Claim credit for a peer's work	3 (1.8%)	162 (98.2%)	5 (3.9%)	123 (96.1%)	1.18
Call in sick in order to take a day off	23 (14.0%)	141 (86.0%)	26 (20.3%)	102 (79.7%)	2.04
Taking extra personal time	32 (20.0%)	128 (80.0%)	54 (43.2%)	71 (56.8%)	7.92[1]
Purchase shares upon insider information	18 (11.1%)	144 (88.9%)	14 (10.9%)	114 (89.1%)	0.00
Authorizing subordinates to violate company policy	8 (4.9%)	154 (95.1%)	18 (14.3%)	108 (85.7%)	7.54[1]
Fail to report a co-worker's violation of company policy	42 (26.8%)	115 (73.2%)	44 (35.5%)	80 (64.5%)	2.49
Falsifying reports	3 (1.8%)	162 (98.2%)	10 (7.9%)	117 (92.1%)	6.19[1]
Hiring competitor's employees to learn trade secrets	42 (26.1%)	119 (73.9%)	46 (36.8%)	79 (63.2%)	3.80[2]
Fail to report a co-worker's violation of law	21 (13.0%)	141 (87.0%)	25 (20.2%)	99 (79.8%)	2.70
Divulge confidential information to parties external to the firm	7 (4.2%)	158 (95.8%)	11 (8.7%)	116 (91.3%)	2.42
Taking longer than necessary to do a job	15 (9.2%)	148 (90.8%)	28 (22.2%)	98 (77.8%)	9.51[1]

(1) Significant at .01 level or better.
(2) Significant at .05 level or better.
(3) Significant at .10 level or better.

SOURCE: From Bucar, B., & Hisrich, R. D. (2001). Ethics of Business Managers vs. Entrepreneurs. *Journal of Developmental Entrepreneurship*, Vol. 6(1): 59–82. Reprinted with permission.

Strategy in Action

The Truth According to Google

Google, Inc., is widely recognized as the world's leading search technology company. "The perfect search engine," says Google cofounder Larry Page, "would understand exactly what you mean and give back exactly what you want." Given the state of search technology today, that's a far-reaching vision requiring research, development, and innovation to realize. Google is committed to blazing that trail. Even though Google is the leader in the field, the company's goal is to provide a much higher level of service to all those who seek information, whether they're at a desk in Boston, driving through Bonn, or strolling in Bangkok. Here is Google's philosophy about the Internet, and these values are likely to guide the way individuals, businesses, and technologists view it into the future. Google describes these as the "Ten Things Google Has Found to Be True":

1. **Focus on the user and all else will follow.** From its inception, Google has focused on providing the best user experience possible. While many companies claim to put their customers first, few are able to resist the temptation to make small sacrifices to increase shareholder value. Google has steadfastly refused to make any change that does not offer a benefit to the users who come to the site: The interface is clear and simple, pages load instantly, placement in search results is never sold to anyone, and advertising on the site must offer relevant content and not be a distraction.

2. **It's best to do one thing really, really well.** Google's entire staff is dedicated to creating the perfect search engine and works tirelessly toward that goal.

3. **Fast is better than slow.** Google may be the only company in the world whose stated goal is to have users leave its website as quickly as possible.

4. **Democracy on the web works.** By analyzing the full structure of the web, Google is able to determine which sites have been "voted" the best sources of information by those most interested in the information they offer.

5. **You don't need to be at your desk to need an answer.** The world is increasingly mobile and unwilling to be constrained to a fixed location. Whether it's through their PDAs, their wireless phones or even their automobiles, people want information to come to them. Wherever search is likely to help users obtain the information they seek, Google is pioneering new technologies and offering new solutions.

6. **You can make money without doing evil.** Google is a business. The revenue the company generates is derived from offering its search technology to companies and from the sale of advertising displayed on Google and on other sites across the web. However, you may have never seen an ad on Google. That's because Google does not allow ads to be displayed on our results pages unless they're relevant to the results page on which they're shown. Google firmly believes that ads can provide useful information if, and only if, they are relevant to what you wish to find. Google has also proven that advertising can be effective without being flashy. Google does not accept pop-up advertising, which interferes with your ability to see the content you've requested.

(Continued)

(Continued)

7. **There's always more information out there.** Google's researchers continue looking into ways to bring all the world's information to users seeking answers.

8. **The need for information crosses all borders.** Though Google is headquartered in California, our mission is to facilitate access to information for the entire world, so we have offices around the globe.

9. **You can be serious without a suit.** Google's founders have often stated that the company is not serious about anything but search. They built a company around the idea that work should be challenging and the challenge should be fun. There is an emphasis on team achievements and pride in individual accomplishments that contribute to the company's overall success. Give the proper tools to a group of people who like to make a difference, and they will.

10. **Great just isn't good enough.** Always deliver more than expected. Google does not accept being the best as an endpoint, but a starting point. Google's point of distinction is anticipating needs not yet articulated by our global audience, then meeting them with products and services that set new standards. This constant dissatisfaction with the way things are is ultimately the driving force behind the world's best search engine.

SOURCE: www.google.com. Reprinted with permission.

Writing a Code of Ethics

It is never too early in the formation of a new venture to write a code of ethics. Even if there are no employees, or just one or two, the organization always has several stakeholders: customers, suppliers, other businesses, and community members. Once written, the document can and should be revisited each year, and as the firm grows, more information can be added to it. Codes of ethics should contain the following types of information (Alford, 2005):

- Purpose
- Policy
- Procedures (with examples of behaviors)
  o   Honesty and fairness
  o   Conflicts of interest
  o   Purchasing and selling goods and services
  o   Discrimination, harassment, and professional work environment
  o   Confidentiality of compensation information
  o   Labor and employee relations matters
  o   Confidentiality and insider trading
  o   Intellectual property
  o   Immigration law
  o   Compliance with antitrust laws

- Environmental
- Accurate and complete records
- Workplace safety
- Bidding, negotiation, and performance on contracts
- Reporting suspected violations
  - General policy
  - List of designated personnel
  - Complaint procedures
- Training
- Review procedures
  - Employee input
  - Timeline

Failures and Foibles

Do's and Don'ts on Strategy From a CEO

Paige Arnof-Fenn is the founder and CEO of Mavens & Moguls, a strategic marketing consulting firm, whose clients include Fortune 500 companies as well as early stage and emerging businesses. She notes that from her experience, there are no short-cuts to launching a new venture. You must do the hard work to understand your customers, competitors, market conditions and risks. She presents the following principles that apply to start-ups as well as Fortune 500 companies, whether they sell consumer products, professional services or technology products.

These lessons can help aspiring entrepreneurs and managers avoid the failures and foibles common to strategic planning and implementation.

1. *Stop selling and start sharing.* People are much more interested in what you have to say when you're sharing your knowledge, your passion and your experience to help them solve their problems. Focus on being interested in them, and don't worry so much about being interesting. It's amazing how interesting you are when you're paying attention to your customers' needs. People buy from those they like, trust and identify with. Building rapport creates that trust and credibility. Just remember, it's about the relationship, not the sale. Nobody likes to be sold, but everyone likes to buy.
   Do: Listen to what your prospects and customers say with their words and body language.
   Don't: Pull out a brochure or sales sheet unless they ask for it.

2. *Differentiate or Die.* What makes you unique vs. the others in the market? Make sure there's something special about your product or service other than the price. Own something important in your customers' hearts and minds. Being good is no longer good enough—you have to find something where you're great. Use your imagination and creativity to set yourself apart from the crowd. I once worked with a business owner who always wears red. She works in a male-dominated field where everyone has basically the same credentials so at least she's easy to spot at events. "The lady in red" gets most of her work by referral, which is a great way to build a business.
   Do: Talk to real customers and ask them for a report card.
   Don't: Chase last week's/quarter's/year's trend.

(Continued)

(Continued)

3. *Solve Problems People Will Pay For.* Revenue is validation. Are customers voting with their wallets? Are your products or services the "nice to have" thing or the "have to have" thing? Be very important to your most important customers—they should think of you first for any needs in your category. Also, make sure you have more than just a "one off" good idea. Although great businesses start with great ideas, not all ideas are company-worthy. Many of the dot-coms forgot that the business model must actually work, that cash flow matters and that it's not just about building awareness but about making the sale. Janet Jackson got plenty of attention for her wardrobe malfunction in the 2004 Super Bowl, but did that sell more of her products?

Do: Test, tweak and try again.

Don't: Ask your friends or family and call it "research."

4. *Leverage the Evangelists.* There are people out there using your product or service who would be glad to tell others about your business. If you can make them happy, they'll help you spread the word to other like-minded customers. And here's something to keep in mind: They may be using your product or service for purposes other than the ones you initially intended, so make sure you really understand what they like and dislike about your business and, more important, why. And remember, it's not about pedigree or job title—your champions can come from anywhere. At one of the startups I worked for, a hair stylist made a key introduction for our company. Friend-raising can, in fact, lead to fundraising, so make friends before you need them.

Do: Make it easy for your evangelists to try your product or service.

Don't: Discount the negatives. There may be an important insight buried within.

5. *Be Visible.* Wasn't it Woody Allen who said that 80 percent of success is just showing up? Invisibility is not a good business strategy—if people don't know you exist, then guess what? You don't. You don't have to run a Super Bowl ad to get noticed, but you do have to be active in the communities you cater to so people know where and how to find you. Whether you have a technology business, a consumer products company or a professional services firm, you're in the relationship business. If there are businesses that target your same customer base, then find creative ways you can each leverage your contacts and databases to multiply your outreach. Best-kept secrets are just that: secrets.

Do: Put your mouth where your money is, too.

Don't: Hide in your office or behind your computer online.

6. *Create Extraordinary Experiences.* The relationships you have with your customers are based on the cumulative experiences they have with your employees, product, service and business. If your brochure or website makes one claim but the reality is very different, it's the first-hand knowledge that will be remembered by your customers, so make sure you deliver on the promises you make every time you connect with your customers. Is it such a surprise that most of the airlines are going bankrupt while Jet Blue and Southwest are profitable?

Do: Consistently reinforce your key messages in everything you do.

Don't: Forget that every employee, partner and affiliate is an ambassador, too.

7. *Put Passion Above All Else.* Customers are savvy—they know when something is genuine or if you're just going through the motions. So do your employees, partners and affiliates. If you don't enjoy what you are doing, find something else to do! It's hard to compete with someone who gets up feeling excited every day and who's full of ideas about their business. To them, what they do doesn't feel like work. Enthusiasm is contagious, so determine what it is you enjoy doing and then share your gift with others whose talents may lie somewhere else. When everyone plays to their strengths, the results are superior.

Do: Work you love and believe is important.

Don't: Waste time. It's your most precious commodity.

Review Question

1. How can innovative companies stand out in a competitive market?

Summary of Chapter Objectives

1. Understand the importance of planning as an ongoing activity central to entrepreneurship, the four reasons why entrepreneurs and managers of new ventures should plan, and the strategic entrepreneurship perspective
   - Systematic planning is a formal process that is well worth the investment of time and effort. It provides the road map for the new venture. *Strategic planning* requires taking a long-range view of the venture and developing the vision to guide operations. It involves identifying opportunities and threats in the external environment and assessing how the venture's internal and external strengths and weaknesses can be leveraged to take advantage of the opportunities and minimize the threats. The four reasons why strategic planning should be done are:
   - The probability for business success increases.
   - Managerial leaders can more effectively adapt to change.
   - Planning helps provide a meaningful context and direction for employee work.
   - Planning helps align controls to key objectives.

2. Know how to create a strategic vision for the new venture; learn how each component of the vision contributes to the development of the strategic plan.
   - Having a vision enables the venture to launch with a purpose, and it helps it keep going under circumstances that are unanticipated, including crises that threaten the firm's survival. The vision that the entrepreneur and management team creates at start-up will probably look different one year

or five years later because it will evolve to reflect changes internal or external to the organization.

- The areas of inquiry that shape the components of the strategic vision include the opportunities and obstacles confronting the new venture, how progress will be tracked, the difference the new venture intends to make, and the contributions of the key members of the organization that will support the vision.

3. Understand the important benefits of managing company values and ethics.
   - While founders and managers consider compliance with the law one reason for considering values and ethical behavior, there are several practical and rewarding aspects to the process of actively managing ethics in entrepreneurial organizations.
   - Managing ethical behavior leads to several positive outcomes, including building employee loyalty, reducing hiring and trainings costs, driving sales, building customer loyalty, maintaining loyal vendor relationships, and reducing loss of suppliers and unexpected cost increases.

4. Learn how to create a code of ethics to guide firm behavior in support of the overall strategic vision
   - The Sarbanes-Oxley Act is a new requirement for businesses, and one result has been that the ethical commitments of the code of conduct for a new venture act as a signal to potential investors, employees, and customers that these are good firms with which to do business.

CASE 4.1   JetBlue

While much of the industry was crippled by September 11, and while United Airlines and US Airways fell into bankruptcy, JetBlue has been a dramatic example of what can happen when the right entrepreneur with the right idea . . . comes along at the right moment.

Salter, 2004, p. 67

Years before starting the airline, David Neeleman, the founder of JetBlue and now the CEO and director, scrutinized the reasons that airline start-ups fail. Getting started was the easy part. The barriers to entry were relatively low in the mid-1990s—an airline could get off the ground for about $10 million. New entrants leased a few aging jets from a relatively unknown airline, paid for a new coat of paint, and then hired the pilot and crew. At first, the airline would offer limited routes at outrageously cheap fares, using bare bones advertising. The airline would then rely on word-of-mouth promotion, fueled by the extremely low fares, to gain additional business. But then the troubles would begin.

All airlines have high fixed costs due to the expense of leasing and maintaining aircraft. A new airline is in a poor position to bargain for reasonable lease terms at airports. It may be forced to pay higher fuel and insurance costs based on its new entrant status. The only way to cover the high costs is to sell as many tickets as cheaply as possible in hopes of breaking even. This business model is hardly sustainable and can lead to a downward spiral.

The leased planes may begin to break down due to their age, causing maintenance costs to skyrocket, not to mention the effect on the already limited customer base when flights must be canceled due to mechanical problems. The airline would begin to be seen as "cheap, but unreliable"(Peterson, 2004, p. 41). The larger

existing airlines would see their opportunity to eliminate a small start-up airline that is stealing even a small amount of their market share. The larger players can easily operate with low margins, or even at a loss, in the short-run to match the prices offered by the start-up, causing customers to return to the airlines they know. Predatory pricing, as it is called in the industry, is extremely effective in running start-up airlines out of business, and larger airlines return to their traditional pricing once the smaller airline has been extinguished.

Neeleman studied these stories and felt that he could do it differently. He knew the only way to avoid this vicious cycle, which he had seen played out again and again, was to provide a start-up airline with enough money in the beginning to weather the brutal combat that was sure to ensue. An old joke in the airline industry captures this reality, "How do you make a little money in the airline business? Start out with a lot" (Peterson, 2004, p. 42). Neeleman calculated the necessary buffer amount of start-up capital to be 10 times what most new airlines invest. In fact, he refused to start his airline without reaching a goal of $200 million.

Once he had the money, Neeleman decided to avoid other problems that had plagued start-ups, such as high maintenance costs. He would use some of the large initial investment to purchase all new planes that would be more reliable, more efficient, and less expensive to maintain. This would also allow the airline to customize passenger entertainment options from the beginning. Assuming strong growth from the start, Neeleman planned to purchase several planes at once to gain a volume-based price break.

Finally, following Southwest's example, Neeleman wanted to "have the lowest costs in the airline industry" (Peterson, 2004, p. 43). He felt that he could even surpass Southwest Airlines by focusing on technology to gain operational efficiencies. All reservations would be electronic, and all unnecessary paperwork would be eliminated.

Neeleman understood that cash is king and that profits are crucial to maintaining a successful business, but he also wanted to make JetBlue a leader in customer service. His commitment to service has paid off—in 2005, JetBlue was the No. 1 airline on the Brand Keys' Customer Loyalty Index.[2] JetBlue was named Best Domestic Airline for Value by the readers of *Travel + Leisure* magazine, as part of their 2006 World's Best Values Awards survey ("JetBlue Named," 2006). Neeleman likes to joke about this saying, "when we first started the airline we said, 'This will be the best customer service company in the country, and it's going to be in New York,' and everyone just laughed at us" (Hira, 2004, p. 198). This commitment to service is what many analysts feel has buoyed the company's profits over the years.

The Airline Industry

The airline industry has struggled in recent years, especially due to high fixed costs, increasing fear of terror attacks, and the rise of regional carriers such as JetBlue. The newer, smaller jets used by regional carriers can travel greater distances and are much faster than the older turboprop planes. Regional jets are also more cost-efficient, allowing carriers like JetBlue to operate in previously underserved markets (*Airlines Industry Profile*, 2005). Larger carriers such as Delta Airlines and American Airlines have created several regional divisions to compete in the changing market.

Several factors—including airport capacity, route structures, weather, technology, and rising fuel and labor costs—have significantly narrowed airline margins over the past decade (*Airlines Industry Profile*, 2005). Traditional carriers turned to higher prices, especially for business customers. However, in 2000 and 2001, corporations began to look for ways to cut costs

and began limiting business travel to reduce expenses, relying more heavily on technology such as video and teleconferencing (*Airlines Industry Profile*, 2005). In an industry where even a short slowing in revenues can have a major effect on the airline's finances, the low-cost business model of budget airlines has a clear advantage.

Despite the strength of the low-cost carrier business model, the rise of JetBlue was highly unlikely. In fact, 58 jet airlines have opened since deregulation in 1978, and all but one, Midwest Express, have since closed their doors (Peterson, 2004, p. xix). In 1999, the low-cost carrier segment was a mere 10 percent of the air travel business, and of that 10 percent, 90 percent was Southwest Airlines. By 2004, budget airlines carried 30 percent of air travelers, and JetBlue was ranked in the country's top 10 airlines (Peterson, 2004, p. xix).

Low-cost airlines have provided a balanced solution to the issue of rising airline ticket prices. They offer not only tickets for a lower price but also customer service and other amenities passengers value, using a business model that has led Southwest Airlines to make a profit for 30 consecutive years (*Airlines Industry Profile*, 2005). JetBlue has also been growing successfully over the last five years, and not without competition. Atlantic Coast Airlines, once affiliated with United Airlines, has reinvented itself as Independence Air. United Airlines recently created a budget airline of its own called Ted, and Delta Airlines created its version of a budget airline, called Song. The industry is changing rapidly, trying to shed some of the high fixed costs inherent in its traditional business model.

Although JetBlue has been extremely profitable, reaching $1 billion in revenue in 2003, it is still a small airline when compared with American Airlines ($17.4 billion), United ($13.7 billion), or Delta (with $13.3 billion) (Salter, 2004). But JetBlue plans to continue growing at a rapid pace, adding a new plane every 10 days in 2005.

JetBlue's Keys to Success

The success and growth of JetBlue are directly related to the airline's rigorous recruiting and training program, its ongoing commitment to technology, and its understanding that a quality customer experience must extend from the time customers purchase their tickets to the time they leave the destination airport, luggage in hand. Stuart Klaskin, a Coral Gables, Florida-based aviation consultant, explains the successful formula of JetBlue:

> They've redefined what is expected of a startup airline . . . They said, Let's completely wipe the slate clean. And from a technology standpoint and a customer service standpoint, they have done things that most other people in the airline industry have only thought about. (Overby, 2002, p. 72)

Rigorous Recruitment and Training

David Neeleman was a diligent student of the flight industry, first working at a travel agency and then starting Morris Air—a Salt Lake City-based charter airline—in the early 1990s before joining Southwest Airlines for a brief period. He studied the reasons that start-up airlines failed over time and sought out ways to avoid these pitfalls.

When it came to recruiting the in-flight crew, Neeleman had a clear sense of the people he *did not* want to hire. He feared that airline attendants who had been laid off from some of the major airlines might be disillusioned about the job. Instead, he welcomed applicants from a wide range of fields. In fact, the first class of recruits included "a sixty-year-old retired New York City firefighter, a nightclub singer, and a mortician" (Peterson, 2004, p. xiv). Today, the odds of being hired by the airline are 80 to 1.

JetBlue employees do not earn the highest salaries in the industry, however, the stock purchase program, 401(k), and profit sharing, coupled with numerous other tangible and intangible benefits such as free vacation flights and personal growth opportunities, have led to low turnover (Jackson, 2005, p. 54). Each employee receives extensive training when he or she first joins JetBlue, not only on procedures but also on customer service and the company's values. Employees are also given the opportunity to participate in professional development opportunities throughout their JetBlue career.

Ongoing Commitment to Technology

The commitment to staying on the cutting edge of technology served as a pillar of JetBlue's success. Neeleman and his partner, David Barger, the COO, feel that technology is essential in creating a positive customer experience from ticket purchase to arrival. John Kasarda, an airline industry expert at the University of North Carolina's Kenan-Flagler Business School, commends JetBlue, saying, "They took what was cutting edge in terms of digital business and translated it to aviation. It was surprising somebody hadn't done it sooner" (Overby, 2002, p. 73).

Ticketing: The Beginning of the Experience

Neeleman was the innovator who brought electronic ticketing to the airline industry when he operated Morris Air.

> One day, soon after they got their license, Neeleman heard someone musing about 'Why can't we be more like a hotel, where you just show up with your confirmation number and get your room? Why go through all this ticketing nonsense?' Neeleman picked up on the thought: Why *couldn't* an airline simply take reservations and charge people's credit cards, and when they got to the airport, they'd get their boarding pass? (Peterson, 2004, p. 15)

Neeleman recognized that the cheap direct flights he intended to offer were simple transactions that wouldn't need to involve a travel agent. So, he brought the idea to some of his technically savvy employees, who developed the first electronic ticketing system. Although it is standard across all airlines today, this concept was brand new in 1993. The system also integrated several operational aspects, including Internet booking and revenue management, as well as reporting functionality (Overby, 2002).

From the beginning, JetBlue offered a simple Web site customers could use to book travel. Customers can book either on-line or by phone. All fares are one-way, and there are no Saturday stay-over fees or other restrictions. All ticketing is electronic and nonrefundable. Customers who are unable to fly as planned can change their ticket for a fee much lower than other airlines charge (Peterson, 2004, p. 121).

JetBlue's business model not only saves customers hassle, but also makes financial sense for the start-up. By using incentives to drive customers to the Web site for booking tickets instead of contacting a customer service representative, JetBlue saves significantly on staffing costs. "A reservation taken over the phone costs the airline, on average, four dollars; the same itinerary booked on its Web site costs twenty-five cents" (Peterson, 2004, p. 122). The straightforward ticketing system made it much cheaper to train the representatives the company *did* hire. It also made booking tickets a faster process. By not using travel agencies to distribute its tickets, JetBlue also saves money by avoiding costly commissions.

The Plane: The Chance to Make Customers for Life

The large initial investment that Neeleman made in the company, as well as the tremendous amount of capital raised from outside investors, allowed the start-up airline to purchase brand new planes—a fact that gave the company a tremendous benefit from the very beginning. New planes incur less maintenance costs, and they can be fitted with cutting edge features from the beginning, such as satellite TV.

JetBlue decided to install satellite TV to provide cable programming to every seat on each of its planes. Called LiveTV, this new technology was created by a joint venture of Harris Corporation and the Sextant Corporation (Peterson, 2004, p. 87). Installing this feature served two purposes: first, it surprised and delighted JetBlue customers with an unexpected feature and, second, it provided a service that other airline giants couldn't easily match.

JetBlue has also made a significant investment in technology behind the scenes, also unmatched by competitors. JetBlue maintains a paperless system for most business processes, from the first paperless cockpit and "Blue Performance," a program to track operational data (updated with every flight), to the company's intranet, which shares information with all JetBlue employees (Overby, 2002).

JetBlue recently introduced a new way to reroute planes due to inclement weather and other disruptions, called an operational recovery system. When the airline is faced with a situation such as a major weather development, the software can produce various solutions based on guidelines that the airline selects as most important (for example, no delays longer than three hours). The software calculates not only ways to reroute planes to fit the set guidelines but also the cost associated with each solution. This program will be essential for maintaining order as the airline grows (Salter, 2004).

Baggage Claim: The Final Impression

As the last piece of the customer's JetBlue experience, the baggage claim could make or break the customer's impression of the overall experience. Barger felt strongly that "no matter how good the flight was, what [the customer will] remember is that it took forty-five minutes to get their bag" (Peterson, 2004, p. 122). Committed to serving its customers throughout the entire travel experience, JetBlue mandated that the first bag would arrive on the baggage carousel within 10 minutes of the plane's arrival at the gate and that the last bag would arrive within 20 minutes.

When the Department of Transportation reported a 12 percent increase in mishandled luggage between August 2003 and 2004, Barger knew that JetBlue had to react. Keeping with its commitment to technology, the company rolled out BagSuite, a new baggage reconciliation and data warehouse software to be deployed to all airports JetBlue serves. This new product is expected to reduce annual costs for mishandled bags by 30 percent (Croft, 2004). Whereas larger airlines wait for the government to mandate better baggage handling, JetBlue sees the early investment as key to maintaining the high customer satisfaction for which it is known.

The Future of JetBlue

To keep pace with demand, JetBlue is beginning to grow at a rate unprecedented in the airline's short history. JetBlue added 7 to 10 employees each day in 2005 (Peterson, 2004, p. xix). In 2005, the combination of strong competition, high fuel prices, excess capacity, and the lingering fear of terrorism led to lower earnings and poor share prices for all airlines. And despite Neeleman's goal to be the lowest cost airline, the extra amenities JetBlue provides, coupled with its traditionally low fares, mean that JetBlue has higher operating costs than Southwest Airlines—costs that have led to lower profit margins (Johnson, 2005). (See Table 4.3.) However, Neeleman doesn't view high fuel prices and the more competitive market as all bad. He sees the difficult environment as a challenge for losing competitors and those without a solid business model.

Table 4.3   JetBlue Operating Expenses per Available Seat Mile

	Year Ended December 31		
	2003	2002	Percent Change
	(in dollars)		
Operating expenses:			
Salaries, wages, and benefits	1.96	1.97	(0.4)%
Aircraft fuel	1.08	.92	16.7
Landing fees and other rents	.50	.53	(5.4)
Aircraft rent	.44	.49	(11.3)
Sales and marketing	.39	.54	(27.0)
Depreciation and amortization	.37	.33	13.1
Maintenance materials and repairs	.17	.11	56.4
Other operating expenses	1.17	1.54	(24.2)
Total operating expenses	6.08	6.43	(5.5)%

SOURCE: *JetBlue's 2003 Annual Report on Form 10-K.* JetBlue Investor Relations/Annual Report. April 23, 2004. Retrieved from http://investor.jetblue.com/ireye/ir_site.zhtml?ticker=jblu&script=700

JetBlue's double-digit operating margins may be a thing of the past as airplane repair and maintenance costs increase with aging planes (Bond, 2004). Also, the addition of a new type of plane in 2005 was expected to add operating costs around training, as well as complexity. But nonetheless, the airline is still filling about 85 percent of its seats (10 percent higher than the industry average), and passengers are paying slightly more to fly JetBlue than their competitors (Newman, 2004). Delta Airline's low-cost subsidiary, Song, has cut fares on some of JetBlue's most competitive routes, but JetBlue has kept its balance. For example, between New York and Orlando, JetBlue filled 89 percent of its seats whereas Song filled 72 percent (even with a cheaper fare by $5) (Newman, 2004).

Critics feel that JetBlue is bound to begin looking like other airlines, especially with low turnover, meaning the labor costs will certainly rise as employees are given raises. As the planes continue to age, maintenance costs will increase. But Neeleman continues to prepare JetBlue for the future by maintaining cutting edge technology.

Although Neeleman and Barger are the most public leaders of JetBlue, they have also assembled a management team with deep and broad industry experience. This allows Neeleman to be the public face of JetBlue without needing to oversee every aspect of the company. The fact that the culture is bigger than Neeleman's leadership suggests the company may continue its successful run well into the future.

SOURCE: This case was written by Laurel Ofstein, DePaul University.

Discussion Questions

1. How did Neeleman challenge the standard operating procedure of the airline industry?

2. Did Neeleman have a strategic vision or plan for JetBlue? If yes, how did he follow this plan as he built his business?

3. What did JetBlue offer that was different from existing airlines?

4. What were the keys to JetBlue's early success?

5. How can JetBlue remain a leader in the low-cost carrier industry?

CASE 4.2 Haldiram: A Family Entrepreneur Mastering the Intense Competition in the Indian Snack Market

Pankaj Agrawal, CEO of Haldiram-Delhi, smiled to himself as he finished reading the latest (February 27, 2003) market research report on the snack foods market in India. While small, unorganized companies still dominated India's snack foods market, the report stated that the organized, branded products market was experiencing strong growth. According to the report, "In the branded chips segment, U.S. multinational, PepsiCo India Holdings Pvt. Ltd. with its Ruffles/Lays, Cheetos, and Hostess brands, and

Haldirams, a major Indian player dominate the market" (Phookan, 2003).

Indeed, Haldiram had become an undisputed leader in the snack foods industry in India, with an estimated turnover of 3.5 billion rupees[3] and an estimated brand valuation of 15 billion rupees (Kukreja, 2002). It was a household name synonymous with authenticity in the *namkeen* and *mithai* markets (see Exhibit 1—A Note on Indian Meals and Snacks), and was known as the "Taste of Tradition." It was said that Haldiram was to namkeen and mithai what Cadbury was to chocolates. The Haldiram brand was ranked among the top 100 of "India's Most Trusted Brands 2003" survey done by A. C. Nielsen.

As Agrawal contemplated the future of Haldiram, he saw three strategic opportunities: (1) expansion of Haldiram-Delhi's product line in India, (2) international expansion of Haldiram-Delhi's lines, and (3) expansion in India's fast-food business in which there appeared to be huge opportunities. How should the company leverage its past successes to enable growth? These were the issues he planned to discuss with his father in the coming week.

Haldiram—Then and Now

Haldiram's story began in 1936, when Gangabisanji Agrawal (alias Haldiram Agrawal) opened a namkeen shop in Bikaner in the State of Rajasthan, in Northern India. The namkeens, salty snacks that were made from chickpeas, pulses (legumes, such as dry beans and lentils), oils, ground nuts, and spices, were prepared in the traditional Northern Indian way known as the Bikaneri style, using techniques that dated back to the 19th century and had been passed down through generations. In 1941, the shop began using the brand name, Haldiram. Using a team of experienced Bikaneri namkeen makers and competing on the basis of superior and uncompromising quality, Haldiram served namkeens directly to customers, as well as through the trade.

Following on the success of namkeens, Haldiram expanded into mithai. As it did with namkeens, Haldiram made all the mithais in a traditional manner, with expert cooks using the freshest, purest, and original ingredients each day. Even the spices were ground in special spice grinders to give the original Bikaneri flavor, which few others could deliver. With a spirit of hard work and great dedication, which became a hallmark of the subsequent generations of Haldiram, the founder tested each product daily for quality and taste.

Over the years, Haldiram had expanded into other regions of India on the basis of its family tree. Each succeeding generation of the family had taken Haldiram into a new region and into new cities within a given region. Representing three different lines of the family, the Haldiram Group was composed of three companies that operated independently but shared the same brand name. First, Haldiram Manufacturing Company Ltd. was based in Delhi (founded in 1983 by the third-generation Manohar Lal Agrawal) and catered to the Northern Indian market. Haldiram Foods International Ltd.-Nagpur served the western and southern regions and was founded in 1989 by the third-generation Shivkisan Agrawal. Finally, Haldiram Bhujiawala Ltd. was based in Kolkata and focused on the Eastern India market. Founded in 1958 by the second-generation Rameshwarlal Agrawal, it had a history of bitter relationships with the other two units and operated in total isolation.

Within India, all three Haldiram groups relied on word-of-mouth advertising and spent very little on traditional media. Haldiram's philosophy was to tap the needs of the lowest common denominator, using very affordable prices. Each family group offered a similar product line, although each claimed to have adapted the taste to the specific domestic region targeted by the group (see Exhibit 2). The three companies also operated under slightly different brand names: *Haldiram* by the Delhi unit, *Haldiram's* by the Nagpur unit, and *Haldiram Bhujiawala* by the Kolkata unit. Although the Delhi and Nagpur companies did consult each other regularly and serviced a total of about 600,000 retail outlets, each company claimed that the quality of its products was distinctly different from those of the other group companies. This strategy had worked well in India because each of the family divisions operated in a clearly demarcated region; few customers knew that, in reality, Haldiram was three different companies. Consequently, despite a history of family feuds, the brand continued to be reinforced in the minds of the Indian consumers.

Despite their differences, the strategies of all three companies emphasized a core commitment to the snack business, a dedication to quality, and a desire to be a leader in the markets it served. All three companies stood by the customer service motto, "You name it—we have it." Each had also developed a strong international presence by extending its products to the Indian emigrant market in different nations, where their markets overlapped in the absence of any territorial agreement. Unfortunately, the common brand used by the independently operating family groups was beginning to create confusion in the minds of international consumers, so by resolution, the three companies had begun seeking differentiation through packaging and logos.

Within India, Haldiram-Delhi was the biggest of the three companies. In 2002, the Delhi unit had an annual turnover of 1,750 million rupees, as compared to 750 million rupees sales for the Nagpur unit and 1,000 million rupees in sales of the Kolkata unit (Kukreja, 2002). In recent years, Haldiram-Nagpur had been distinctly aggressive in diversifying into related sectors such as processed milk, bakery, and ice creams. It planned to introduce a new "Mo'pleez" brand name for the international market, with a slogan "Marching Ahead . . . For a Global Presence." Within India, the Nagpur unit was expected to launch an exclusive chain of restaurants under varying brand names such as Abhinandan (welcome), Hot Spot, and Thaath Baat (pomp and show). It was also working to set up an amusement park.

Haldiram-Delhi: A Look Back

"My father, Manohar Lal Agrawal, singlehandedly founded the Delhi unit of Haldiram as an independent firm in 1983, when he had migrated from the family town of Bikaner to start a small shop in Chandni Chowk, the main hub of commercial center in Delhi," explained Pankaj Agrawal, CEO and managing director of Haldiram-Delhi. "In 1985, he decided to modernize Haldiram's marketing system with a view to transform traditional Indian foods into international recipes, and to attract foreign buyers. While the brand name quickly became famous in India on the basis of product quality, the growth in the international markets was slow because of the limited shelf life of the product."

"Around 1990," continued Agrawal, "all three family factions of Haldiram independently decided to upgrade their production systems, introducing the most sophisticated production and packaging technologies. This enabled the shelf life of *namkeens* to be extended from under a week to almost six months, which not only opened up the international market, but also [offered] an opportunity to carve a larger presence in the domestic market. In 1991, Haldiram-Kolkata opened a state-of-the-art manufacturing center, with a showroom above the premises for across-the-counter sales, which proved to be a runaway success. In April 1992, we [Haldiram-Delhi] opened our first manufacturing center and showroom at Mathura Road, New Delhi.

"Prior to then, wholesalers and shopkeepers used to come and buy from the shop . . . the family didn't have any sales force or any marketing network. But with the new manufacturing center and showroom, Haldiram-Delhi began marketing its products broadly with upgraded packaging. The Haldiram brand name gained wide publicity, and the distribution network and the market rapidly expanded. To leverage these developments, we launched syrups and crushes in 1993, which were an instant success."

Agrawal continued, "In 1996, Haldiram-Delhi started a restaurant at Mathura Road based on the fast-food concept. Until then, Haldiram was essentially a sweet shop mix supplier, making namkeens and mithais. The restaurant carried a broader, though selected, range of Indian snacks, like ice creams, samosas, chole bhature (Northern India), pao bhaji (Western India), dosas and idlis (Southern India), and Bengali sweets (Eastern India). The restaurant instantly became a leading Indian snack fast food center in Delhi . . . it surpassed all our expectations. So another showroom-cum-restaurant was added at Lajpat Nagar, Delhi.

"Then in 1997, Haldiram-Delhi bought land in Gurgaon in the adjoining State of Haryana, which was seen as a suburb of Delhi and where several foreign multinational corporations had shifted their headquarters. The land bought was situated on the fast-growing Delhi-Jaipur national highway. The plan was to shift all the production to Gurgaon and to build a restaurant and a sweet shop in front of the plant for giving more exposure to the brand name. My charge was the design and construction of the Gurgaon unit. When it became operational in 2001, I also took over as CEO of Haldiram-Delhi.

"At present, the fast food business is growing more than the sweets. Our brand name got even more popular because of this fast-food thing. Starting the restaurant at Mathura Road was a turning point for our business, although in terms of revenue, I would say that namkeens are about 70 percent of our total turnover, sweets are about 20 percent, and the fast-food segment is about 10 percent."

Haldiram-Delhi: Vision for the Future

By 2003, Haldiram-Delhi had evolved over the previous 20 years from namkeens and salty snacks to a sweet shop, to a branded sweet mix marketer, to a popular fast-food chain. Commented Agrawal, "There was no real defined vision for moving into fast food. It was simply that we wanted to serve the best to the customers. That was our only vision." He added, "We didn't focus it like we had to start a fast-food restaurant in 1996. It just happened. Our main expertise was—and still is—Indian sweets and namkeens." Agrawal continued, "Nor was there any real vision for deciding how many restaurants to open, or how to grow into a regional fast-food chain. From the start,

Haldiram-Delhi has concentrated on namkeens and sweets . . . the rest happened because the opportunity was ripe in time. Now, the time is such that the growth in fast food is more than the growth in sweets."

Fast Food in India

Pankaj Agrawal observed that the Indian fast-food industry was "totally unorganized . . . there are no Indian fast-food chains about which we can say that he is our competitor or anything like that. Thus, there is a huge business opportunity to become a leader in the Indian fast-food segment. Haldiram is emerging as a multi-cuisine restaurant for the whole family. We want to focus on our own North Indian foods, *chats* and all. We don't want to start a specialty South Indian restaurant or go into that line. We want to specialize into this mix of North Indian plus South Indian . . . if a customer specifically wants to have South Indian food, then he or she might go to a South Indian restaurant if he or she finds the quality is not good. If each and every member of the family wants to have different things, then Haldiram's is definitely their choice."

To better serve entire families, the firm was looking into (1) controlling its costs and (2) focusing more on customers' demands by studying their needs and wants. "For example," stated Agrawal, "the cook comes early in the morning and makes the products so that by the time the restaurant is opened for the day, everything is prepared. Once the customers start coming in, we can serve them very quickly. But there is still room for improving the efficiency of the persons who are making, for instance, *chole bhaturas,* by using ready-made (frozen) *chole.* If they use ready-made chole, they can be more focused on frying the bhaturas, and then can possibly be done faster, increasing their efficiency.

"Haldiram is also very focused on serving customers well. In India, traditionally, there has hardly been any management within the restaurant business. And we are not from a restaurant background. We didn't have any restaurant experience . . . we don't have any professional degree or anything relating to restaurants, or how to manage them. But Haldiram has become a trendsetter for better restaurant management because we have treated customers as part of our family. The customers have taught us how to manage the restaurants . . . and we have gotten quite fast in serving them. We haven't done any study, but we don't take more than three to four minutes to serve customers after they reach the service counter.

"However," he continued, "there is still a need to better understand what customers want. We used to make 50 to 60 different products, but we learned that the customers were not interested in all of those products. There are some key products for which the customers come to our place . . . those products are our strengths. We are most well known for namkeens . . . for them, customers will come from very far-off places. On the other hand, a customer won't come to our place to eat pizza or burgers . . . they will go to McDonald's or Pizza Hut.

"For us," continued Agrawal, "McDonald's offers an exemplary business model . . . no other Indian food company is comparable. McDonald's has 30,000 restaurants around the world, and I am impressed with their systems and the way they grow . . . how they can replicate their systems all over the world. Like McDonald's, we are developing our own internal systems first. Until and unless, we are strong in-house, we don't want to expand. We don't want to give out franchises, because this is the time when each and every company will give, and we can see that every fast-food restaurant is giving out franchises. McDonald's has 50 restaurants in India, and Narula's has 20 restaurants. Each and every fast-food giant has a number of restaurants. We don't want to expand so fast. Also, we are looking for a distinctive format of company-owned and operated franchisees. Like today, we manage each and every outlet personally. Thus, we can learn from it and at the same time, it doesn't affect our brand name also because everything is done in-house."

Snack Foods in India

The total snack foods market in India consisted of more than 1,000 snack items and 300 types of sweets, which varied regionally according to preferences in taste, form, texture, aroma, size, and shapes and fillings. The Northern Indian region accounted for about 50 percent of the total Indian market and was the most developed (Achievers' Resources, 2001).

While sales in the unorganized sector had been quite flat in recent years, the revenues in the organized sector had been growing at about 15 percent annually. The organized sector concentrated primarily on the urban markets, while the unorganized sector led in India's large and growing rural markets. The unorganized sector was immensely diverse and relied on easily accessible indigenous technology, with nonstandardized recipes and product quality, few links to testing facilities, unorganized distribution channels, storage deficiencies, and low entry barriers.

According to Jagdeep Kapoor, managing director of Samsika Marketing Consultants, three factors were driving the growth in the branded sector: "Branded players are making the right moves in terms of product offering and pricing, ethnic snacks are convenient and appropriate accompaniments for hard and soft beverages, and growth is being spearheaded by teenage consumption" (Bhushan, 2002). The branded players relied on quality control systems, standardized raw material sourcing, and upgraded packaging, enabling prices to be set at 25 percent or more over the nonbranded products. Reportedly, the market for branded chips had been growing at about 20 percent annually (Phookan, 2003).

In particular, PepsiCo loomed as a large and formidable competitor, given its resources and interest in the Indian market. Entering the Indian market in 1989, PepsiCo's focus was on the "bridge" snack foods—a hybrid between Western and Indian snack foods with products priced at about 30 percent premium over the local competitors. Its snack foods offerings included Ruffles/Lays, Cheetos, and Hostess brands and Lehar *namkeens* (the latter was exclusively sourced from a local player, Bikanervala). Its current president, chief financial officer, and a member of PepsiCo's Board of Directors, was India-born Indra Nooyi. Nevertheless, according to Agrawal, "Haldiram does not put Pepsi in the namkeen segment, but instead into the snack segment. If you take only the namkeen segment, we are still the leader. Pepsi is not near us in the country, but as, and when, we diversify from namkeens to other kind of snacks like potato chips or extruded snacks (e.g., Cheetos), Pepsi has more know-how and knowledge about it because they have been into that business for a long period. So, in that area it will be very difficult for us to compete with them in terms of technology, in terms of marketing and everything else."

PepsiCo's snack foods were distributed through its soft-drink distribution channel, which initially targeted India's 50 largest cities, then extended to 150 cities, and eventually secured distributors in more than 400 cities. Its potatoes were grown using five patented varieties of hybrid seeds by contract farmers in Punjab and other states, including Uttar Pradesh, Madhya Pradesh, Maharashtra, and Karnataka. To reduce the costs and time delays in serving the Western and Southern India markets from the Northern Indian plant, it also established a plant in Pune.

By 2000, after acquiring the dominant Uncle Chipps brand in 1998,[4] with annual revenues of 1,500 million rupees, PepsiCo held a 30 percent share of the 5,000 million-rupee packaged snack food market and about a 90 percent share of the packaged potato chips market. The overall snack food market in India stood at 20,000 million rupees, of which 75 percent was in the unorganized sector.

PepsiCo's strategy in India focused on attempting to overcome resistance to higher prices by offering a range of package sizes from 35 gram sachets to 400 gram economy packs, which were downsized versus comparable standard packs of its competitors. The 35 gram sachets, priced at 5 rupees (about 11 U.S. cents), proved to be quite popular, growing at least three times more than "regular" sizes and helping to drive market penetration and distribution. PepsiCo also placed an emphasis on attractive retail displays and made a greater push through more frequent retail outlet visits by its sales agents. Finally, PepsiCo reportedly invested 10 percent of its revenues in advertising, seeking to communicate the message that moments shared with its brands made consumers' day-to-day lives special and fun.

In addition to PepsiCo, Haldiram-Delhi's competitors in Northern India included Nathu's and Bikanervala (Bikano brand). Nathu's Sweets, founded in 1936 in Delhi, was a manufacturer, retailer, and exporter of sweets, namkeens, and other related products. It was currently managed jointly by the fourth-generation husband-and-wife team of Anand and Navita Gupta. Nathu's used mostly modern technology and strived to develop recipes to suit contemporary trends, while continuing the traditional tastes and recipes. Nathu's was known for its innovation and introduction of new products. In recent years, Nathu's has expanded into franchisee-managed restaurants that offer more than 500 items, ranging from traditional Indian snacks to Westernized food items such as pizzas, burgers, and sandwiches.

Bikanervala was a family of *Halwais* (snack food and sweets makers), which founded a sweet shop in Bikaner, Rajasthan in the 1850s. In 1950, a part of the family migrated to Delhi and set up a roadside *khomcha* (temporary shop) in the Moti Bazar. Bikanervala offered traditional recipes perfected over the generations, exotic ingredients, and experience in the art of making ethnic sweets and namkeens. Eventually, the khomcha grew into a regular shop, Bikaner Namkeen Bhandar, in the Chandni Chowk and came to be popularly known as Bikanervala.

Bikanervala formed its exclusive agreement to produce namkeens for PepsiCo's brand,

Lehar, in 1995, opening a new plant in Faridabad, Haryana, to enable high-volume production. The collaboration also gave Bikanervala a significant visibility in the cities, where PepsiCo was gaining strength (in smaller towns and villages, PepsiCo's sales of branded packaged foods were more limited). Upgrading its Delhi plant in 1997 to manufacture its own Bikano brand of products, Bikanervala sought to exploit the changing lifestyle in India that introduced vast potential for the snack foods industry. With an increasingly busy lifestyle, people had little time to spend in the kitchen preparing snacks for guests—it was becoming "much easier to empty biscuits and namkeen packets into plates and serve them immediately" (Sen, 1998).

Bikanervala also engaged in exporting its products to several markets through exclusive overseas distributors, particularly in the Anglo cultures (United States, United Kingdom, Canada, Australia) and the Middle East, and in 2000, became the first Indian food company to become ISO9002 certified. Bikanervala also opened outlets throughout India and diversified into the fast-growing packaged spices, cookies, and syrups markets. It had also launched its own Web site to expand its market reach and presence, and it formed agreements to supply its branded products to several organizations, including Indian Airlines and the Indian Railways, to further increase the company's visibility. In 2001, it secured another exclusive supply contract with Mother Dairy (a dairy company) to diversify into the packaged namkeens market with a "Aa Jaa Kha Jaa" (come on, eat up) brand.

In 2001, Bikanervela's turnover had reportedly grown to 500 million rupees, with 30 million rupees coming from exports. The company developed a new vision to "put the standardized traditional Indian sweets, namkeens, and vegetarian fast food of various Indian regions firmly on the world map." The new goal was to double the sales to 1 billion rupees by 2004. The CEO and managing director, S. S. Aggarwal explained the strategy as follows, "We will add to our product mix, improve our marketing strategies and increase our presence in the retail market" (Bhushan, 2002). Indeed, by 2002, the company had a network of 500 dealers who delivered packaged sweets and namkeens at conventional grocery stores in most North India markets. Its snacking outlets were, however, limited to Delhi and Bikaner, and included six traditional Bikanervala outlets, which exclusively carried its products, and 15 new Bikano Points, which carried both Bikanervala's own packaged products and branded products from select firms such as Nestlé and Kwality Walls. The company also planned to introduce snacking outlets internationally and entered into an agreement with Dubai's leading supermarket chain, Al Maya Lal's Group of companies, to introduce Bikano Points beginning in 2003 (Bhushan, 2002). Meanwhile, several more brands existed in other regional markets of India, including Peppy (western India) and Hello (central India). While several large Indian companies, such as Indian Organic Chemicals, Greenfield Process Food, and Premnath Monga Industries, had tried unsuccessfully to enter the traditional snack foods market during the 1990s, additional competition came from the unorganized sector, which was particularly prevalent in small towns and villages. In small towns, there were typically dozens of local manufacturers marketing various namkeens and sweets; and in big metro areas such as Delhi, one could find many manufacturers in each and every neighborhood. Agrawal noted, "Quality-wise, they cannot compete with us, but price-wise, especially considering our whole supply chain cost, distribution cost, and retailer margins, it is very difficult to compete with them. As one goes into the interiors (small cities), one finds that the customers want good quality but they cannot afford it. They want something of cheaper price. Out there, we have a limited market share."

*Haldiram-Delhi: Striving for
Operational Excellence*

"From Day One of the Gurgaon unit," Agrawal emphasized, "I watched over everything and put a top priority on overseeing the implementation of all the systems. Systems were one area in which we were not very strong . . . we had some internal weaknesses that we wanted to overcome. We had the opportunity to make changes in Gurgaon . . . trying various experiments to get the results we sought. We experimented with new systems in each and every area of management, including purchasing, finance, maintenance, and production. We felt that if the changes were successful in Gurgaon, then we could adapt them in the other, older units at Mathura Road, Lajpat Nagar, and Chandni Chowk, where the people had gotten very used to working in a particular fashion.

"We developed everything ourselves. We did not bring in any professional experts or consultants to help in planning new systems because we know our people better than any external agency," asserted Agrawal. "We also realize that we are still developing. Haldiram is not a company that is 100 or 200 years old with all of its systems and everything in place. We are still a very small company—a family-owned company and a complete family business. Yet, we are moving toward more professionalism. We are already in process, and step-by-step, everything is going to happen. We are still learning every day and trying to achieve improvements that we can replicate in the other units, like packaging and the process of manufacturing a product.

"We did it ourselves . . . we could not hire food technologists because if we did, we would have to disclose our recipes. While it's true that firms such as Coca-Cola use food technologists without disclosing its recipe, Coca-Cola does not disclose its formula to the bottling plants—it simply prepares its pre-mixes at one place, and then dispatches them to distributors all over the world. Moreover, I wanted to learn everything on my own. I wanted to see each and every product . . . how it was manufactured and how it tasted. So, this was the best way for me to learn. If I hired a professional, then he would be doing everything on his own, and it wouldn't increase my knowledge. So, that is the reason . . . I want to get involved in each and everything."

Haldiram-Delhi's Three Strategic Issues

"I discuss everything with my father because he still has more practical knowledge than I do. He has been in this business for more than 40 years. So before implementing anything, I first discuss it with him," Agrawal said. He identified three important issues that needed to be resolved:

1. *Expansion of Haldiram-Delhi's product line in India.* A number of national and foreign firms (e.g., PepsiCo) appeared to be eyeing the market opportunities created by Haldiram. After all, Haldiram had been the first to brand its namkeens and mithais in India and the first to introduce packaging and presentation of ready-to-eat snacks. Its success had been driven by branding and marketing traditional products with which Indian consumers were already familiar. But, to retain its market share in India, should the firm expand its product line? If so, should it focus on traditional Indian foods (e.g., samosas) or Western-style foods (e.g., potato chips, which appeared to be experiencing strong growth, particularly within the teenage market and younger consumers)? And, if the latter, how should Haldiram compete with the larger, wealthier, and more professionally managed PepsiCo?

"We also have a need to succeed using just average people," stated Agrawal. "That way, the competitors would not be able to use their financial muscle to take the initiative out of Haldiram. Why would, for instance, Pepsi, need our people when they have their own highly qualified people? Our people are not as well qualified as their people are."

2. *International expansion of Haldiram-Delhi.* Haldiram had created a popular snacks brand that transcended regional and national boundaries, in an industry that was only gradually beginning to become global. While Haldiram was primarily known for its Northern Indian snack items, Agrawal knew that internationally, a substantial proportion of Indian emigrants were from Southern India. Consequently, he wondered, should Haldiram diversify into Southern Indian snack items and market them internationally? If so, how should this be done, given the three family factions of Haldiram and the already emerging confusion among customers in the international markets?

Agrawal felt that if it were to expand internationally, it would need to improve its packaging and distribution systems. "Consider the characteristics of a product like Rajkachori, which requires 10 different kind of inputs, including yogurt and three different kinds of spices. Many of the inputs and the final product don't have a long shelf life. On the other hand, foreign fast-food products are becoming available in India very rapidly . . . many Western companies simply package burgers or pizzas, freeze it, and send it across. We could go to the international market with frozen products because the cold chains exist."

3. *Expansion in the fast-food business.* According to Agrawal, "We have been quite successful in the fast-food business, although it has been hard work. But I am encouraged by what we have achieved. And there is a huge business opportunity to become a leader in the Indian fast-food segment. But . . . how would we do this?

If you are going to franchise, then you have to limit your variety. You cannot give each and every product. So, we would be focusing only on our core products and our main products like Indian chat, papri chat, golgappas, and Indian snacks like chole bhature, pao bhaji, and tikkis, and give out franchises for that, along with the sweets. We would want to promote both of these products together in a branded format like Haldiram's.

"Second," he continued, "we would not want to go far from Delhi so that we could have a good control and face the initial problems more effectively. Because this is such a new area for us, so we have to start in Delhi to see how it goes . . . the customers' reactions, the turnover in franchisees, profits, and so on. If everything is in place and we succeed, then there is huge opportunity to target and expand into other areas in the Northern region . . . we can go to sub-metros like Chandigarh, Gurgaon and Noida.

"One thing is clear, though," reflected Agrawal, "apart from food, there is no business that we can or we are looking for. It is only related to food. That's the main expertise. If we go into manufacturing of anything, like televisions, there is no point doing that. We are also not going into any areas that have huge competitions. We would not make any money there. So, what's the use? It is better to develop your own line and make money in that . . . expand your brand name."

SOURCE: This case was written by Vipin Gupta, Simmons College; Nancy Levenburg, Grand Valley State University; and Pankaj Saran, EMPI Business School, Delhi. Used with permission.

Exhibit 1   A Note on Indian Meals and Snacks

According to Madhu Gadia (2000),

Lunch is usually eaten around 1:00 p.m. and it is typically the main meal of the day. After that is siesta time. If the situation permits, Indians never miss an afternoon nap. Around 5:00 p.m. is teatime. Children are served milk or sherbet (sugared, flavored beverage) while adults drink tea and eat fried spicy snacks. India is the home of a variety of salty and spicy hot snacks that have no equivalents in other cultures. This is often the time friends visit to share snacks and gossip or to discuss the news of the day. The more important or rare the friend, the greater the number of snacks served. Indians take pride in serving a number of dishes at meals or teatime.

Even after more than twenty years in the United States, I really miss a good snack when I go shopping. I will often say, "I wish there were someone selling *samosa* and *chai*." You can find coffee and even *chai* now but all the snacks served with it [in the United States] are typically sweet. In India, snacks are abundant. *Chat, samose, dahi bade,* and *pakore* are commonly sold on the street. The best part of going shopping is to stop and have a plate of *chat* on the way back home. As I am writing this, my mouth is watering as I am thinking of the hot and spicy taste of *samosas* with tangy hot chutney sold at the corner shop. You don't have snack to fill your stomach but to make your mouth and taste buds come alive. I never remember it ruining my dinner. The street foods of India are unique. With *pani puri* in the north, *bhel* in Mumbai and *bhaji* in the south, the street foods are part of the Indian culinary world.

Term	Definition
Chole bhature	*Bhaturas* are fried pastries. *Chole* is a mixture, often prepared in a pressure cooker, containing garbanzo beans, onion, tomato, and several spices, including garlic powder, cumin seeds, mint, turmeric, chili powder, bay leaves, cloves, and garam masala (like allspice, a mix of spices).
Golgappas	*Golgappas* are made from wheat flour. The wheat flour is made into small flat circles (same size as a cookie) and deep fried. Golgappas may be stuffed with potatoes, green peas, chopped onions, green chilies, and spices (e.g., coriander).
Mithai	In Hindi, *mithai* indicates several different types of sweets, some of which are sugar confections (solids) and some of which are puddings (semi-solids).
Namkeen	*Namkeen* means salty. A namkeen is a salted bread, made with wheat flour, water, and cardamom, which is fried in ghee (clarified butter).
Pao bhaji	Potatoes, mixed vegetables, onions, tomato, green chilis, and spices are fried and served with buttered buns.
Papri chat	A combination of crispies, chopped potatoes, and garbanzo beans, tossed in yogurt and tamarind chutney, served chilled.

(Continued)

(Continued)	
Rajkachori	Deep-fried mini-balloon bread filled with chickpeas, yogurt, tamarind sauce, mint chutney, and cilantro chutney.
Samosa	Traditionally, a triangular deep-fried meat or vegetable patty served as starters or snacks.
Tikkis	*Tikkis* are fried pastries (small balls) that may be made from mashed Paneer (a mild-flavored Indian cheese), spices, cashews, and raisins.

Exhibit 2   Haldiram Mission Statements

Haldiram Delhi (www.haldiram.com): "Our perpetual consistent quality, best packing strategy, vast market coverage and the number of years of experience have given us a cutting edge vis-à-vis our competitors. Our natural ilk to improve our performance and quality with each passing year has taken us way ahead of our nearest competitor. The people at Haldiram's are very sensitive and customer friendly about the complaints, which in fact is a rare occurrence from the customers and dealers."

Haldiram's Nagpur (www.haldirams.com): "Haldiram's products inherit the matchless quality. Zero impurity and world class packaging are the hallmarks of each and every Haldiram's Product. To top it up the trump card of reasonable prices and efficient marketing strategy is the key to success. Haldiram is quality conscious; it has always advocated the principle of superior input superior output. We believe in treating customers with trust, dignity, and respect. We believe in fair business practices and in doing our part to save the environment."

Haldiram Kolkota (www.haldiramfood.com): "The quality of salty snacks, sumptuous sweets, made to traditional standards, endeavored stress on quality, packing, shelf life, competitive price and with special emphasis on consumer's satisfaction. . . . To say the least, the lingering taste of Haldiram is among the best in the world of Indian sweets and namkeens."

Discussion Questions

1. Did Haldiram have a strategic long-term vision when it began? Does each of the Haldiram factions have its own strategic plan now?

2. In your analysis of the Haldiram stores and based on the facts of the case, how would you recommend the Haldiram stores move forward?

3. How did Bikanervala's new vision of putting their products "firmly on the world map" give them a competitive edge?

4. How would you resolve the issues facing Haldiram-Delhi?

Notes

1. As recounted by Amy Curtis-McIntyre, in S. Peterson, *Blue Streak* (New York: Penguin Group, 2004), p. 59.

2. See Brand Keys Web site (http://www.brandkeys.com/awards/leaders.cfm) for the complete listing.

3. One Indian rupee is approximately equal to .023 U.S. dollars.

4. In the early 1990s, Delhi-based company Amrit Banaspati was the market leader in the packaged potato chips market with its Uncle Chipps brand and approximately 50 percent market share.

References

Achievers' Resources. (2001, January). *Opportunities for selected Canadian value-added food products.* New Delhi, India: Canadian High Commission.

Airlines industry profile (Yahoo! Finance). (2005, February 22). Retrieved February 3, 2006, from http://biz.yahoo.com/ic/profile/airlin_1600.html

Alford, J. M. (2005, January 13–16). *Finding competitive advantage in managing workplace ethics.* Paper presented at the U.S. Association of Small Business & Entrepreneurship. Indian Wells, CA.

Barney, J. B. (2001). Is the resource-based "view" a useful perspective for strategic management research? Yes. *Academy of Management Review, 26,* 41–56.

Becker, L. C. (1977). *Property rights: Philosophical foundations.* London: Routledge.

Bhushan, R. (2002, November 14). Snacking gets cracking. *Business Line* (The Hindu Group of Publications). Retrieved from http://www.blonnet.com/catalyst/2002/11/14/stories/2002111400060100.htm

Bond, D. (2004, November 1). Don't blame JetBlue. *Aviation Week & Space Technology,* p. 27.

Bucar, B., & Hisrich, R. D. (2001). Ethics of business managers vs. entrepreneurs. *Journal of Developmental Entrepreneurship, 6*(1), 59–82.

Cascio, W. F. (1998). *Applied psychology in human resource management.* Upper Saddle River, NJ: Prentice Hall.

Croft, J. (2004, December). Saving private luggage. *Air Transport World,* pp. A10–A12.

De Carolis, D. M. (2003). Competencies and imitability in the pharmaceutical industry: An analysis of their relationship with firm performance. *Journal of Management, 29,* 27–50.

Delmar, F., & Shane, S. (2003). Does business planning facilitate the development of new ventures? *Strategic Management Journal, 24*(12), 1165–1185.

Devero, A. (2003). Corporate values: Stimulus for the bottom line. *Financial Executive, 19*(3), 20–23.

Gadia, M. (2000). *New Indian home cooking.* New York: Berkeley Group.

Gundry, L. K., & LaMantia, L. (2001). *Breakthrough teams for breakneck times: Unlocking the genius of creative collaboration.* New York: Dearborn Books.

Hasnas, J. (1998). The normative theories of business ethics: A guide for the perplexed. *Business Ethics Quarterly, 8*(1), 19–42.

Hill, C. W. L., & Jones, T. M. (1992). Stakeholder-agency theory. *Journal of Management Studies, 29,* 131–154.

Hira, N. A. (2004, November 15). Customer service. In New York. Who knew? *Fortune 150*(10), 198.

Hitt, M. A., Ireland, R. D., Camp, S. M., & Sexton, D. L. (2001). Strategic entrepreneurship: Entrepreneurial strategies for wealth creation. *Strategic Management Journal, 22*, 479–491.

Ireland, R. D., Hitt, M. A., Camp, S. M., & Sexton, D. L. (2001). Integrating entrepreneurship and strategic management action to create firm wealth. *Academy of Management Executive, 15*(1), 49–63.

Ireland, R. D., Hitt, M. A., & Sirmon, D. G. (2003). A model of strategic entrepreneurship: The construct and its dimensions. *Journal of Management, 29*(6), 963–989.

Jackson, L. A. (2005, January). When the love is gone. *Black Enterprise*, p. 54.

JetBlue named Best Domestic Airline for Value by readers of Travel+Leisure Magazine (Press release). (2006, February 16). Retrieved February 17, 2006, from http://www.jetblue.com/learnmore/pressDetail.asp?newsId=398

Johnson, K. (2005, February 4). Analyst differs on EasyJet's course. *Wall Street Journal*, p. C3.

Kukreja, S. (2002, December 11). It all snacks up. *The Economic Times*. Retrieved from http://economictimes.indiatimes.com/cms.dll/articleshow?artid=30884141

Miller, C. C., & Cardinal, L. B. (1994). Strategic planning and firm performance: A synthesis of more than two decades of research. *Academy of Management Journal 37*(6), 1649–1665.

Moore, G. A. (2002). *Crossing the chasm*. New York: HarperBusiness.

Newberg, J. A. (2004, Spring). Corporate ethics codes as competitive advantage. *Research@Smith, 4*(3), 2.

Newman, R. (2004, October). Preaching JetBlue. *Chief Executive*, pp. 26–29.

Overby, S. (2002, July 1). JetBlue skies ahead. *CIO*, pp. 72–78.

Peterson, B. S. (2004). *Blue streak: Inside JetBlue, the upstart that rocked an industry*. New York: Portfolio.

Phookan, M. (2003, February 27). The snack foods market in India. *STAT-USA*. Retrieved from http://www.stat-usa.gov/

Porter, M. E. (1985). *Competitive advantage*. New York: Free Press.

Rouse, M. J., & Daellenbach, U. S. (1999). Rethinking research methods for the resource-based perspective: Isolating sources of sustainable competitive advantage. *Strategic Management Journal, 20*(5), 487–494.

Salter, C. (2004, May). And now the hard part. *Fast Company*, pp. 66–75.

Sen, A. (1998, April 5). Snack food-makers mint money while consumers smack their lips. *The Indian Express*. Retrieved from www.theindianexpress.com

CHAPTER 5

Market Entry

Positioning the Firm for Strategic Advantage

There will come a time when big opportunities will be presented to you, and you've got to be in a position to take advantage of them.

—Sam Walton, founder of Wal-Mart, Inc.

A business has to be involving, it has to be fun, and it has to exercise your creative instincts.

—Richard Branson, founder of the Virgin brand

Objectives:

1. Learn how to develop your value solution based on your overall strategy

2. Understand the key drivers that are integral to buyers' demands and expectations within your industry

3. Know how your own value solution is matched and compared against these drivers within your marketplace

4. Learn the value of the perceptual map and how the map is used to maintain and exceed your competition in your industry

5. Learn how to develop and gain an appreciation for a "Go-to-Market" strategy that is based on your value solution, the drivers in the industry, and your competitive positioning

6. Use the strategic plan outline to develop organizational-level strategies, industry-market strategies, management team strategies, and financial strategies for the new venture

7. Conduct a TOWS analysis to consider the new venture's strategic position

8. Explore new approaches that shift the focus of the new venture's strategy from direct competition to the creation of new value

Speaking of Strategy

Travelocity and Innovation—How CEO Michelle Peluso and Her Team Make Decisions

Renee Montagne (host): In our business news today, how one CEO makes tough decisions. Our series on management decisions ends today with a conversation about strategy. Business executives decide every day how to respond to a changing marketplace, where to invest, where to cut back and what direction to take a company. Michelle Peluso launched her own start-up six years ago. Now, just 33 years old, she is CEO of Travelocity. It's one of the biggest on-line travel agencies in a growing industry. This year consumers are expected to spend $63.5 billion on travel through the Internet. *Morning Edition's* Steve Inskeep spoke with Michelle Peluso about how she and her team make decisions.

Ms. Michelle Peluso: I've always really admired people who have exceptionally talented people around them. I think it says a lot about their confidence that they've put strong people around them and let them act. But at the same time, clearly, you know, it's incumbent on me—I'm the CEO of the company—to understand deeply what's going on in all aspects of our business and to question things where I think, you know, we're off-track.

Steve Inskeep: Do you make decisions quickly or slowly?

Ms. Peluso: Quickly. If I didn't answer that question quickly, it would seem very hypocritical.

Inskeep: If you said, "Um" . . .

Ms. Peluso: Right. I don't know. Uh-huh.

Inskeep: . . . we would know something about you.

Ms. Peluso: Quickly. I trust my instincts. I remember once hearing someone tell me when you're in the 40 to—you know, 60 to 80 percent comfort range, decide to move on.

Inskeep: 60 to 80 percent comfort range. How do you measure that?

Ms. Peluso: You need analytical data behind the big decisions you make, so you need smart people in a room. You need to debate pros and cons, but, you know, in some cases, the last piece of analysis, the last piece of data isn't always necessary. And so, you know, if you're comfortable with what the data is saying and you kind of have a general agreement and your instinct feels right, then you go with it.

Inskeep: You know, I'm thinking you might be in a business where it is better if you decide things quickly because your customers decide quickly whether to stay with that site, wait for it to finish downloading, or move on to the next thing.

Ms. Peluso: Sure. Indecision is paralysis, and taking risks is really critical. At the same time, what's really important culturally is making sure that if we make a decision and it's the wrong decision, that we react really fast and that we don't punish each other for making a bad decision or for taking a risk. It can be paralyzing for the average employee if they feel like the CEO is saying, "Hey, let's take some risks," but what that really means is we only want to hit home runs. That's never the case, so balanced with risk has to be acknowledgment of when you don't succeed, there's great lessons to learn. Learn them, move on.

Inskeep: Granting that you've probably moved on from whatever decisions these were, can you describe a risk you took that didn't pay off and forced you to turn around and go back?

Ms. Peluso: Sure. Well, back in—I mean, so many, of course. Back in the early days of Site59, which is a company I started that Travelocity acquired in March of 2002, you know, right before the Internet bubble kind of burst, we were looking at not just last-minute travel packages, which is what we really focused on in the end, but we were also looking at things like staying in town, last-minute gifts, kind of a broader range, and we really started to invest in some of those business areas, and at the end of the day, it wasn't the right decision. We needed to focus on that which we thought we would do particularly well, last-minute travel packages. But, you know, we recouped really quickly, and we moved on, and it was clearly the right thing to do.

Inskeep: How did you recoup?

Ms. Peluso: We scaled back some of the investments that we were making. We took the team that was focused on those areas and really reinvigorated them and focused them back on the core business, and that we had learned a lot. I mean, that was critical, too, to make sure the employees who were working in those areas understood that we learned an enormous amount from what they had done, and we would really incorporate that into accelerating the core business.

Inskeep: You have recently taken a different approach to your customers. You've redesigned your Web site, right?

Ms. Peluso: Yes, that's absolutely right. We really thought that putting the great images of travel front and center would help kind of inspire consumers as they were purchasing their on-line travel. One of the things that we found was that our competitors were focusing a lot on discounts and 70 percent off, and frankly, even our own Web site looked a little bit like a Turkish bazaar with kind of all sorts of deals screaming at you. And one of the things we wanted to do was to differentiate ourselves dramatically from our competitive set.

Inskeep: How did it even come to your attention as CEO that there was a problem?

Ms. Peluso: People came to our site and our competitors' sites, and we asked them: Can you really differentiate? What feels different about this Web site versus another? Frankly, a lot of consumers thought we all kind of looked the same. So we really needed to make sure that that first impression stands out, that it's different.

Inskeep: As a CEO, after all this market research was done, did somebody bring the information to you for a final decision?

Ms. Peluso: Sure. The consumer experience team, along with some others from the marketing department and the research team, came forward with their recommendations, a series of options, and their recommendation backed up by analytical data on what consumers said they

(Continued)

(Continued)

wanted. And we also talked to suppliers. What are the kinds of things that suppliers want us to merchandise about travel?

Inskeep: Probably hard to quantify this, but how much money did you think was riding on that decision?

Ms. Peluso: It is hard to quantify. Certainly, there were millions of dollars of development put into overhauling the entire site, but it's more than that because if you get it wrong, clearly your conversion or your sales can suffer.

Inskeep: Can you give an example in which you had to make a decision where you were balancing the short-term gain of your company against the long-term benefit of the company?

Ms. Peluso: Oh, sure. I mean, all the time. You know, we really work hard on making decisions for the long run. A really recent example is there are some competitors out there—I guess they're competitors—that have come up with—it's called, you know, MetaSearch, and they've come up with this notion of everything's just about price so, you know, we'll screen and scrape Travelocity and put the prices in and put everybody's price in and . . .

Inskeep: Screen and scrape meaning that . . .

Ms. Peluso: They'll just . . .

Inskeep: . . .their site will search your site for the best price . . .

Ms. Peluso: Exactly.

Inskeep: . . .along with a bunch of other sites.

Ms. Peluso: Right. And in the short term, maybe that can produce some incremental business for us because they refer people back to our site to buy, but I actually think strategically, it's a real mistake. I think that travel's about great deals, as I said earlier, for sure, but it's about a lot more than that. And, you know, we certainly don't want people using our brand in a way that we think is not good for us, not good for consumers, not good for suppliers.

Inskeep: Is it also that if you competed only on the question of getting the lowest price, somebody can always match you or even beat you on that. You need to build up a brand and a Web site and a look that people know and trust and respect.

Ms. Peluso: That's absolutely the case. And frankly, sometimes we don't want to be surrounded by competitors who we think don't have as strong of a value proposition as we do, and so we'll show you the total price of a car, including all those hidden taxes and fees, right up front. You know, we don't want to be on a list where some of our competitors don't show all those fees, and we seem more expensive. So that's a great example where maybe in the short run, it would have produced incremental revenue and incremental bookings, but, you know, we've strongly decided not to participate with the Travelocity brand because we think over the long run, it's not the right thing for our business.

Inskeep: Michelle Peluso is the CEO of Travelocity. Thanks very much.

Ms. Peluso: Bye now.

Montagne: This is *Morning Edition* from NPR News. With Steve Inskeep, I'm Renee Montagne.

SOURCE: April 14, 2005, Interview of Michelle Peluso with Steve Inskeep, Renee Montagne, host. WBEZ-Chicago, National Public Radio, from *Morning Edition*. Reprinted with permission of the National Public Radio via Copyright Clearance Center.

Table 5.1   Designing Your Value Solution

Benefits of Product/Service	Value Solution (What Problem(s) Does It Solve?)	For Whom? (Target Audience)
Benefit 1:		
Benefit 2:		
Benefit 3:		
Benefit 4:		

Designing Your Firm's Value Solution(s)

Prior to putting together any type of messaging regarding how the entrepreneur will deliver on the strategy, it is necessary to establish the firm's unique selling point—otherwise known as the value solution. This is directly related to developing the firm's strategy as presented in Chapter 4.

In that chapter, you had the opportunity to learn the benefits that win customers and how to sustain your competitive advantage. Begin defining your value solution along the similar categories of value and cost-benefits of customer convenience, price, productivity, simplicity, convenience, and image. Under these categories, think about how your company, your service, and/or product is different from anyone else's. To further perceive and develop your value solution, begin by considering the following:

• What solution or need does your product/service fill in the eyes of your customers? Why would they want your product/service? How does the solution improve the lives of your potential customers? Go ahead and develop a full list based on these questions and then also consider:

• Would you buy this product? Why or why not? If not, this may give you an insight into potential weaknesses, areas that you need to improve and enhance before placing your product/service in the marketplace. Essentially, you could reverse these weaknesses and turn them into a value solution that makes a difference in how customers perceive and buy your product/service.

From there, you can then start to determine who will most benefit from your product and/or service. All this information can then be mapped out using Table 5.1.

If you are having difficulty in listing the benefits, examine further how the categories of customer convenience, price, productivity, simplicity, and image can then be differentiated from the competition. For example:

• *For customer convenience,* who within your firm's industry is emphasizing customer convenience? Where are there gaps? How does your primary market currently go about buying existing products or services of this type? How can your new venture create a solution or solutions to offer customer convenience?

- *For price*, how does your pricing strategy compare to others in the industry? Is pricing a major buying criterion for your customers? If so, how can you make price a key differentiator (while keeping your viability and business expenses in mind)?

- *For productivity*, how does your product/service improve or enhance the productivity and efficiency of your market? How can you make sure that efficiency is perceived as a key marketing or selling point of what your firm offers or how it conducts business?

- *For simplicity*, how does your product or service meet some of the basic needs and solve the current problems of your customers?

- *For image*, how do your potential or current customers perceive the benefits of your business? What are their sources of information? Word of mouth? Trade publications? The Internet? How can you build or improve the image of your product/service solutions?

By answering these questions, you can then further develop your value solution(s) and refine it to communicate your message directly to where your market would look and find information related to your business.

The Innovator's Toolkit: Market-to-Market Creative Connections

This tool, in which creative connections are forged between the intended market and an unrelated market, will help the entrepreneur to generate ideas for positioning the new venture, for promoting its products and services, and for developing and extending the value solution.

1. Business description
Write the nature of the business in a word or a short phrase.

2. Attribution list
List all the features, (e.g., characteristics, services, products, promotion methods, value offered) that you associate with this business in a column on your paper. If the business is not yet in existence, list your intended features. If it is an already established business, list the features it already provides.

3. Select a different type of business
Pick an industry or business type that is distinctly different from yours or the one you are considering, and write the name of it at the top of the next column on the page.

4. Attribution list for different business
List all the features, (e.g., characteristics, services, products, promotion methods, value offered, etc.) that you associate with this business. Write as much as you know about what this business does or could provide.

5. Make creative connections

- What do the attributes of the "different business or industry" suggest for your business or industry? For your value solution?
- What could you put in place in your business that has been successful or a competitive advantage in the different business? How can information from a different industry partner assist you in developing your value solution(s)?
- What opportunities did you discover for marketing your product/service? How can these opportunities be integrated into how you market your value solution?

Discussion Questions

1. To which different business could you compare your business idea or opportunity?

2. What creative connections can be made? Try to list at least three new connections.

The Key Drivers Integral to Buyers' Demands and Expectations Within Your Industry

Once you have defined your firm's strategy and value solution(s), you will find that you will need to revisit and adapt your strategy based on the conditions and context of your industry and marketplace. As customers' needs and preferences change, your firm will need to take a proactive approach in understanding how these changes influence the overall operations and efficiencies of your business. One of the ways to stay ahead and meet the expectations of your customers is to understand the key drivers of your venture within the industry. The categories above are helpful in considering your firm's value solution(s) at the initial launch of your business. However, over time, you will want to adapt these categories to the needs and expectations that drive your customer buying decisions on a daily basis.

Matching and Refining the Value Solution(s) to Marketplace Drivers Over Time

Once the entrepreneur has determined the industry's key drivers over time, those drivers can be assessed based on how well they meet your firm's strategy and value solution(s) (Lehmann & Winer, 2005). Using the grid in Table 5.2, determine how well the strategy and solutions are matched against the key drivers in the market.

Table 5.2 Matching Strategy, Solutions, and Market Drivers

What the Market Demands	Considering Your Strategy and Value Solution(s): How Well Are You Doing?					
	Poor	Needs improvement	Fair	Good	Outstanding	Exceptionally well
Competitive price						
High name recognition						
Superior customer service						
Performance of product						
Knowledge of staff and expertise						

Table 5.2 assists you in benchmarking areas where your firm requires attention or where you lack the internal capabilities and resources to meet the needs of the marketplace. Knowing these weaknesses will help you craft a revised strategy that focuses on those drivers and positions you for the next new innovation (perhaps coming from your organization). While partnering and strategic alliances will be discussed in Chapter 8, the idea of developing a relationship with an outside firm may assist you in finding the key resources to fulfill your strategy and meet or exceed the needs of your customers. In finding a partner to assist with building your resources and capabilities, consider the following three questions:

1. What capabilities do you need to achieve the value solution and key drivers in the industry, and which ones do you lack? (Refer to the second column of Table 5.2.)

2. Which companies have those missing capabilities?

3. Based on cost, quality, and speed, should you acquire those companies or partner with them?

While "how to" partner and build a strategic alliance will be discussed in Chapter 8, discovering what kinds of resources and capabilities you need to implement your value solution and strategy is the first step in the process of building and growing a sustainable, profitable venture. Our next focus will be on how others, including your competition, view your strategy and your operational effectiveness and performance. We will learn the value of the perceptual map and how the map is used to maintain and exceed your competition in your industry

Review Question

1. How do market drivers differ depending on the size of the firm? Across industries?

Matrix Comparisons: Further Examining the Framework

Developing your solution and its match with the key drivers in the industry assesses your internal strengths and weaknesses; also, it is important to look outside, in terms of how others in your market space are performing. Competitive positioning reveals where your company stands in the eyes of any given group of people through the use of matrices. By creating a simple 2×2 matrix diagram, you can easily map out the position of your firm in relationship to its competitors, or its relationship to a firm in a different business or industry. Matrices give us a great way to *visualize* many of the different types of comparisons mentioned in this chapter. Simply take two characteristics of a business and align them on the vertical and horizontal axis. In Table 5.3, we compare expertise and name recognition.

Let us consider the example of an entrepreneur who owns a pet accessories boutique. Pet products and services are one of the hottest new ideas: The American Pet Products Manufacturers Association Inc. estimates that $35.9 billion was spent on pets in the United States in 2005, up from $34.4 billion in 2004 (Pennington, 2005). In this case, the boutique is renowned in its neighborhood, with a steady and loyal clientele. If the entrepreneur wants to compare how her business fares against competing national pet supplies chain in these two categories, she would place her business low on the name recognition scale but higher on the expertise scale. The pet boutique owner may choose to look at the techniques the large chain uses to excel in these areas.

Alternatively, an entrepreneur may choose to plot the position of a firm in a completely different business. Our pet boutique owner, for example, may compare her business to that of another local business such as a gourmet restaurant that has received positive reviews and has even received national publicity. Although her pet boutique is in a different industry, our entrepreneur could look at the strategy of the gourmet restaurant to learn how she could increase her name recognition. Matrices are also a useful tool to quickly identify trends in relationships among business drivers. Is there always a correlation between expertise and name recognition? By creating a visual representation in Table 5.3 of the positioning of a firm, an entrepreneur has another tool in which to survey the competitive terrain in a strategic manner.

Table 5.3   Strategic Positioning of the Firm

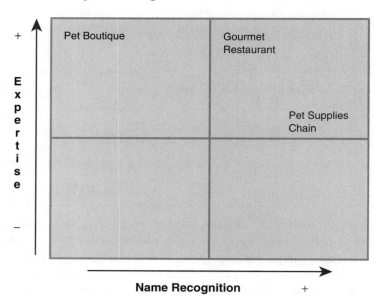

Strategic Reflection Point

Going Beyond the Map—Assessing a Competitor's Will

Even the strongest competitor can be overcome if it is not committed to the market. Similarly, a weak competitor can cause massive damage if it is fanatically committed. At some point, it is crucial to assess competitors' strength of will or commitment. This requires going beyond objectives (what do they want?) to assess the intensity with which they approach the task (how badly do they want it?). Most competitions involve several key times when each competitor has the choice of backing down or continuing the fight. When assessing the likelihood that a competitor will continue to fight (an act that sometimes is not rational from a profit perspective), one should assess the following factors (Lehmann & Winer, 2005).

1. *How crucial is this product to the firm?* The more crucial the product is in terms of sales and profits, number of employees, or strategic thrust, the more committed most companies will be to it. This helps explain why efforts to unseat a market leader by attacking the heart of the market provoke violent reactions, whereas a strategy that nibbles away at secondary markets is more likely to go unmatched. For example, eBay's key product is its on-line auction. Attempts by Amazon.com and others to develop similar auctions are considered to be a strong threat to eBay's viability and are met with increased promotions and advertising, as well as expansion in the number of auction categories.

2. *How visible is the commitment to the market?* It may be difficult for companies to admit they are wrong once they are publicly committed. A good example of this is Exxon's Office Systems Division, which was clearly in trouble for a long time before it was sold in 1985. Also, Coca-Cola held on to New Coke and repositioned it several times, even though it did not sell well.

3. *How aggressive are the managers?* Personality differences exist, and some individuals are more combative than others. This aspect of management may not be detected in the management analysis. Only by knowing how badly a competitor "wants it" can one successfully approach the next task: predicting future strategies.

| **Research in Practice:** | **Pioneers and Followers—Competitive Tactics, Environment, and Firm Growth** |

A form of corporate entrepreneurship called market pioneering occurs when a firm is first to offer a new product/service on the market. The connection between market pioneering and firm performance has received little scholarly attention, and it focused primarily on (1) pioneering as an environment specific phenomenon and (2) firm's performance, as affected by the fit between a firm's pioneer/follower status and its competitive tactics. These phenomena are explored, emphasizing how they are manifested in different industry environments and what pioneers and followers do differently to promote their performance.

A theory that describes how specific competitive tactics relate to firm sales growth rate among market pioneers and market followers is developed in two distinct environmental settings: hostile and benign. To test two proposed hypotheses, data is collected from senior managers of 103 independent, non-diversified manufacturing firms in 75 industries. The main analytical techniques used to assess the data are: cluster analysis, ANOVA, and correlational analysis. The findings suggest that market pioneers grow at the same rate as market followers.

In hostile environments, pioneering may enable firms to break out of the dominant price-based mode of competition and grow despite charging high prices. Pioneers in hostile environments are better served than followers from a wide geographical distribution of their products. It is recommended that followers in hostile environments reduce their cost structures in order to maintain low price strategies. The results also suggest that, in benign environments, offering products with warranties superior to those of competitors may have positive effects on sales growth, more so among pioneers than followers.

SOURCE: J. G. Covin, D. P. Sleven, and M. B. Heeley, "Pioneers and Followers: Competitive Tactics, Environment, and Firm Growth," *Journal of Business Venturing* 15, no. 2 (2000): 175–210.

Developing the Go-to-Market Strategy

It has been said, "If you don't know where you are going, any road can take you there." To eliminate such disorientation and provide direction, an entrepreneur should begin with the vision that was developed in Chapter 4 and create the "Go-to-Market" (GTM) strategy for what will be the firm's launch. A full GTM strategy encompasses the channels that a company uses to connect with its customers and the organizational processes it develops to guide customer interactions from initial contact through fulfillment. The right GTM strategy has a significant impact on a company's ability to cost-effectively deliver its value solution to each of its target segments. Companies are becoming increasingly focused and sophisticated in the way in which they compete to create superior customer value. As companies tailor their value solutions to better address customer needs beyond product specifications and to better align their cost of sales and fulfillment relative to those needs, GTM strategy plays a central role.

As we saw in Chapter 4, a powerful vision should continually stretch the corporation's capabilities. For many companies, therefore, the overarching vision is captured in an ambitious aspiration, the time frame of which may be ill-defined and distant. In the 1920s, Ford wanted to put "a car in every home"; in the 1980s, Apple looked toward the future and saw "a computer in every home." By the 1990s, Bill Gates had gone further yet: "a computer on every desk, and in every home, running on Microsoft software." By the end of that decade, this vision had grown to include the Internet. Each of these simple expressions offers a compelling statement that challenges and motivates employees by providing meaning and fulfillment to their work.

Your Go-to-Market Strategy

As you become operational, and to compensate for less-frequent product launches and a focus on solutions rather than specific products, you can now organize your strategic efforts around annual GTM campaigns. A GTM strategy focuses your business on short-term strategic challenges and provides consistent strategic marketing approaches for your products and services. Strategic partners or allies can align their products or services with your GTM strategies to benefit from these campaigns. However, while GTM strategies are intended to make your message to the marketplace more focused and coherent, their short-term focus and vagueness mean partners should take time to understand their benefits. GTM campaigns can be designed using the matrix in Table 5.4, completing each of the cells and offering solutions for your marketplace.

Table 5.4   Go-to-Market Campaigns

GTM Solutions (Areas of Concentration)	Target Audience	Key Products
Strategic Initiative 1: Customer Segment _____		

And continue on with your second and possibly third strategic initiative, customer segment:

Strategic Initiative 2: Customer Segment _____		
Strategic Initiative 3: Customer Segment _____		

Strategy in Action

Ciena Corporation—Developing the Go-to-Market Strategy for a Business Venture

Ciena Corporation is a network specialist, focused on expanding the possibilities for its customers' networks while reducing their cost of ownership. The company's systems, software and services target and cure specific network pain points so that telcos, cable operators, governments and enterprises can best exploit the new applications that are driving their businesses forward. . . .

Ciena Corporation (NASDAQ: CIEN), today announced its go-to-market strategy and new identity incorporating the Company's dramatic business transformation and organizational alignments of the past two years. Ciena's positioning as the "network specialist" grows out of its heritage and strength in solving specific issues in transport and optical networks and applies that specialization to today's most critical applications to solve customers' key business problems. The identity underlines Ciena's relationships with customers and reflects a clear differentiation from competitors.

(Continued)

(Continued)

The Company's repositioning signals a milestone in an evolution resulting from a series of deliberate, strategic acquisitions, the creation of an array of partnerships, and recent moves by the Company to realign its organization and operations. Ciena is building on its heritage as a specialist and its belief that its customers want a close link with a respected partner that has deep experience in supporting customer-driven applications. A strategic specialist must be able to adapt rapidly to a changing environment and embrace its customers' ways of doing business, while bringing to the table innovation, technological expertise and regulatory leadership.

Gary Smith, CEO and president of Ciena, commented, "Ciena has undergone profound change over the last two years during a process where we reexamined the value we bring to customers. We believe that we now have the best of breed products and services to address customers' most critical pain points, and we also have developed the sales and operations infrastructures to support this approach to the market. We believe we now have the breadth of application-specific solutions and supporting customer validation to credibly lay claim to our role as a network specialist; identifying our unique market position and guiding decisions as we go forward."

Ciena's position emphasizes that it will not be all things to all customers, while acknowledging that its efforts might touch many different parts of a network and will evolve as market and customer needs change.

"During their last two years of acquisitions and change, Ciena's aim has not always been crystal clear to the market," said Matt Davis, director of Broadband Access Technology and Service with industry analyst firm Yankee Group. "Articulating this application-driven strategy demonstrates that Ciena is becoming focused on the overall solution—and it may prove to be sustainable in this increasingly changing and diversified communications environment, where content providers try to fit into service networks and service providers seek the best revenue-generation solutions."

The specialist identity places Ciena's core value to the marketplace in its ability to provide customers flexibility and a breadth of offerings, along with the wherewithal and expertise that comes with being an established player in the industry. New channel and sales strategies, competencies gained from its acquisitions, and a broadened portfolio give Ciena the strength to be a valued supplier partner.

The application focus announced today includes five areas of concentration, which will continue to develop as end-user uptake and needs evolve. These include:

- Access infrastructure upgrades for service delivery;
- Storage and Ethernet service value amplification;
- Network scaling for high-bandwidth applications like video and multimedia on demand;
- Core network convergence and automation; and,
- Packet network integration and optimization for enhanced new services.

All four of Ciena's customer segments—service providers, cable operators, government agencies, and large enterprises—are spanned by today's application-focused launch, which is supported by Ciena's demonstrated ability to solve real-world network problems, maximize the business value of enabling services, and boost network economics and improve cost efficiency. This focus builds on the Company's core networking solutions, but specifically targets emerging applications to address new customer demands.

About the Repositioning

To best understand the needs of its customers and how it can better serve the marketplace, Ciena engaged corporate branding leader Hornall Anderson to survey customers, employees, analysts and other industry influencers. The process undertaken by Ciena concluded with testing the positioning among both existing and potential customers. As part of launching its new identity, Ciena also unveiled a new logo, which visually symbolizes a more consultative, adaptable image. The mark features a scripted 'i.e.' within the Ciena name that plays out Ciena's tailored, "as in" application-centric approach to the customer relationship.

In addition, Ciena is supporting the launch with a new customer-facing website (www.ciena.com). Other support will include global trade press advertising targeting all customer segments, focused, integrated marketing campaigns and events, a new digital literature system and sales support collateral. These efforts and ongoing marketing activities throughout the Company will continue to reinforce Ciena's market positioning as the network specialist.

"New services represent an enormous growth area today and in the future. But service providers and enterprises need to know that they can manage their total cost of ownership as they enable enhanced services in their networks," said Smith. "We believe our applications-based approach targeting the critical and high-value network and business issues sets us ahead of the pack in terms of market vision and positioning and we are acting upon that vision in every aspect of our business."

SOURCE: "Ciena Unveils Go-To-Market Strategy and New Identity as Network Specialist" [Press release], October 25, 2004, retrieved from http://www.ciena.com/news/news_3922.htm Reprinted with permission.

Discussion Questions

1. Which industry drivers have affected Ciena Corporation's "Go-to-Market" strategy?

2. In what ways would a GTM strategy differ between a small and large firm?

3. How does the size of the firm influence its strategy?

Failures and Foibles

Not All "Joe" Is Java

Howard Schultz bought Starbucks in 1987 when it was a tiny Seattle roastery and transformed it (and the world of coffee) into one of the world's most successful and innovative companies. Schultz loves talking about the finely tuned "customer experience," and managing that experience is one of the greatest challenges of any business. Starbucks has 8,500 stores and 90,000 employees worldwide. Always on the lookout for opportunities, Schultz puts the customers and their needs first and foremost.

(Continued)

(Continued)

"One day a high profile cable executive came into my office and said, 'Here's a blank check. What would it take to put monitors in every Starbucks store where you could play just one cable channel for a few hours a day?' Although it was a seductive opportunity because of the profit potential, we recognized early on that our customers want to get away from that kind of noise. Our stores are not only an extension of their home and office, but also a respite."

Schultz admits he doesn't always have the foresight to turn down an idea: "I took Starbucks into the magazine business with *Joe*—my idea (produced for Starbucks by Time Inc. Custom Publishing). Nobody read it. Since *Joe* failed I've kept a rack of issues in my office so everyone can see the magazine and realize we shouldn't hide behind our mistakes and we should have the courage to keep pushing by not embracing the status quo. I keep that there as a memento. It was an embarrassing defeat, and we lost a fair amount of money, but sometimes you have to have the courage to fail."

SOURCE: www.starbucks.com; Howard Schultz and Dori Jones Yang, *Pour Your Heart Into It: How Starbucks Built a Company One Cup at a Time* (New York: Hyperion, 1997).

The Strategic Plan Outline

The next section of this chapter presents an outline for the strategic plan. The components of the plan describe in detail how the new venture will carry out its vision. The outline below contains the sections that should be covered in your team's strategic plan. The plan should be tailored to your business needs, and your section headings do not have to be exactly as shown here. The content of your plan should cover these areas, however.

Executive Summary

- Overview of your concept (business and its mission), customers (your market/markets), and your capital requirements (financial strategies)

Concept Description: Organizational-Level Strategies

- What business are you *really* in?
- What is the *mission* of your business (your reason for existence)?
- List your key objectives: What activities will you perform? Where and how will you perform them? What will your business offer, and how will it be special/competitive?
- What are the *key values* of your business? What will its relationships be with stakeholders such as customers, suppliers, employees, and the community?

Analysis of the External Environment: Industry and Market Strategies

- What are the social and economic (and other) trends of your business environment?
- Describe the current climate of your industry (recent trends and performance)
- Who are your key competitors?
- What market(s) do you serve (demographics, psychographics, etc.)? How will you create awareness and sustain your customer base?

Analysis of the Internal Environment: Management Team Strategies

- What are the strengths and experience of each team member?
- What are the knowledge, skills, and abilities you need for your business to perform?
- What do you have? What do you lack (and where can you find it)?
- How will the business be organized (structure and reporting relationships)?

Financial Strategies
- Estimate of start-up costs (investigate similar businesses).
- Investigate financing alternatives (debt/equity financing, listing of possible resources).
- Develop one year minimum (three to five years recommended) of *pro forma* statements. Financial statements include cash flow, income statements, and balance sheet.

Critical Risks and Exit Strategy
- The plan should contain an analysis of critical risks and how the entrepreneur intends to reduce these risks, including financial, organizational, and psychological risks related to the business, the entrepreneur, and the management team, as appropriate.
- Some entrepreneurs include an exit strategy for the business. This is optional, but if you intend to seek external investors, it is recommended to include these for consideration.

References
- Full citations of all sources cited in your strategic plan must be listed here.

Appendices (if appropriate)
- Surveys, copies of supplementary research materials, maps, and so on.

The strategies you develop for your business should build on your perceived strengths, exploit opportunities you identify, and avoid threats. Later, you will learn how to conduct a TOWS analysis of your business to help you develop your strategies. You can also include "must do" and "should do" strategies for the sections above to help you develop short-range and long-range goals for the business.

Strategic Reflection Point

Strategic Direction for ABC Company

The Strategic Direction Sheet for ABC Company (Kerns, 2002) found in Table 5.5 is an illustration of one way that data and information from your visioning work and the components of the strategic plan can be organized. As you begin the strategy development process, constructing this sheet may be very helpful to you.

Table 5.5   Strategic Direction Sheet for ABC Company

Vision "Where are we going?"	Mission "Current Purpose"	Key Results "Our Focus"	Strategies "Taking Action"	Structure "Lining up for results"
• We will become a $21 million business built on quality, innovation, and trust. We meet the needs of our targeted customers for high-quality soft goods. • Our associations are with people who honor commitments, focus on goals and results, and get things done. • Our product offerings are driven by customer needs, the highest industry standards, and our ability to make a fair profit.	We sell high-quality soft goods to our targeted customers. Our commitment to fit, function, and durability sets industry standards and ensures total confidence. All of our company resources are directed, focused, and linked to this purpose.	1. Profitability 2. Average sale per customer 3. Product sales mix targeting 4. Employee satisfaction 5. Customer satisfaction 6. Sales volume 7. Strategic project excellence and action learning	Our strategy for implementing our vision, mission and achieving agreed-upon key results is to involve people in focused performance action plans. These plans call on us to work with a clear purpose, remain focused, and coordinate our efforts. We all need to talk and act in ways that promote performance as we pursue our plans. While we will remain flexible and use strategic projects and learning teams, our energy will be focused on implementing 7 key performance action plans over the next 12 months. Appendix A outlines these plans.	To operate effectively and efficiently, a performance-oriented pyramid of success is reflected in the organizational chart. All personnel are expected to drive our success by achieving agreed-upon goals.

SOURCE: Reprinted from *Business Horizons, 45*(4), Kerns, C. D., An Entrepreneurial Approach to Strategic Direction Setting, pp. 2–5, Copyright 2002, with permission from Elsevier.

Strategic Positioning: From SWOT to TOWS

In stable industries, the Strengths Weaknesses Opportunities Threats (SWOT) analysis remains one of the best ways to think about strategy and selecting a strategic position for the new venture. The goal is to find a sustainable strategic position in which the firm can use its strengths to take advantage of the opportunities available in its industry and markets—while defending itself from threats and masking or correcting its weaknesses. The challenge in identifying weaknesses and developing ways to overcome them can in itself become a strategy. Turning the SWOT into TOWS is about doing the external analysis first—an important distinction when thinking about strategy. When doing such an analysis, it's best to work from the outside in, to do a TOWS analysis (Weihrich, 1982).

Begin by defining the markets in which your firm will sell, the competition that you will face, and the larger industry structure (power relations, business norms, etc) in which your firm will function. For this portion of the analysis, you can use the data you collected in the Knowledge of Industry Checklist (KIC) you completed in Chapter 2. Then turn your attention to the trends and shifts in the external environment: Consider the following factors as you work through the TOWS Analysis.

- Economic factors: The general state of the economy, including inflation, labor market conditions, interest rates, and so on
- Sociocultural factors: Preferences, values, and shifts in consumer trends
- Technological factors: New technologies, technical processes, and the rate of technological change
- Political-legal factors: Regulatory environment, including laws, statutes, and changes in government policies that affect the business

These factors change frequently, so it is necessary to review this analysis at least annually, and more often as appropriate to your industry and the community in which the business resides. Finally, summarize your analysis in a list of opportunities and a list of threats. This is the context in which you must operate. Once you know what the external environment offers you (and the challenges it presents), look inside to inventory your strengths and weaknesses. What skill sets, resources, networks, and so on do you have at your disposal? What are you lacking? Summarize these into a list of strengths and a list of weaknesses. This is what you have to work with.

Finally, map out your TO and WS in a matrix such as the one shown in Table 5.6 and study it to develop a strategy that uses your strengths to take advantage of opportunities, reduce or avoid threats, and overcome weaknesses. It is also highly recommended that you develop a set of strategies and run each through the matrix in Table 5.6, looking for flaws (e.g., lack of management skills in a particular area, low levels of financial resources).

Review Question

1. What questions should you ask to evaluate the external and internal environment of your business?

Table 5.6 TOWS: The Strategic Audit

1. List your perceived strengths (S), weaknesses (W), opportunities (O), and threats (T) inside the matrix.

2. Develop a tactical package around your SO, WO, ST, WT Strategies (your tactical package).

Internal Factors / External Factors	**Strengths (S)** S1 **List internal** S2 **strengths** S3 S4 S5	**Weaknesses (W)** W1 **List internal** W2 **weaknesses** W3 W4 W5
Opportunities O1 **List external** O2 **opportunities** O3 O4 O5	**SO STRATEGIES** How can you use your strengths to take advantage of the opportunities?	**WO STRATEGIES** How can you reduce your weaknesses to take advantage of the opportunities?
Threats T1 **List external** T2 **threats** T3 T4 T5	**ST STRATEGIES** How can you use your strengths to avoid threats?	**WT STRATEGIES** How can you reduce your weaknesses to avoid threats?

SOURCE: Reprinted from *Long Range Planning*, *15*(2), Weihrich, H., The TOWS Matrix: A Tool for Situational Analysis, pp. 54–66, copyright 1982, with permission from Elsevier.

When you complete this analysis, you can consider some of the strategic positions for the new venture:

- The *low-cost* firm that churns out good enough services or products at the lowest possible cost
- The *highly differentiated* firm that creates the highest-quality, best-designed, best-supported, most attractive products or services in its area
- The *narrowly focused* firm that ties itself to a very specific market and serves its needs assiduously, typically with segmented products and services or niche, often customized, products or services
- The *broadly focused* firm that serves a wider market, either with a standardized product or through mass customization

- The firm that *elaborates* a previously chosen position, by penetrating deeper, developing new markets or niches, developing new products, carving out space at the edge of a niche, or raising barriers to competitors wanting to do what your firm does
- The firm that *collaborates* to learn—by licensing your products or services to other, more established organizations in the industry, by outsourcing, or by entering into joint ventures as a way of gaining entry into the marketplace

Review Questions

1. What is the difference between a SWOT analysis and a TOWS analysis?

2. Explain how to complete a TOWS analysis and how to create a tactical package.

Shifting the Focus of Strategy: Creating New Markets Versus Competing Directly

Kim and Mauborgne (1999) spent 10 years researching organizations that have developed fundamentally new and superior value, creating new markets and re-creating existing ones. The researchers found six approaches that enable companies to create new market space. Interestingly, those companies managed to do this by examining familiar information in a new light; accomplishing their goal did not require unique vision or foresight about the future.

The research showed that innovative companies break free from the competitive pack by staking out fundamentally new market space—that is, by creating products or services for which there are no direct competitors. This path to value innovation requires a different competitive mind-set and a systematic way of looking for opportunities, as we have seen in our previous chapters on opportunity recognition and evaluation. Instead of looking within the conventional boundaries that define how an industry competes, managers can look methodically across them. By so doing, they can find unoccupied territory that represents real value innovation. Similar insights can be gleaned by looking across strategic groups within an industry; across buyer groups; across complementary product and service offerings, and across the functional-emotional orientation of an industry.

The change in strategic thinking is described in this way: "Instead of looking within the accepted boundaries that define how we compete, managers can look systematically across them. By doing so, they can find unoccupied territory that represents a real breakthrough in value" (Kim & Mauborgne, 1999, p. 1). This carries valuable and transferable learning for entrepreneurs as they formulate strategy for their new ventures. Table 5.7 presents the six approaches entrepreneurs and managers can use to create new market space.

Table 5.7   Six Approaches to Creating New Market Space

The Conventional Boundaries of Competition	Head-to-Head Competition	Creating New Market Space
Industry	focuses on rivals within its industry	looks across substitute industries
Strategic group	focuses on competitive position within strategic group	looks across strategic groups within its industry
Buyer group	focuses on better serving the buyer group	redefines the buyer group of the industry
Scope of product and service offerings	focuses on maximizing the value of product and service offerings within the bounds of its industry	looks across to complementary product and service offerings that go beyond the bounds of its industry
Functional-emotional orientation of an industry	focuses on improving price-performance in line with the functional-emotional orientation of its industry	rethinks the functional-emotional orientation of its industry
Time	focuses on adapting to external trends as they occur	participates in shaping external trends over time

Summary of Chapter Objectives

1. Learn how to develop your value solution based on your overall strategy
   - Consider defining your value solution along the similar categories of value and cost-benefits of customer productivity, simplicity, convenience, price, and image.
   - You can then further develop your value solution and identify ways you can locate and communicate with your customers, as well as where your market would look to find information related to your business.

2. Understand the key drivers that are integral to buyers' demands and expectations within your industry
   - As customers' needs and preferences change, your firm will need to take a proactive approach in understanding how these changes influence the overall operations and efficiencies of your business.

- To uncover and reveal the most important drivers within your industry, you need to engage in questioning and research that not only reveals the important key drivers but also identifies how well your product or service responds to these key drivers over a period of time.

3. Know how your own value solution is matched and compared against these drivers within your marketplace
   - Once the entrepreneur has determined the industry's key drivers, those driver can be assessed based on how well they meet the strategy and unique value solution.
   - Table 5.2 assists you in benchmarking areas where your firm requires attention or where you lack the internal capabilities and resources to meet the needs of the marketplace.
   - Knowing these weaknesses will help you craft a revised strategy that focuses on those drivers and that positions you for the next new innovation (perhaps coming from your organization).

4. Learn the value of the perceptual map and how the map is used to maintain and exceed your competition in your industry
   - Competitive positioning reveals where your company stands in the eyes of any given group of people through the use of perceptual maps.
   - Perceptual maps are useful whenever a business decision requires knowledge of how people perceive issues and when the success of company policy or action requires a desired response.

5. Learn how to develop and gain an appreciation for a "go-to-market" strategy that is based on your value solution, the drivers in the industry, and your competitive positioning
   - A full "go-to-market" strategy encompasses the channels that a company uses to connect with its customers and the organizational processes it develops to guide customer interactions from initial contact through fulfillment.
   - The right go-to-market strategy has a significant impact on a company's ability to cost-effectively deliver its value solution to each of its target segments.
   - As companies tailor their value solutions to better address customer needs beyond product specifications and to better align their cost of sales and fulfillment relative to those needs, go-to-market strategy plays a central role.

6. Use the strategic plan outline to develop organizational-level strategies, industry-market strategies, management team strategies, and financial strategies for the new venture
   - Organizational-level strategies articulate the mission and key values.
   - Industry and market strategies explore the social and economic trends, the industry climate, key competitors, the markets the new venture serves, and the methods to create awareness by the customer base.

- Management team strategies explain how the new venture will capitalize on the strengths of its members and how it will compensate for what it lacks.
- Financial strategies define the start-up costs, explore financing alternatives and how they will be used, and present at least one year of projections.

7. Conduct a TOWS analysis to consider the new venture's strategic position.
   - The Threats-Opportunities-Weaknesses-Strengths analysis is an innovative approach to analyzing the external environment and applying the new venture's strengths and weaknesses in ways that capitalize on the opportunities and minimize the threats facing the new venture.

8. Explore new approaches that shift the focus of the new venture's strategy from direct competition to the creation of new value
   - Research has shown that the most innovative organizations are moving from competing directly with others in their industry to creating new value that enables them to establish new market space.

CASE 5.1   RentABook.com: A Strategic Analysis

Table of Contents

Executive Summary

RentABook.com is an on-line textbook rental service intent on helping college students keep more of *their* money in *their* pockets. Students simply login to RentABook.com, borrow their textbooks for the term, and return the books after the term is over. A portion of the rental fee is used as a security deposit and is given back to the student once the books are returned. Or, students can choose to keep the book, and RentABook.com keeps their security deposit. Initially, RentABook.com will focus on DePaul University students, with plans to expand to serve college students throughout the Chicago-land area in the near future.

College textbook prices are rising. Right now, DePaul students spend an average of $400 per quarter—$1,200 per year—on books. RentABook.com's unique service helps students save up to 51 percent. RentABook.com also knows how important delivery is to students. Students need their books to arrive on time. That's why RentABook.com guarantees on-time delivery. Or if they choose, students can elect to pick up their order at our main location. Customers include the college population who are Internet savvy and have limited disposable income.

Our management team consists of current DePaul students with backgrounds in different aspects of business—accounting, finance management, and marketing. Our team members' student status gives us personal insight into our customers' needs and interests as well as first-hand experience with the current book-buying experience. We saw an opportunity to provide more affordable books to students who value affordable prices.

Financial analysis projects that with start-up costs of $31,500, RentABook.com can generate net profits of $5,215 in year one, $19,514 in year two, and $25,000 by the third year. Such growth potential makes RentABook.com an attractive investment. Our management team is seeking $15,000 in initial bank loans. The rest of the funding will be secured using personal investments and credit.

Organizational-Level Strategies

What Business Are We Really In?

RentABook.com is in the textbook rental *service*. But RentABook.com is really in the business of saving students money. That puts RentABook.com in indirect competition with other money-saving services targeting students—student rates for phone service, gym membership, parking, and so on.

Mission Statement

Our service is for students who want quality, affordable textbooks available for delivery or pick-up. Our domain name is RentABook.com, and our mission is to provide competitive prices and on-time delivery so that students can avoid the hassles of bookstores and other on-line retailers. We stand apart from others because of our unique services for a student community that values affordable prices

Students can log on to www.RentABook.com and borrow the books they need for a nominal fee and a security deposit (Visa, Master Card, AmEx, Check, Money Order, PayPal). If books are ordered no later than a certain date, they will be delivered before the first day of the semester. Students can choose to waive shipping costs by electing to pick up their books at 245 N. Southport Ave. in Chicago. At the end of the quarter, students will receive their security deposits back after books are returned. If students decide to keep their books, they can e-mail RentABook.com, and we will retain their security deposit.

Key Values

Our key values include:

- Dependability—Our customers trust us to deliver their books on time. We must do what we can to uphold their trust.
- Service—Our customers deserve impeccable customer service. We must fulfill their requests to the best of our ability.
- Affordable price—Our company is built on the foundation of providing students with the most affordable textbooks available.

To provide the most affordable books for our customers, we must establish a good rapport with our suppliers. A good rapport includes paying our suppliers on time and taking advantage of price discounts as much as possible. Because we rent our books to students, we do not need to purchase a large quantity of books every semester; we purchase only enough books to maintain a steady inventory each semester.

Industry and Market Strategies

Advertising

Price is the most important factor students take into account when deciding where to purchase their books. We must show how incredibly affordable it is to borrow books at RentABook.com. Instead of simply telling students how affordable RentABook.com is, show students the difference in cost between purchasing books at our competitors versus renting books at RentABook.com.

We need to show students the benefits of choosing RentABook.com. A side-by-side comparison shows what students can afford to buy when they shop with competitors versus how much more they can purchase with the savings they get with RentABook.com. What would college students buy with the money they saved using RentABook.com? The way we are planning to execute our advertising strategy is to post 8½ × 11-inch, four-color posters on bulletin boards throughout DePaul University. Leaflets will also be passed out in the front foyer of dormitories and student-populated apartments. We are also considering half-page ads in the *DePaulia*, the weekly university newspaper.

Social Trends

The most recent trend is that more and more college students are shopping on-line. College students are one of the populations that are most dependent on the Internet. About 86 percent of college students use the Internet, and 81 percent report having made a purchase on-line (Pastore, 2000b) "Internet has become an integral element of college life" (Pastore, 2000b). In 1999, e-commerce purchases done by college students totaled $2.2 billon, an increase of 18 percent from the previous year (Mack, 2000). Textbooks are one of the main things that college students buy on-line; they ranked sixth among products purchased on the Internet. Of the college students that purchase items on-line, 42 percent purchased textbooks (Ebenkamp, 2000). College students aren't the only ones purchasing school supplies on-line; 26 percent of parents doing back-to-school shopping plan to do so via the Internet, and of these, 20 percent plan to purchase textbooks on-line (Pastore, 2000a).

Economic Trends

One of the major concerns of college students is the high-priced textbooks in the bookstores. All U.S. college students together spend an average of $105 billion per year on their texts. On average, most full-time college students who purchase their books from a bookstore spend $500 per quarter (Freemna, 1999). The average cost of a textbook is about $62, according to the National Association of College Bookstores (Hardin, 2000). Many bookstores claim to offer used books to save students money, but 59 percent of students who searched for used textbooks in the fall 2003 quarter/semester didn't find any available for their classes (Calpirg, 2004).

Climate of Industry

The textbook industry is successful because of high demand. The battle for the textbook market exists between brick-and-mortar college bookstores and on-line bookstores. They compete for the $2.7 billion textbook market (Csar, 1999). More and more students are turning to the Internet to purchase their textbooks because

of the lower prices and other things such as convenience. Gross sales of textbooks, in the month of August 2003, totaled about $668 million ("As Fall Buying," 2003). Although 20 percent of college students don't purchase any textbooks at all because of the high prices, the majority of students do. Some of the factors that influence students to purchase the textbooks are the difficulty of the classes, the amount of assignments from the textbooks, and also the extent that the instructor uses lectures based on the textbooks.

Key Competitors

The textbook industry is one of the most successful industries. That is why there are so many competitors. RentABook.com's key competitors are: Barnes & Noble, Amazon.com, e-campus.com, varsitybooks.com, and the library.

Barnes & Noble is one of the most successful bookstores in the industry. It operates many stores nationwide. Barnes & Noble is also affiliated with textbooks.com, which is an on-line retailer (Freemna, 1999). For that reason, and also because of the current stores the company is opening on DePaul University's campus, we consider Barnes & Noble our top competitor. The company's total revenue for 2004 was $6.55 billion, with a 12.9 percent annual growth (*Barnes & Noble: Key statistics*, 2004). Barnes & Noble has the competitive advantage of being both an on-line retailer and bricks-and-mortar bookstore. It is a nationwide, successful, and well-known company.

Amazon.com, the on-line e-tailer, is also successful. Part of its success is due to the fact that Amazon has first mover advantage of being an on-line bookstore. Amazon.com has a well-known, trusted global brand name and reputation (which contribute to the company's success), knowledge of customer buying habits, and a high rate of continuing customers. This company sells more than just textbooks. Other things include apparel and accessories, electronics, toys and games, music, and things for the home and garden. Amazon's 2004 total revenue was $6.92 billion with a 33.8 percent annual growth (*Amazon.com Inc.: Key statistics*, 2004).

E-campus.com is an on-line retailer of discounted textbooks, both new and used. Besides textbooks, e-campus.com sells college logo merchandise, electronics, computers, office and general supplies, music and gifts. Dave Thomas, Wendy's founder, backs up this company, which opened for business on July 2, 1999. A major drawback for this company is the fact that it filed for bankruptcy in June 2001. After filing for bankruptcy, the company was bought by George Valassis, who was an investor (Tatge, 2001).

Varsitybooks.com, an on-line retailer, focuses on selling textbooks. Also known as Varsity Group, the company gets its books from Baker & Taylor, which is a leading U.S. book distributor (*Varsity Group Inc.: Profile*, 2005). This company began in 1998 and calls itself a college marketing company. It has both on-line and off-line advertising (Mack, 2000). One of the company's strategies, which it considers a competitive advantage, is to hire student campus reps to spread the word. The marketing strategy also includes radio spots, campus newspapers, and sponsorships (Csar, 1999). Varsitybooks.com spends in the $5 million to $10 million range on advertising campaigns. This company also supplies its books to more than 240 educational institutions. Total revenue for 2004 was $37.7 million, up 49 percent from 2003 (*Varsity Group Inc.: Profile*, 2005). The library is also one of our competitors because some students rent their books from the library. DePaul University's library offers students the opportunity to rent some of the books that are required for classes. Although this is good option for students because they don't have to purchase their books, the library offers only a limited selection, and only two or three books are in stock for each class. Another pitfall for the library is that these books are gone fast and can be checked out for only four weeks. There is an option to renew the book, but only if no one is on a waiting list, which is uncommon because most students want to save some money by renting the books available. There is also the disadvantage of not being able to keep the book. Many students keep textbooks that are related to their majors for future reference, and renting them from the library doesn't give them that option. Students also have to pay a fee if the book is overdue, lost, or damaged.

One of the ways that RentABook.com will compete with the other competitors is by offering the students more options. We will give students the option to rent or buy their textbooks. From the survey, we saw that many students use the bookstore's buy-back program, which shows that they are not interested in keeping their textbooks; therefore, we are giving these students the option to rent their textbooks for a cheaper price. As students, we also know that many students like to keep their textbooks, especially those related to their majors, so we are giving these students the option to purchase textbooks that they would like to keep. We are aware that although our prices will be cheaper than most college bookstores and Barnes & Noble, they might not be cheaper than Amazon, e-campus, or Varsity Books, but we will compete with these textbook retailers by offering students the option to pick up their textbooks from our location.

This option will save them the shipping charges, and it will guarantee them that they will get the correct book on time, which is the major reason some students don't buy their textbooks on-line; it is also the biggest concern for those who do shop on-line, according to our perceptions and those of students to whom we have talked. We will also focus on other student concerns to improve our service and differentiate ourselves from other competitors. Other concerns include availability of textbooks and convenience. We will have a variety of textbooks on all DePaul courses, and if we run out, we will order from our suppliers as orders come in to have them available to students. We will also make our service convenient by making our Web site easy to use and by having the books ready to be picked up at our location (which will be near by the Lincoln Park Campus of DePaul).

Target Market

RentABook.com's target market is college students, who are Internet savvy and have limited disposable income. RentABook.com is concerned with the buying behavior and trends of all college students, but it focuses on DePaul University's college students. Sales from other students will be welcomed and appreciated, but our first-year plan is to focus on DePaul University's college students and do most of our advertisement at DePaul University. Small advertisements, such as handing out flyers, will be done at other nearby universities to gain awareness, but not a lot of money will go toward advertisement at those universities. We chose to focus on DePaul students because of the easy accessibility; because we are all students at this university, it will be easy to advertise our business and reach our target market there.

One of the ways that we will maintain a customer base is by sending e-mails to our continuing customers, which will be done weeks before their school quarter begins. The e-mails will remind them of our business, and sending these notes a couple of weeks before a new quarter starts is a good idea because that is when most students purchase their textbooks. We will also offer them promotions, such as saving 15 percent, to encourage them to shop with us instead of our competitors.

There are different ways that RentABook.com can create awareness. One of the ways that we will do so is by starting an advertising campaign in the spring quarter to let people know we are opening open in the fall quarter. Because we will be focusing on DePaul University students, it will be easier for us to reach the majority of this population in the spring quarter. We will also create awareness by word of mouth. As RentABook.com's owners, we have the advantage of being DePaul University's students; therefore, we will be able to talk about our business to our friends and faculty, hoping they will mention our business to their friends, relatives, and anyone else that will benefit from our business.

Student Survey Results

Our management team decided to create a survey (Appendix 1) and test our target market's book-buying behavior. The survey was handed out to more than 100 students from various backgrounds, ages, and majors. What our team was attempting to do was to determine how our target market was going to respond to a new and unique product. An entrepreneur can be more confident about the product with the approval of the consumer ahead of time.

When students were asked where they buy their textbooks, 60 percent said they used the DePaul bookstore. The Internet was a close second, coming in at 30 percent. The rest of the students bought their books from their friends and other peers. We find these results to be in our favor because even if we only have 30 percent of our target market, that would be enough to start our company. However, we also hope to shift those numbers, so more and more students shop on-line at RentABook.com.

Also, when students were asked whether they ever purchased books on-line, 64 percent answered yes. We find that these results are in our favor as well because the majority of students have already used an on-line service at some point and are familiar with the process. The only potential drawback is that some of the students may have been dissatisfied with their on-line experience and may have decided not to purchase books on-line anymore.

Although most students purchase their books at the bookstore, more than 79 percent were willing to give our service a try. Because students are so comfortable using the Internet, they are not opposed to shopping on our Web site. When students were asked whether they would consider purchasing their books from an on-line service, an overwhelming 79 percent answered yes and 10.5 percent answered maybe.

These results made us ecstatic because we realized how comfortable our target market was with using new products and shopping on-line.

Our team also wanted to know how much, on average, a student spends on books every quarter. We found out that the average amount was about $400. Because most students take about four classes per quarter, we figured that a single textbook costs about $100. This comes out to about $1,200 a year spent on textbooks alone, whether the university is on the quarter system or the semester system. Our service was created especially to alleviate the problem of students paying too much for textbooks.

When we asked students to rate the most important factor they consider when purchasing textbooks, not to anyone's surprise, the most important factor was price. Convenience and availability came second and third. We think that price was the most important factor because demand for textbooks is inelastic. No matter how much textbooks go up in price, students will still purchase them for their classes. Also, students do not have a lot of disposable income, so every penny counts. That is why price is by far the most important factor, and that is exactly what our company will provide.

TOWS Analysis

To help us develop strategies for the start-up and launch of RentABook.com, we have conducted a TOWS analysis. In the analysis (Table 5.8), we identified the threats and opportunities facing our business, as well as our internal strengths and weaknesses that we can use to leverage the opportunities in the industry and marketplace and reduce or avoid the threats.

Management Team Strategies

As a group, the participants in RentABook .com have agreed on making the business relationship a general partnership. It was agreed that all the founding members would divide money shares into equal portions, and most decisions would be made as a team. The reason this is done

is to ensure that no decision impact's just one team member's future. If a decision is made, it is made as a team, and because the company is a general partnership, all assume equal liability for the company. There is no future consequence to a specific person for the team's error or. As a disadvantage to this partnership, although most decisions are made as a team, some decisions will be made individually when it come to the different sectors of the business, and if the decision is a wrong one, it will reflect on the whole team and company as the general partnership assumes a team liability instead of an individual one.

Location

RentABook.com is a company that does not possess large amounts of capital, so the team has decided that the location of the warehouse and operations would be in one of the team member's household. The consequence of this decision is that a lot of money is saved. The expenses of rent and most utility bills are saved in this decision. All that is needed for the company at first is a location to store books and a place to have your systems ready to run. Although a warehouse is being considered for our future projections, to start up we would like to have a secured location. As an advantage to using a team member's apartment, we have the fact that it is located in the heart of the target market, which in this case would be Lincoln Park. This location gives RentABook.com the opportunity to reach out further to the customer and create a better relationship. The major disadvantage at the start will be the available storage space of the household. Although the inventory will not be as big to start as it will be in the future, some space will be needed to store the inventory that is at hand.

Strengths and Experience of Team

Although the team members and founders of RentABook.com are students, they have a lot of strengths that are beneficial to the company and the strategies that will be enacted. First, all the team members have knowledge and practice in

Table 5.8   TOWS Analysis for RentABook.com

Internal Factors / External Factors	Strengths (S) S1 Access to market S2 Understanding of market S3 Diverse management team S4 Resources to advertise to market S5 Strong business skills	Weaknesses (W) W1 Little available capital W2 No experience W3 No storage facility for inventory W4 No competitors to learn from W5 Full-time students, little time to dedicate
Opportunities O1 First entrant to market O2 No competitors O3 Price important to market O4 Large market O5 Students need books	**SO STRATEGIES** How can we use our strengths to take advantage of the opportunities?	**WO STRATEGIES** How can we reduce our weaknesses to take advantage of the opportunities?
Threats T1 Books & editions change often T2 Competitors can enter market T3 Inventory wear and tear T4 Large players in industry T5 On-line only courses	**ST STRATEGIES** How can we use our strengths to avoid threats?	**WT STRATEGIES** How can we reduce our weaknesses to avoid threats?

SOURCE: Adapted from *Long Range Planning, 15*(2), Weihrich, H., The TOWS Matrix: A Tool for Situational Analysis, pp. 54–66, copyright 1982, with permission from Elsevier.

all the fields that are required to run the business, and these are finance, accounting, marketing, and management. We all have experience in most of these courses and also possess working experience in all of these fields. Second, as RentABook.com is a company created for students, we are students, and we are aware of the needs that students have wanting to purchase a textbook, and that is price. In other words, we are a part of our target market, and as a result, we know the needs of our customer. Third, because we are students and know the key factors involved in a student's decision, we will know how to reach and catch the attention of our potential customers. Finally, our competition is well known by the team because we used to be customers of these companies. With all these strengths put together, RentABook.com could be a great asset and benefit for the student population.

Structure of RentABook.com

One of the major advantages in the management of RentABook.com is that we will have no employees to start. This will give the company no worries on an hourly pay or salary for others apart from the team. As a consequence of this, the team members of RentABook.com will be their own employees. As stated before, most decisions within the company will be made as a team, but some members will focus more on a certain department. The team members assigned to each department are the ones who are most knowledgeable and experienced in the field. As a consequence of this analysis, the team has been structured as follows:

Andres Ayala and Maria Mendoza: Management

Arby Gonzales: Accounting and marketing

Staci Oliyar: Finance

With the experience of each member in his or her assigned area, RentABook.com will have a major strength in each department, and as a consequence of this structure, the ideas provided to the team as a whole will be more efficient and organized, and with all this in mind, the whole team will give advice and agree on a certain decision as a whole.

What Does RentABook.com Need From the Team?

The main concern before opening a business is money, but once the money is there, the individual or team has to analyze many other things if their business is to be successful. Our team needs to know how to reach out to the student market and let them know that RentABook.com has opened. In other words, a well-thought-out marketing strategy needs to be created so our market o knows that we provide an affordable service. Because our main goal and mission is to provide students with an affordable price that beats out our

competition and saves money, we need to make sure that this is what happens. Without providing an affordable and low price, the company is lying to the market and will not be successful. Finally, we need to create a customer-company relationship within RentABook.com. For our service to survive throughout the years, we need to prove that we are a company that cares about the customer. By doing all this, our customers will give good words of trust and advice about our company to other incoming or current students. Furthermore, the good reputation of RentABook.com would create a good following of loyal customers.

What Does RentABook.com Have and Lack?

As a team, we have decided that to create a bigger inventory, the team members will donate their own books to the company. Although this will not create a big inventory, it will augment the inventory that we purchase. We also have the advantage of technology on our side. Because our business is basically run from the Internet, the fact that we have a Web site gives us a way to reach our customers in the comfort of their own homes. On our advertisements, we will post our Web site for the customer to visit and rent books, and this also creates a way of advertisement for RentABook.com. By students visiting the Web site alone, they will know that this company exists, and they will tell their friends about it, and with this, our Web site creates a word of mouth around our target market population. Our team possesses the skills needed to run the business. Without the skills and strategies of every one of the members, RentABook.com would not have been created. All of these strengths will be essential and beneficial in the running of RentABook.com.

Although we do possess major strengths and abilities that will benefit us when the business is in progress, our company does lack some items that could be beneficial. There is a lack of inventory within our reach because our start-up capital is not as high as other companies. As students, we do not posses a lot of money, and as a solution to our lack of capital and inventory, we have decided to apply the strategy of just-in-time inventory. Although we will have a good enough stock of books to start up, when someone requests a book that is unavailable in the inventory, RentABook.com will order it the minute the order is received. This will create a bigger inventory for us throughout the future and also allow us to save some money on inventory. As an effect of not having a big inventory, we lack the ability of having a warehouse or storage area. Although this could be beneficial to us, it also creates the advantage of saving us money. Finally, we do not have any employees but ourselves. Because the company provides its service mostly through our Web site, we do not need to have employees at the start. This also saves us money and gives us the opportunity to invest the cash into other beneficial assets for the company. Although we do lack these things at first, in the future, they are essential to the running of our business, and they are things that will be examined in detail after the success of our business.

Financial Strategies

Start-Up Costs

The following is a list of the start-up costs that our company is anticipating to incur in the first year of our existence. These costs include our domain name, which we will have to purchase for at least five years, as well as a server and the appropriate software to host and run our Web site to the best of its ability. We will also need a fast Internet connection to be able to manage the traffic on our Web site. The T-1 connection is one of the fastest, and we chose it because we do not want students to get frustrated at our slow connection and go to another Web site. We will also have Microsoft Commerce Manager® and PayPal® on our Web site for further convenience. Microsoft Commerce Manager will help us build our storefront, including shopping carts, inventory searches, shipment tracking, and the ability to use any major credit card securely on our Web site. We will also need our initial inventory, and the fees for the partnership agreement and legal fees. The partnership agreement will ensure that we are all protected from a legal perspective.

Start-Up Costs

• Five-year domain name:	$350 for initial cost $7.25 per year thereafter
• Intel Xeon processor and server: (Includes all the proper Web software and disaster recovery)	$5,000 purchase price
• T-1 Internet connection 1.54 MBps	$3,348 per year
• Microsoft Commerce Manager	$300 per year
• Fees for using PayPal	$0–$3,000 2.9% + $0.30 $3,000–$10,000 2.5% + $0.30
• Initial textbook Inventory	$20,000
• Shipping supplies	$500
• Legal fees	$300
• Partnership agreement	$99
• Advertising campaign	$1,200 per year
• Licensing	$400
Total Start-Up Cost:	**$31,497**

Our total start-up costs came out to $31,497. In our opinion, these figures are very feasible for a team of four, and we will easily be able to raise the above amount to start our company. We realize that this list may be incomplete, due to the fact that many companies incur unanticipated costs along the way. We are prepared for the fact that there may be additional costs involved with starting our business, and we are willing to be flexible enough to adjust our figures where necessary.

Financing

Our company will have a debt/equity structure for the financing of our company. The equity financing will come from team members themselves as well as our friends and family. The team will come up with $6,000 in personal savings as well as another $6,000 collected from family and friends for a total of $12,000. The rest will be debt financing. Our team will apply for a small business loan from a bank for $15,000. We think that we will be able to get such a loan because the loan amount is not very large, and we can provide the collateral. Our suppliers will also provide some of the debt financing with a $5,000 credit for our inventory for a total of $20,000. This brings our total to $32,000, which is a little bit above our initial start-up costs. Finally, our team is prepared to use credit cards in the event that we incur unanticipated costs. We will use the credit cards as a last resort.

Pricing Strategy

Our pricing strategy was designed to save our customers money. We can keep our price so low because we can get up to six turnovers on a textbook before it becomes obsolete. Usually, the publisher will release a new edition every two years or so. This will give our company a chance to turn over the book six times before a new edition comes out. (Three quarters per year times two years.) This analysis does not include the December session or summer school classes.

In that case, our turnover would be even greater. When a book does become outdated, we will either ship it back to the publisher or sell it on our Web site at a deep discount. We will not be renting old editions of textbooks.

Our company's strategy is to save students 30 percent on every book they buy compared to the price a bookstore charges. For example, if a book is sold for $100 at the bookstore, then we will be offering the book for $70. The security deposit will be 30 percent of the $70 purchase price. In this case, the security deposit will be $21 ($70 × .30). The rest of the purchase price will be the rental charge (only $49). If a student decides to keep the book, we will keep the security deposit, and the student still gets the book for $70. If a student does decide to return the book, we refund the security deposit and the student only pays $49 to rent the book. Overall, each student saves 51 percent on every textbook rental versus if they bought the book at the bookstore.

The Numbers

RentABook.com's strategy for making extra profit is to use the deposit money to invest in 30-day Treasury bills. Because every month we will have a surplus of cash from deposits, we can increase our profits by using that money to invest in low-risk bonds. At the end of the 30-day period, the deposit will either be refunded to the customer, or in case the customer chooses to keep the book, the money will go back into the company.

In the first fiscal year of our company's existence, we project that we will end up with a net profit of $5,215 (Appendix 2). Taking into account all of our expenses, the first two quarters we will experience a loss of ($17,334) and ($5,945), respectively. However, by the time spring quarter ends, our company will be making a profit of $11,160. Our net profit for the year will be $5,215.

By year two, we project a net profit of $19,514. Overall, our company will grow at a steady rate as we gain recognition among the student population. The reason for our company's rapid growth of 274 percent from year 1 to year 2 is the fact that we will not be taking into account any more start-up costs. Our expenses from the first year onward will all be minimal, such as the upkeep of the Web site, Microsoft Commerce Manager fees, and fees for using PayPal. We predict a steady growth of our company as students begin to use our services across universities in the Chicagoland area. If our company keeps growing, within the next couple of years, we will be adding extra expenses such as renting a warehouse and hiring new employees.

SOURCE: This strategic plan analysis was written by students Anastasiya Oliyar, Maria Mendoza, Arby Gonzalez, and Andres Ayala of DePaul University. Reprinted with permission.

Discussion Questions

1. What is your perception of the concept of RentABook.com? Does it seem to you to have potential for market success?

2. Sh166ould additional research be conducted for the plan? Are there other factors the team should consider?

3. How can RentABook.com use its strengths to leverage some of the opportunities and to avoid the threats in its industry and market?

4. How can the company reduce its weaknesses to more effectively embrace the opportunities and avoid the threats?

5. What specific strategy do you recommend RentABook.com develop?

Appendix 5.1
Student Book-Buying Behavior Survey

Thank you for taking the time to participate in this survey. This survey will be used to gauge students' book-buying behavior.

Please answer the following to the best of your ability.

1. On average, how much money do you spend on textbooks per quarter?

2. Where are you most likely to get your textbooks?

    [ ]   School Book Store

    [ ]   Internet

    [ ]   Borrow from Friends

    [ ]   Purchase Used Books from Other Students (via bulletin boards)

    [ ]   Other _____ Why?

3. Have you ever purchased books online?

    [ ]   Yes

    [ ]   No (continue to #6)

4. If yes, please rank the most important factors for your purchases with 1 being the most important and 3 being the least.

    [ ]   Price   [ ]   Convenience   [ ]   Availability

5. Please rank your biggest concerns when purchasing books online.

    [ ]   Security   [ ]   Receiving books on time

    [ ]   Service   [ ]   Receiving the correct book

6. Do you utilize the School Book Store's book buy-back system?

    [ ]   Yes   Why/why not?

    [ ]   No

7. Would you consider borrowing your textbooks through a textbook rental system? Why/why not?

Thank you for your time.

Appendix 5.2
RentABook.com Financial Statements

Winter Q

Revenues	$18,690
Pub. Exp.	$20,025
Sec. Liab	$4,494
Loss	($5,829)

Spring Q

Revenues	$18,690
Pub. Exp.	$3,975
Sec. Liab	$4,494
Profit	$10,221

Autumn Q

Revenues	$18,690
Rev. from old ed.	$9,345
Pub. Exp.	$3,975
Sec. Liab	$4,494
Profit	$19,566
OPERATING PROFITS	$23,958

INCOME STATEMENT x1

REVENUES		
WQ	$14,196	
SQ	$14,196	
AQ	$14,196	
Sale of Old Ed.	$9,345	
Total Revenues		$51,933
EXPENSES		
Inventory	$27,975	
Domain Name	$358	
Server	$5,000	
Internet Connection	$3,348	
Mgt Software	$300	
Shipping Supplies	$500	
Ad & Promo	$1,200	
Legal	$300	
Licensing	$400	
Partnership Agreement	$99	
Total Operating Expenses		$39,480
NET PROFIT		$12,454

YEAR x2

Winter Q

Revenues	$22,361
Pub. Exp.	$23,958
Sec. Liab	$5,367
Loss	($6,964)

Spring Q

Revenues	$22,361
Pub. Exp.	$4,792
Sec. Liab	$5,367
Profit	$12,203

Autumn Q

Revenues	$22,361
Rev. from old ed.	$11,180
Pub. Exp.	$3,975
Sec. Liab	$5,367
Profit	$24,200

OPERATING PROFITS	$29,438

INCOME STATEMENT x2

REVENUES		
WQ	$16,994	
SQ	$16,994	
AQ	$16,994	
Sale of Old Ed.	$11,180	
Total Revenues		$62,163
EXPENSES		
Inventory	$32,725	
Domain Name	$7	
Internet Connection	$3,348	
Mgt Software	$300	
Shipping Supplies	$500	
Ad & Promo	$1,200	
Total Operating Expenses		$38,080
NET PROFIT		$24,083

YEAR x3

Winter Q

Revenues	$27,476
Pub. Exp.	$29,438
Sec. Liab	$6,594
Loss	($8,557)

Spring Q

Revenues	$27,476
Pub. Exp.	$5,888
Sec. Liab	$6,594
Profit	$14,994

Autumn Q

Revenues	$27,476
Rev. from old ed.	$13,738
Pub. Exp.	$3,975
Sec. Liab	$6,594
Profit	$30,645

OPERATING PROFITS $37,082

INCOME STATEMENT x3

REVENUES		
WQ	$20,882	
SQ	$20,882	
AQ	$20,882	
Sale of Old Ed.	$13,738	
Total Revenues		$76,383
EXPENSES		
Inventory	$39,301	
Domain Name	$7	
Internet Connection	$3,348	
Mgt Software	$300	
Shipping Supplies	$500	
Ad & Promo	$1,200	
Total Operating Expenses		$44,656
NET PROFIT		$31,727

References

Amazon.com Inc.: Key statistics (Yahoo! Finance). (2004). Retrieved March 11, 2005, from http://finance.yahoo.com/q/ks?s=AMZN

As fall buying season opens. (2003). *Educational Marketer.* Retrieved March 1, 2005, from http://www.publishers.org/highered/index.cfm

Barnes & Noble Inc.: Key statistics (Yahoo! Finance). (2004). Retrieved March 11, 2005, from http://finance.yahoo.com/q/ks?s=BKS

Calpirg. (2004). *Rip-off 101: How the current practices of the textbook industry drive up the cost of college textbooks.* Retrieved March 9, 2005, from http://calpirg.org/CA.asp?id2=11987&id3=CA&

Csar, T. (1999). Online textbook industry competes with local bookstores. *The Guardsman Online.* Retrieved March 11, 2005, from http://www.ccsf.edu/Events_Pubs/Guardsman/f981207/uwire06.shtml

Ebenkamp, B. (2000, April 10). Book buying 101. *Brandweek, 41,* p. 22. Retrieved February 25, 2005, from Business and Company ASAP database, DePaul University Library.

Freemna, L. (1999). Battle of the (college) books gains intensity. *Advertising Age, 70*(35), 16. Retrieved March 1, 2005, from ABI/ Inform database. DePaul University Library.

Hardin, A. (2000, March 6). Online textbook discounts disputed. *Crain's Cleveland Business, 21*(10), 3.

Kerns, C. D. (2002). An entrepreneurial approach to strategic direction setting. *Business Horizons, 45*(4), 2–6.

Kim, W. C., & Mauborgne, R. (1999). Creating new market space. *Harvard Business Review, 77*(1), 83–93.

Lehmann, D. R., & Winer, R. S. (2005). *Analysis for marketing planning* (6th ed.). Burr Ridge, IL: Irwin.

Mack, A. M. (2000, August 7). Textbook case. *Brandweek, 41*(32). Retrieved March 1, 2005, from FirstSearch database.

Pastore, M. (2000a). Back-to-school shopping goes high tech. *ClickZNetwork: Retailing.* Retrieved February 27, 2005, from http://www.clickz.com/stats/sectors/retailing/article.php/450461

Pastore, M. (2000b). US college students use net for shopping. *ClickZ Network: Demographics.* Retrieved February 27, 2005, from http://www.clickz.com/stats/sectors/demographics/article.php/432631

Pennington, A. Y. (2005, November 16). 8 perpetually hot businesses. *Entrepreneur.* Retrieved February 15, 2006, from http://www.entrepreneur.com/article/0,4621,324539,00.html

Schultz, H., & Yang, D. J. (1997). *Pour your heart into it: How Starbucks built a company one cup at a time.* New York: Hyperion.

Tatge, M. (2001). Where's the bucks? *Forbes.* Retrieved March 2, 2005, from Business and Company ASAP database, DePaul University Library.

Varsity Group Inc.: Profile (Yahoo! Finance). (2005). Retrieved March 11, 2005, from http://finance.yahoo.com/q/pr?s=VSTY

Weihrich, H. (1982). The TOWS matrix: A tool for situational analysis. *Long Range Planning, 15*(2), 54–66.

PART II

Entrepreneurial Strategies for the Growing Venture

CHAPTER 6

Financial Resource Capabilities

While deals often fail in practice, they never fail in projections.

—Warren Buffett[1]

Objectives:

1. Know the differences between debt and equity financing: two similar but separate audiences

2. Understand the financing stages along the life cycle of the business

3. Understand the most common sources of financing available for your business

4. Know the differences between venture capital and angel investment

5. Learn how investors conduct a due diligence analysis and what they commonly look for when examining your business

Strategy in Action

Raging Bull

At 21, William Martin started his first company—not bad for a first job. As a college student with almost no money, Martin and two friends created the on-line financial company, Raging Bull. So how did Martin and his partners get from the dorm room to a $2 million investment from CMGI, a highly successful venture capital firm?

After his freshman year at the University of Virginia, Martin took an internship at Goldman Sachs where he learned from the partners and attended industry events such as Goldman's Internet conference. This experience motivated him to think differently about the potential of Internet.

"On the bus home from Manhattan, I would think about the Net and what kinds of businesses might work there." Back in Charlottesville for his sophomore year, he recruited other Internet enthusiasts to help him set up an investment-discussion board. His roommate, a graphic designer, created the site's look and feel. Fellow members of the university's investing club helped with content by writing daily market recaps. By the next summer, Martin decided to try making Raging Bull a viable competitor of Silicon Investor and Yahoo!—the industry leaders. He amassed $30,000 from savings and credit-card loans to finance a business expansion and moved Raging Bull to the basement of his parents' New Jersey home. A co-conspirator, Rusty Szurek, 21, passed up a summer job and moved in with him.

"We spent the summer making changes, adding features, and watching how the changes affected traffic," Martin says. Over the summer, the number of registered users grew from a few dozen to 15,000, and Martin made his first big capital investment: a $7,000 Sun Microsystems server.

As September 1998 approached, classes beckoned. Martin, worried that Raging Bull would wither without his full-time attention, wanted to continue building the business. He had a hard time convincing his partners to bag their studies. Even worse, the team was running out of money. Just then, the company got some much-needed media attention. "Within days," Martin says, "we had eight interested investors. It was crazy. Our only asset was that Sun server."

One suitor was @ventures, the venture-capital arm of CMGI, an Internet conglomerate based in Andover, Massachusetts. CEO David Wetherell, 44, discovered Raging Bull while surfing the Web during a vacation. "I was looking for applications that had the potential to grow quickly," he says. When CMGI asked to see a business plan, Martin and his pals pulled an all-nighter to write one. The next morning, Wetherell requested a one-on-one with Martin.

A few days later, Martin found himself at Wetherell's house, hammering out a deal. "That night," Martin remembers, "I called Rusty and Greg [Wright, 22, another partner] and said, 'You're not going back to school.'" It was the perfect opportunity. They started hiring employees—including Stephen Killeen, 36, formerly a senior vice president at Fidelity Investments and at DLJ Direct, who serves as president and CEO. By March of that year, Raging Bull had 15 employees and 85,000 registered users.

SOURCE: From Kirshner, S., "First companies are serious business," in *Fast Company* (25), June 1999, p. 168. Reprinted with permission via Copyright Clearance Center.

Discussion Questions

1. What role do you think business plans play when attracting funding?

2. If you were Martin, what additional information would you want to know about CMGI and the value they would bring in exploiting this opportunity?

3. What initial questions and information would you want to have prior to formulating a "deal"?

The Differences Between Debt and Equity Financing: Two Similar but Separate Audiences[2]

Once you have an idea of the start-up costs, you will need to decide how to finance your new venture. On the entrepreneurial front, there are two fundamental types to consider: equity financing and debt financing.

Equity financing deals with an exchange of money for a share of business ownership. In this type of financing, you receive funds without incurring debt, meaning that you do not have to repay a specific amount of money at any particular time. However, the major disadvantage of this form of financing is the dilution of your ownership interests and the possible loss of control that is associated with sharing of ownership with additional investors.

Debt financing deals with borrowing money that is to be repaid over a period of time and most likely with interest. This type of financing can be either long term (repayment due over more than one year) or more short term (repayment due in less than one year). Your obligations are limited to repaying the loan, and as opposed to equity financing, the lender does not gain an ownership interest in your business. In start-ups and in smaller firms, personal guarantees[3] are likely to be required on most debt contracts. From the lender's perspective, the debt-to-equity ratio[4] measures the amount of assets available for repayment of a debt in the case of default by the entrepreneur. If you have too much debt, your firm may be considered overextended/risky, and this may impair your chances of future investment.

However, too much equity financing may show that you are not making the most productive use of your capital. That is, the capital is not being used advantageously as leverage[5] for obtaining cash to operate your business effectively and efficiently. Lenders, using industry benchmarks, will also consider the debt-to-equity ratio in assessing whether the company is being operated in a creditworthy manner. For many start-up firms, the owners need to monitor their cash flow and guard against any shortages that can influence the business in taking excess debt. Again excessive debt can impact the firm's ability to obtain needed capital for the future growth of the business.

Strategy in Action

On Understanding Debt Versus Equity

Too many entrepreneurs assume loans are the first form of financing they should look into for their emerging ventures. But the prospect of taking on long-term debt for your small business can appear quite daunting when first put through an analysis of sales, costs and breakeven. Many entrepreneurs feel borrowing money isn't nearly as attractive as securing equity investors, but they know that securing venture capital partners might be unrealistic, given the size and scope of their enterprise. Most hesitations regarding loans focus on issues of being locked into periodic installments, having to pay large interest costs over time, tying up vital company assets as collateral and jeopardizing profit margins. So how do equity and debt stack up to each other, and what are the trade-offs you should consider?

Debt	Equity
• Take on Creditors	• Take on Partners (Dilution of ownership)
• Low Expected Return	• High Expected Return
• Smaller Funding Amounts	• Larger Funding Amount
• Periodic Payments	• No Short Term Payments
• Maturity Date	• Open-Ended "Exit" Date
• More Restrictions	• Less Restrictions
• Personal Guarantees	
• Adherence to pre-determined financial ratios	

Now you're ready to assess the relative merits of each form of funding for your specific business.

Partners/creditors. Whoever provides your firm with funding will, to some degree, become part of your management team. An equity partner will have direct input into decision-making—a lender doesn't have this access. As stated before, a lender may require personal guarantees and performance measures. These requirements may feel like a lender has decision-making abilities.

Company returns. Equity partners will likely expect your venture to generate after-tax annual profits of 35 to 45 percent on the equity they invested. Creditors are only concerned with your ability to generate pre-tax cash flow to cover periodic interest expenses on the debt.

Funding amount. Equity partners can provide your firm with more up-front capital to allow you to fund all the projects necessary to achieve your growth objective. What a lender can fund is based solely on your ability to make loan installments, and that will likely be quite small early on in the life of your business.

Payments. Equity doesn't get "paid back" each month or each quarter—it represents partners in the firm. But lenders will expect loan repayment to begin the month after you close escrow on the loan.

Maturity. Equity partners have no guarantees on when they may get their funds plus a (hefty) return out of your business. It could be after an acquisition, a subsequent round of funding or the IPO. Creditors, however, are removed from the balance sheet at a set date upon the final payment on the loan.

Restrictions. Both funding types can require contractual terms that limit your use of funds and the types of policies implemented, but lenders often have much more restrictive loan provisions than do equity investors.

You must examine each of these trade-offs in detail before deciding which is best for your firm. Then you can establish a set of funding priorities to guide you in your negotiations with potential equity or debt funding sources.

Review Questions

1. What are the trade-offs entrepreneurs should consider between debt and equity financing?

2. In what situation would you choose debt versus equity? And vice versa?

3. What role does an entrepreneur's aversion to risk play in choosing between debt and equity?

Speaking of Strategy

Terra J. Sinkevicius and S & S Kid Express, Inc.

Terra Sinkevicius is the owner, founder, and CEO of S & S Kid Express, Inc., a transportation service company that buses kids to and from school or after-care centers. She is a wife and mother to one son. Terra has 10 years experience in driving children. She holds a bachelor's degree in liberal arts and science with a minor in Mandarin Chinese from De Paul University in Chicago, and she has completed several business courses associated with her degree, including finance management, business writing, and business psychology. Terra is also the reserves librarian for an academic library in Chicago.

The idea for her business came about because she was fed up with the buses she had used to get her son to school. The yellow buses are suffering through budget cuts, which when mixed with increasing enrollment in many school districts, makes them more of a nuisance than anything. And the private companies that she hired to transport her son to school were "incompetent," in her words.

"And I said, the only way I'm going to make sure that he can get to school and get picked up is to start my own company," said Sinkevicius.

So she created a business plan for the company as a class project, took it to a bank for a loan, and was denied. "I knew it would get denied," she said. But the lender did give her nearly 20 recommendations for improving her business plan. She then tweaked the plan and worked with Accion Chicago, a small business lender, for three months before getting it [her loan] approved in June.

That is when she went out and got her "babies," the two buses that currently anchor her transportation service. She also hired drivers (called field managers because of their added responsibility for marketing, selling, and supervising) and has built an extensive client list, which is growing quickly. "I've been getting calls every day because of the flyers and word-of-mouth," she said, "And that's really big because that's how you grow; that's where the expansion will come from.

"Our mission is to provide safe, reliable, quality transportation services to school age children with or without special needs, who are traveling from home to school, from school to home or after-care programs. The initials S & S stand for "Safe & Secure" kids on the roadway.

"We offer competitive rates and operate licensed, bonded, and state-inspected small buses customarily used by Yellow School Bus Companies. Each child is treated with respect and dignity by our company drivers, and is safely secured before and during any road trip."

Her hope is to buy more buses in the future and expand the area she can cover. It is an excellent start for someone who is a student, full-time worker, entrepreneur, and parent. "One thing that appeals to me about this kind of business is that I don't have to quit my day job to do it," Sinkevicius said.

One would think it would be very time consuming to do all that and raise a child. "Not yet," she says, with a laugh.

SOURCE: Reprinted from *Epicentre,* Newsletter of the Coleman Entrepreneurship Center at DePaul University, Autumn 2004. Used with permission.

Understanding the Financing Stages Along the Life Cycle of the Business[6]

One of the ways to understand all the different financing stages that a business may go through during its life cycle is to imagine your business emerging on a timeline. At the initial stages, you are at the opportunity identification and evaluation stage. As your opportunity develops around a sound business model and strategy, your business begins to gain legitimacy and credibility, especially in the eyes of investors and lenders. As part of their agreements with you, they may determine a number of milestones and goals/objectives that need to be made prior to additional investment.

The first stage is the *seed* stage: The focus is on evaluating the opportunity, and typical activities of the entrepreneur include doing the prior market and industry analysis, developing and enhancing the product/service, and assembling a management team. Most of the funding in this stage is from personal savings, contributions of friends and family members, and, in many cases, the use of personal credit cards.

The next stage is called *Series A* and usually comes when the business is in launch mode. In many cases, the firm has seen its first revenues but is not profitable. Firms at this stage have demonstrated market potential and are ready to look for external investors.

After the launch of the business, when the model and strategy have proven successful, firms then move into the *Series B* stage. At this time, funding is needed to hire more management and staff, to develop and enhance the operational and marketing plan, and to begin to seek alliances with other firms that would complement the founding firm's product/service offering. External and outside investors can also be critical during this stage in bringing in additional funding as well as expertise to the business.

Beyond Series B stage, the firm may also look into securing a line of credit from a commercial bank, especially when sales and revenues are starting to grow. The business most likely needs working capital because monthly cash flow is often at the breakeven point. Investors are usually not involved at this stage. Assistance from the bank allows the business to further expand its operations, but both profits and lines of credit are not enough to support the development of assets and other internal processes and capabilities needed to maintain a stronger revenue base. The firm at this stage is ready for a *Series C* round, which will allow the business to expand its operation and to command a significant competitive position within its respective industry.

Most emerging ventures go from seed to Series B stages, and then owners make plans to sell or to make an initial public offering (IPO) of common stock (to be discussed in future chapters). Those who don't sell or make an IPO usually take on short-term debt, referred to as "mezzanine" or "bridge" financing. This debt is used to support or sustain additional growth opportunities while the firm prepares for an acquisition, an IPO, or even a management buyout. In some cases, ventures have a separate *Series D* round (even rounds E, F, and G) to grow their firms before considering a mezzanine or bridge round.

While the business transits from one stage to another, it will need to be reassessed. More rounds of financing carry the risk that the entrepreneur's control and stake in the business will be overly diluted. Careful consideration is required at each stage based on the overall business strategy, growth opportunities and plans, and the firm's exit strategy.

Speaking of Strategy

Paul White, Novazone

Novazone Inc. was not a thriving business when Paul White joined it in late 2003. In fact, the company had cash-flow problems that threatened to quash the launch of its new ozone-sterilization devices. To buy the business and turn it around, White needed substantial capital resources. He also needed investors who could see past the present situation and buy into his vision of Novazone as a world-class supplier of high-end industrial equipment.

"Novazone had customers like Procter & Gamble, Coca Cola, Colgate-Palmolive and Neutrogena," says White, 43, now president and CEO. "But the company was perpetually running out of money."

The risks were enormous when he offered to buy the struggling company, but so was the upside potential. White bought the company at a relatively low price but had to convince investors that it was worth much more. "What we did was fairly complex," admits White, who jumped into entrepreneurship after several years as a venture capitalist for Fremont Ventures in San Francisco.

To get money in the door quickly, White offered a series of convertible bridge loans to angel investors. These loans allowed White to purchase the company without giving up any ownership until the company's health improved. In other words, White borrowed money from investors with the promise to convert it into company stock at a later-determined price. The loan arrangement bridged the gap between when White needed the cash and when he could reposition the company with stronger sales and a higher valuation.

Right on Time

For entrepreneurs, a key benefit of bridge financing is the time it buys between investment and valuation, according to Peter Townshend, a partner at law firm Allen Matkins Leck Gamble

& Mallory LLP in Del Mar Heights, California. Townshend, who specializes in preparing the legal documents companies need when they bring on new investors, says he has been preparing more bridge loans lately.

The purpose of the loan is to get a little bit of money in when it's needed most. That money typically comes from smaller investors, such as angels. "Entrepreneurs will try to get money in quickly from supportive parties who might not have enough money to make a round," says Townshend. He also likes the flexibility of convertible bridge loans. "For a company that's not in the position to raise bank debt, there hasn't been much between a bank loan and pure equity capital," Townshend says. In his opinion, the convertible note is the perfect middle ground: "It's quick to close and can be as easy as a single loan document."

The loans are short term—typically six months to two years, according to Townshend, and by definition are meant to be converted into stock rather than repaid.

Rewarding Investor Risk

If this sounds like the answer to your financing prayers, be warned: Bridge loans make some investors queasy. "For the investor, it's a little like buying a car without knowing how much it costs," Townshend explains. To overcome investors' apprehension, companies typically make it very attractive for investors to take that additional risk. Terms on bridge loans can include not just interest, but also "warrant coverage"—essentially a free grant of stock options that can be exercised later.

"[Investors want to] earn a little interest on their loans—maybe 5 percent—but they'll also earn a discount on the eventual stock purchase. Or they'll get additional warrants—maybe 25 percent warrant coverage," Townshend says. That would give a $100,000 investor the option to purchase another $25,000 worth of stock at the same discounted price, but at a later time— perhaps as much as five years later. At Novazone, early investors who entered into convertible notes were treated to interest, warrants and a discount on the eventual stock price. All in all, individual investors lent the company more than $3 million—enough for White to buy the company, with plenty left over for working capital and new marketing efforts.

Sales started pouring in immediately. By the third quarter, Novazone's sales pipeline had grown 250 percent. By late 2004, Novazone was profitable, with annual sales approaching $10 million.

The Conversion

As White had hoped, Novazone's rapid growth began to attract the attention of venture firms, which led to a large VC investment and the conversion of the loans into stock within the year.

"That was the tricky part," White recalls. When a VC firm started to negotiate a major investment into Novazone, some of the original terms of the bridge loan were called into question. The firm complained that White had given up too much to the loan holders. Fortunately, those loan holders knew what a great deal they were getting and were willing to compromise. "There was a lot of room for renegotiation," says White. "In the end, everybody took a cut—the note-holders included. But they all bought into the idea that it was the right thing for the company."

(Continued)

(Continued)

On paper, the original investors (that is, lenders) were rewarded with exceptional returns on their money. "It was only on paper—a conversion return," says White, "but it was unanimous that it was a good deal for the angel investors."

The Right Fit

Who should make use of convertible bridge notes? Entrepreneurs who are raising money from less sophisticated investors should certainly consider it, says Townshend. "It's perfect for the rich uncle who has no idea what the right price is for equity. He wants to put money in now and leave the negotiations to a more sophisticated investor."

Although it is rare for institutions to use bridge notes, the process is so straightforward that Townshend expects even professional investors to begin using them more in the future. "Eventually, bridge rounds may replace equity rounds completely," he predicts.

That would certainly be welcome news for entrepreneurs. Convertible bridge loans make very good sense for entrepreneurs who can do a lot with a little: When the initial money can be used, as in Novazone's case, to rapidly improve a company's position or value, the entrepreneur stands to benefit from a higher valuation for the company. The best part? Bridge loans are relatively simple documents. While you'll still want an attorney involved in drafting the document, taking money through a bridge note is not nearly as complicated as selling stock in the company.

Nonetheless, Townshend warns entrepreneurs not to use convertible notes indiscriminately. Company owners should not mislead bridge investors about the company's plans to raise additional money and convert the loan to stock. Convertible bridges should only be used when a major financial event—like a larger round of equity fund raising—is on the horizon.

As Townshend puts it, "The trick is not to let your bridge turn into a pier."

SOURCE: David Worrell, "Bridge the Gap: When Risks Are High and Cash Needs Are Immediate, a Convertible Bridge Note Provides a Solution Everyone Can Live With," *Entrepreneur*, May 2005, http://www.Entrepreneur.com/article/0,4621,320957,00.html Copyright © 2005, Entrepreneur.com; all rights reserved. Republished with permission from Entrepreneur.com.

Further Descriptions of the Common Sources of Financing From a Debt Perspective[7]

There are several sources to consider when looking for financing. It is important to explore all of your options before making a decision.

Personal savings: The primary source of capital for most new businesses comes from savings and other personal resources. While credit cards are often used to finance business needs, there are usually better options available, even for very small loans.

Friends and relatives: Many entrepreneurs look to private sources such as friends and family when starting out in a business venture. Money is often loaned interest-free or at a low interest rate, which can be beneficial when getting started.

Commercial banks: The most common sources of funding, banks and credit unions, will provide a loan if you can show that your business plan is sound. The principal types of loans available from a commercial bank include:

Working-capital lines of credit are the most common form of secured loan available to growing businesses. They are tied directly to the receivables or inventory levels of the borrowing company. These loans provide funds that can increase as sales increase, while providing the bank with collateral that can easily be liquidated (that is, turned into cash in case of default on the loan).

Working-capital financing is normally contracted for a year and may be renewed for additional periods by the lender. The borrowing arrangement will have a stated maximum amount and will be limited to an agreed-on percentage of the assets being pledged as collateral. The interest rate on these lines of credit will usually be variable and fluctuate with the prime rate. There are two primary types of working-capital lines:

Accounts-receivable financing is certainly considered a source of financing but is arguably not the most attractive option. Accounts-receivable financing takes a company's best receivables at a significant discount and, consequently, outsources a firm's receivables. Usually, the indirect (customer satisfaction) and direct cost (discount) of receivable financing outweighs the benefit of immediate cash flow. Therefore, most businesses seek alternative forms of financing. Traditionally, accounts-receivable financing has been employed primarily by large textile companies and is usually limited to between 75 and 85 percent of the eligible receivables balances (typically receivables less than 90 days old). Thus, when sales are made, a significant portion of the unpaid invoice can immediately be converted into cash. As amounts are collected from the customer by the company, the loan is paid down or new receivables are pledged as collateral for the loan. Receivables financing thus provides a revolving line of credit in which funds are continually advanced, repaid, and readvanced. The key factors in obtaining receivables financing are determining the receivables that are eligible for the loan and the percentage that will be advanced. The bank will conduct a thorough investigation of your business, reviewing such items as your customers' credit histories, the types of receivables, and the quality of the accounts. The better the condition of your receivables (e.g., a small number of accounts outstanding more than 90 days and good customer credit ratings), the more the company will be allowed to borrow against those accounts. You should have a credit résumé for each of your customers to aid in this process.

Inventory financing, like accounts-receivable financing, provides a revolving line of credit. Funds are advanced to the company on the basis of a certain percentage of eligible raw material and finished-goods inventories. Advances are generally not made on work-in-process inventory because of its unfinished state and limited liquidation value. Because inventories are less "liquid" assets than accounts receivable, the amount advanced under an inventory loan is not as great as in the case of a receivables loan. Amounts advanced under an inventory loan vary dramatically with the nature of the inventory, ranging from 30 to 70 percent of the value. On some sophisticated inventories that would be hard to dispose of, lenders may be unwilling to lend at all. Inventory loans come due as the products are sold; thus, they are often used in tandem with a receivables line of credit to provide financing until proceeds of the sale are collected. Inventory financing presents special problems for both borrower and lender. The latter must ascertain the liquidation value of the inventory and be assured that it is secured in a safe location before advancing funds. Therefore, there may be additional administrative procedures, such as monthly reports and calculation of obsolescence rates, turnover rates, and gross profit margins, to justify the borrowing base. In addition, improved procedures for controlling the inventory may have to be implemented, sometimes even to the extent of locating inventories in independent bonded warehouses, to satisfy the bank's conditions.

Equipment term loans provide a company with funds to purchase new equipment, or they may be used to obtain cash by borrowing against the appraised value of equipment already owned. From 60 to 80 percent of the equipment value may be borrowed with this kind of loan (so the company will have to make a down payment with its own cash). By not loaning on the entire value of the equipment, the bank improves its ability to recover its investment in case of default. These loans are generally repaid in monthly or quarterly installments over one to five years (a period that reflects the expected life of the equipment). Interest rates may be fixed or variable, depending on the bank and the credit situation of the borrower. Borrowers are often given an equipment line of credit, allowing them to purchase various pieces of equipment over an agreed-on period of time without making a separate loan agreement for each item.

Equipment leasing is increasingly being used as a method of financing. Equipment leases provided by commercial banks are generally long-term rather than short-term leases. The bank purchases the equipment needed and enters into a noncancelable agreement to lease it. The payments required may be sufficient to cover the cost of the equipment and financing; the lease payment may even be variable and fluctuate with the prime rate. Even though the bank owns the equipment, the user, or lessee, is usually responsible for the insurance, maintenance, and any associated taxes.

A *financing lease,* or *capital lease,* on the other hand, is treated as a borrowing, and the lessee is considered the owner of the equipment. A financing lease usually provides for the sale of the asset to the lessee at a nominal or prearranged price. Regardless of the type of agreement, the advantage usually sought in equipment leasing is that 100 percent of the cost of the equipment can be financed. However, the bank may require you to maintain a security deposit equal to 20 to 30 percent of the equipment cost, which would negate this advantage. Depending on whether this deposit pays you interest and when it can be freed up, leasing may still be a more attractive alternative than a term loan.

Commercial real estate loans and commercial term loans. Commercial real-estate loans usually extend from 10 to 25 years and provide up to 75 percent of the property value. These loans are comparable to mortgages on residential property. Interest rates are usually fixed, and payments are made monthly. The payments may fully amortize the loan, or there may be a balance still unpaid at the end, called a balloon payment, which must be either paid off or refinanced. If the value of your real estate has appreciated since it was purchased, you can convert that into cash by obtaining a second mortgage. A second means just that—the lender is second in line for the collateral in case of a default. Thus, the interest rate on a second mortgage is normally higher than on a first.

Commercial term loans are often given to firms with strong financial histories. With this type of loan, there is no direct relationship between the amount of the loan and an individual asset of the company (unlike working-capital financing). However, the assets of the company are generally pledged as collateral. Banks monitor these loans by requiring the company to maintain certain financial ratios. If these loan covenants are not met, the bank can call the loan (require immediate repayment). Loan covenants are individually negotiated and may cover such items as working capital levels, the current ratio (ratio of current assets to current liabilities), the debt-to-equity ratio, future profitability, and levels of equity. They may also restrict payment of dividends, additional borrowings, or capital expenditures without having prior bank approval. If the financial position of the company is extremely solid, the bank may be willing to make these loans on an unsecured basis (that is, with no collateral).

Short-term commercial loans are usually written for a period of from 30 to 90 days, primarily to meet seasonal needs, such as a buildup of inventories. These loans are expected to be liquidated once the temporary need is past. Medium- and long-term commercial loans are usually for a period of more than one but not more than 10 years. The amount advanced ranges from 40 to 50 percent of working-capital needs, supplementing any short-term financing. Interest rates vary with the creditworthiness of the applicant and are normally 0 to 4 percent above the prime rate.

Government-guaranteed loans are loans guaranteed against loss to the lender by the Small Business Administration (SBA), an agency of the federal government. The guarantee is for up to 85 percent of a maximum of $150,000 of loan proceeds (75 percent of loans above $150,000 to a maximum of $1 million). Because of the reduced risk of loss, the interest costs on such a loan are usually less than for a comparable commercial loan. However, you must meet specific criteria to be eligible. Normally, personal guarantees are required, and loans are on a secured basis. For a complete description and variety of loan programs offered by the SBA, see their Web site at www.sba.gov.

Revolving lines of credit provide your company with a committed source of money against which it may borrow as long as certain negotiated conditions are met. Like commercial term loans, a line of credit may be collateralized by a general pledge of all of the assets of the company, or it may even be unsecured. It will always involve strict loan covenants. With a revolving line of credit, the borrower may draw the funds as needed, with interest charged only on the outstanding funds. There is usually no defined repayment date, although generally the lines are expected to be repaid in full once a year for at least a 30-day period. Banks typically charge an annual commitment fee of 0.25 to 0.50 percent of the unused portion of the line. Most businesses will get this financing only when they have an established track record.

Failures and Foibles

Truth and Consequences

When physical therapist Jodi Medell opened a running store in Santa Fe, New Mexico, she had time on her side. Her home had sold, and as a result, Medell had a critical ingredient in any start-up financing plan: collateral to secure a loan, the lack of which can ground even the most inspired idea. She also found a supporter in a local banker, a fellow runner who thought Medell's vision was well-suited to the Southwestern town; the nearest such store was an hour away. "Everything fell into place," recalls Medell, 33. "My house was on the market for a while. Right before I desperately needed money for collateral, it sold."

Getting collateral was only half the battle. Although it took just three months from the time she drafted a business plan until she received an SBA loan from a local bank, in that short period, Medell learned the harsh reality of start-up financing. To begin with, she qualified for only two-thirds of her loan request, despite putting up the money from her home, her car and life insurance for collateral. She also had the daunting task of developing a three-year financial plan. Lacking a business background, Medell struggled with the estimates. "It was phenomenal how much paperwork I had to go through," she says. "You spend so much energy trying to get funding that you're wasted before you even open."

The rigors of the credit process didn't end with the launch of her store, The Running Hub. The $98,000 loan was mainly for inventory, and she needed approval before accessing funds. "I had to copy my invoices and send them to the bank so they had proof it was going back into the inventory," says Medell.

Despite the strings attached to her financing, Medell is one of the lucky ones. While there may seem to be a boundless supply of business credit, little is flowing to start-ups. Even SBA dollars generally fund existing companies, not start-ups like Medell's. And other programs for unbankable entrepreneurs have such strict requirements that many people don't qualify.

Complicating the credit search are misconceptions about start-up financing. One of the most common myths is that the strength of a business idea can secure a bank loan when assets are scarce. "My first question is, 'How much do you have [available] to put in?' I make it clear that I will not be their venture capital partner," says John Milbauer, chair of Minnesota's Lino Lakes State Bank, which requires an owner's equity investment of 25 percent of project costs. Unfortunately, entrepreneurs are so obsessed with financing, they often neglect details like critiquing the business plan. Even a banker may not uncover flaws in the strategy, particularly when the borrower is a strong contender in terms of credit history and collateral. "If people have good credit and are willing to put up their house, they will get the loan," says Therese Flaherty, director of the Wharton Small Business Development Center in Philadelphia, "but they may not be able to generate the payback."

There was no danger of Jamila Payne, 26, falling into that trap. Payne was a recent college graduate when she launched a mail order clothing business, Milla by Mail Direct. Without collateral, traditional credit sources were out of reach. But instead of plunging headfirst into a frustrating credit search, she planned her business to the smallest detail. By the time Payne needed a loan, she had incorporated her company, drafted a business plan and saved $8,000. Impressed with her initiative, a nonprofit lending group accepted her in its program for entrepreneurs 30 and younger. Payne got $15,000 and completed a 10-week training program, an invaluable experience for the young business owner.

SOURCE: Crystal Detamore-Rodman, "Don't Waste Your Time Looking for Money in All the Wrong Places: Here's the Truth About Startup Financing," *Entrepreneur's Be Your Own Boss*, October 2003, http://www.entrepreneur.com/mag/article/0,1539,311169,00.html Copyright © 2003 Entrepreneur, all rights reserved. Republished with permission from Entrepreneur.

Review Questions

1. Discuss the financing options at each stage of the business life cycle.

2. What are the most common sources of financing? Cite the costs/benefits of the various funding sources.

3. What are the advantages of seeking bridge or mezzanine loans?

Preparing Your Information for the Lender

If you do decide to pursue debt financing and have targeted a lender interested in your business and its strategy (i.e., reviewed business plan, held preliminary discussions on type of loan), the lender will most likely request the following information:

- Copies of tax returns, for both the company and yourself
- Explanations of significant variances in past operating results
- Most recent financial results
- Revised financial projections, using assumptions requested by the lender
- Names of customers, suppliers, and business consultants who can be contacted by the lender
- Copies of important corporate documents, such as existing loan and stock agreements, minutes of board of directors meetings, and major contracts

To review an example of a loan request package, go to http://www.redfcu.org/forms/business_loan_packet.pdf.

When reviewing a loan request, the lender is primarily concerned about repayment. To help determine its likelihood, many loan officers will order a copy of your business credit report from a credit reporting agency. Therefore, you should work with these agencies to make sure they present an accurate picture of your business. Using the credit report and the information you have provided, the lending officer will consider the following issues:

- Have you invested savings or personal equity in your business totaling at least 25 percent to 50 percent of the loan you are requesting? Remember, no lender or investor will finance 100 percent of your business.
- Do you have a sound record of credit worthiness as indicated by your credit report, work history, and letters of recommendation? This is very important.
- Do you have sufficient experience and training to operate a successful business?
- Have you prepared a loan proposal and business plan that demonstrate your understanding of and commitment to the success of the business?
- Does the business have sufficient cash flow to make the monthly payments?

Selecting the Lender

As you discuss your loan request with potential lenders, you should be evaluating their suitability to your needs at the same time. Important items to consider include the following:

- Responsiveness to credit needs. Can the lender respond quickly as your credit needs change?
- Reliable source of credit. Can the lender continue to supply your needs as you grow or if there is a slight downturn in your business?
- Knowledge of your business. Do the people who will work on your account understand your business and its industry?
- Decision-making authority. Who makes the ultimate decision on your loan request?
- Experienced personnel. Can the people on your account offer constructive advice?

Review Questions

1. What factors will loan officers consider when they review your loan package application?

2. Why is it important for an entrepreneur to interview a banker and understand the culture?

3. What analysis and preparation should be done by an entrepreneur to prepare a winning loan application?

Equity Investors: Angel Investors and Venture Capital Firms

These individuals and firms help expanding companies grow in exchange for equity or partial ownership and usually have stringent requirements for investing. Generally, they are as follows:

- The business must have a strong management team.
- The business must have definite growth opportunities.
- The business should have some unique characteristic, such as special technology, patents, or key individuals.
- The potential growth of the business must be reasonably predictable within a given time.
- The potential for gain must be greater than the associated risk.
- If a company meets these criteria, it should consider seeking venture capital financing.

On the angel investment side, these investors characteristically make informal arrangements; do not finance ventures as a profession; are not family, founders, or friends; and usually invest in businesses located close to their homes. Angels are often individuals who have succeeded in the same or a related industry or have been service providers to smaller or newer businesses, such as attorneys or accountants. It is common for angels to want some nonfinancial rewards, for instance, to develop a rewarding relationship with the entrepreneur and to serve in some sort of consultation role. Angels prefer to find competent and trustworthy entrepreneurs and to work with the founders in the business's early start-up stages by infusing seed money or first-stage funding. Angels' behaviors, practices, and points of entrance into the funding cycle are complementary to many of venture capitalists' habits.

Entrepreneurs gain access to angels through capital intermediaries and business brokers or by connections into informal networks, frequently composed of service providers or successful business founders. For some business owners, the nature of the approach to angel capitalists is at times a drawback. Whether the initial access to the angel is direct or indirect, the entrepreneur should seek legal advice in reference to securities laws before any overtures are made or conversations take place. Angel capital has the "patience money" feature. Angels show more flexibility in both the holding term and the liquidity of their investments. Angels appear in many guises, but most often, they are successful, middle-aged individuals. Angels pool their resources occasionally to act as a group of investors rather than individually, but the angel-type preferences and behaviors hold true whether the deals are made by one person or a consortium. To locate angels, check the directory on the Angel Capital Association Web site, www.angelcapitalassociation.org. For assistance in forming an angel group in your community, contact the Kauffman Foundation: www.kauffman.org.

Speaking of Strategy

An Interview With Kathleen Elliott, Angel Investor

What are the top three mistakes entrepreneurs make when approaching angel investors?

Mistake 1: Entrepreneurs enter into the funding process without adequate knowledge of the types of companies that are likely to be attractive to angel investors.

Like any investor, angel investors invest in order to achieve a return on their investment. This implies that a company should be in an attractive and growing industry, will demonstrate rapid growth, have a scalable business model, and achieve a significant level of revenue and profit in five years, or so, that will enable the investor to have a positive return on their investment. This implies that the entrepreneur understands the concept of an "exit strategy." Furthermore, angels invest in order to *grow* a company; they are not investing to pay off accumulated debts or deferred salaries of founders.

(Continued)

(Continued)

There is something very alluring to entrepreneurs about the concept of angel investing (and rightly so—who wouldn't want a white knight in the form of an angel helping you to grow your company?) But the truth is that probably less than 5 percent of all businesses attract outside capital. Therefore, entrepreneurs should self-select early on in the process of building their company to determine whether they are building the type of company that would appeal to an angel investor. Otherwise, they will waste a lot of time barking up the wrong tree wooing investors who are unlikely to invest in their company, when their time could be much better spent building their business.

Mistake 2: Focusing too much on "valuation"—the value that an outside investor assigns to your company.

If, in fact, your company is attractive to outside investors, the next step is to place a value on your enterprise. In the early stages of a company, this is more art than science. It is a process of estimation based on future potential and is subject to negotiation between the entrepreneur and the investor. There is typically no public information on this for an entrepreneur to benchmark against, as the investors base valuation numbers on other deals they see and the projected rate of return. Often times, entrepreneurs will get hung up on the fact that they do not think the investor is putting an appropriately high enough value on the enterprise and negotiations will break down.

For an early stage company, its valuation is not the most important piece of the equation. Finding an investor who will help you to grow your company and build value is much more important than an arbitrary number.

Mistake 3: Not owning the financials.

Most entrepreneurs start a company based on their technical expertise. Their backgrounds typically are not steeped in sophisticated financial analysis. So, when the time comes to put together revenue forecasts and financial statements to present to investors, entrepreneurs rely on the help of others, and may not spend the amount of time necessary in understanding and believing in the numbers that are being presented, and more important, the assumptions that are behind the forecasts. Understand your forecasts, know the numbers, know what is do-able and achievable; otherwise you will find that those hard-sought meetings with investors will quickly spiral out of your control. Related to this is not having a well-thought out marketing plan and knowing who your target customers are and how they make decisions.

I have to add another issue, and that is communication. If an entrepreneur raises an early round of capital, it is quite likely that more rounds of funding will follow. Your current investors are your best source for follow-on investment, as well as introductions to other investors. If they do not hear from you on a regular basis, are not kept up to date on your progress, or are not fully informed when things fall below expectations, you will have a very hard time cultivating them to invest more funds, or to make important introductions to other sources of capital.

What "homework" and preparation should be done before approaching an angel?

This relates to understanding the process (as mentioned). Know what investors' hot buttons are. Learn the investment lingo, such as exit strategy, pre and post money valuation, liquidation preferences, etc. Know who your customer is and how they make purchasing decisions.

Seek out other entrepreneurs who have raised outside funding and ask them about the process. You should seek out a mentor or adviser who is familiar with your industry space and has had experience in raising outside capital.

When you meet with an investor, know who you are meeting with, what is their industry background, what other types of companies have they invested in. Seek out entrepreneurs who know your potential investor to get a sense of how they will work with you in building your company. You could be starting what will be a very long relationship, so make sure the chemistry is right.

On the future of angel financing. . . .

It has been my understanding that angel funding has been larger than [venture capital] funding by a factor of two to three times over the past several years.

As venture capital funds grow larger, it implies that venture capital will operate even more so in the rarefied world of Google-type companies—the billion-dollar blockbusters.

About Kathleen Elliott

Kathy is a co-author of the best-selling "how to" book for aspiring women entrepreneurs entitled, *The Old Girls' Network: Insider Advice for Women Building Businesses in a Man's World* (Basic Books, August 2003). She serves as a board member of *The Capital Network (TCN)*, formerly the Technology Capital Network at MIT, a nonprofit organization that matches entrepreneurs with investors and provides educational forums for entrepreneurs. She was a Forum Committee member for Springboard/New England, a venture capital conference for women entrepreneurs, and a Steering Committee member of the Commonwealth Institute's Emerging Women Entrepreneurs Program, an innovative program that helps women entrepreneurs launch high-tech companies. She helped to start 8Wings, which was an angel investment group focused on investing in women-led companies.

SOURCE: Interview with Kathleen Elliott conducted by Jill Kickul, December 10, 2005. Printed with permission.

Research in Practice: Venture Capitalists and Angels

Venture capitalists and angel capitalists exhibit great differences in their approaches to evaluating risk and to avoiding risk. Venture capitalists' combined sets of expectations and attitudes may explain, at least partially, the complex deal structures that exist in terms of timing, exit strategies, and debt and equity provisions (for a description of defining a deal, see explanatory term sheet in Appendix A). Venture capitalists make investments as professionals who focus on initial public offerings for the enterprises they choose, with clear exit strategies in place from the beginning. In 2004, the software and biotechnology industry sectors captured 24 percent and 19 percent, respectively, of venture capital investment. Other industries also gaining momentum are the medical devices and equipment, semiconductors, and networking and equipment sector. Figure 6.1 shows the number of companies receiving venture capital from 1997 to 2004, and Figure 6.2 provides the amount invested by venture capitalists in these firms (data from National Venture Capital Association, PricewaterhouseCoopers, Thomson Venture Economics).

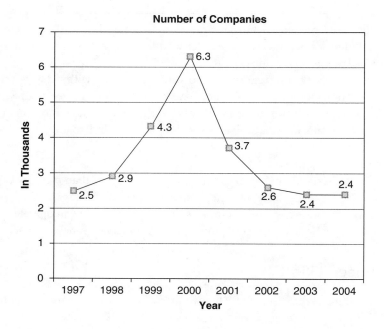

Figure 6.1   Investments, Venture Capital, Number of Companies

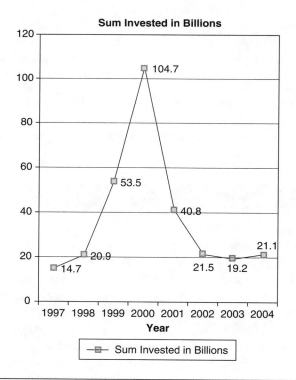

Figure 6.2   Investments, Venture Capital, Billions of Dollars

Strategic Reflection Point

Perspectives on Raising Venture Capital

There is no doubt that it is a nearly impossible time for entrepreneurs to raise venture capital. Weak public capital markets have sidelined many venture capital fund managers, leading most of these investors to focus exclusively on follow-on financings to existing portfolio companies. Only the "best of the best" new companies are attracting such funding and usually with tougher terms and lower valuations than they would have seen a few years ago. The process is also likely to take a lot longer than ever before.

Accordingly, entrepreneurs need to prepare themselves when approaching venture capitalists. Always an important factor, preparation has become critical today. Increasingly, several "must have" factors have become an essential part of the necessary preparation. In short, an entrepreneur whose goal when approaching venture capitalists is to be funded must have:

A Dress Rehearsal. You need to rehearse your presentation many times, using a "moot court," with different audiences asking different questions and replicating the actual meeting you will have with the managers of the venture capital firm. Make sure your rehearsal audiences, such as lawyers, accountants, business school professors, and entrepreneurs who have raised venture capital, have the background and training to ask the right questions—including the tough ones—and are able to evaluate your responses critically. Do your homework on the venture capital firm and learn what the "hot buttons" may be so you can address key issues in your presentation. As the saying goes, "You never get a second chance to make a first impression." The rehearsals will help you survive the first meeting and get to the next steps. Be prepared for the tough questions and don't be scared, intimidated or upset when the really hard ones start flying at you. If the team at the venture capital firm doesn't ask tough questions, they are not "engaged" in your presentation. If they are not engaged enough to beat you up a little, then there will probably be no next steps and no deal.

A Mentor. It's always helpful to have a venture-capitalist coach who has either raised such funding or who has advised on or negotiated venture-capital transactions. The mentor or coach can help you stay focused on the issues that are important to the venture capitalist and not waste his or her time. The mentor can reassure you during the difficult and time-consuming process and teach you to remain patient, optimistic and level headed about the risks and challenges you face.

A Detailed Game Plan. Prepare a specific presentation that isn't too long or too short—usually 15 minutes is about right. Don't attempt to "read" every word of your business plan or put every historical fact of your company on a Power Point slide. Keep it crisp and focused and be prepared for questions and to defend your strategic assumptions and financial forecasts. Remember that every minute counts. Even the small talk at the beginning of the meeting is important, because the seasoned venture capitalist is sizing you up, learning about your interests and looking for the chemistry and the glue that is key to a successful relationship.

Your Team Available to Meet the Venture Capitalist. Don't overlook the "personal" component of the evaluation. In many cases it can be the most important factor considered in the final decision. The four "Cs"—camaraderie, communication, commitment and control (over your ego)—may make or break the outcome of the meeting. Any experienced venture capitalist will tell you that, at the end of the day, the decision depends upon the strength of the people who will be there day to day to execute and manage the company. The venture capitalist will look for a

(Continued)

(Continued)

management team that is educated, dedicated, and experienced, and, ideally, one that has experienced some success as a team prior to this venture. The team should also be balanced, with complementary skills and talents, so that all critical areas of business management are covered—from finance to marketing and sales to technical expertise.

Passion, Not Rose-Colored Glasses. Many entrepreneurs fail to make a good impression in their initial meeting with the venture capitalist because they come on too strong or not strong enough. The experienced venture capitalist wants to see that you have a passion and commitment to your company and to the execution of the business plan. However, the investor does not want to be oversold or have to deal with an entrepreneur who is so enamored of an idea or plan that he or she can't grasp its flaws or understand its risks.

A Way to Demonstrate Personal Commitment. All venture capitalists will look to measure your personal sense of commitment to the business and its future. Generally, venture capitalists won't invest if an entrepreneur's commitment is only part-time or his or her loyalty [is] divided among other activities or ventures. In addition to fidelity to the venture, the investor will look for self-confidence, a high energy level, a commitment to achievement and leadership, and a creative approach to problem solving. You will also have to demonstrate your personal financial commitment by investing virtually all of your own resources into the project before you can ask others to part with their resources. Remember, any aspect of your personal life, whether good, bad or seemingly irrelevant, may be of interest to the venture capitalist in the interview and due diligence process. Don't get defensive or be surprised when the range of questions is as broad as it is deep—venture capitalists are merely trying to predict the future by learning as much as possible about your past and current situation.

An Open and Honest Exchange of Information. One sure deal killer for venture capitalists involves your trying to hide something from your past or downplaying a previous business failure. These seasoned investors can and will learn about any skeletons in your closet during the due diligence process and will walk away from the deal if they find something that should have been disclosed at the outset. A candid, straightforward channel of communication is critical. A previous business failure may be viewed as a sign of experience, provided you can demonstrate that you've learned from your mistakes and figured out ways to avoid them in the future. On a related note, you must demonstrate a certain degree of flexibility and versatility in your approach to implementing your business plan. Venture capitalists may have ideas about the strategic direction of the company and will want to see that you are open-minded and receptive to their suggestions. If you are too rigid or too stubborn, they may view this as a sign of immaturity or that you are a person with whom compromise will be difficult. Either can be a major "turn-off" and a good excuse for them to walk away.

A Big Market and a Big Upside. Make sure your business plan and your presentation adequately demonstrates the size of your potential market and the financial rewards and healthy margins that strong demand will bring to the bottom line. A venture capitalist that suspects your product or service has a narrow market, limited demand and thin margins will almost always walk away from the deal. If your target market is mature, with a number of already established competitors, the venture capitalist may feel the opportunity is limited and will not produce the financial returns that they expect. In short, these investors are looking for a company that has a sustainable competitive advantage, demonstrated by a balanced mix of products and services that meet a new market need on both a domestic and overseas basis. Remember that most venture capitalists want a return of 60% to 80% for seed and early-stage or post-launch deals and at least 25% to 35% on latter-stage and mezzanine-level investments. An entrepreneur's business plan and presentation must demonstrate that the venture capitalists' money will be better served in your company than in other investments.

An Understanding of What Really Motivates the Venture Capitalist's Decision. David Gladstone, a seasoned venture capitalist and author of the *Venture Capital Handbook,* writes: "I'll back you if you have a good idea that will make money for both of us." That one sentence captures the essence of the venture capitalist's decision-making process. You must have a good idea—one that is articulated in a business plan that expresses the risks and opportunities and how your management team will influence the odds of success and survival. Then, it must make money for both of you. The venture capitalist wants deals in which both the investor and the entrepreneur can enjoy the upside and the scale isn't weighted in favor of one over the other. Finally, the "I'll back you" component reminds you that in exchange for capital and wisdom, venture capitalists expect to have some control, with "checks and balances" built into the structure of the deal and the governance of the company and protection [built] into the documents, to ensure that their investment and ability to participate in the growth and success of the company are protected.

An Exit Strategy. The saying, "Begin with the end in mind," clearly applies to venture capital deals. Investors aren't looking for a long-term marriage. Rather, they will be focused on how you intend to get their original investment and return on capital back to them within four to six years. Your business plan and oral presentation should include an analysis and an assessment of the likelihood of the three most common exit strategies, namely: an initial public offering (IPO), a sale of the company, and a redemption of the venture capitalist's shares by the company directly. Other exit strategies include restructuring the company, licensing the company's intellectual property, finding a replacement investor, or even liquidating the company.

So there you have it: a list of the 10 "musts" that you, the entrepreneur, must have in order to prepare for your encounter with the venture capitalist investor, an encounter that could be a critical factor toward setting your company on the path of considerable growth. Study the "must have" list carefully. Then gather together all the musts to assure that you've prepared properly to achieve the goal of securing funding.

SOURCE: Used with Permission, Andrew J. Sherman, Partner, Dickstein Shapiro Morin & Oshinsky LLP, April 1, 2003, http://eventuring.kauffman.org/eShip/appmanager/eVenturing/eVenturingDesktop?_nfpb= true&_pageLabel=eShip_articleDetail&_nfls=false&id=Entrepreneurship/Resource/Resource_293.htm

A Due Diligence Checklist

Below is an example of the many questions and level of analysis an investor may go through in examining your business venture.

- What is the company's corporate structure? C Corporation, S Corporation, LLC, or LP? Does this model allow for a liquidity event and/or return on investment?
- Is there an exit strategy?
- Is the corporate structure overly complicated? If so, why, and might it be simplified?

(Continued)

(Continued)

- How many existing shareholders? Too numerous, and, if so, why?
- Does the corporate structure fit with the business model?
- Does the corporate structure allow for growth?
- What is the founder share allocation? Do they have a large enough stake to have the incentive to succeed, but not so large as to ignore board and other advisors? Is the founders' stock vested over time?
- Who is on the board of directors? Do they have the right background for the company? Are there a sufficient number of outside directors? How are board members compensated?
- Does the company have a board of advisors and, if so, who is on the board? Do the advisors actively participate in the company's development? How are advisors compensated?
- Has the company been involved in any litigation or been threatened with litigation?
- Does the company have all required permits and licenses?

Financial Assumptions

- Has the company completed one-, three- and five-year financial projections?
- Have the financial documents been properly developed according to applicable accounting rules?
- Has the company used an outside, independent accounting firm to compile, review, or audit financials?
- How good are the assumptions? (rate of growth, acceptance rate, pricing, multiple revenue streams, costs)
- Are revenues realistic?
- When does the company reach cash flow positive, and what cash requirements will it take to get there?
- Has the company already received funding, and, if so, how much; what are pre-money valuation and terms?
- What are the follow-on funding requirements and sources? Has the company properly anticipated future needs, and is it already working on those?
- Have all tax returns been properly filed?
- What is the company's debt carry? What are the ratios?
- Is the company's current valuation aligned with its current stage of development and market potential?

Market Assessment

- Does the company's product or service address a new or existing market?
- Is the product or service platform-based, with the opportunity for additional products or services? Or is this potentially a one-trick pony?
- Does the company have a well-thought-out sales and marketing plan?
- Does the company have key relationships in place, or is it working on the same, with marketing and/or sales partners?
- Does the company have or need key joint venture relationships?
- Is the company focused on the appropriate market development, or are they trying to do too much at one time?

- Have they chosen the right first market?
- Does their product or service represent a market push or pull?
- What is the potential market size?
- Have they conducted thorough market research to support their financial assumptions, revenue model, and valuation?
- What is their stage of development? Concept, alpha, beta, or shipping?
- If the company has already introduced its product or service into the market, what is the number of current and potential customers?
- What is the length of its sales cycle?
- What are the channels of distribution?
- Does the company's product or service have a seasonal aspect?
- Is this a stable market and are COGS stable?

Competitive Analysis

- Who are the company's competitors?
- Has the company realistically assessed its competitors?
- What is the company's market differentiator? Is this enough to make them superior to competition from the customer's perspective?
- Is this a market or product consolidation?
- How entrenched are the competitors?
- What is the financial stability of competitors?
- What does the market share look like?
- How will this company win?
- Has the company done a detailed feature-by-feature analysis?

Management Team

- What is the caliber pedigree of the team?
- What is the team's overall track record?
- Do they have the combined requisite skills and experience?
- Do they recognize limitations in management, and are they seeking candidates?
- Is the management open to discussion and suggestions on improvement to their business model?
- Has the management team been previously funded?
- How are management and all other employees being compensated?
- Does the company have an option plan, and have options been granted to all employees? What percentage do the founders have as compared to other key management?

Technology Assessment

- Do they have market requirements and functional specifications?
- At what stage is development? Concept, alpha, beta, shipping?
- Does the company have any usability studies?
- Does the company have adequate intellectual-property protection? Does it need it?

(Continued)

(Continued)

- Is the company relying on being first to market, rather than on any IP position, for competitive advantage, and is this realistic?
- What is product quality assurance like?
- Is it proprietary architecture or open-source code?
- Do they have adequate systems in place to identify and protect IP?
- Who in the company is focused on these issues?
- Has the company properly set up relationships and documentation to ensure ownership of all intellectual property?
- Does the company own all necessary intellectual property through internal development or licenses?
- Do any other companies have potential claims to the IP resulting from previous employment relationships or for any other reason?

Operations

- Does the company have an operating plan or outline of the same if early stage?
- Has the company considered all aspects of operation to successfully launch a product or service?
- Does the operating plan anticipate growth? Is anticipated growth realistic?
- Has the company received any citations or notices of violation?
- For more mature companies, does each division of the company have an operating plan, and are they compatible?
- Does management meet regularly to ensure compliance with plan or make needed adjustments?
- Has the company been able to stay on plan?
- Does the plan take into consideration all cash needs and anticipated cash flow?
- Does the company have an alternative plan if assumptions do not hold, such as for product rollout, cash needs, and market response?

Comparables

- Recent IPOs (10Ks, annual reports)
- Recent companies funded in this space
- Third-party (including government) databases, reports, publications, and market analysis
- Comparable financial models

Things to Look Out For

- Unrealistic valuation (or revenue model)
- Affects percentage ownership
- Affects possible subsequent rounds
- May end up with "down-round" on next financing
- Complicated investment terms
- Preferred fine, but be careful of other complicated features such as rights of first refusal; onerous liquidation preferences; registration rights; no lock-ups; co-sale

- Heavy debt
- New investment dollars should be used for advancing the company, not for paying old obligations
- Missing key assumptions about market or financial model
- One-trick pony (one-product or -service company)
- No board per se
- Inexperienced management
- Poor advisors

For the full Due Diligence Checklist, refer to Appendix B.

SOURCE: Checklist reprinted with permission from The Kauffman Foundation, www.kauffman.org (2004), "Angel Investment Groups, Networks, and Funds: A Guidebook to Developing the Right Angel Organization for Your Community." Author: Susan Preston, Kauffman Foundation.

The Innovator's Toolkit: Catching the Investor's Attention

Below is a sample presentation outline which you may find helpful as you prepare your presentation:

Table 6.1   Preparing Your 10-Minute Pitch to Investors

INTRODUCTION (1–2 minutes)	• Know how you will greet your audience. • Briefly introduce yourself (you will add more detail about yourself when discussing the management team later). • Identify how you will grab their attention right up front: tell a brief story illustrating the need, ask them to imagine a different reality, share a startling statistic, and connect the idea to them. • Provide a very high-level overview of the need, your solution, and the benefits of investing.

INDUSTRY (2 minutes)	• Who is the target market?
	  o How large is it? (don't inflate; quantify with data)
	  o Size, rate, or growth and projected growth of the industry
	  o What dynamics impact this market? How will those dynamics impact the demand for your solution?
	• Who is the competition?
	  o In what industry are you competing?
	  o Who will you be competing against…today and tomorrow?
	  o Why will customers come to you instead of your competitors? (what are your competitive advantages and disadvantages)
	  o What are the barriers to entry?
	  o How might that relationship change over time? (future partners, mergers, acquisitions, or acquirers)

(Continued)

Table 6.1 (Continued)

PRODUCT/SERVICE (2 minutes)	• What is the problem/opportunity/need that you are addressing?
	  o How large is it? (quantify with data)
	  o Who is it a problem for? (use a real-life example)
	• What is your solution?
	  o What are you offering? (don't recap every feature)
	  o How does it meet the need?
	  o How are you uniquely solving the problem?
	  o Why can't it be solved another way?
	• What is your business model?
	  o How will you make money? (support with specific projections)
	  o What is your projected revenue stream?
	  o Where might there be shortfalls? (how will you handle them)
	  o Expected pricing and how it compares to competition
	  o Breakeven in sales/units

MANAGEMENT (2 minutes)	• Who is your management team?
	  o Why should we invest in you? in your team?
	  o What track record/experience do you have in this industry? in starting a new business?
	  o Your relevant experience (but not your life history!)
	  o Your management team's qualifications
	  o Recent company history

FINANCING (2 minutes)	• Your summary financials
	  o What do you need and how will you spend it?
	  o What are your projected gross margins, breakeven, cash-flow forecasts, sources, and uses of funds?
	  o What is the Return on Investment (ROI) for investors?
	  o Do you want debt or equity?
	  o Equipment, inventory, and so on?
	  o Announce the availability of your full business plan

END (final 1 minute)	• Recap the need/opportunity and your solution (and competitive advantage). • Recap what you need from your potential investors (funds solicited) and your promise to them (ROI).

SOURCE: Adapted from Mary Shapiro, Simmons School of Management, Silverman Business Plan Competition (2005). For additional recommendations, please refer to Appendix C.

Review Questions

1. Describe the differences between angel and venture capital financing.

2. What are angels and venture capitalists looking for in a business that they are considering providing financing?

3. Describe, in detail, the components of presenting your business plan.

All Told, Why Entrepreneurs Don't Get Funding[8]

While going through the process of seeking funding for new ventures, here are nine of the common mistakes entrepreneurs make along the way, counting down from the least common to the most common mistakes.

1. *Minimize competition in target market.* Many entrepreneurs are eager to show investors why their product or service will fulfill an unmet need within the marketplace so they fail to discuss current market competition. However, this will turn investors off. From their viewpoint, a market without competition has no customers to demand your product or service.

2. *Future performance-focused.* Although investors want to hear your plan for future performance and the metrics you will use to measure success, they also want to understand what your company has done in the past. Past performance is a precursor to future performance and speaks volumes about a company's track record.

3. *Failure to tailor management biographies to the current stage of business.* Detailed biographies of each member of the management team must be discussed. Each biography should include the current responsibilities of the management member and should be tailored to the current stage of the company. These biographies should change as the company proceeds to move through its life cycle.

4. *Asking investors to sign a nondisclosure agreement.* Most investors refuse to sign a nondisclosure agreement. Once you understand that this is nearly universal, you can decide what you will and will not disclose as part of your discussions. Proprietary technology is something that you would not disclose in detail, but the strategy and concept must be described.

5. *Including investor feedback in your business plan.* It is better to solicit comments from a number of reliable sources and include a generic interpretation of common concerns.

6. *Claiming first-mover advantage.* If you are going to claim first-mover advantage—that is, if you claim that you are the first to market in your area of business—which we don't recommend that you do, you must demonstrate that your strategy can substantiate this claim.

7. *Proprietary technology overload.* It's not enough to simply reiterate the fact that your company possesses some extraordinary proprietary technology. Rather, an entrepreneur must describe in detail how this technology will be exploited to satisfy a customer's unmet needs.

8. *Inaccurately defining market size.* Investors will be turned off by presenters who provide too much information that is useless in determining the accurate market size in which the company will operate. Do your research and provide the

potential investor with a relevant market size and, more important, a plan to gain a significant market share within this market.

9. *Aggressive financial projections.* After the Executive Summary, the financial section of the business plan is the most eagerly read by potential investors. It is imperative that this statement should be reasonable, well thought out, and internally consistent with the company's strategy. If possible, present comparative numbers to substantiate your financial projections. However, these numbers are not always available. In that case, it is best to provide conservative, well-reasoned assumptions.

Summary of Chapter Objectives

1. Know the differences between debt and equity financing: two similar but separate audiences
   - *Debt financing* involves borrowing money that is to be repaid over a period of time, usually with interest. Debt financing can be either short term (full repayment due in less than one year) or long term (repayment due over more than one year). Excessive debt may impair the new venture's ability to acquire financing in the future.
   - *Equity financing* describes an exchange of money for a share of business ownership. This form of financing allows you to obtain funds without incurring debt, in other words, without having to repay a specific amount of money at any particular time. The major disadvantage is dilution of control for the entrepreneur.

2. Understand the financing stages along the life cycle of the business
   - Seed stage: the first funding benchmark. This is the initial capital used to do product or service development, patent filings, market research, and business partner recruitment. Typically, seed stage financing comes from the entrepreneur's personal savings and contributions from family members and friends.
   - Series A stage: Start-up financing. The new venture has its first revenues but still demonstrates no profitability. This is the stage when outside investors may be brought into the firm.
   - Series B stage: After successful launch, the venture proves the viability of its business model. Funding is needed to develop the marketing plan, to hire more staff or management team members, and to establish strategic alliances.
   - Additional Stages: C or even D and E rounds of financing focus on commercial loans, lines of credit, IPO, and bridge financing.

3. Understand the most common sources of financing available for your business
   - Personal savings, loans, or equity investment from family and friends, bank or other commercial loans, lines of credit, working capital, and equipment or other capital leasing are all common sources of financing for start-up and early growth stages.

4. Know the differences between venture capital and angel investment
    - Venture capitalists are professional investors, only rarely investing seed capital. These investors are interested in firms with high growth potential, and in exchange for investment, they require a proportion of ownership.
    - Angels are usually experienced business people who are often interested in seed investments as well as later stage investments. They usually prefer to serve in a consulting role.

5. Learn how investors conduct a due diligence analysis and what they commonly look for when examining your business
    - Review the Due Diligence Checklist. The areas for investigation include: financial assumptions, market assessment, competitive analysis, management team, technical assessment, and operations. It is important to prepare effectively for investor reviews and analyses.

CASE 6.1   Benchmark Mobility, Inc.

In 2000, Ronald Reed launched his home health-care equipment company, Benchmark Mobility Inc., with just $1,800. But his capital needs accelerated so quickly that within a few years, his personal savings, credit cards and home-equity funds were no longer up to the task. "I was sitting on a couple hundred thousand dollars of business I couldn't do anything with because I had outgrown my personal credit," says Reed, 36.

Reed understood that securing growth capital would prove difficult. Reed worked his way through the Yellow Pages, but was turned down by every large bank he contacted. Their concern was universal: his lack of assets to secure the loan. "For us to have $3 million in sales, we might only have $50,000 of inventory at any given time," Reed reveals. "Now that's a huge gap, and most banks aren't comfortable [granting] a quarter-million-dollar credit line without having a building and a large amount of inventory to substantiate that. Even though the company is making a great deal of money and cash flow is pretty well-diversified through different payers, the banks don't see us as their ideal client." Two years and 21 banks later, the Indianapolis entrepreneur still didn't have financing. In the meantime, his financial situation had grown progressively worse. "There were times I wasn't sure I was going to make payroll," he recalls. Frustrated, he asked the Central Indiana Small Business Development Center for help. One of the smaller banks it recommended came through with a $250,000 line of credit. "That's a bank I never would have considered," Reed admits. "I assumed a bigger bank would have more money to take chances on [small companies] vs. a smaller bank that I assumed would have to have fewer loans that are risky. But it was the opposite—we had to go to a small bank strictly because they were the only ones willing to listen."

David vs. Goliath

It seems like every bank today calls itself a small-business lender and promises specialized attention and loans to support a wide range of commercial needs. But there are important distinctions in the way banks of different sizes approach small-business lending, as Reed's credit search illustrates. For starters, small lenders are less driven by financial formulas and more inclined to consider individual factors, such as the business's management, in making their loan decisions. Their lending styles appeal to borrowers weary of the widespread consolidation that has created increasingly larger banks and, many argue, cookie-cutter service.

Loan decisions at large banks, meanwhile, are rarely made locally. Financing applications are sent off to the bank headquarters for analysis, and the decision is ultimately based on the applicant's computerized credit score, not the judgment of local loan officers. By virtue of size, however, the largest lenders have sophisticated credit products to support an entrepreneur's evolving financing needs, such things as loans for international trade. Some even have [venture capital] units.

Each banking group clearly has distinct advantages. For business borrowers, it often boils down to a choice between the big-bank credit arsenal and the personal service of a community lender. "A more sophisticated loan plan or investment plan is something you look to the larger institutions to do," says James Ballentine, director of community and economic development for the American Bankers Association. "But a community institution says, 'We can provide you with greater customer service because we know the area that you're in and have historical knowledge of this community.'"

In truth, many fledgling entrepreneurs turn to smaller lenders out of necessity. "You have small businesses that are in different stages of their lives. The newer firms that don't have long histories of audited financials or histories of paying their suppliers on a regular basis really need that experienced community lender who doesn't rely on the standard financial ratios to make credit decisions," explains Jonathan

Scott, associate professor of finance at Temple University's Richard J. Fox School of Business in Philadelphia. "[The answer] may not always be yes, but at least it's not a matter of, 'We'll type this data into the computer and we'll get our decision.'"

While community banks can provide flexibility, they may, however, have a difficult time keeping pace with the financing needs of their business borrowers. What's more, some small banks lack the in-house expertise to offer government-guaranteed financing, such as SBA [Small Business Administration] loans. Although most community banks are at least familiar with SBA loans, many cannot provide the quick turnaround of larger, more practiced lenders. Says Gina Woods, business advisor at the Central Indiana Small Business Development Center, "What's so nice about going to a [large bank] is that they do SBA loans all the time."

Credit Culture

Access to the right kind of credit is just one factor in choosing a bank. Equally important is the bank's credit culture, or the policies and principles that direct lending activity. For instance, many large banks focus on businesses of a certain size, meaning that if your company falls outside those parameters, you probably won't get the same level of service as a larger, more valued customer. That isn't as much of a problem at a smaller bank. "The big advantage is that I have access to executive management, and executive management has been receptive when I have had a potential opportunity," Reed says of his bank.

And of course, there is the issue of underwriting flexibility. While banking industry insiders say that increased competition has forced large banks to become more flexible, "community banks, if they know a community well, are perhaps more willing to deviate from [their lending] formulas," says Ballentine.

Nonetheless, there are very different approaches, even among community banks. "Some community banks are more specialized in real estate lending," Scott stresses. "Others want a balance between real estate and small-business lending." And while community banks often champion entrepreneurial ventures shunned by large lenders, some are more risk-averse than others. Scott witnessed this firsthand when he referred a hair salon owner to a local community bank for financing. The businesswoman wanted to move to a new commercial location, a historic building that presented some zoning challenges. Scott's recommended bank passed on the credit request. "They were somewhat conservative," he says. The business owner pitched the loan deal to another community bank, one that was less concerned about the zoning issues. It ultimately approved financing.

While a bank's size does influence its commercial lending culture, as Scott's example illustrates, it doesn't tell the whole story. "You need to shop around to find out what bank fits your needs," Ballentine urges. "It's good to go to both large and small institutions to see the kinds of services they are providing."

SOURCE: Crystal Detamore-Rodman, "Just Your Size: Don't Make Assumptions About a Bank's Lending Methods Based on Size Alone—Here's How To Find the Bank That Can Help You Cash In," *Entrepreneur*, April 2005. Copyright © 2005, Entrepreneur.com; all rights reserved. Republished with permission from Entrepreneur.com.

Discussion Questions

1. Not all money is created equally. Discuss the pros and cons of securing bank debt.
2. Reed spent a significant amount of time searching for debt financing. What alternative forms of financing should he have sought or at very least, what forms of financing should he have considered?
3. Start-up funds are not enough to sustain a growing business. Discuss the analysis Reed should have employed as his business began to grow.

CASE 6.2 Adam Makos and *Ghost Wings:* Making History by Sharing History

Ghost Wings magazine is the evolution of a newsletter that was started in 1994 by Adam and Bryan Makos, along with their friend, Joe Gohrs. The men turned their aviation hobby (an interest that stems from their grandfathers' service experiences) into a business. The business evolved over the course of several years from a circulation of 10 to 20 into the magazine, *Ghost Wings,* launched in 1999 with a circulation of 10,000 and growing. Adam calls it "a small idea and a simple project [that] has taken a turn for the best." This turn led to Adam Makos being named one of the 2003 Global Student Entrepreneur Award Winners, sponsored by Saint Louis University.

Adam didn't plan to found his own business. The newsletter wasn't even intended to be a long-term project. Adam, Bryan, and Joe spent a lot of time together growing up and dabbled in several little hobby-like ventures over the years. The newsletter was just "the one that just happened to stick." The Makos's sisters, Erica and Elizabeth, have also joined the *Ghost Wings* staff in recent years. Erica is a junior in college, and Elizabeth is a junior in high school. Although the staff is predominately made up of the Makos siblings, Adam doesn't consider the magazine a family business. He says, "It's just based on a common interest in military history."

The magazine's topic is a passion for Adam and his family and friends. The magazine tells the stories of American veterans, primarily those connected to military aviation from World War II, Korea, and Vietnam. According to Adam, "We really started our newsletter, and then later our magazine, with a simple, I guess you could say blinded goal, of using our publication as a vehicle to tell the stories of American veterans. So there really wasn't much in the way of a long-term profit forecast, long-time distribution plan, or even a very complex set-up. We kind of jumped into it feet first, just with our enthusiasm driving us."

"In my opinion there are two ways to really start a magazine, a newspaper, a publication. One would be to have a lot of start-up capital, a well-developed and properly hired staff— basically with all of the facets of the business lined up before you start producing your product. In our case, we followed what could be thought of as another avenue, in that it started as a ground floor kind of thing—just a couple thousand dollars chipped in by the staff members—we were all volunteers. No plans for distribution other than what we could do through our own personal selling. Basically, we didn't really start from a position of strength in the marketplace."

Looking back, Adam has learned that a lot of models are available to guide new business ventures. "In our case we followed none of them." Asked for advice he would give to new entrepreneurs on evaluating and setting up their business, Adam reflects, "I would say there's really no need for people, when they're starting their own business, to reinvent the wheel at every step. A business, at least a business that will succeed, requires innovation. But at the same time, when you're starting up, study your competitors, study the industry, and basically you can try to take everything upon your shoulders . . . or you can look at what others are doing and see what they're doing right, what they're doing wrong, and how they do it, and then pattern your business development from the examples of others."

After producing the newsletter for about five years, the *Ghost Wings* staff decided that they would put together their first issue as a magazine. They created the magazine in Microsoft PowerPoint® software which, according to Adam was "terrible for professional publishing and design. We designed the magazine all wrong." After they created the magazine content they met with Christine Nichols, a retired catalog editor and family friend, to show her their magazine. Christine helped point them in the direction of a printer and allowed them to use her local publishing resources.

The *Ghost Wings* staff financed the first issue of the magazine themselves. The staff worked out of Adam's basement and used the family computer, so the only expense was the printing costs. As a senior in high school, Adam had been saving up for a car but decided to forgo the purchase to fund the publishing of the first issue of the magazine. Since the first issue was such a success, Adam was able to use the proceeds from the first issue to fund the second issue, and so forth.

Although they were a very small business with limited resources, their uniqueness helped market them. As high school students at the time, the *Ghost Wings* staff relied on the story that surrounded the magazine for publicity— "the story of a group of young people producing a magazine to honor generations other than their own. Basically to honor our grandfathers, and our parents' generations." A few stories appeared in the local newspapers, veterans newsletters, and aviation industry publications, and the orders began to trickle in. *Ghost Wings* also did some direct selling at air shows. Adam believes this opportunity was directly related to the magazine's success. He says, "We were fortunate because a number of air-show operators, like those at the Mid Atlantic Air Museum, let us come in and set up a small table in the middle of a parched runway to sell our magazine. Without their generosity, who knows if we would have lasted until issue two?"

Adam went to college just as the magazine was starting to "gain legs." He found that, no matter how well he could multi-task, school required a lot of his attention and time. "One can't expect to remain fully committed to a business, obviously, when you've got school to contend with." Adam went back home every Friday night to dedicate his weekends to the magazine. The group's passion for the subject prevented

burnout through the balancing act of school and the business. He says, "In the case of our group, working on the weekends was not really work. It was fun, it was an adventure, and it was a path of discovery for us . . . because we're all great history fans, and our work dealt with interviewing and telling the stories of veterans. So it was our work, but it was also our recreation."

As a liberal arts student, Adam's work on the magazine did not have a direct connection with his college work. He found that the faculty didn't show much interest in sharing their knowledge or assisting him in growing his business. In fact, he even received discouragement from some. "They would say, 'hey, your subjects are dying really quickly.' I actually had one professor say, 'It's nice that you're doing this magazine, but you'd better consider all your options because how are you going to have any content, how are you going to have any stories when the WW II veterans are gone? It's a nice thing you're doing but I don't see much longevity in it.' . . . and I was thinking, well, you obviously haven't cracked the pages because we tell the stories of WWII veterans, Korean War veterans, and Vietnam War veterans. Of course, 'the greatest generation,' as they're called, is passing along, but America has had millions of men and women who have served, and those stories are really not going anywhere."

Adam faces the challenge of building a reputation as a serious business with a staff made up solely of young people. He sees a double standard in the market's reactions to his work, "As much as people might sing the praises of young entrepreneurs, other people don't always take a young person in a business role very seriously." Adam also found that without a business education and real world experience, he had to teach himself as he went along. If he could go back in time and start over, Adam says he would have done an internship in the office of a major magazine to learn a little about operations from the professionals. Without this background to draw on, Adam says, "we had to basically chart our own course. That's a much slower process."

The staff does all of the publishing—the writing, the selling, the accounting, as well as spin-off projects—themselves. Although Adam would like to expand the staff, it has been difficult to find other young people who share the passion for World War II and Korean War history.

The news and popular culture influence topics in the magazine. In addition to historic stories, the articles focus on topics that have been brought up by forms of popular media: books, TV, and movies. The staff also keeps up to date by attending conferences, museums, and other aviation-related events. Adam says, "We're creating the same publication we would like to see as enthusiasts, and I think that's one of the ways we stay really current."

The *Ghost Wings* staff now spends much of their time reevaluating the future direction of the magazine. They intend to launch a new magazine because the current magazine serves such a small niche. In the case of *Ghost Wings,* the focus is on aviators, who represent 10 percent or less of those who have served in the U.S. military. Adam says, "It's almost a niche within a niche." Adam fears that this decision will change the entire dynamic of the business. "The business could change literally with the snap of a finger, and that's basically where we're at right now."

Adam feels the magazine's success has just begun. When asked to provide advice to other entrepreneurs, Adam offers caution instead. "Do your homework before you jump into a business. Don't open your coffee shop before you've studied Starbucks. You need to know the industry—everyone from your smallest competitors to your largest competitor and how each of those levels of business have operated, how they've survived, how they've grown, and how they've died, in many cases. So I guess the biggest word of caution, word of advice, word of insight, would be to stay passionate about the topic you want to start. When you're passionate, the creativity will flow. But don't let your creativity and your enthusiasm hurry you down the path too quickly or obscure your vision of the greater picture."

SOURCE: Case prepared with the assistance of Laurel Ofstein, who conducted the interview with Adam Makos, winner of the Global Student Entrepreneur of the Year Award, 2003. Printed with permission.

Discussion Questions

1. Discuss the implications of assessing the trade-offs of changing a venture's tactical strategies.

2. How do young entrepreneurs convince stakeholders that age doesn't matter? What can young entrepreneurs do to minimize the negative perception of age?

3. What role does luck play in today's new ventures? Is there such a thing as luck?

4. How do you fund an "accidental" business venture?

Appendix 6.1 Explanatory Term Sheet Sample

This term sheet summarizes the principal terms with respect to a potential private placement of equity securities of _____ (the "Company") by a group of investors led by _____ .
This term sheet is intended solely as a basis for further discussion and is not intended to be and does not constitute a legally binding obligation.

PROPOSED TERMS FOR PREFERRED STOCK FINANCING OF (THE "COMPANY")

Amount: $ _____ at [First] Closing; [$ _____ at Second Closing prior to _____ , 200 __]

Type of Security: Series _____ Preferred Stock ("Preferred")

Price per Share: $ _____ ("Original Purchase Price")

Investors: _____ (collectively, the "Investors")

First Closing: [First] Closing on or around _____ , 200 _____

Capitalization: Outstanding   Pro Forma

Common Stock
Preferred Stock
Options
    Reserved
    Outstanding and unexercised
    Available for grant
Warrants
Convertible notes/other securities

(Continued)

(Continued)

Comment: Dividends typically range from 7% to 10% of the Original Purchase Price. Most dividends are noncumulative.

Comment: This is a simple participating preferred, which means that the funds remaining after payment of the Preferred's Original Purchase Price will be shared equally by the Common and Preferred shareholders. As drafted, this provision is very favorable to investors because there is no cap on the amount they are to receive.

RIGHTS, PREFERENCES, PRIVILEGES, AND RESTRICTIONS OF PREFERRED

Dividends: Holders of Preferred shall be entitled to receive, prior to any payment of dividends to holders of the Common Stock of the Company (the "Common Stock"), annual dividends payable in the amount of $_____ per share when and if declared by the Board of Directors *[or, which shall cumulate from year to year annually on the anniversary date of the closing whether or not declared by the Board]*.

Liquidation Preference: In the event of any liquidation or winding up of the Company, the holders of the Preferred will be entitled to receive in preference to the holders of Common Stock an amount ("Liquidation Amount") equal to the Original Purchase Price *[or: plus all cumulated dividends]*. After payment of the Original Purchase Price *[or: plus all cumulated dividends]* to the holders of the Preferred, the remaining assets shall be distributed ratably to the holders of Common and Preferred on a common equivalent basis *[ratably to the holders of Common Stock] [or] [ratably to the holders of Common and Preferred on a common equivalent basis until the holders of Preferred have received a total return in the liquidation of three times the Original Purchase Price after which any remaining amounts will be distributed ratably to the holders of Common]*. A merger, acquisition, or sale of substantially all of the assets of the Company in which the shareholders of the Company do not own a majority of the outstanding shares of the surviving corporation shall be deemed to be a liquidation.

Conversion

▲ Optional: The holders of the Preferred will have the right to convert their Preferred at their option, at any time, into shares of Common Stock. The total number of shares of Common Stock into which the Preferred may be converted initially will be determined by dividing the Original Purchase Price by the Conversion Price. The initial Conversion Price will be the Original Purchase Price. The Conversion Price will be subject to adjustment as provided in paragraph (iv) below.

208

▲ Automatic Conversion: All of the Preferred will be automatically converted into Common Stock, at the then-applicable Conversion Price, in the event that (x) holders of a majority of the Preferred consent to the conversion to Common Stock or (y) upon the closing of an underwritten public offering of shares of the Common Stock of the Company at a public offering price per share (prior to underwriting commissions and expenses) of not less than [2 to 5] times the Original Purchase Price in an offering of not less than $20,000,000 (the "IPO").

Comment: The purpose of forcing conversion is to clean up and simplify the Company's capitalization structure at the IPO. Company will want as much flexibility to force conversion (which generally means a 50% threshold), particularly if trying to do IPO in volatile markets when market conditions may cause the offering price to fall below the per-share price that will force conversion. May need to address majority threshold if representing investor that does not own a majority of the preferred. Alternatives include a supermajority threshold or a series vote.

Antidilution Protection: The Conversion Price of the Preferred will be subject to adjustment to prevent dilution in the event that the Company issues additional equity securities at a purchase price less than the applicable Conversion Price. [Ratchet alternative: The Conversion Price of the Series _____ Preferred will be subject to a "full ratchet" adjustment to reduce dilution in the event that the Company issues shares at less than the Conversion Price. The then-effective Conversion Price shall be reduced to the price paid for such newly issued shares.] The Conversion Price of the Preferred will be subject to adjustment on a broad-based weighted average basis. The Conversion Price shall not be adjusted because of (a) conversion of the Preferred, (b) securities issued to a commercial lender or lessor which is approved by the [entire] board, (c) the sale or grant of options to employees, directors, or consultants to purchase up to _____ shares of common stock [or the sale or grant of options to purchase shares approved [unanimously] by the Board of Directors], (d) issuances in acquisitions of another company or assets unanimously approved by the Board, and [(e) any other issuance that is approved by the [entire] Board.] The Conversion Price will also be subject to proportional adjustment for stock splits, stock dividends, recapitalizations, and the like.

Comment: Broad-based weighted average as shown is most typical and favorable to the Company. An alternative is a narrow-based weighted average formula which looks only at the outstanding stock (as opposed to all stock on a fully-diluted basis). Other, more rare, alternatives include a "ratchet" provision which is quite onerous from the Company's perspective as it provides that, upon a down round, the Conversion Price of the Preferred is adjusted downward to the issuance price of the dilutive financing. Another provision, the so-called "pay-to-play" provision, is burdensome to the investors because it requires that investors must participate in dilutive rounds to retain antidilution protection for their shares.

(Continued)

Voting Rights:

Other than Directors. The holders of a share of Preferred will have a right to that number of votes equal to the number of shares of Common Stock issuable upon conversion of Preferred.

Directors. The size of the board shall be set at _____. The holders of Preferred shall be entitled to elect _____ directors. The holders of Common shall be entitled to elect _____ directors. The remaining directors shall be elected by the Preferred and Common voting together.

[Redemption at Option of Investor: At election of the holders of at least 50% of the Preferred, the Company shall redeem [1/3 of the Preferred on the fifth anniversary of the Closing, 1/3 on the sixth anniversary of the Closing and 1/3 on the seventh anniversary of the Closing], each at a redemption price equal to the Original Purchase Price [plus a rate of return equal to 10% per year on the Original Purchase Price [or: plus all cumulated dividends] minus the amount of any dividends previously paid to holders of Preferred.]

Protective Provisions: Consent of the holders of a *[majority]* of the outstanding Preferred Stock shall be required for: (i) any amendment or change of the rights, preferences, privileges, or powers of, or the restrictions provided for the benefit of, the Preferred; (ii) increases or decreases the authorized number of shares of Common or Preferred Stock; (iii) any action that authorizes, creates, or issues shares of any class of stock having preferences superior to or on parity with the Preferred; (iv) any action that reclassifies any outstanding shares into shares having preferences or priority as to dividends or assets senior to or on parity with the preference of the Preferred; (v) any amendment of the Company's Articles of Incorporation or Bylaws that adversely affects the rights of the Preferred; (vi) any merger or consolidation of the Company with one or more other corporations in which the shareholders of the Company immediately after such merger or consolidation hold stock representing less than a majority of the voting power of the outstanding stock of the surviving corporation; (vii) the sale of all or substantially all the Company's assets; (viii) the liquidation or dissolution of the Company; (ix) the declaration or payment of a dividend on the Common Stock (other than a dividend payable solely in shares of Common Stock);

Comment: The Company will typically resist a redemption feature on the theory that the expected liquidity will be achieved when the Company goes public or is acquired. The investors may insist on the redemption feature to force the Company to cash them out at some point if the other liquidity options (an IPO or acquisition) have not occurred.

Comment: Need to consider threshold vote required: The Company will generally favor a simple majority threshold; however, if we represent the investors and the investors do not hold a majority of the outstanding preferred stock, may need consider a supermajority threshold or a series vote.

[(x) the license by the Company of any of its technology of such a manner as to have the same economic effect as a sale or disposition of all or substantially all of the assets of the Company;] (xi) the repurchase by the Company of any shares of its capital stock, except redemption or repurchase of shares of common stock from employees or consultants upon termination of their employment or service pursuant to agreements providing for such repurchase; or (xii) changes the authorized size of the Company's Board [unless required during a future financing].

RIGHTS AGREEMENT

Registration Rights:

Demand Rights: If, at any time that is six months after the Company's initial public offering [or: If, at any time on or after two years from the Closing Date], holders of at least [40%] of the Preferred (or Common Stock issued upon conversion of the Preferred or a combination of such Common Stock and Preferred) request that the Company file a registration statement for all or any portion of the Common Stock issued or issuable upon conversion of the Preferred, having an aggregate offering price to the public of not less than [$5,000,000], the Company will use its best efforts to cause such shares to be registered, provided, however, that (a) the Company shall not be obligated to effect any such registration within 90 days prior to the filing of, and [90 to 180] days following the effective date of, a registration statement pertaining to an underwritten public offering of the Company's securities, (b) such registration obligation shall be deferred not more than six months from the date of receipt of request from the initiating holders if the Company furnishes the initiating holders with a certificate of the Chairman of the Board stating that in the good-faith judgment of the Board, it would be seriously detrimental to the Company and its shareholders for such registration statement to be effected at such time, provided that the right to delay a request may be exercised by the Company not more than once in any 12-month period, and (c) the Company shall not be obligated to effect more than [two] such demand registrations. Any such registration shall be firmly underwritten by an underwriter of nationally recognized standing.

Comment: Generally, holders of 30% to 50% must demand registration.

(Continued)

(Continued)

Registrations on Form S-3: Holders of at least 20% or more of the Preferred (or Common Stock issued upon conversion of the Preferred or a combination of such Common Stock and Preferred) with proceeds of at least [$5,000,000] will have the right to require the Company to file one registration statement annually on Form S-3 with respect to Common Stock issued upon conversion of the Preferred.

Comment: Registrations on Form S-3 not possible until one year after IPO; shorter form, much less expensive. Typically, offering must be between $1 million and $5 million.

Piggyback Registration: The Investor [and _____, and _____ (collectively, the "Founders")] will be entitled to "piggyback" registration rights with respect to offerings registered by the Company, subject to the right of the Company and its underwriters, in view of market conditions, to reduce (but to no less than 30% of any offering after the IPO) the number of shares of the Investor [and Founders] proposed to be registered. *[All shares proposed to be registered by the Founders shall be cut back prior to any reduction of the number of shares proposed t o be registered by the Investor.]*

Comment: Limit underwriter "cutback" after IPO; typically 20–30%.

Comment: Founders may be given limited or subordinate rights. Important to define Founders who will have this right and who will be subject to Right of First Refusal and Co-Sale Agreement (see below).

Registration Expenses: The registration expenses (exclusive of underwriting discounts and commissions) of all demand registrations, Form S-3 registrations, and piggyback registrations will be borne by the Company.

Transfer of Registration Rights: The registration rights may be transferred to a transferee (other than a competitor of the Company) who acquires at least 10% of the Investor's shares. Transfer of registration rights to a partner, affiliate, or related entity of Investor will be without restrictions as to minimum shareholdings.

Other Registration Provisions: Other provisions will be contained in the Rights Agreement with respect to registration rights, including cross indemnification, the agreement by Investors if requested by the underwriter in a public offering not to sell any Common Stock that they hold for a period of 180 days following the effective date of the registration statement for the IPO or 90 days following a subsequently public offering (subject to all directors, officers, and holders of 1% or more of the Company's securities entering into similar agreements), the period of time in which the registration statement will be kept effective, underwriting arrangements, and the like.

Comment: Underwriter "lockup" provisions are typically 180 days for IPOs. Some investors want no more than 90 days agreed to in advance to preserve ability to negotiate a shorter lockup period with underwriters. This may, however, create a burden later in getting numerous investors to agree to extend the period at the time of the IPO.

Comment: Condition "lockup" on agreement of officers, directors and holders of 1% or more of the Company's securities being subject to same restrictions.

Comment: If we represent the Company, we will want to be able to grant rights pari passu with the registration rights contained in the Rights Agreement. Investors should agree to this if the new rights holders are cut back prior to any investor being cut-back.

Granting of Subsequent Registration Rights: The Company shall not grant registration rights to any third party that are superior to [or pari passu with] the registration rights set forth in the Rights Agreement without the prior written consent of holders of a [majority] of the Preferred.

Comment: Depending on composition of investors, may want a threshold other than a simple majority. Company will probably prefer a simple majority threshold.

Comment: The Company will want simpler termination language, such as, "upon any three-month period when the Investors can sell all of their shares pursuant to Rule 144."

Termination of Registration Rights: The registration obligations of the Company shall terminate five years after the initial public offering. In addition, the registration rights will terminate if (i) the Company has completed its IPO, (ii) an Investor (together with its affiliates, partners, and former partners) hold less than [1%] of the Company's outstanding Common Stock (treating all shares of convertible preferred stock on an as-converted basis) and (iii) all such stock held by an Investor (and its affiliates, partners, and former partners) may be sold under Rule 144 during any ninety (90)-day period.

Information Rights:

Comment: Information rights and inspection rights should have the same percent threshold. Will want threshold high enough so that each small investor does not have these rights, but each primary investor does have these rights.

So long as an Investor holds not less than [5% to 15%] of the total Preferred issued in the financing (or Common Stock issued upon conversion of the Preferred or a combination of such Common Stock and Preferred), the Company will deliver to the Investor audited annual and unaudited quarterly financial statements. So long as the Investor holds not less than _____ % of the total Preferred issued in the financing (or Common Stock issued upon conversion of the Preferred or a combination of such Common Stock and Preferred), the Company will timely furnish the Investor with budgets and monthly financial statements. These obligations of the Company will terminate upon a public offering of Common Stock [or at such time as an Investor has converted more than [50%] of its Preferred into Common Stock].

Comment: Sometimes information rights and inspection rights will terminate if an investor begins converting some of its preferred stock.

(Continued)

(Continued)

Inspection Rights:

The Company shall permit an Investor that holds not less than _____% of the total Preferred issued in the financing (or Common Stock issued upon conversion of the Preferred or a combination of such Common Stock and Preferred) to visit and inspect the properties of the Company, including its corporate and financial records, and to discuss its business and finances with officers of the Company during normal business hours following reasonable notice.

Comment: Important to define the investors who will have this right (generally the same as the ones who have information and observation rights) and which issuances of equity securities will not trigger this right.

Right of First Refusal:

In the event the Company offers equity securities (other than (i) options reserved at the Closing under the Company's option plans, (ii) upon conversion of outstanding Preferred, (iii) upon exercise of outstanding options or warrants, (iv) in connection with an acquisition or a public offering that is approved by the [entire] board [, including the _____ director], or (v) in connection with an equipment lease or commercial lending arrangement that has been approved by the [entire] board [, including the _____ director], each Investor who holds not less than _____% of the total Preferred issued in the financing (or Common Stock issued upon conversion of Preferred or any combination of such Preferred and Common Stock) shall have a right of first refusal to purchase such portion of those equity securities as to maintain its pro-rata ownership interest in the Company. This right shall terminate upon the closing of an IPO or an acquisition of the Company [or at such time as an Investor has converted more than [50%] of its Preferred into Common Stock].

Comment: Sometimes investors will want right to subscribe for more than their pro-rata portion, including, in some rare cases, all of a future financing.

Miscellaneous Provision: Amendment/Waiver of Rights Agreement

No right may be waived and the Rights Agreement may not be amended without the approval of the Company and the holders of a [majority] of the Preferred.

Comment: Depending on composition of the investors, may want to adjust threshold, though Company will prefer a majority threshold.

RIGHT OF FIRST REFUSAL AND CO-SALE AGREEMENT

Right of First Refusal: Except for gifts to a spouse or children, or transfers to the estate of a deceased shareholder, or transfers of up to [1% to 10%] of all of the Founder's stock (including all preferred and common stock), a Founder may not transfer any shares of the Company's capital stock now owned or hereafter acquired without first offering it to the Company and then to the Investors. [If an Investor does not exercise its pro-rata right, other Investors that exercise their right may purchase the non-participating Investor's portion.]

Comment: The percent of stock that Founders may transfer free of any restrictions ranges from 1% to 10%; generally, 5% is standard.

Put Right: In the event a Founder transfers his shares in violation of this Right of First Refusal and Co-Sale Agreement, the Investors shall have the right to put a pro-rata portion of their shares to such Founder.

FOUNDER STOCK-RESTRICTION AGREEMENT

Each Founder will execute a stock-restriction agreement with the Company pursuant to which the Company will have a repurchase option to buy back at cost a portion of the shares of stock held by such person in the event that such shareholder's employment with the Company is terminated, prior to the expiration of _____ months from the date of the Preferred Stock Purchase Agreement (the "Measuring Date"). A portion of the shares will be released from the repurchase option based upon continued employment by the Company as follows: [_____% will be released from the repurchase option as of the date of the Preferred Stock Purchase Agreement; an additional _____% will be released from the repurchase option on the first anniversary of the Measuring Date, and an additional % will be released on the completion of each month thereafter].

Comment: The release of Founder's shares from Company right of repurchase is highly negotiated at the time of first venture financing. Generally, the Founder will be given some credit for work done prior to financing so not all Founder's shares will be subject to right of repurchase. The Founder's remaining shares will be released from the repurchase option either monthly thereafter (which is typical) or some portion one year after the financing and then monthly thereafter.

(Continued)

(Continued)

OTHER AGREEMENTS AND CONDITIONS

The Preferred Stock Purchase Agreement: The purchases of the Preferred will be made pursuant to a Preferred Stock Purchase Agreement reasonably acceptable to the Company and the Investors, which agreement shall contain, among other things, appropriate representations and warranties of the Company, covenants of the Company reflecting the provisions set forth herein and appropriate conditions to closing which will include, among other things, qualification of the shares under applicable Blue Sky laws, the filing of Amended and Restated Articles of Incorporation, and receipt of an opinion of counsel. The Preferred Stock Purchase Agreement shall provide that it may only be amended and any waivers thereunder shall only be made with the approval of the holders of a majority of the Preferred.

Comment: You will need to think through the representation and warranties. Generally, Investors want cleaner reps and warranties with fewer qualifiers (knowledge and materiality), while the Company will want fewer reps and warranties and more qualifiers.

Proprietary Information and Inventions Agreement: Each officer and employee of the Company will enter into a proprietary information and inventions agreement with the Company.

Key Man Insurance: [$1,000,000] policy on the lives of each of the Founders, with the Company as beneficiary [but with proceeds to be applied to redemption of Preferred Stock at the election of holders of the majority of Preferred].

Comment: Key-man insurance is good source of funds for redemption in early-stage company, if investors have requested the right of redemption.

Finders: The Company and the Investors shall each indemnify the other for any broker's or finder's fees for which either is responsible.

Expenses: The Company and the Investors will each bear their own legal and other expenses with respect to the transaction (except that, assuming a successful completion of the transaction, the Company will pay reasonable legal fees and expenses incurred by counsel to the Investors, up to $_____).

Comment: Investor's counsel usually capped between $10,000 and $30,000.

Comment: If representing the Company, try to delete bracketed language re [in their sole discretion].

The Closing: The Closing of the purchase of the Preferred will be conditioned upon the following:

▲ Completion of due diligence to the satisfaction of the Investors [in their sole discretion];

▲ Compliance by the Company with applicable securities laws;

▲ Opinion of counsel to the Company rendered to the Investors in form and substance satisfactory to the Investors and their counsel;

▲ [Other material conditions];

▲ Such other conditions as are customary for transactions of this type.

CORPORATE INVESTORS

Comment: Should receive careful consideration when a corporate investor is investing.

Confidentiality [and Standstill]: Each corporate investor will enter into a confidentiality agreement covering standard information disclosed by the Company [and a standstill agreement for a period of five years] [and will enter into a voting agreement agreeing to vote all shares [in the event of a merger or acquisition of the Company or a sale of all assets] in the same manner as the majority of all other shareholders]. Further, to avoid conflicts of interest, any director [or observer] affiliated with such investor may be excluded from any portion of any Board meeting when the majority of the other Board members deems it to be appropriate to protect the interests of the other stockholders.

(Continued)

OTHER MATTERS

In consideration of the Investors' commitment of substantial resources to perform and complete a due-diligence review of the Company, the Company agrees that during the period between the acceptance of this Term Sheet and _____, 200____, the Company shall not enter into or continue discussions with any third party, either agent or principal, concerning a possible investment, public offering, merger, acquisition, or other business arrangement. If for any reason the Investors decide not to proceed with this investment, they will provide immediate written or verbal notice to management of the Company, and all terms, including the "exclusivity" outlined above, will terminate upon such notice.

This offer will expire if not accepted by _____.

Agreed and Accepted

_____   [Investors]

[Company]

Date: _____   Date: _____

Counsel for the Company is:

Counsel for the Investors is:

SOURCE: www.kauffman.org (2004), "Angel Investment Groups, Networks, and Funds: A Guidebook to Developing the Right Angel Organization for Your Community." Author: Susan Preston, Kauffman Foundation. Reprinted with permission.

Appendix 6.2 Due Diligence Checklist Table

The documents and materials itemized below constitute a list of materials which should be reviewed for any financing. Keep in mind that many early-stage companies will not have some or many of these documents, as certain events may not have occurred. Request should be made for all documents or disclosures listed below.

TITLE OF SECTION AND SUBSECTION	DOCUMENTS REQUESTED	SHOULD HAVE	DATE RECEIVED	DATE DELIVERED	REVIEWER'S INITIALS	COMMENTS
I.	**General corporate materials (The Company, all subsidiaries, partnerships and joint ventures).**					
A.	**Business Plan**, including executive summary, market analysis and plan, operational plan, and complete financials.					
B.	**Minutes**					
1.	Minutes of stockholders' meetings, including those of any predecessor corporations.					
2.	Minutes of board of directors, including those of any predecessor corporations.					
3.	Minutes of permanent committees of the board, including those of any predecessor corporations.					
4.	Authorizing resolutions relating to this offering and related transactions.					
C.	**Charter Documents**					
1.	Articles or Certificate of Incorporation, as amended to date, including current drafts of pending charter amendments and recapitalization documents.					
2.	Drafts of documents related to proposed reincorporation.					
3.	Bylaws, as amended to date.					
4.	Good standing (and franchise tax board) certificates.					
5.	List of jurisdictions in which the Company or any of its subsidiaries or affiliates is qualified to do business,					

(Continued)

(Continued)

TITLE OF SECTION AND SUBSECTION	DOCUMENTS REQUESTED	SHOULD HAVE	DATE RECEIVED	DATE DELIVERED	REVIEWER'S INITIALS	COMMENTS
D.	**Corporate Organization**					
1.	List of officers and directors.					
2.	Management structure organization chart.					
3.	Stockholders' lists (including list of optionees and warrant holders), including number of shares and dates of issuance, and consideration paid.					
4.	Information regarding subsidiaries, i.e., ownership, date of acquisition of stock and/or assets, all closing binders relating to acquisitions.					
5.	Information regarding joint ventures or partnership, i.e., partners, date of formation, all closing binders relating to joint ventures or partnerships.					
6.	Agreements relating to mergers, acquisitions, or dispositions by the Company of its subsidiaries or affiliates of companies, significant assets or operations involving the Company or any of its subsidiaries or affiliates since inception, including those of any predecessor or subsidiary corporations.					
E.	**Capital Stock**					
1.	Stock records, stock ledgers and other evidence of securities authorized and issued.					
2.	Agreements relating to the purchase, repurchase, sale or issuance of securities, including oral commitments to sell or issue securities.					
3.	Agreements relating to voting of securities and restrictive share transfers.					
4.	Agreements relating to preemptive or other preferential rights to acquire securities and any waivers thereof.					
5.	Agreements relating to registration rights.					

TITLE OF SECTION AND SUBSECTION	DOCUMENTS REQUESTED	SHOULD HAVE	DATE RECEIVED	DATE DELIVERED	REVIEWER'S INITIALS	COMMENTS
6.	Evidence of qualification or exemption under applicable federal and state blue sky laws for issuance of the Company's securities.					
7.	Documents relating to any conversion, recapitalization, reorganization, or significant restructuring of the Company.					
II.	**Litigation**					
A.	Any litigation, claims, and proceedings settled or concluded, including those of any predecessor corporations and subsidiaries.					
B.	Any litigation, claims, and proceedings threatened or pending. Please include potential litigation—e.g., employees who may be in breach of non-compete agreements with prior employers.					
C.	Any litigation involving an executive officer or director, including executive officers or directors of predecessor corporations and subsidiaries, concerning bankruptcy, crimes, securities law, or business practices.					
D.	Any consent decrees, injunctions, judgments, other decrees or orders, settlement agreements, or similar matters.					
E.	All attorneys' letters to auditors, including those of any predecessor corporation and subsidiaries.					
III.	**Compliance with Laws**					
A.	Any citations and notices received from government agencies, including those of any predecessor or subsidiary corporations, or with continuing effect from an earlier date.					
B.	Any pending or threatened investigations and governmental proceedings.					

(Continued)

(Continued)

TITLE OF SECTION AND SUBSECTION	DOCUMENTS REQUESTED	SHOULD HAVE	DATE RECEIVED	DATE DELIVERED	REVIEWER'S INITIALS	COMMENTS
C.	All material governmental permits, licenses, etc., of the Company presently in force, together with information regarding any such permits, licenses, etc., which have been canceled or terminated, required to carry out the business or operations of the Company or its subsidiaries or affiliates, including such permits, licenses, etc. required by foreign, federal, provincial, or local authorities, and any evidence of exemption from any such permit or license requirement.					
D.	All documents filed with the SEC or any state or foreign securities regulatory agency, if any.					
E.	Any material reports to and correspondence with any government entity, municipality or government agencies, including the EPA and OSHA, including those of any predecessor corporations or subsidiaries.					
IV.	**Employee Matters (Including items regarding any predecessor or subsidiary or affiliated corporations and all items presently in force and drafts of any pending amendments or new items)**					
A.	Employee agreements.					
B.	Consulting contracts.					
C.	Employee benefit and profit-sharing plans, including stock option, stock purchase, deferred compensation, and bonus plans or arrangements.					
D.	All other employee compensation, bonus, incentive, retirement, benefit (e.g., Life or health insurance, medical reimbursement plans, etc.), or similar plans.					
E.	Employee Confidentiality and Proprietary Rights Agreement.					
F.	Officers and directors questionnaires.					
G.	Contracts with unions and other labor agreements.					

TITLE OF SECTION AND SUBSECTION	DOCUMENTS REQUESTED	SHOULD HAVE	DATE RECEIVED	DATE DELIVERED	REVIEWER'S INITIALS	COMMENTS
H.	Loans to and guarantees for the benefit of directors, officers or employees.					
I.	"Key person" insurance policies.					
J.	Listing of employees by office and department.					
K.	Affiliation agreements with advertising agencies or public relations firms.					
L.	Stock ownership of directors and of the five most-highly compensated officers.					
V.	**Real Property**					
A.	Deeds.					
B.	Leases of real property.					
C.	Other interests in real property.					
D.	Any documents showing any certification of compliance with, or any deficiency with respect to, regulatory standards of the Company's or any of its subsidiaries' or affiliates' facilities.					
E.	Financing leases and sale and lease-back agreements.					
F.	Conditional sale agreements.					
G.	Equipment leases.					
VI.	**Intellectual Property Matters**					
A.	List of all foreign and domestic patents, patent applications, copyrights, patent licenses and copyright licenses held by the Company.					
B.	List of any trademarks, trademark applications, trade names, or service marks.					
C.	Claims of infringement or misappropriation of others' patents, copyrights, trade secrets, or other proprietary rights.					

(Continued)

(Continued)

TITLE OF SECTION AND SUBSECTION	DOCUMENTS REQUESTED	SHOULD HAVE	DATE RECEIVED	DATE DELIVERED	REVIEWER'S INITIALS	COMMENTS
D.	Copies of all agreements in-licensing or acquiring any technology, including without limitation software licenses, patent licenses, or other technology licenses, or any development or joint-development agreements.					
E.	Copies of all agreements out-licensing or selling any technology, including without limitation any software licenses, patent licenses, or other technology licenses, or any distribution, OEM, VAR or sales-representative agreements.					
VII.	**Debt Financing**					
A.	All debt instruments, credit agreements, and guarantees entered into by the Company, including lease financing, which are currently in effect.					
B.	All material correspondence with lenders, including all compliance reports submitted by the Company or its accountants.					
C.	Any loans and guarantees of third-party obligations.					
D.	Any agreements restricting the payment of cash dividends.					
VIII.	**Other Agreements**					
A.	Marketing agreements.					
B.	Management and service agreements.					
C.	Forms of secrecy, confidentiality, and nondisclosure agreements.					
D.	Contracts outside the ordinary course of business.					
E.	Indemnification contracts and similar arrangements for officers and directors.					
F.	Agreements with officers, directors, and affiliated parties.					
G.	Any agreements with competitors.					

TITLE OF SECTION AND SUBSECTION	DOCUMENTS REQUESTED	SHOULD HAVE	DATE RECEIVED	DATE DELIVERED	REVIEWER'S INITIALS	COMMENTS
H.	Any agreements with governmental agencies or institutions.					
I.	Any agreements restricting the Company's right to compete or other agreements material to the business.					
J.	Any material insurance arrangements (including property damage, third-party liability, and key employee insurance).					
K.	Agreements requiring consents or approvals or resulting in changes in rights in connection with change-of-control transactions.					
IX.	**Financial Information**					
A.	Audited/Unaudited financial statements, including those of any predecessor corporations.					
B.	Interim financial statements.					
C.	Budget plan, including revisions to date with respect to the budget plan for the current fiscal year for the Company and its subsidiaries and affiliates.					
D.	The Company's long-range strategic plan, any other documents concerning its long-range plans, and any information concerning the Company's compliance therewith.					
E.	Disclosure documents used in private placements of the Company's or any of its subsidiaries' or affiliates' securities, or institutional- or bank-loan applications since inception.					
F.	Any other material agreements with creditors.					
G.	Significant correspondence with independent public accountants, including management letters.					
H.	Any reports, studies and projections prepared by management on the Company's or its subsidiaries' or affiliates' business, financial condition, or planned operations, including business plan.					

(Continued)

(Continued)

TITLE OF SECTION AND SUBSECTION	DOCUMENTS REQUESTED	SHOULD HAVE	DATE RECEIVED	DATE DELIVERED	REVIEWER'S INITIALS	COMMENTS
I.	Any reports and studies prepared by outside consultants on the Company's or its subsidaries' or affiliates' business or financial condition.					
J.	Reports and materials prepared for the Company's board of directors or a committee there of.					
K.	Contracts with investment bankers and brokers.					
X.	**Tax Matters**					
A.	Federal, state and local tax returns, including those of any predecessor corporations.					
B.	Audit adjustments proposed by the IRS.					
XI.	**Acquisitions/Divestitures**					
A.	Acquisitions or divestitures (including related documentation).					
B.	Current plans or negotiations relating to potential acquisitions or divestitures.					
XII.	**Public Relations**					
A.	Annual reports and other reports and communications with stockholders, employees, suppliers, and customers.					
B.	Advertising, marketing, and other selling materials.					
XIII.	**Press Releases and Clippings**					
A.	Analyst reports.					
XIV.	**Miscellaneous**					
A.	Supply copies of all market research or marketing studies concerning the Company's business conducted.					
B.	Significant agreements currently in draft stage.					

SOURCE: www.kauffman.org (2004), "Angel Investment Groups, Networks, and Funds: A Guidebook to Developing the Right Angel Organization for Your Community." Author: Susan Preston, Kauffman Foundation. Reprinted with permission.

Appendix 6.3
Additional Guidelines for Presenting Your Business Plan

The objectives for making your presentation are to:

- Summarize the main points of your business plan.
- Convey your commitment, integrity, competence, and passion.
- Anticipate and answer questions judges may have.

To accomplish those objectives, this appendix offers guidelines regarding your content, visuals, delivery skills, and responses to questions.

Content

Some general strategies when structuring your content:

- Do not rehash your entire business plan. You want to hit the highlights and stay on the big picture. Be careful about delving into details.
- Punctuate the need for your business idea, how you will fill it, what your competitive advantage is, and why you are the person who can make it happen.
- Make the structure of your presentation obvious. Give them an agenda up front. Segue to the next topic with explicit bridge statements (i.e., "Next I'd like to talk about . . ."). Provide a summary as you conclude each section (i.e., "So you can see that this will provide the three benefits of . . .").
- Anticipate questions or concerns and imbed them in your speech (i.e., "I anticipate that you are concerned about . . ."). This makes you look proactive and smart, whereas by waiting for that objection or concern to be brought up in Q&A, you could look defensive.

Notes

You are not expected to memorize your presentation. However, you do not want to read from your notes and lose the credibility eye contact establishes.

You also don't want to have your visuals so textually dense that your verbal speech is moot.

- You can use 4 × 6 index cards, which you will try to avoid holding and place to the side for easy reference.
- Use large-font bullets to highlight critical information.
- Avoid using a script at all costs.
- When referencing your notes, pause and then resume talking with solid eye contact.

Visuals Aids

Remember the purpose of visuals: to reinforce (not mirror) your verbal message, to organize the message for the audience, and to increase their retention of the message. So . . .

- Project only key points (your speech will impart the details and supporting information).
- Follow the 6 by 6 rule: no more than 6 lines of text with 6 words per line.
- Use color, font, and text size (40- to 44-point for titles, 24-point at least for body) consistently, and to avoid clutter and aid in organization.
- Reduce glare by having a dark background (i.e., blue) with lighter text (i.e., yellow).
- Use "talking titles": a slide's title can make the one main point of that slide (i.e., "Management team brings 50 years' experience") with bullets supporting it in the body.
- First slide is your title slide: Include any of the following: your name, management team names, product name, company name, logo, visual of product, date.
- Second slide can include an agenda, or the agenda stated as your main points of need/opportunity-solution-benefits.
- Slides 3 to 4: One of them should summarize your management team, and the other your financials.
- Final slide: what do you want to sear into their brains? This slide contains your main points, again possibly describing opportunity-solution-benefit.

Your Attire as a Visual

Use your attire to project your credibility and competence. Some guidelines:

- Dress more formally than your audience.
- Wear solid dark clothes with one splash of color.
- Avoid jewelry that is shiny or noisy.
- Do not wear shoes that can easily come off or have too high a heel that may cause you to sway.
- Make sure your face and particularly your eyes can be easily seen.

Delivery

Your body can also project your credibility and competence. Use your nervous energy to energize your delivery by channeling it into the following behaviors:

- Eye contact:
  o Consider your speech as a series of one-on-one conversations.
  o Look at each person for three to five seconds to establish connection.
  o Do not speak unless you are looking at someone . . . pause if you are looking at your notes or at the PowerPoint® image.

- Body:
  o Have upright posture, keep chin raised.
  o Keep feet quiet unless you make a purposeful move around the stage.

- Hands:
  o Use slow gestures to convey confidence.
  o Include a few large gestures (such as to your PowerPoint® image) for visual variety.
  o Make sure your hands are quiet between gestures (by your sides, held at your waist, etc.). It's the pause between that amplifies the power of the gesture.

- Movement:
  o Own the entire stage by moving across it.
  o Move deliberately: at least three slow steps, then a pause.
  o Move up to the audience, back to the PowerPoint® image, over to the computer console.

- Voice:
  o Think of yourself as telling a story that requires variety in pace, pitch, and intensity to create interest, emphasize points, and build to a climax.
  o The slower you talk, the more confident you sound.
  o Prevent pitch from creeping upward by keeping your chin down.
  o Keep breathing to keep your voice strong and full.
  o Imbed pauses (audiences like these!) while you move or read or adjust your PowerPoint®.

Question and Answer

Your goal in the question and answer period is to:

- Answer as many questions as you can (versus repeating your entire presentation in response to only the first one!).
- Continue to build your credibility and competence.

To do so, consider:

- Stand still and listen as the person asks the question (it is OK to pause to think of your response, so don't be formulating it as they talk).
- Rephrase their question (versus "parroting" it back word for word) to make sure you understand it correctly and that everyone else in the audience has heard it.
- Answer briefly while including the entire audience in your eye contact.
- If you don't know the answer, say so. Don't make it up. You can offer what you do know (i.e., "We didn't look at that option, but what we did do is . . .").
- If the response would reveal confidential information, say so and be quiet.
- Resist the urge to mentally label a person who asks very direct or hard questions as a troublemaker or someone who is trying to attack you (i.e., "Do you really believe that you can do xyz??"). Their sharp or aggressive tone could just be their communication style, or it may indicate that this topic is a strong area of concern. Don't be overwhelmed or get defensive. Just answer the question.
- Try to anticipate as many questions as possible ahead of time by asking colleagues or by identifying your weak points and crafting a response.
- Convey confidence by moving toward the questioner versus backing away and by maintaining good eye contact.

Special Note: Many presenters run out of time and have to cut their presentations short. This is usually due to the speaker trying to cram too much information or too many introductions into a short period of time. The three most common mistakes presenters make are:

1. Not practicing their presentation ahead of time

2. Using time-consuming audiovisual materials

3. Spending too much time on management and company history

Notes

1. In the Berkshire Hathaway, Inc., Chairman's Letter to Berkshire Hathaway Shareholders, March 3, 1983.

2. Adapted from SBA: Financing Basics Web site, http://www.sba.gov/financing/basics/basics.html; Kauffman eVenturing Web site (Finance and Accounting: Funding Sources), http://www.eventuring.org; Lister, K. & Harnish, T. (1995). *Finding Money: The Small Business Guide to Financing.* New York: Wiley Publications.

3. For more on *debt to equity,* see the Business Owner's Toolkit, http://www.toolkit.cch.com/text/P06_7305.asp.

4. For more on *personal guarantees,* see the Business Owner's Toolkit, http://www.toolkit.cch.com/text/P10_3376.asp.

5. For more on *leverage,* see the Business Owner's Toolkit, http://www.toolkit.cch.com/pops/P99_10_2000_02.asp.

6. Adapted from David Newton, "From Seed Stage to Mezzanine, a Breakdown of the Key Financing Terms and What They Mean to You," *Entrepreneur,* July 16, 2001, retrieved from http://www.Entrepreneur.com/article/0,4621,291079,00.html. Copyright © 2005, Entrepreneur.com; all rights reserved. Republished with permission from Entrepreneur.com.

7. Adapted from http://www.sba.gov; http://www.eventuring.org; K. Lister and T. Harnish, *Finding Money: The Small Business Guide to Financing* (New York: Wiley Publications, 1995).

8. Adapted from "Growthink's Top Nine Business Plan Mistakes," http://www.growthink.com/businessplan/resources/BusinessPlanMistakes.pdf Accessed December 12, 2005.

CHAPTER 7

The Evolving Management Team

Good leaders make people feel that they're at the very heart of things, not at the periphery. Everyone feels that he or she makes a difference to the success of the organization. When that happens people feel centered and that gives their work meaning.

—Warren Bennis

People are definitely a company's greatest asset. It doesn't make any difference whether the product is cars or cosmetics. A company is only as good as the people it keeps.

—Mary Kay Ash, founder of Mary Kay cosmetics

The great leaders are like the best conductors—they reach beyond the notes to reach the magic in the players.

—Blaine Lee, founder of FranklinCovey

Objectives:

1. Recognize that managing the growing new venture requires a distinct set of leadership skills

2. Learn the factors to consider when building the management team, including how to find the right people for the needs of the new venture

3. Understand the role of an advisory board and how to find the right advisers for the new venture

4. Learn about the corporate governance role of a board of directors and what to look for in potential outside independent directors

5. Understand the major forms of business ownership, the benefits and disadvantages associated with each one, and the factors an entrepreneur should consider when choosing a form of ownership

Strategy in Action

Potbelly Sandwich Works—Teamwork That Works

Potbelly Sandwich Works began in 1977 as a small antique store. To supplement the antique-dealing side of the business, the couple who owned it decided to make sandwiches for their customers. What began as a lark turned out to be stroke of genius. Soon, people who couldn't care less about vintage glass doorknobs were stopping by to enjoy special sandwiches and homemade desserts in this unusual atmosphere. As the years passed, the lines grew. Booths were added, along with ovens for toasting sandwiches to perfection, vista-coolers, napkin dispensers, hand-dipped ice cream, and live music. Over the last two and a half decades, the little antique shop has grown into a unique sandwich restaurant with 78 stores in eight states and the District of Columbia.

Bryant Keil purchased this antiques shop-turned-sandwich joint in 1996, and he has come to believe that Potbelly's success "has as much to do with people as product" (Meyer, 2005). While every Potbelly detail is published in a thick manual, Keil acknowledges that ultimately the customers' experience comes down to the "smiling, happy" workers who serve them. "We have a book as big as anybody else's book that delineates every microcomponent of our business. But the reality is, you don't refer back to the book very often," Keil said. "If you train people to make good choices, and the choice is ultimately to exceed customer expectations, you end up making the right decisions" (Meyer, 2005). The key to instilling such enthusiasm and loyalty in employees starts with the attention that is paid to the environment of the organization. Potbelly's describes its store atmosphere as warm and homey: "We are proud to say that our stores are 'real' environments—you won't find any plastic laminate surfaces, fluorescent lighting or unnatural materials in our dining areas. Instead, through use of warm lighting, natural wood, marble, antique fixtures and signage, as well as live music, we create a welcoming place where our customers are happy to meet friends and see familiar faces. We strive to make each location the local, neighborhood sandwich shop of the community it serves. Everyone at Potbelly is committed to providing the highest levels of service we can achieve. We attract the brightest and the best people who share and embrace Potbelly's values. We offer ongoing learning and development opportunities along with coaching and mentoring in a positive, stimulating and open work environment. Our team members feel good about themselves and the work that they do, they take pride in the company and are committed to giving great customer service" (Meyer, 2005). According to the company's Web site (http:www.potbellys.com), the array of benefits offered to employees is impressive: Besides a competitive salary, Potbelly's staff members receive a stock option opportunity; 401K with company match; incentive plans; medical, dental, vision, life, and long-term disability insurance; paid time off; training programs; and free Potbelly food. In addition, the company articulates other advantages that are not often associated with

(Continued)

(Continued)

organizations in its industry: quality of life, a fun work environment, smaller crews, great live music, and no late nights or rowdy bar crowds. It also makes a rather unusual promise to its staff: Your clothes won't smell like grease from fryers or grills because there are no fryers or grills.

It seems clear that Keil's attention to the environment in which employees work—and to which customers are attracted—has led to the extraordinary attention employees pay to the details involved in creating a memorable customer experience. Furthermore, bringing in and retaining skilled people to Potbelly's board and management team have spurred the growth of the business. Potbelly seems well positioned for growth as it has recently expanded its management team talent to include William Moreton, chief executive of the Wendy's International Baja Fresh chain, who joined Potbelly as president and chief financial officer in June 2005.

Potbelly's provides benefits similar to Starbucks, so it is not surprising that Potbelly has received financial backing from Starbucks Corp.'s Chairman Howard Schultz and from investment firms Maveron, William Blair & Co., Oak Investment Partners, Oxford Capital Partners, and Benchmark Capital Management Co. Potbelly has raised more than $50 million to fund its expansion, closing its latest $15 million round in March. The company has signed leases on more than 30 new locations and is targeting sales of $100 million this year, up from $70 million in 2004 (Meyer, 2005). The company has chosen not to franchise at this point in time, preferring to expand with company-owned stores that are opened and run by store managers acculturated in Potbelly's mission and values. The investment in people throughout this organization has led to a cohesive team that embodies these values and brings them into the customer experience.

Up and Running: Managing the Growing Firm

The motivations and behaviors that are associated with successful start-ups can be very different from those that are required to manage a successful firm. New ventures are frequently launched by entrepreneurs who are passionate about a particular product or service, but who may have very little interest in management of an established organization (Willard, Krueger, & Feeser, 1992). Entrepreneurial leadership draws on components of transformational, team-building, and value-based leadership that enable the leader to mobilize the capacity to meet the challenges of new venture formation (Gupta, MacMillan, & Surie, 2004). Leaders will need to do the following (Gupta et al., 2004, p. 246):

1. extract exceptional commitment and effort from organizational stakeholders;
2. convince them that they can accomplish goals;
3. articulate a compelling organizational vision;
4. promise that their effort will lead to extraordinary outcomes;
5. persevere in the face of environmental change.

The transition from the entrepreneurial founder to the professional management team has been widely researched and linked to stories in the popular business press. For example, Auletta (1999) discussed several entrepreneurial start-ups, including Point cast, in which the founders resigned when it became apparent that their skills did not fit the needs of the growing firm. The life cycle perspective on the formation and growth of new ventures includes the influences of firm age, size, and growth stage on the specific set of managerial and leadership skills that are required (Boeker & Karichalil, 2002). Entrepreneurship strategy researchers have described the "leadership crisis" (Greiner, 1972) that occurs when the new venture outgrows the abilities of its founder or founding team. Some founders do not have the competencies needed by the growing organization, and they may require professional management and delegation (Certo, Covin, Daily, & Dalton, 2001; Finkelstein & Hambrick, 1996). For example, the finance vice president (or maybe even the founder performing this role) who was adept at establishing controls and reports in the new venture may not be proficient at the very different tasks of cultivating the financial community, managing currency fluctuations, or dealing with complex tax problems (Hambrick & Crozier, 1985, p. 35).

Which is more likely to lead to founder departure—rapid growth or low growth? New ventures tend to be more focused on growth than on earnings or profitability (Boeker, 1992; Eisenhardt & Schoonhoven, 1990), so low growth may be an indicator that the founders do not have the appropriate skills to manage the firm. Rapid growth, however, may also indicate a strong need for new managers with different capabilities (Wasserman, 2001). Thus, a paradox is presented: "Is founder departure more likely when a firm is growing rapidly and the need for professional management is most urgent, or when the firm is growing more slowly or declining and there is pressure for founder replacement?" (Boeker & Karichalil, 2002, p. 819). Both perspectives were supported in a study of 78 semiconductor firms, in which two sets of causal factors influenced founder departure in opposite ways: the size and growth (very high and very low) of a new venture accelerated the rate of founder exits, and these pressures were ameliorated when founders were owners and board members as well as handling their particular position and functional responsibilities (Boeker & Karichalil, 2002). One of the most interesting implications of this study is that it offers a contrast to studies of top management succession in established firms. These firms have viewed rapid growth as an affirmation of the approaches taken by their top managers, and this, in turn, lowered top management turnover (Finkelstein & Hambrick, 1996). Another interesting finding was that complexity of leadership increases more directly with growth in the number of employees than with growth in sales (Boeker & Karichalil, 2002).

Research on successful new ventures has shown that teams perform better than one individual. This is why venture capitalists and other investors look for a balanced team when evaluating a potential firm. One of the best ways to begin preparing an organization for growth is to identify the abilities and skills that are critical to its success in the first two to three years (Dingee, Haslett, & Smollen, 1997) and to build a team that allows the founder to compensate for areas in which he or she is not as strong. In a young, fledgling company, it is not likely that the entrepreneur will have the resources to hire full-time management or even employees to perform all the functions. However, talent can be brought in on a part-time or contractual basis, and eventually some of these individuals may join the firm in a more permanent role. Here are two key questions to ask related to the entrepreneur's and the management team's (if one exists) skills:

- What is the depth of the team's knowledge and extent of their reputations in the types of markets, technologies, and operations in which the new venture will be active?
- What are the team's management skills in the three key areas of marketing, finance, and operations (Dingee et al., 1997)?

As the entrepreneur determines what skills are lacking to successfully grow the new venture, it is time to begin thinking about whom to bring on board. Hiring well is one of the most important activities in the entrepreneurship process. Hiring well means firing less often. Did you know that the term *firing* comes from the popular practice in the Middle Ages of burning someone's possessions and dwelling to ostracize them from the village? It makes the phrase, "you're fired," much more vivid, doesn't it? Here are some considerations when hiring team members and employees:

- Hire the person, not the position. It is difficult to fit somebody into a predefined box, and in entrepreneurial organizations, each person is required to do whatever it takes to help the new venture accomplish its goals. The "it's not my job" mentality has no place in the young, growing firm. Also, people bring with them to the organization a wide repertoire of skills that are often untapped. Find out what team members and employees like to do in their spare time and what approaches they might suggest to perform their work. The goal is to have everyone bring their "whole selves" to work, including their creativity, ingenuity, and productivity.

- Avoid the killer of innovative thinking: the attitude that "I already know all there is to know about this company, because I (or we) started it." This is a common pitfall of entrepreneurs, and even though many are diplomatic enough not to actually say the above words to employees or team members, the attitude hangs in the air and discourages any diversity of viewpoints. Here's a test: If the entrepreneur announces that a decision needs to be made and asks for input but nobody volunteers an idea, it's likely that the others fear the entrepreneur's reaction to any information they might provide. This is also the case if somebody volunteers an idea, but it's one the entrepreneur has already stated.

- Hire people smarter than you. An entrepreneur who is intimidated by people with expertise she or he does not possess, and who therefore hires only those who are less informed or educated, must have great feelings of inadequacy that will hamper venture growth.

- Provide clear expectations to the management team and to employees. If these individuals did not contribute to the strategy (mission, values, code of behavior, etc.) of the firm, it should be articulated and explained fully to them. Do not expect people to mind-read what they are supposed to do.

- Build the kind of company for which you would like to work. What type of environment, leadership style, teamwork, and so on would you like to be surrounded by every day? This should become the blueprint for building the organization that has the right people and the organizational culture in place to carry out its desired strategy.

Is it always better to bring in team members with significant entrepreneurial experience? In a study of nearly 100 businesses in the United Kingdom (Ucbasaran, Lockett, Wright, & Westhead, 2003), researchers found that where one or more entrepreneurs have prior entrepreneurial experience, these individuals may try to dominate those who are inexperienced entrepreneurially, thus reducing cohesion and creating conflict-induced team turnover. One inference from this study is that teams that introduce members who have prior entrepreneurial experience should be aware of both the assets and potential liabilities associated with this experience. The fact that one or more team members have been through the process does not necessarily mean they can replicate previous contributions (and strategies) with the same success in the future (Ucbasaran et al., 2003). Therefore, it makes sense to think carefully about the kinds of skills that are needed and not bring someone on board simply because they have prior entrepreneurial experience. The key is to determine whether they have the right kinds of experience and whether they will fit into the existing management team culture.

Speaking of Strategy

Six Principles for Retaining Loyal People and Partners

- Preach what you practice. Communicate the vision, goals, and values of the organization. Practice what you preach is also required.
- Partners must win also. Enable your vendors and partners to participate in win-win venture.
- Be selective in hiring. Select people with values consistent with the firm's. Membership on the team is selective.
- Use teams of talented people. Use small teams for most tasks and give them the power to decide. Provide simple rules for decision-making so teams can act.
- Provide high rewards for the right results. Reward long-term values and profitability. Provide solid compensation, benefits, and ownership.
- Listen hard, talk straight. Use honest, two-way communication and build trust. Tell people how they are doing and where they stand.

SOURCE: Thomas H. Byers and Richard C. Dorf, *Technology Ventures: From Idea to Enterprise* (New York: McGraw-Hill, 2005), p. 277.

The Innovator's Toolkit:	Creating a Collaborative Team Environment

As the entrepreneur builds the management team, here are some questions that trigger personal reflection and lead to the construction of an innovative and productive team environment. This tool can be used with management team members or with newly hired employees. It is a proactive way of creating the desired new venture culture (Gundry & LaMantia, 2001).

- It is important to me that as a team we . . .
- When it comes to working as a team, I really value . . .
- When it comes to customer satisfaction, I really value . . .
- In difficult times, I really value . . .
- Important values I think we need to hold as a team are . . .
- I think it is important that we all agree to . . .
- One thing I am most frustrated by about teams is . . .
- In team meetings, I think it is important that we . . .
- I want to be a part of a team that operates in this way . . .

Review Questions

1. How does leading an entrepreneurial venture differ from leading in a corporate environment?

2. What challenges are involved in transitioning from the entrepreneurial founder to the day-to-day business manager?

3. How should an entrepreneur approach building the management team?

Building an Advisory Board: Seeking Advice and Advisers

Entrepreneurs need good advice, and early in the formation of the new venture, they will likely ask the questions, "From whom can I get the best advice?" and "What should I look for in an adviser?" Not all advisers are effective. Some guidelines for selecting the right people for the specific new venture stage of development are provided below.

Six Tips for Finding the Best Advisors for Your Business[1]

1. *Recruit advisors for short-term objectives.* Startup business models evolve and change. Don't recruit advisors who will help you with future products or future markets. Focus on the short-term and determine what skills, introductions and knowledge you will need to accomplish your immediate business objectives. Your advisors should help you fill the gaps for the next six months, not six years.

2. *Advisors can help establish credibility.* One of your needs as an entrepreneur is to establish business credibility. This will help you attract customers, partners, key employees, financiers and other essential ingredients to get your business off the ground. Picking the right advisors will help you establish credibility. In fact, it is often easier to persuade industry luminaries and prominent experts to join your advisory board than it is to persuade operational executives who are not used to the idea of devoting personal time to serve on boards. Keep in mind, however, that industry luminaries are not likely to roll up their sleeves and help you with basic startup issues like meeting payroll and paying rent.

3. *Look for advisors in unusual places.* One traditional place to find advisors is by getting referrals from the SBA's SCORE (Service Corps of Retired Executives) program, a national mentoring service for entrepreneurs. However, to find advisors who are specialists in your business, you will need to be more creative. If your business has industry conferences or training workshops, this is one place to start looking. Open the Yellow Pages and call "competitors" from different regions or different neighborhoods that you can learn from. Ask your relatives and friends if anyone they know has started a comparable business. Talk to potential suppliers for introductions. You should also try using online services such as Micromentor, a free matching service for entrepreneurs and business mentors.

4. *A free lunch is often a better motivator than equity.* Some advisors will ask for equity in your business in exchange for advice and introductions. Others will be satisfied if you pay for lunch now and then. In my experience, the advisors who prefer a free lunch are better than the advisors who demand equity. As a gesture of gratitude, you may decide to give a particularly helpful advisor some equity in your company over time, but do not be in any rush to do so. If you have attracted a top advisor who is asking for equity, make sure you structure the compensation over a payment schedule (such as quarterly or annual) rather than upfront.

There is no standard compensation scheme for advisors, because it depends on how many advisors you need, how much time they will devote and what kind of company you have. For example, a rule of thumb for high-growth ventures is 1.0 to 2.5 percent of share capitalization for all advisors contrasted with 10 to 20 percent reserved for senior executives and key employees. If you have five advisors, you should consider 0.2 to 0.5 percent of share capitalization as compensation per advisor.

If you are too early-stage to put together an equity compensation plan, you should consider making a small cash payment to your advisors. For example, you can cover their expenses to attend meetings, or you can allow them to submit expense reports for sales and marketing activities that are tangentially related to your business. (If you do this, don't forget to specify an expense limit.) These are variations on the free lunch concept and tend to motivate advisors more effectively than equity, particularly while the company's business model is not yet proven and the value of the equity is difficult to pin down.

5. *Don't treat advisors like employees or suppliers.* It's not easy to hold advisors accountable. They are not like employees whom you are paying with a steady paycheck. They are not like suppliers who are billing you for services rendered. Even if

you are paying them, it is difficult to hold advisors accountable in practice. This is because most advisors have income from other sources and will treat your business as a part-time hobby or casual business interest. Since they are usually not fiscally responsible in the same manner as a company officer or director, they can easily walk away if they do not perform up to expectations.

6. *Set term limits.* Much like board members have term limits, advisory board roles should also have term limits such as 12 months or 24 months. It is awkward and may even be potentially damaging to your business's reputation to kick out an advisor if he or she is not performing. Setting term limits makes the transition happen naturally. In my experience, most advisors make their most valuable contribution shortly after they sign on and are excited about their involvement. After some months, they get distracted with other matters and it takes effort to keep them motivated. Some advisors will become very involved with your business, will take on the role of passionate advocates, and will want to renew their engagement. If you cannot afford to do so, don't be discouraged. If you treat your advisors well, they will continue to help you without any formal compensation and title and will expect nothing in return but the satisfaction of watching your business grow.

Research in Practice: The Role of Advice and Advisers

The National Small Business Poll (National Federation of Independent Business, 2002) of 750 firms included a study of the role of advice and advisers. Small business owners gather a continuous supply of information to help them manage their enterprises. In the process, they draw on many sources. Some are internal to the firm, including employees and register slips; some originate outside the firm such as periodicals and customers. Some sources provide personalized advice such as one-on-one counseling; some sources provide generic information on Web sites and in books. This poll examined the outside advisers whom owners solicit for advice and the types of advice they seek. Here are the key findings:

- Two thirds (66 percent) of small business owners have one person with whom they are likely to consult before making a critical business decision. In 56 percent of those cases, that person will be a family member. In order of frequency, these owners consult a spouse, a partner/co-owner, a professional adviser/counselor, an employee, and a son.

- One third (34 percent) of small-business owners have no one person to whom they turn prior to making a critical business decision. About 55 percent of these owners handle the decision "solo." The rest either change the adviser with the situation/decision or routinely consult with several people. In the last 12 months, 84 percent of small employers sought advice from one or more counselors (people not in the firm and not the firm's customers). The average number of advisers was three and one-half, and they provided advice on an average of five topical areas.

- Accountants were the group most likely to provide solicited advice (59 percent); next, were family members (44 percent), lawyers (39 percent), other business owners (34 percent), suppliers (31 percent), and insurance agents and brokers (30 percent).

- The advice solicited from counselors was commonly taken. However, a relationship between taking the advice and paying for the advice appeared. Owners were more likely to take advice if they had paid for it.

- Small businessmen and women often did not pay for the advice they received, or they paid for it indirectly through purchase of other goods and services. Payment was tied to the type of adviser. Lawyers charged 75 percent of those soliciting them; suppliers charged 3 percent.

- "Accounting, bookkeeping, and taxes" was the subject on which advice was most frequently sought. About 73 percent reported that they asked for advice on one or more matters in the last year. Other areas that were frequent topics of inquiry included: legal questions (56 percent); computers, software, Web sites, and telecommunications (53 percent); and industry-specific technical matters (48 percent).

Boards of Directors: Corporate Governance Considerations

As discussed in the previous section, there are many good reasons to establish an advisory board for the new venture. If the venture is a corporation, a board of directors must be appointed. The key difference between advisory boards and boards of directors is that the latter have legal responsibilities and voting authority in the company. Advisory boards do not. One thing to keep in mind is that without the voting authority that directors have, some entrepreneurs may be less inclined to take the advice of advisory board members, and likewise, some advisers might not take their role seriously. However, both are useful to entrepreneurs. Members of advisory boards and boards of directors can accelerate the new venture's development in four major ways (Telecommunications Development Fund, 2002):

- Access: Board members can supply networking and contacts to attract capital investment and to recruit employees and other members of the management team. In time, this access will extend to developing strategic partnerships and selling to high-visibility customers.

- Credibility: Outsiders will assume the new venture has experienced assistance, and that it is worth considering. This will be helpful when trying to attract capital and management talent.

- Mentoring: An effective board provides the entrepreneur with mentoring and guidance through prosperous and difficult times. Ideally, the board should always include at least one member whom the entrepreneur trusts and with whom he or she connects on a personal level.

Who should be selected as outside directors? The ideal member should meet at least five of the criteria below. Try to find members who do not duplicate one another's experiences. An ideal member:

- Is a mentor and trusted confidant
- Has built a management team
- Has attracted equity investors and debt financing
- Has created revenue and achieved positive cash flow
- Has developed strategic partnerships

- Is knowledgeable about your industry
- Is experienced in the key operational challenges the venture will face in the next year or two
- Has recent, successful experience in specific corporate functions and industries
- Complements, rather than duplicates, the strengths of the current management

Board members can be recruited through professionals the entrepreneur has already met, such as accountants and attorneys. Other entrepreneurs, local professional groups and trade associations, executives of successful companies, and former colleagues from prior employers can also help locate board members.

In summary, here are some thoughts from entrepreneurs about setting up and operating a board (Telecommunications Development Fund, 2002):

The Entrepreneur

1. Don't look at the board as an adversary.
2. Don't think you can do it on your own.
3. Invest in your board as a group and in each director as an individual.
4. Don't be a dictator; don't think you have all the answers.
5. Tolerate uncertainty.
6. Keep your sense of humor.

The Directors

1. Go slow. Start with a three-person board.
2. Work with people you like.
3. Find smart, experienced directors who want to help.
4. Seek out a mentor.
5. Recruit other CEOs.
6. Make sure to have at least one true outside independent director.
7. Pick directors who will tell you what you need (not what you want) to hear.
8. Don't let directors become disengaged.

The Entrepreneur's Communications

1. Be honest—disclose, disclose, disclose.
2. Go to your board early with problems.
3. No surprises . . . use green, yellow, and red flags.
4. Avoid conflict within the board.
5. Learn to listen to what your directors have to say.
6. Write out how the board will operate and what you expect from directors.

Failures and Foibles

Knowing When to Hire and Delegate

Lillian Vernon, founder of Lillian Vernon Corporation, a retail gift catalog and Internet sales company, started her mail-order catalog business in 1951 in a male-dominated industry controlled by well-established giants. Lillian Vernon Corporation is now a leading national catalog and on-line retailer that markets gifts, housewares, and gardening, seasonal, and children's products. The company, along with Time Life, a leading direct marketer of music and videos, is a division of Direct Holdings Worldwide. Through hard work and perseverance, the company has grown tremendously. In 2005, the company mailed 101 catalogs in 22 editions. Since 1951, 130 million orders have been shipped. The catalogs average 96 pages with more than 700 products in each edition. The company shipped 4.2 million packages in 2004. Lillian Vernon has become a household name, recognized as part of popular American culture and featured on numerous television programs, including *C.S.I.*, *Saturday Night Live*, *David Letterman*, *Conan O'Brien*, *The Daily Show*, *MADtv*, and *Jeopardy*. According to an Opinion Research poll, more than 47 million Americans are familiar with the Lillian Vernon name. Lillian Vernon says she still uses the tools that have always been the cornerstone of her success. Here is what happened as the company grew and she realized that she needed help in growing the company to reach its potential:

"Decision making at Lillian Vernon has always been entrepreneurial—the spirit of the entrepreneur controls all my major moves. I pride myself on examining each situation from all angles, gathering the important facts and acting on my best judgments. Good old-fashioned common sense—the core ingredient of an entrepreneur—has been invaluable in my decision-making process. Still, a smart entrepreneur needs the guidance and input of professional managers to make educated, sound business decisions. We have grown the company by combining the best qualities of entrepreneurship and professional management.

"When you're an entrepreneur, your business is like your child—a creation of your own making. Every morning, I was the first one in the office, reviewing the bills, signing the checks and putting out fires that ranged from a crisis in the warehouse to quality control issues. I approved every word of catalog copy and took phone orders from my customers. For the first 19 years, the business grew gradually, allowing me to continue directing all aspects of the operation. But between 1970 and 1984, Lillian Vernon grew from $1 million in sales with a small base of customers to sales of $115 million with millions of customers nationwide. As a result, I could no longer handle every job myself.

"I knew that my company could only grow if I faced the challenges inherent in growth. I set my course on becoming a manager. I also hired managers who were on the same wavelength— with an entrepreneurial spirit and a willingness to act and make decisions independently. The two aspects of my business that I value most are my employees and my mailing list. I've purposely kept our management team lean. I'm always available to discuss operations, but I encourage my executives to make their own departmental decisions.

"One of the most difficult decisions of my career came when my company experienced unabated growth. Sudden growth can push a company to that fine line between success and failure, and such was the case in 1983 when we grew 80 percent in a short period. Our computer system couldn't handle the influx of orders, and an update to accommodate the workload would

(Continued)

(Continued)

cost millions. Although we continued to buy products for a growing business, our inability to ship quickly resulted in a massive buildup of inventory. We needed more staff to get the job done. Suddenly all my company's assets were tied up in inventory and equipment and there was an insufficient influx of cash to meet all our financial obligations. I had to take a step back and assess where we were, where we were going and what actions were required. I was determined to save my company and, again, common sense led me to the only feasible course of action: I took out a loan to pay my bills. Carrying debt was a foreign concept to me, but at that time it was necessary.

"In the end, I paid back the loan ahead of schedule and shored up our operations. Nonetheless, it was a sobering experience. Entrepreneurs don't dwell on their mistakes: They learn and move forward. From that time on, I have closely monitored my company's growth rate. Four years after this crisis, in August 1987, Lillian Vernon Corp. became a public company. We were in the middle of building our new national distribution center in Virginia Beach then and everyone advised me to wait. But once again I followed my own rule of "Do it now!" Had I waited, the October 1987 stock market crash would have forced a lengthy postponement of our public offering.

"My company continues to prosper. We've moved to new headquarters and, as always, my simply furnished office has a desk facing the door so that I can see our bustling operation and be a part of it. I'm always in the office when I'm in town, and I continue to travel more than 200,000 miles each year to source new products for our nine catalogs. My vice presidents and senior buyers accompany me on these trips, and I've learned to value and trust their instincts as well as my own. After all, success is a team effort. I may have planted the garden, but it's taken a team of entrepreneurial-minded professionals to keep it growing." (Vernon, 1999, p. 13).

SOURCE: Vernon, L. (1999). Entrepreneurs and professional managers. *Management Review, 88*(2), 13. Reprinted with permission granted via Copyright Clearance Center.

Review Questions

1. How should an entrepreneur approach building the advisory board?

2. What are some of the ways a board can accelerate the development and growth of a new venture?

Forms of Ownership: Legal Structure of the Organization

Sole Proprietorship

Sole proprietorship is the quickest and easiest business structure to adopt. If you don't incorporate and don't have a partner, you are automatically a sole proprietor. Legally, you and your business are the same. As a sole proprietor, your net profit is taxed at personal income tax rates, and you are personally liable for any debts or losses you incur. If you run a one-person business that has limited liability, you may not need to bother with the expense and time of incorporation or any other more complex form of organization. Sole proprietorship can also be a good choice for businesses in the start-up phase because it does not have a lot of legal requirements.

As a sole proprietor, you may still need to register your business. Business licensing differs from state to state. Some, like California, require nearly all businesses to register; others have relatively few requirements. If, however, you are doing business as a sole proprietor under a trade name rather than your personal name (*City Architects,* as opposed to *Allison Smith, Architect*), you will likely need to get a business certificate or register as a DBA (Doing Business As). This allows your customers, your suppliers, the government, and anyone else with whom your business deals to know who the real owner of the business is.

"Doing Business As"

You may choose to register as a DBA even if the law doesn't require it. A DBA can help you open a business bank account and may reassure some clients that you have lasting power. In most cases, you register for a business certificate (DBA) at the county clerk's office. In a few cases, you register with the state or city, but a call to the county clerk will resolve the question.

Benefits:

- The least expensive and least complicated business structure to form

Disadvantages:

- Owner personally liable for debts and losses
- No other type of liability protection

Corporations

Although incorporation requires more paperwork and expense than sole proprietorship, it does give you one critical benefit—protection from liability. A corporation is a separate legal entity from the person (or people) who owns it. The corporation, not the owner, enters into business deals, owns property, borrows money, and engages in other business activity. Because the corporation is involved in these business deals, you and your personal assets will, in many cases, be protected from liability if something goes wrong.

For businesses with more than one owner, incorporating can often protect you from the actions and misdeeds of your co-owners. In a partnership, each partner is personally liable for the business-related actions of all the partners.

Benefits:

- You can gain access to benefit plans only available to corporations.
- Ownership is easily transferred. The continuity of the business is not influenced by shareholder withdrawal.

- Being incorporated also creates a positive image for your company. When you are trying to raise capital, obtain credit card merchant status, win certain kinds of new customers, or do business in foreign countries, incorporation can be important for the impression and assurance it provides.

Entrepreneurs should be aware that corporate liability protection is not absolute. If you are interested in incorporation because of the protection it promises, look at the following exceptions:

1. It cannot protect you from your own bad acts. Being a director of a corporation does not protect you from personal liability from the wrongs you personally commit. For example: You run a package delivery service, and you fill in for a driver who has called in sick. If, in the process, you run into a busload of people, you are personally liable for the damage.

2. It cannot protect you from things you personally guarantee. Banks and some corporate creditors often require personal guarantees from people in a corporation. So if your business were to fail, you would be personally responsible for repaying these debts. In addition, you don't want to become personally liable inadvertently . . . so be certain your name, title, and company name are on anything you sign.

3. It cannot protect you from owing governmental trust fund taxes (withholding taxes and sales taxes). When taxes are held in trust, all officers and anyone who has check-signing authority are jointly liable to the government for these taxes. That means that as a principal, you cannot hide behind the corporation and will be personally liable for these taxes if they are not paid.

4. It cannot protect you from some state laws. New York, for example, has a law which says that the 10 largest shareholders of a corporation are personally responsible for unpaid employee wages. If a restaurant operates for three years and goes out of business, the owners and principals are personally responsible for any unpaid salaries.

5. It cannot protect people in certain professions. Professionals including doctors, lawyers, and accountants are personally liable in any lawsuit.

Disadvantages:

- This form of ownership is subject to the most fees and requirements: it's the most expensive way to form an organization.
- Double Taxation: The corporation is taxed on its income, and the stockholder is taxed when dividends are received.
- Shareholders have final control. This will limit the owner's independence and control.

S Corporations

S Corporation status gives you the liability protection of a corporation and allows you to pay taxes on the same basis as a sole proprietor or partnership (i.e., you pay tax at the personal rate, and your profits are your salary). In S Corporations, the number of corporate shareholders is limited to 75, all shareholders must be U.S. citizens, and shareholders must be individuals rather than other corporations or estates. The only exception is tax-exempt, charitable organizations.

Many tax and legal experts recommend S Corporation status for smaller entities and start-ups. It can provide you with corporate liability protection and potentially reduces your tax burden (because corporate income is taxed at one level instead of two). In addition, if your business experiences a loss in its first year, you can generally pass that loss through to your personal income tax return. There are other potential tax advantages as well, including the ability to deduct (as an investment interest expense) interest you incur to buy S Corporation stock.

On the downside, S Corporations are limited in terms of the amount of deductions for fringe benefits such as heath insurance, group term life insurance, deferred compensation plans, and so on. Whereas a C Corporation can deduct these benefits for all owner-employees, an S Corporation cannot deduct them for an owner-employee who owns 2 percent or more of the corporate stock. For example, a C Corporation can deduct 100 percent of its owner-employees' health benefits, while at present, S Corporations can deduct only 30 percent (the same as a sole proprietorship). Deductibility will be raised, in stages, from today's 30 percent to an eventual 80 percent over 10 years.

To become an S Corporation, all shareholders must file and sign IRS Form 2553. Shareholders pay income tax on their share of the corporation's income, regardless of whether or not they actually received the money. If the corporation suffered a loss, shareholders can claim their share of that loss. Most states follow the federal pattern of not imposing corporate tax on an S Corporation but instead taxing the shareholders. Be aware, however, that some states tax an S Corporation the same as a C Corporation. You might want to contact the tax division of your state treasury department to find out how this is handled in your state.

Benefits:

- Corporate liability protection for shareholders
- Profits are taxed at the personal rate
- Potential to write off losses against personal income tax

Disadvantages:

- Requires more paperwork and is more expensive than partnership or sole proprietorship
- No benefit deduction for owner-employees with 2 percent or more of corporate stock

C Corporation

The main difference between a C Corporation and other business structures is that a C Corporation files and pays corporate income taxes directly. In other words, a C Corporation is considered an entity separate from its shareholders and must pay taxes on income left over after business expenses. There are a number of instances where it is beneficial to become a C Corporation. If you plan to keep profits and other chunks of cash in the bank to finance your growth, repay debt, or make other capital expenditures, C Corporation status makes sense. This is because C Corporations can take advantage of lower initial corporate income tax rates. For profitable companies, C Corporation status has the ability to provide greater flexibility in terms of planning and controlling federal income taxes. C Corporations also can deduct the cost of certain fringe benefit packages.

If you form a C Corporation, be aware that you run the risk of being taxed twice on your profits—once as a corporation and a second time as an individual when you dispense those profits as dividends or when you liquidate the corporation. This is one of the major disadvantages of a C Corporation. Let's say, for example, your company has profits of $100,000 for one year. First, the corporation will have to pay tax on it. Then, if you parcel that money out to yourself or other owners, the IRS may treat it as dividends and will tax you as an individual. If you wait until the next year to take all or part of that money as salary, you will already have paid corporate tax on it during the year it was profit and will then pay tax as an individual when you give it to yourself as salary. Many tax and financial experts can come up with ways to plan for profits to avoid or limit this type of double taxation. You should speak with your accountant or tax adviser to come up with the most flexible program for your company.

Another tax-related benefit to C Corporation status is its ability to treat the cost of fringe benefits as fully tax deductible. Whereas a C Corporation can deduct benefits (such as heath insurance, group term life insurance, deferred compensation plans, etc.) for all owner-employees, an S Corporation cannot deduct them for an owner-employee who owns 2 percent or more of the corporate stock. A C Corporation can deduct 100 percent of its owner-employees' health benefits, while at present, S Corporations can deduct only 30 percent (the same as a sole proprietorship). Owners of C Corporations can also borrow from the corporation's retirement fund and have access to certain benefit packages that S Corporations do not permit.

General Partnership

If you have business partners, you have the option of forming a partnership instead of incorporating. Should you choose this route, experts highly recommend that you formalize this relationship by creating a written general partnership agreement that will protect all parties involved. It is possible to have a partnership without a formal agreement, in which case you will be governed by the Uniform Partnership Act, but this allows for little flexibility or protection in events such as one partner leaving. A written contract, on the other hand, will spell out exactly what each partner's rights and responsibilities are.

The chief benefit of a general partnership is that you have someone with whom to share the business burden. It will also probably cost less and require less paperwork to form a partnership than a corporation. In addition to the written partnership agreement, you may have to file a partnership certificate registering the company's name and perhaps obtain a business license as well. These requirements vary from state to state and locality to locality, so check with your county clerk's office to find out the specific requirements for your region.

If you do form a partnership, each year, you have to file a partnership information return that tells the IRS and state officials how much the partnership earned or lost and how those gains and losses are to be divided among the partners. The partnership itself does not pay income taxes. Instead, the partners report this information and pay taxes on their shares on their personal returns, as an individual does in a sole proprietorship.

The downside of partnerships is that you are personally responsible for your partner's liabilities related to the business. One partner can take actions—such as signing a contract—that legally bind the partnership entity, even if all the partners were not consulted. Each partner is also personally liable for injuries caused by one partner on company business. In other words, if one partner causes an accident while making a delivery with the company van, all partnership assets, as well as each partner's personal assets, are at risk. Of course, a partnership can protect itself against such risks by carrying the proper insurance.

Benefits:

- A way to share the business burden
- Simpler paperwork and less cost than incorporation

Disadvantages:

- All partners are personally liable for the business actions of a single partner. Liability is unlimited.
- Transferring ownership requires the consent of all the partners.
- A majority vote of partners is required for control.

Limited Partnership

Limited partnerships are typically used for real estate investing or in situations where a business is looking to finance expansion. For most small businesses, forming a general partnership or an S corporation will meet their needs. In circumstances where they are appropriate, limited partnerships provide many of the benefits of partnerships and corporations. They provide a way for small businesses to raise money without taking in new partners, forming a corporation, or issuing stock.

A limited partnership must have one or more general partners, who have the same responsibilities and liability restrictions as they would in a general partnership. In addition, there are one or more "limited" partners, typically investors not involved in the day-to-day activities of the company. These limited partners are not personally liable for debts of the partnership, and they get the same tax advantages as a general partner. However, they do have significant restrictions. They can not, for instance, be involved in the management of the company (with few exceptions). If they are, they may become personally liable for the partnership's debts. Creating a limited partnership can be as complex and costly as forming a corporation. It is advisable to hire an attorney to assist you in conforming to the various filing requirements in your state.

Benefits:

- Ability for partnerships to raise money without involving outside investors in day-to-day business decisions
- Limited personal liability and greater tax advantages for limited partner

Disadvantages:

- Complex and costly filing procedures
- General partners still have personal liability for company's debts and actions

Limited Liability Company

Yet another business structure option has been created as a hybrid of the corporation and the partnership—the limited liability company. A limited liability company (LLC) has the liability protection of a corporation but the tax status of a partnership. In other words, although you get liability safeguards similar to those of a corporate shareholder, you pay taxes at the personal rate on your share of the profits or use the loss to offset other income. While an LLC has many of the same characteristics as an S corporation or a limited partnership, it is, in many cases, more flexible. For example, it is possible to use an LLC to bypass the restrictions on S corporation ownership, to allocate profits differently from ownership interests, or to get around the general partner's personal liability in a limited partnership. Every state, with the exception of Hawaii and Vermont, allows limited liability companies. States have different sets of restrictions, however, so it is advisable to check with your state department of taxation first to find out the applicable state laws and if your company would qualify to be an LLC.

Filing to form an LLC can be extremely complicated, and the paperwork needs to be completed meticulously, so you probably want to hire an attorney to help you. You need to follow the state rules that govern formation of an LLC in your state and to file the proper forms with the correct state bureau. You also will need to observe IRS guidelines in your LLC operating agreement (governing the relationships and responsibilities of the LLC owners) so that you qualify for taxation as a partnership rather than a corporation. Another new structure, the limited liability partnership, provides benefits similar to those in an LLC to professional partnerships.

Benefits:

- Liability protection similar to a corporation but tax status of a partnership
- Potentially greater flexibility than an S corporation or a limited partnership

Disadvantages:

- Extremely complicated filing procedure that requires strict adherence to state and federal guidelines
- Not yet available in all states

Nonprofit Corporation

The primary benefit of being a nonprofit (or not-for-profit) corporation is that you are exempt from paying income taxes. You must qualify for tax-exempt status under the IRS Code Section 501(c)(3). Should you attain this status, not only is your corporation exempt from paying taxes, but people, corporations, or other organizations that contribute to your corporation can take a tax deduction for those contributions. There are other benefits, too. For example, if you do a lot of mailings, you can qualify for the lower nonprofit postal rate. Plus, there is the positive image a nonprofit connotes: It tells people that you're in business not for the money but for a higher purpose.

Typically, tax-exempt status is reserved for corporations formed for religious, charitable, literary, scientific, or educational purposes. This could include child care centers, museums, research institutes, dance or music groups, places of worship, schools, community groups, and others. Of course, you don't make money from a nonprofit company; once you put assets in, they become property of that corporation and must be dedicated to specific nonprofit purposes. And you can't sell the business to get your money back. A nonprofit company goes on; if it is sold, liquidated, or otherwise ends, the assets must be passed to another nonprofit corporation. There are other responsibilities and restrictions in running a nonprofit business, too numerous to list here. If you are seriously considering forming a nonprofit corporation, you might want to get in touch with legal or tax counsel that specializes in this area.

Benefits:

- Tax-exempt status
- Contributions tax deductible
- Helps project an altruistic image for company

Disadvantages:

- Tax advantages limited to companies formed for religious, charitable, literary, scientific, or educational purposes

Review Questions

1. Which of the different forms of business ownership seems most appropriate to your business?

2. What are the benefits and disadvantages?

┌─ **Strategic Reflection Point** ─────────────────────────────

Entrepreneurial Leader Behaviors

Instructions

You are probably aware of people in your organization or industry who are exceptionally skilled at motivating, influencing, or enabling you, others, or groups to contribute to the success of the organization or task.

We might call such people "outstanding entrepreneurial leaders."

Below are several behaviors and characteristics that can be used to describe outstanding entrepreneurial leaders. Each behavior or characteristic is accompanied by a short definition to clarify its meaning.

Using the above description of leaders as a guide, rate the behaviors and characteristics on the following pages. To do this, on the line next to each behavior or characteristic write the number from the scale below that best describes how important that behavior or characteristic is for a person to be an outstanding entrepreneurial leader.

Scale

1 = This behavior or characteristic **greatly inhibits** a person from being an outstanding leader.

2 = This behavior or characteristic **somewhat inhibits** a person from being an outstanding leader.

3 = This behavior or characteristic **slightly inhibits** a person from being an outstanding leader.

4 = This behavior or characteristic **has no impact** on whether a person is an outstanding leader.

5 = This behavior or characteristic **contributes slightly** to a person being an outstanding leader.

6 = This behavior or characteristic **contributes somewhat** to a person being an outstanding leader.

7 = This behavior or characteristic **contributes greatly** to a person being an outstanding leader.

An example is shown below. If you believed that being tall *inhibited* a person from being an outstanding leader, you would write 1, 2, or 3 on the line to the left of "Tall," depending on how much you thought being tall inhibited outstanding leadership. If you believed that being tall contributes to a person's being an outstanding leader, you would write 5, 6, or 7 on the line to the left of "Tall," depending on how much you thought being tall contributed to outstanding leadership. Finally, if you believed that being tall had no effect on whether a person was an outstanding leader, you would write 4 on the line to the left of "Tall."

Fill in each blank below with the scale value (1 through 7) you feel best describes how important the behavior or characteristic is to being an outstanding entrepreneurial leader.

_____	A. Tall	= Of significantly above average height
_____	1. Diplomatic	= Skilled at interpersonal relations, tactful
_____	2. Positive	= Generally optimistic and confident
_____	3. Improvement-oriented	= Seeks continuous performance improvement
_____	4. Inspirational	= Inspires emotions, beliefs, values, and behaviors of others, inspires others to be motivated to work hard
_____	5. Integrator	= Integrates people or things into cohesive, working whole
_____	6. Encouraging	= Gives courage, confidence or hope through reassuring and advising
_____	7. Decisive	= Makes decisions firmly and quickly
_____	8. Enthusiastic	= Demonstrates and imparts strong positive emotions for work
_____	9. Intellectually stimulating	= Encourages others to think and use their minds; challenges beliefs, stereotypes, and attitudes of others
_____	10. Informed	= Knowledgeable; aware of information.
_____	11. Effective bargainer	= Is able to negotiate effectively, able to make transactions with others on favorable terms
_____	12. Foresight	= Anticipates possible future events
_____	13. Intuitive	= Has extra insight
_____	14. Convincing	= Unusually able to persuade others of his/her viewpoint
_____	15. Confidence builder	= Instills others with confidence by showing confidence in them
_____	16. Team builder	= Able to induce group members to work together
_____	17. Performance-oriented	= Sets high standards of performance
_____	18. Ambitious	= Sets high goals, works hard
_____	19. Visionary	= Has a vision and imagination of the future
_____	20. Autonomous	= Acts independently, does not rely on others
_____	21. Independent	= Does not rely on others; self-governing
_____	22. Risk taker	= Willing to invest major resources in endeavors that do not have high probability of success
_____	23. Self-interested	= Pursues own best interests

SOURCE: Reprinted from V. Gupta, I. C. MacMillan, and G. Surie, "Entrepreneurial Leadership: Developing and Measuring a Cross-Cultural Construct," *Journal of Business Venturing* 19 (2004): 241–260. Printed with permission.

Summary of Chapter Objectives

1. Recognize that managing the growing new venture requires a distinct set of leadership skills
   - Transformational, team-building, and value-based leadership enables the entrepreneurial leader to gain commitment from stakeholders, convince them that the goals are reachable, articulate a meaningful vision, link effort to extraordinary outcomes, and persevere in the face of change.

2. Learn the factors to consider when building the management team, including how to find the right people for the needs of the new venture
   - It is critical to hire well in the new venture, and this includes management team members as well as employees. Hire the person, not the position, and hire someone smarter than you.
   - Avoid killing the innovative thinking of new members, and provide clear expectations to everyone. Just because someone has prior entrepreneurial experience doesn't make that person the right fit with the new venture.

3. Understand the role of an advisory board and how to find the right advisers for the new venture
   - Not all advisers are effective. Not all advisers take their roles seriously and offer the important advice and connections that an entrepreneur needs.

4. Learn about the corporate governance role of a board of directors and what to look for in potential outside independent directors
   - Directors provide access, credibility, and mentoring to the entrepreneur and the new venture.
   - Directors should have knowledge of your industry, should have experience in acquiring equity or debt capital investment, should know how to develop strategic partnerships, and should have skills that complement—not duplicate—those of the management team.

5. Understand the major forms of business ownership, the benefits and disadvantages associated with each one, and what factors an entrepreneur should consider when choosing a form of ownership
   - Entrepreneurs can select from the sole proprietorship, the corporation (C Corporation and S Corporation), the partnership (general and limited), the limited liability company, and the nonprofit corporation.
   - There are benefits and disadvantages to each, as well as implications for capital investment, taxes, and internal management relationships in the new venture.

CASE 7.1   College Nannies and Tutors: Taking Care of Business—and Families

College Nannies, as it started, now College Nannies and Tutors, is a professional search company. This is how it works: A family will contract with the company to recruit, interview, screen, and eventually place a nanny or a tutor with their family. The nanny is employed by the family, and the tutor is employed by the company. Joseph Keeley, a 2003 winner of the Global Student Entrepreneur of the Year Award, Great Lakes region, founded the company while a student at the University of St. Thomas in St. Paul, MN. He explains,

"The whole premise is that we place active role models with the children, whether it is after school to help them with homework, get them to different activities, or full-time in the summer when they're home from school and parents are both working. Our service enables them to be involved in a lot of different things and also to have someone [whom] they can look up to. It's safe, and we provide someone who has the level of responsibility that the parents are looking for, as well.

"In 2003 we had about 75 nannies [whom] we placed—that was our third year in business. Tutors is something we're just starting out with, so right now we only have a couple tutors. We're taking that fairly slow because we're working on some tutor training and the different curriculum assessment tools that we would need.

"In a year or two, we will probably have anywhere from 100 to 150 nannies and probably 20 tutors. In the company we have about four people who are involved at any given time with the business internally."

Joe's Decision to Become an Entrepreneur

"I was a freshman in college and I needed a summer job. I was a hockey player at the university at the time, and I was introduced to a family of two physicians—the dad was a former college hockey player. They had two boys [who] both played hockey and they were looking for a big brother of sorts to be with them during the summer because both parents had a demanding work schedule. So I got a summer job as a nanny (or a "manny," if you will). The job involved getting the boys up in the morning, taking them to baseball, to hockey practice, to their friends' houses. We'd go golfing, we'd go to the pool, we'd maybe do some reading or some educational thing—kind of had a blast.

"After that first summer I met a lot of people in the neighborhood through organizing little pick-up baseball games or whatever it may have been. A lot of parents in the neighborhood were expressing the same need. There seemed to be a disconnect between the families I was meeting and some of my friends [who] were working construction, or something that was just filling their time for the summer. They weren't really getting too much more above the paycheck. These families I had met started asking me if I knew of others who could perform this service. I would respond, `Yeah, I know someone and I'll find them,' and I came to be known as the person [whom] people could call."

From the Initial Idea to a Business

Joe's idea for College Nannies was an outgrowth of his experience with families. Once it started to grow, did he evaluate the merit of this idea in any way?

Joe recalls, "Yes. One benefit was being a student. I could take it very slow because it wasn't my sole livelihood. Anything you do above and beyond being a student, everyone thinks is wonderful. It's when you're doing it and you're not a student that it becomes even more real. I did a lot of research on what was out there. Ironically, I found that there were a lot of nanny placement services around the country—every major city seems to have a few. And many are very good. Some are more focused on running a business, and others just more focused on cash, and I really wanted to have a combination of the two. Most of them were focusing on what I like to call "Mary Poppins–type" placements: full-time, 40 hour a week, infant care. And although now I will find that for any given family, I thought there was a niche there to develop, not only just [to place] college students, but to also place college graduates.

"Not every family needs a full-time person—they may just need someone for the summer, and in that summer, it would be a different type of individual. Often, the school-aged kids are very active. They are running a hundred miles an hour, going to different activities—they need someone not only to keep up with them, but also to understand the activities and someone [whom] they can look up to, more importantly. There's a whole mentorship component to it, as well as educational. College students, my main recruitment base, seem to be a good fit for that. It involved a lot of research and talking to families. My business is far different now than it was when I first started, and I'm sure we'll continue to change in the future. It's continual evaluation, I guess."

The Role of Entrepreneurship Education in Building the Business

"I had the privilege of being in a highly ranked entrepreneurship program at University of St. Thomas in St. Paul. Actually, I was kind of a critic of the entrepreneurship degree when I got to school. You know, there's the age-old question of whether you can teach that. I knew I was going to go into business, but I wasn't quite sure about what specific discipline.

"So, as I got this idea, and it started to snowball into the future, I thought, well, I'll just connect some people, and then we started talking about potential liability and the need to determine what kind of structure I was going to have. I had all these questions. So I went to the entrepreneurship department and said, 'I think I'm going to start a business.' I talked with them, and so that was a tremendous asset—not only in the beginning, but all throughout school. I always had a very educated board of directors, or advisers, of professors. If we were working on a case study in class, it was always something that I could relate back to the business. And in some cases, in my entrepreneurship classes, doing projects—we'll do a fictitious marketing plan for Dell computer. But it meant even more, even to my team members, if we did it on something that would actually be implemented, so they would usually rise to the occasion. We would work on the business in class. It was kind of a constant work in progress with everyone.

With that in mind, I always focused on not trying to lose out on anything while I was in school. So growing slow, especially when you're working with kids, is pretty important because you can't just do a shotgun approach and hope something works. You shouldn't have too many chances to slip up when you're dealing with children.

The advantages of starting a business when you're a student are that there really isn't a lot of pressure. It seems that in society in general, whenever you're a student, if three people standing there are about the same age, [someone] asks them what are they doing and they say, 'I'm a student.' People say, that's great—you could be the 10th-year senior, and everyone thinks it's great that you're in school! It's when you're out of school that you have the pressure of answering the question, 'what are you going to do?' Being a student and having a business . . . everyone just thought that was the greatest thing.

"It truly did increase the value of my education because I had something that was my own case study, that was molded from classes and experiences, and I think it made my education much more relevant than the average undergraduate experience would be. I'm sure you're going to have a far different experience five years into the workforce, and you're going to be able to recall those experiences instead of just going right into an MBA program out of undergrad. I had that kind of ongoing experience, so that was definitely an advantage.

"As far as the disadvantages, I would have to say in any business, whether you're a student or outside of school, starting something can be pretty lonely. For the most part, unless you have a partner or significant growth, it's just you. Although you may have a lot of people to bounce things off of, it's overwhelming and it's all that you end up thinking about. You need some strong things in your life to be able to put that away.

"I kind of see it as a rollercoaster in a way. If your average employment is kind of a level field that keeps going fairly linear, I would say that small business, or any business for that matter, the lows may never be as low if you have a regular employment situation. It gets to be those points when you're extremely lonely, you don't feel you know what you're doing, you think, is this ever going to work? Part of you wants it to not work so you can just forget about it—you'd sell it for a dollar if someone would take it. But then there are the times when the highs won't ever be as high—I guess it's kind of those extremes that you have to have a little bit of both.

"With being a student, come the accolades and things. Whenever you do something above and beyond being a student, everyone thinks it's great. But there's some added pressure to it, I think, as well because your peers may think you're ungodly successful and are making boatloads of money, and in actuality, you probably haven't even paid yourself yet, if you are cash-positive.

"Initially, there was some word of mouth, and there was no mystery that I was 20 when I was coming. I think there were some credibility issues that I had to deal with. I'd come to their door to do an initial family meeting, and I'm

sure some of them were thinking, whoa—you're young—if they didn't know how old I was. I would talk to them on the phone about the process, and they were really excited about it (oh, you guys are very well-organized). I've had the comment before when I've come to the door and introduced myself, that they initially thought that I was their nanny.

"The Entrepreneurship program catered well to getting some real skills that I would need. Toward the tail end of my college career, they opened up a 24-hour entrepreneurship, practicing entrepreneurship lab—an incubator of sorts. We had access to copiers, phones, computers, fax machines . . . so that was certainly helpful. It was actually an office space. The first year, I had no need for an office to interview individuals. I'd just meet them at coffee shops or school, and I would meet with families at their homes. But it's kind of difficult when you're initially incorporated out of your dorm room. So, they were great. They definitely gave me more resources than I expected.

"Leveraging the fact that you're a student is probably the greatest resource that anyone who has a business, or even without a business, has. People will bend over backwards for students because either, one, they remember the way it was and remember it's difficult to get going and people like that mentorship or, two, they don't pose a threat to anyone. If you would call a company right now and say, I'm a student and I like your company. I'd like to come get an informational interview. Their head is going to get so big, they pat you on the back . . . but if you're out of school they're going to wonder what your agenda is. So I think leveraging the fact that I was a student in that business [was helpful] and for many people that caught their eye. That was definitely one of the most important things."

Getting the Balance Right: Building the Business Team

All start-ups are complex, but Joe Keeley feels his is especially challenging because he is sending screened individuals into homes with children

"Addressing the insurance and legal issues—all the stuff that might not be fun for an entrepreneurial-minded marketer—it's really difficult, balancing everything that you have on your plate. You need to work on your business and on systems, and the concept of it—but if you spend all your time doing that, you don't spend any time servicing your customers and getting sales and things. It's finding that balance of knowing what you should be doing and is it the right decision. No one ever knows. It's kind of that sense of unknown which may be one of the exciting parts of it, but at the time, it just feels really overwhelming.

"Initially, I had an attorney who was from my hometown [who] was practicing law in the Twin Cities. I talked to him, and he did some pro bono work to help me set up the corporation, setting up my bylaws and things.

"The initial marketing was just from some cash that I put into the business. It was under a thousand dollars, what I initially put into it. There was no outside financing. Since I graduated, an investment group in the Twin Cities that focuses on growth management, turnarounds, and a number of different consulting services has put a first stage of capital in it. When you're out of school and you have office space and you're working on development of a business, as well as continuing with your customer base, there are a lot of other issues and expenses that come up as you address a lot more of these legal and insurance issues. I've moved into their offices and work with them.

"We're moving toward franchising the concept, which is a pretty significant financial, as well as organizational endeavor.

"Right now, I have a full-time person, the placement coordinator for the Twin Cities. I still assist her, but it frees me up to put systems into the business—in any franchise, there needs to be a set way things are done and forms and trademarked names and software. So we're in the process of putting our franchise package together. Then we will have a couple of these offices in the Twin Cities, and then we'll go to other major metro markets because there are the same dual-income working parents in Chicago as there are in the Twin Cities. So we will expand that way, hopefully. Our goal is to have upwards of around 150 franchises in the next three to four years. We have gotten some interest from some people just finding us on the Web and hearing about us either through the award or different articles or things.

"The business was initially started as College Summer Nannies, so that's all that I did. Parents will be quick to tell you what they want, what they need. They'll ask you, can you do this for me? Then all of a sudden, you have a new service. I think that is one advantage of being a small business—you can move very quickly, and if you want to start a new service tomorrow and it's kind of along the same business lines, you can.

"I think that's a strength of small business, of entrepreneurial-based firms, but I find it ironic that I'm in the middle of putting in systems, putting in accountability and software, that there's a process it goes through. Because it's a strength, but it's also that way of thinking and some other things that come along with it that can be a weakness. You find yourself trying to mimic some larger firms, especially with a franchise. It's a system, so you're kind of taking a little bit of that away by putting in policies and procedures. But in order to grow, that's what you need. All of these big companies and big franchises have systems that take longer to make decisions because they wouldn't like to be shooting from the hip.

"I don't think I'll be big business any time soon. It's definitely a very mission-driven company, and it needs to be because, as I mentioned before, it can get very lonely. There are days when you are flying 10,000 feet, and other days you just need to be put into a bucket and brought home. But at the end of the day, this is definitely about people. And the most difficult families to deal with can also be the most rewarding. You place someone and the kids love this person and it's a great job and the family's so happy. So, in any business, there needs to be something more than just financial reward. There needs to be something there, at least for me.

"I think, on just a surface level, it is pretty rewarding, although on a day-to-day basis, it seems like you're always a little bit lost and you're never going to get there. But you need to just stop and take a look back to see that you have come a long way and realize that. So that can be fairly rewarding. And, depending on your definition of success, unfortunately, a lot of people measure that financially. It's certainly a part of business—you have to pay the bills if you haven't got that component figured out. But it can be measured differently. Making a difference in the lives of children and families and students, in particular, has been something that is extraordinarily rewarding. And of course, at the tail end of college, with all the different awards and the student entrepreneurship award and the conferences we got to go to was certainly a nice boost to keep going with that.

"It's really nice that I can make up [my own hours]—if I have a lot of things to do, I can do some of it at home, I can work on a Saturday. I can take a Monday morning off and get some personal errands done, when I have friends that have little to no autonomy and room to move in their cubicles right now. They work 50 hours a week, whatever it might be, and, regardless of whether they're being productive or not, need to be there. If you're productive at seven or eight [o'clock] at night, you can do it then if you have your own business. It's kind of calling your shots. Although I've not been in the corporate work environment, I have a feeling just getting the sense from some of my peers, I might be in for a rude awakening since this is what I'm used to now."

What advice would Joe give to college students thinking about entrepreneurship?

"I think that if someone has an idea that they think might work, or might—even at the smallest level—create a job for themselves for income substitution—that they should definitely do it,

because you'll learn a tremendous amount just by doing that. Even if it's just differentiating yourself on paper so you can get a better job that you're looking for. Or having fun, or getting more out of your education, which I think was a priceless experience for me. Even if it's a simple service business and you just want to supplement your summer income.

"You know someone only makes $4,000 or 5,000 if they work a full-time job in the summer. If it's income, find something that you can do on your own, and you never know what it could snowball into. There are opportunities all over. Everyone seems to have an idea. I would encourage someone to go for it and access your resources that you have available, especially at universities because people are not teaching to be rich. They're teaching because they want to, and the really good [professors], especially [those] I find in the entrepreneurship department, certainly do their fair share of research and things, but they're teaching because they love to. They love the excitement that they get out of students. And they can be great resources.

"A lot of people say, 'why do you need to go into entrepreneurship if you're going to open your own business? 'You don't need your degree for that.' But you can learn a lot of the hard skills of managing risk and those skills. Those [skills] apply to corporations as well—especially when you see companies that want to be entrepreneurial and look at new lines of business because they want to change. Having those skills and working on your own are absolutely things that companies are going to want. I think they call it 'intrapreneurship' within a company.

"I was a critic initially of the program, and the major itself, but ironically, I'm now one of the biggest advocates. It's kind of the question of whether entrepreneurs are made or born. I think the answer to that question is, yes—they are both. There are a lot of different ways an idea can take shape—you can go from scratch, or maybe in a small service business you have a job and eventually take over. I see anxiety of entrepreneurship students when they see other people [who] have businesses or someone like me in school. You don't have to have an idea to learn things and to find it fascinating."

SOURCE: Case prepared with the assistance of Laurel Ofstein, who conducted the interview with Joseph Keeley, winner of the Global Student Entrepreneur of the Year Award, Great Lakes Region, 2003. Printed with permission.

Discussion Questions

1. What leadership skills did Joe exhibit in managing his growing company?

2. How should Joe change his leadership style to prepare to manage future franchises?

3. What type of advisers did Joe have to help build his business?

Note

1.   Listing from A. Advani, "6 Tips for Finding the Best Advisors for Your Business," *Entrepreneur,* July 6, 2004, retrieved from *http://www.entrepreneur.com/article/0,4621, 316289,00.html* 2004. Copyright © 2005 Entrepreneur Magazine; all rights reserved. Republished with permission from Entrepreneur.

References

Advani, A. (2004, July 6). *6 Tips for findings the best advisors for your business.* Retrieved from http://www. entrepreneur.com/article/0,4621,316289,00.html

Auletta, K. (1999). Push comes to shove in the valley. *Management Today, 17*(3), 58–62.

Boeker, W. (1992). Power and managerial dismissal: Scapegoating at the top. *Administrative Science Quarterly, 37,* 400–421.

Boeker, W., & Karichalil, R. (2002). Entrepreneurial transitions: Factors influencing founder departure. *Academy of Management Journal, 45*(3), 818–826.

Byers, T. H., & Dorf, R. C. (2005). *Technology ventures: From idea to enterprise.* New York: McGraw-Hill.

Certo, S. T., Covin, J. G., Daily, C. M., & Dalton, D. R. (2001). Wealth and the effects of founder management among IPO-stage new ventures. *Strategic Management Journal, 22,* 641–658.

Dingee, A. L. M., Haslett, B., & Smollen, L. E. (1997). Characteristics of a successful entrepreneurial management team. In S. E. Pratt (Ed.), *Pratt's guide to venture capital sources* (pp. 23–28). Wellesley Hills, MA: Venture Economics, Inc.

Eisenhardt, K. M., & Schoonhoven, C. (1990). Organizational growth: Linking founding team, strategy, and growth among U.S. semiconductor ventures, 1978–1988. *Administrative Science Quarterly, 35,* 504–529.

Finkelstein, S., & Hambrick, D. C. (1996). *Strategic leadership: Top executives and their effect on organizations.* St. Paul, MN: West.

Greiner, L. E. (1972). Evolution and revolution as organizations grow. *Harvard Business Review, 50*(4), 37–46.

Gundry, L. K., & LaMantia, L. (2001). *Breakthrough teams for breakneck times: Unlocking the genius of creative collaboration.* New York: Dearborn Books.

Gupta, V., MacMillan, I. C., & Surie, G. (2004). Entrepreneurial leadership: Developing and measuring a cross-cultural construct. *Journal of Business Venturing, 19,* 241–260.

Hambrick, D. C., & Crozier, L. M. (1985). Stumblers and stars in the management of rapid growth. *Journal of Business Venturing, 1,* 31–45.

Meyer, A. (2005, May 9). Potbelly's leader: People stoke growth. *Chicago Tribune.* Available from http://www.benchmark.com/news/sv/2005/05_09_2005a.php

National Federation of Independent Business (NFIB). (2002). National small business poll. *Advice and Advisors, 2*(5). Available from http://www.nfib.com/object/3447844.html

Telecommunications Development Fund. (2002). *Building your board: A corporate governance guide for entrepreneurs.* Washington, DC: Author.

Ucbasaran, D., Lockett, A., Wright, M., & Westhead, P. (2003). Entrepreneurial founder teams: Factors associated with member entry and exit. *Entrepreneurship Theory and Practice, 28*(2), 107–127.

Wasserman, N. (2001, August 3–8). *Founder-CEO succession and the paradox of entrepreneurial success.* Paper presented at the annual meeting of the Academy of Management, Washington, DC.

Willard, G. E., Krueger, D. A., & Feeser, H. R. (1992). In order to grow must the founder go: A comparison of performance between founder and non-founder managed high-growth manufacturing firms. *Journal of Business Venturing, 7*(3), 181–194.

CHAPTER 8

Building Networks and Strategic Alliances

I feel like my role is to connect the dots . . . I'm a conductor of a world class orchestra.

—Paige Arnof-Fenn, founder and
CEO of Mavens & Moguls

80 percent of success is showing up!

—Woody Allen, film director

Objectives:

1. Understand the benefits and outcomes of creating and sustaining strategic alliances

2. Learn how to determine the best "fit" among partners and resources in your environment and industry in forming your strategic alliances

3. Understand the value of investing in the social capital that can drive your business

4. Know the different types of networks and groups that you can use to build your social capital and the variety of networking strategies used by entrepreneurs

Speaking of Strategy

**A Conversation With Julie E. LeMoine,
President and Founder of U C How Technologies**

Julie LeMoine is an innovator and leader in technology and business. Her career includes 20 years of designing Internet and security products and services for intelligence agencies, National Security Agency (NSA), and Fortune 100 companies. Ms. LeMoine is a serial entrepreneur and member of the VoIP Security Association Technical Advisory Board, The Commonwealth Institute, and the Lahey Women's Health Initiative Task Force; she is a Springboard presenter alumna. In 2004, Ms. LeMoine was named one of the Top 10 Women to Watch in Technology and Science in New England.

Julie has been a technology leader, business leader, and team builder in information security and Internet-based solutions, including 20 years of defining and designing "first-time ever" Internet and security protocols, products, and services for the military, intelligence agencies, NSA, and Fortune 100 companies. She founded U C How Technologies to harness and integrate the current technology in information security and communication/collaborative techniques. One of the results is the SDE Server™, the company's flagship product, a highly secure, business-centric, persistent, collaboration platform that enables users to meet on-line where they communicate and share images, files, and applications within the context of their specific work content and needs.

Briefly describe your latest venture

U C How Technologies is a technology company that helps the enterprise avoid the most perilous of IT [information technology] issues, hacking, eavesdropping, and perhaps worst of all, possible noncompliance [with] government and other security regulations. U C How helps enterprises save thousands to millions in IT dollars and operations costs by rapidly deploying secure communication capabilities across the organization. U C How's Secure Private Office platform deploys in weeks and works in conjunction with ongoing security and communications strategies. It enables the enterprise to use the latest advanced communication tools such as chat, live file sharing and Voice Over Internet Protocol (VoIP) as well as their own or third-party software securely. All services are secured and logged. And, it fosters more efficient and effective business interactions across a diverse set of operating conditions.

The Secure Private Office was named one of the top three collaboration environments to consider for financial institution usage and as one of the best 30 software products to emerge in 2003 by Forrester Research. The technology has also been cited by the Yankee Group as one of the few options in collaboration and communication that is secure as well.

How did you choose to partner with your two largest partners, Concordant and Prescient?

Sales for any high-tech start-up come in two primary ways, direct or via channel. As a technology company with a software product line that resulted from our customers' needs, our focus has been to sell via channels as much as possible. Basically, our goal is to sell via established partners' sales and marketing arms. This sales strategy is something we used very successfully at the previous company I cofounded. This path is not without its issues, including trying to keep mind-share and promote sales via channels sales representatives who sell more than our software and/or services. However, the benefits are significant, including a reduction in cost, enabling a smaller company to remain focused on technology that customers need; reduced pressures to establish a significant sales and marketing arm; as well as the ability to capitalize on a partner's well-known brand name. One good channel can make a start-up company. This can be critical for a company such as U C How Technologies that is entirely customer funded and has yet to take external funding from investors or the like.

U C How Technologies sought out and partnered with the telecommunications company, Prescient World Wide for precisely the reasons stated above. They had a fully established sales rep force of over 200 external sales reps that sell the companies telecom services. We were a good fit for them as we brought a value-add service to their new VoIP services that would differentiate them in the market. These capabilities [that] U C How brought to the Prescient VoIP service offering could not be duplicated by them in time to capitalize on their value in the marketplace. So, both companies saw real value in . . . the partnership. We were introduced to Prescient by one of the U C How advisory board members. We negotiated a partnership that was equal footing as far as intellectual property (IP) as we both brought software products to the table, each with significant IP. We defined a revenue split of approximately 75 percent / 25 percent, where U C How would receive 25 percent of the sales of our joint product offering if their sales channel sold the joint offering.

Additionally, it made sense for U C How to partner with companies that will be able to staff and also benefit from the delivery of our technology to customers. One such partner for U C How is Concordant. We are a small technology company but become instantly bigger in service and support with partners like Concordant. This partnership gives us the flexibility to grow our customer base without having to hire as rapidly as might otherwise be necessary. Concordant is ranked by the Boston Business Journal as No. 13 in the state of MA for IT service providers. We partnered with them due to their focus on security and compliance consulting and their expertise in the health care technology. U C How's software is 100 percent HIPAA security compliant, making health care an industry that we can quickly support with the right introductions and partners. Concordant's excellence in both security and health care made them a perfect partnership choice as a partner to provide deployment and complementary consulting around our software for customers. The partnership allows us to mitigate risk of overhiring and opens more customer doors as well.

What have been some of the benefits and outcomes from the partnerships?

I addressed the benefits above, but the outcomes have varied. For example, the Concordant partnership brought the opportunity to present "Secure Collaboration in Health Care" at the annual Mass Data Health Care Consortia conference. I co-presented with Concordant, which lent us their credibility as a trusted IT service provider in health care. The contacts made at that conference are still ongoing. Concordant also made a PR announcement around our partnership that was also great for exposure.

The Prescient partnership brought new capabilities to the Secure Private Office software. We accomplished the tight integration with Voice over IP (VoIP) services, one of the hottest growing services in software today. U C How also secured VoIP. These two new features alone have greatly increased the value of our product line offering. Prescient and U C How shared in the funding of this integration, and as a result, this defrayed our costs. Additionally, we entered into an exclusive with them for the first six months. This exclusive guaranteed a certain amount of revenues to U C How, regardless of sales. This is a benefit but also held us back from working with other VoIP vendors. So, exclusives have to be weighed very carefully, and the terms need to be very clear.

(Continued)

(Continued)

What are some "must-haves" that you need to know about a potential partner before deciding to do business together?

- *Must* have a real partnership agreement, with all terms around meeting, updates, sales, payment, forecasts sharing, pricing, all of it spelled out clearly. This does not have to be long, but it needs to be very clear and to the point. Get signature at the CEO level.
- Identify the POCs (Point of Contact) that matter for your efforts with them and establish a good rapport with them.
- Make sure you feel you can get some amount of mind-share from them or you [are] wasting your time.
- Understand the "win-win-win" of it all. You win, they win, the customer wins.
- You should understand the way in which the partner will influence your bottom line. Make sure you are as clear as possible about how your products or services will be sold in combination with their products and services. Will this partner bring in revenues in some way, whether it is by introductions to new customers or channels, or will they sell your services or products directly?
- Is your partner ready to make the impact in the same time frame you are expecting or needing it to occur? This is very critical. If your partner is not ready, and you are counting on some kind of action in the early days, you can be left in a very unsatisfactory partnership. Hash out the timing, be as realistic as possible.
- Realize you do not know the inside of your partners' business, from good to bad. They are not you, and they will keep many things to themselves. Even if you share as much as possible, do not think you are getting all the insight you expect
- Understand what motivates them to sell for you and with you so you can push those buttons. For example, see if you can [provide incentives to] their sales force in some way.
- Understand their market and the way they sell as much as possible if you are selling with them or they are selling your services. It may be entirely different. Will their market resonate to your message or do you need to adjust?
- Trust, some level of trust must be there; don't go into business with a company or group you feel may have questionable integrity. It is your name and your company's reputation on the line.

SOURCE: Interview by Jill Kickul. Printed with permission.

The Benefits and Outcomes of Creating and Sustaining Strategic Alliances

With the emergence of enabling innovations and their direct impact on industry-wide advancement, small, independent entrepreneurial firms are faced with increasing competition and increasing barriers for advancement. The ability of small enterprises to leverage assets and vie with existing competitors has become exponentially difficult as resources are getting scarcer while competition remains fierce (Maynard, 1996). Realizing the very scope of these threats, few companies can compete without some form of organizational relationship (Jarratt, 1998). As a result, more and more entrepreneurs are quickly realizing the benefits of aligning with complementary partners and forming strategic alliances (Koza & Lewin, 1998).

A strategic alliance is a partnership, usually a business partnership that is strategic because it is entered into by design, with forethought, to be of benefit. A strategic alliance can be thought of as a value-added partnership made up of independent companies that, together, manage the flow of goods and services along the entire value-added chain. But being a member of a strategic alliance is more than being just another link in a chain. All good strategic alliances maintain themselves as a network first. In a network, as we have seen, information and services flow in more than one direction, and there is the possibility of reconfiguring the alliances as opportunities present themselves.

As Figure 8.1 illustrates, strategic alliances represent the *balance* between being entirely on your own in the marketplace and being completely swallowed up by the competition.

In terms of resource dependency (Pfeffer & Salancik, 1978), the development of interfirm alliances is a means by which organizations can support and facilitate their business initiatives, capabilities, and resources. In the formation of organizational relationships, distinct, value-adding expectations remain present between each allying firm. Originally, such arrangements were common in enabling a small firm to provide for a necessary and calculated growth, lacking

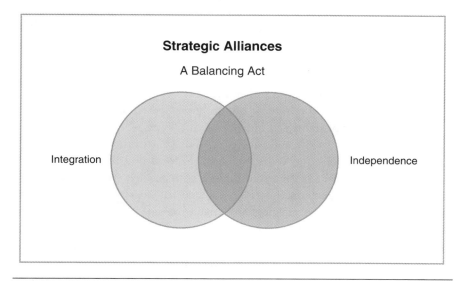

Figure 8.1   Strategic Alliances: Integration Versus Independence—the Balancing Act

the issues associated with a typical expansion (Varadarajan & Cunningham, 1995). In general, perceptions exist that entrepreneurs have typically experienced a greater need and realized benefit from partner relationships as a result of their general lack of financial resources and expertise. Therefore, it is critical for the success of the relationship that internal strategic congruence and understanding exists within the management team of each firm before an interfirm alliance is defined.

Because entrepreneurs generally have less resources (both financially and in terms of subject expertise) to draw on, innovations within their particular product or service is an area where benefits can clearly be seen. In a study by Angela Larson (1991), seven alliance partnerships were examined. In this study, all of the firms were able to benefit from product advances. Benefits seen in this study included advancement into new market segments and shorter product-development lead times. By capitalizing on these benefits, entrepreneurs can lower their entry cost and expedite their speed to entry, usually resulting in increased market shares. Moreover, access to new products can allow a firm to concentrate on its most competitive products while adding multiple related product applications (Doz & Hamel, 1998).

In addition to product improvements, technology advancements are another area where benefits are generally seen and expected from long-term alliances. Benefits tend to be realized through R&D collaboration, interfirm groups, and mutual assistance in such areas as distribution system design, software development, customized just-in-time inventory systems, and prototype testing (Larson, 1991). Gomes-Casseres (1994) provides an example of how a strategic alliance enabled a smaller firm to obtain a competitive edge. Mips Computer Systems, a relatively small computer firm, operated in the same market as IBM and Hewlett Packard. Because of scale economies, only a few of the producers in the market would ultimately survive. To obtain a large market share and influence the industry standard, Mips created various alliances. These partners were able to contribute to production capacity, market presence, technological competencies, and finance. With these alliances, Mips was able to attain a sizable market share (Gomes-Casseres, 1994). As shown by Mips, entrepreneurial firms are more apt to obtain a sizable market share by forming a strategic alliance.

In addition to product innovations and technological advancements, assistance with future strategic planning can often be a critical area where rewards are seen. As discussed by Miles, Preece, and Baetz (1999), smaller firms can often be limited in their managerial skills due to their tendency to focus on specific technological rather than general business concerns. Aligning with partners can give the smaller, entrepreneurial firm greater access to see the internal workings of a more structured company. In addition, alliances may enable the smaller, more niche-focused firm to draw on subject matter experts that may not exist in their company. This can help firms make sure all aspects of the business receive the appropriate amount of attention and detail, contributing to future success.

Even with driving forces behind organization relationships, alliances can lack self-culmination and maintenance. To ensure some level of entrepreneurial success, strategic alliances must be goal oriented, mutually focused, and communications compatible (Brush, 1996). Alliances should be grounded in trust and mutual understanding, with each firm's business model and strategy acknowledged, to succeed in adding value to its participants (Morgan & Hunt, 1994). Crucial in business relationships, these criteria fuel enterprise communication and cohesion, smoothing the seams of a venture between two similar yet separate entities.

Harbison and Pekar (1998) further suggest that the decision to pursue an alliance should begin with a clear statement of the strategic objective. Koza and Lewin (1998) contend that any interfirm alliance should be embedded in a firm's strategic portfolio. Establishing long-term strategic goals helps an entrepreneur to clearly understand the gaps between what can be accomplished internally and what may need outside partnership to accomplish. This understanding of strategic direction gives entrepreneurs confidence in their choice of partners and helps them to experience many of the benefits of a strategic alliance.

Organizational strategies exist between firms that possess characteristics pertinent to their current entrepreneurial objectives and business model. Relationships among firms in various markets are characterized by a chain of connections classified as technical, planning, knowledge, social, legal, and economic (Holmund & Kock, 1996). Only among these bonds can the necessary social, cultural, and ideological relationships be forged, fostering a framework of increased organizational ability across industrial barriers (Liljander & Strandvik, 1993).

How do these relationships evolve, and how are they sustained over time or the life cycle of the organization? Taken from a study by Kickul and Gundry (2000), here is the view of one CEO, who echoed the words of others in the sample:

> We are strong believers in the Japanese concept of 'Keiretsu.' We have a cadre of long-term suppliers that we value. When we are in a hurry, they give us priority. When there is a problem, they always make it right. We understand their abilities, limitations, and quirks, and do things to make their jobs much simpler and easier. Most of all we LISTEN to them and they listen to us. (p. 359).

Review Questions

1. What are some of the visible benefits of forming and developing a strategic alliance with another similar or different organization?

2. What are some examples of how you have seen these benefits realized by both firms (creating a win-win partnership)?

3. Before embarking on a strategic alliance, why do you think it is important that an interfirm alliance be embedded within the entrepreneurial firm's strategic portfolio?

| Research in Practice: | NFIB National Small Business Poll—Strategic Alliances |

How important are strategic alliances to entrepreneurs and small businesses? The value of forming and sustaining these alliances is well understood, but just how many companies actually form these, and with whom or what types of organizations are they formed? A poll on this topic was conducted by the National Federation of Independent Business (NFIB), the nation's largest small business advocacy group, representing the consensus views of its 600,000 members in the District of Columbia and all 50 state capitals.

The NFIB reported that about 64 percent of small manufacturers and 63 percent of small businesses in general (all industries) currently hold or have held some type of alliance. The most utilized alliance type by small manufacturers is a long-term production agreement and the most utilized by small businesses is a licensing agreement. This is interesting because it suggests that many entrepreneurs seek very specific types of alliances to further a particular growth strategy, as in the case of licensing, for example.

The study also showed that businesses that form alliances are just as likely to have three or more of them (about 50 percent). Moreover, once an alliance is formed, companies are not likely to discontinue that alliance or stop using alliances altogether (10 percent or fewer of the companies polled). Alliance use by small manufacturers varies based on the size of the manufacturer, ranging from 53 percent use by those with less than 10 employees to 71 percent use by those with 20 or more employees. Interestingly, small manufacturers do not seem to favor alliances with larger businesses over ones with similar/smaller businesses, although there are notable exceptions based on the type of alliance. Licensing agreements, product or service-based R&D alliances, and purchaser-supplier alliances tend to be formed with larger businesses. Only long-term outside contracting relationships tend to be more often formed with similar/smaller-sized partners.

How do alliance opportunities arise? The research suggests that these tend to be formed with partners who are drawn from either prior social or business relationships. More than 36 percent of the manufacturers and 40 percent of small-business owners report a prior social relationship with their most recent alliance partner and greater than 25 percent of the manufacturers held a previous alliance relationship. Almost 50 percent of the responding business owners had known their alliance partners for more than 5 years.

A majority of both small manufacturers and small-business owners indicate that their alliances are profitable, have exceeded expectations and have increased their ability to compete. Eighty-four (84) percent of all the small manufacturers and 76 percent of the small-business owners report positive alliance experiences and that the latter have exceeded expectations and have increased their ability to compete.

SOURCE: Based on NFIB, 2004, "Small Business Poll," *Strategic Alliances,* Volume 4, Issue 4, Washington, D.C., p. 1.

Review Questions

1. While many entrepreneurs experience a positive experience in joining forces with others, what can be several of the negatives of aligning with other firms?

2. What initial piece of advice would you give entrepreneurs as they are developing their first alliance?

Strategy in Action

Achieving Best "Fit" Among Partners and Resources

How do you choose partners that will really help your organization get key resources? To start, look for areas where you have abundant resources. These resources can be physical, such as land, but they may also include people and information. In particular, look for resources that you are currently underutilizing so that they are, in effect, surplus. This is what you bring to a potential partnership. Then, identify areas where you are lacking in resources, personnel, or access to information. These are the resources you need from a partner.

Consider also the external factors—the opportunities and threats. Consider how your business environment is changing and who will be your competitor(s) in the next decade. Begin by conducting a strategic analysis of the market sectors and target audiences that make the most sense for your business. What are the most profitable areas? Where is the greatest growth? Understand clearly where you are so that you can find the partners that best complement you.

Look at the changing competitive environment and assess how it will affect you. Assess the impact to your business of consumer behavior, competitor behavior, and government policies.

Overall, the difference between what you have and what you need is your *resource gap*. Identifying your resource gap helps you choose your partner (also review your TOWS from Chapter 4). You will look for someone who complements you—someone who has what you lack and lacks what you have. Some critical points underlying your strategic alliance:

- There must be a strategic intent for the alliance, and that intent must be linked with your abilities.
- You should know what resources you have and how to make the most of them.
- What you have an excess of, or aren't optimizing, is what you bring to the partnership.
- What you lack that is critical to attaining your vision is what you are looking for in a partner.
- If you have a capacity, how can someone else make use of it? Making an inventory of your attributes prevents missed opportunities.

Now that you have completed your resource gap, you are ready to locate those partners that would best complement your business. Where you need to do your research will depend on the kind of business you are in, so consider checking with professional and industry organizations, professional service providers such as accounting and law firms, and parallel businesses in your industry—a beautifully presented magazine might team up with its printer for mutual branding opportunities, for example. Even direct competitors can establish a noncompetitive relationship, pooling resources and ideas that help each other.

Many entrepreneurs are so wildly passionate about their business and vision that they assume other people are as high energy and as ready "to do whatever it takes to get the job done." This may not be so; it is smart to get references from people who have worked with the potential strategic partner.

(Continued)

(Continued)

Here are some useful sources of information to help make an inventory of potential partners:

- Acquaintances—customers, suppliers, and so on
- Industry associations
- Chambers of commerce, World Trade Council
- Diplomatic missions (for foreign companies)
- Government
- Economic development authorities
- Libraries and the Internet
- Annual reports
- Investment bankers
- Venture capital groups

Something to consider: if you are interested in a particular organization, buying one share in the company entitles you to information.

With Whom Should You Partner?

Understanding your resource gap helps you make a short list of potential partners. First, and more important, you are looking for a partner with a complementary resource situation. Your partner should also have:

- a history of successful relationships,
- personal chemistry with you, and
- a willingness and ability to contribute.

You are looking for someone who is your opposite in resources but a good match in terms of organizational culture. When you have done all of the analyses, the following questions should be considered:

1. What's your gut feeling about the partner you are considering?
2. Is there synergy in terms of goals and objectives of the partnership?
3. Is there a natural fit in terms of values, integrity, and personality?
4. Do your potential partners have a solid understanding of your objectives and goals, and are they genuinely excited about joining forces for a partnership?

When you think you have identified a possible partner who fits a profile, it is then time to ask yourself and your team the more difficult questions: Does this organization seem like a good fit? Are its people the best at what they do? Could I get someone even better?

If you compromise, you will probably end up spending a lot of time and energy holding up your end of the relationship. If you have a big-name strategic partner who doesn't live up to promises of bringing in customers or making managers available to the alliance, you may find yourself in a bind. Research has shown that for an alliance to be successful, three factors have to be *different* but complementary (Doz & Hamel, 1998):

1. Resources

2. Technology

3. Employees

In this way, each partner needs the other to fill their resource gap. Partners also need to be *similar* in the following ways (Doz & Hamel, 1998):

1. Perceived need for the venture

2. Ownership of it—risks and benefits should be shared

3. Commitment to it—top-level people often move on or retire; commitment should permeate the organization

4. Communication styles—communication is vital; you must agree on how best to do it

5. Values—openness, respect, and trust of outsiders

Finally, there needs to be understanding. Partners may not necessarily be the same, but they need to agree on certain issues.

In summary, you and your partner must be *different* in some ways, *similar* in others, and have a *mutual understanding*. In effect, you are looking for someone just like yourself who is doing something different. It may seem like an impossible scenario, but together, these criteria simply point you toward choosing someone with whom you can work, both practically and personally (Doz & Hamel, 1998).

Failures and Foibles

Setting the Tone by Planting Weeds

Sam is the CEO and lead entrepreneur of a start-up Internet company. He prides himself on "listening" to people and their ideas. But he also rapidly fires questions at them to assess if they have thought their point through. This is in the manner of, "If you are going to say something you better have thought it through and be able to 'defend' your point." But Sam's style is antithetical to collaboration. Some ideas are just seed ideas that are put out there. Learning to build on one another's ideas and grow an idea is the point. Don't take baby ideas and stomp on them before they have had time to germinate.

(Continued)

(Continued)

Sam did not realize that his style was sending a very clear message about how things get done in the company. He was creating a warfare environment of attack and defend, and it trickled down to other areas of the company of which he was unaware. The "attack and defend" approach was used in software reviews. A software developer had to endure hours of defending his code to reviewers who attacked how and why he created the code the way he did. If the environment was more collaborative, the "we" mentality would take over and the whole team would feel they were ultimately responsible for the code and would approach the "review" differently.

Sam's style was setting the long-term tone for the entire company in ways he did not even realize. The environment Sam was creating worked against collaboration. It made people defend their opinions and ideas at any cost. Openness was gone, because people were protective, thus reducing their willingness to play with ideas and concepts.

"The trouble with the rat race is that even if you win, you're still a rat." —Lily Tomlin

Committing to governing ourselves in meetings and other interactions helps cultivate the kind of team environment that encourages mindful interaction and effectiveness. It creates a sense of safety within people, and when people feel safe, their creativity flows and their willingness to take risks grows.

SOURCE: L. Gundry and L. LaMantia, *Breakthrough Teams for Breakneck Times: Unlocking the Genius of Creative Collaboration* (New York: Dearborn Books, 2001).

Review Questions

1. Within an industry of your choice, where would be the first place to look for a potential partner for a new venture you are considering?

2. What qualities of a potential partner would you want to complement this business? Why?

3. How can you foster a culture of collaboration in your management team? With other stakeholders inside and outside the business?

Understand the Value of Investing in the Social Capital That Can Drive Your Business

All entrepreneurs have heard of financial capital, but many may not have heard of social capital. Social capital is, in fact, very similar to its monetary sibling. It, too, is accumulated by an individual or a business, and it is used, or is available for use, in the production of wealth. Simply, it is the accumulation of resources developed through personal and professional networks. These resources include ideas, knowledge, information, opportunities, contacts, and referrals.

Building Your Social Capital

Social capital refers to connections with outside parties providing access to resources and includes structural, relational, and cognitive dimensions. Its structural dimension subsumes interaction processes, such as those germane to perceptions of legitimacy (Nahapiet & Ghoshal, 1998). Research posits that the location of an entrepreneur in a social network provides various types of advantage (e.g., Granovetter, 1983). In this context, for example, entrepreneurs use informal personal contacts (e.g., potential customers, friends) in addition to formal ones (e.g., consultants, venture capitalists) to obtain information or to access specific resources (e.g., market and industry information, financial support).

In the book, *Achieving Success Through Social Capital*, Wayne Baker comments, "Studies show that lucky people increase their chances of being in the right place at the right time by building a 'spider web structure' of relationships that catch information" (as quoted in Misner, 2004). Baker further comments, "Success is social; all the ingredients of success that we customarily think of as individual—talent, intelligence, education, effort and luck—are intertwined with networks" (as quoted in Misner, 2004).

To begin to understand the various individuals and their knowledge resources, use the following Information Network Component Tool to identify them through their various roles/activities and strengths that you can learn from and use to build your business.

The Innovator's Toolkit: Information Network Component Tool

1. Individuals in the business or profession where you want to launch and grow your business:

Name and Contact	Strengths/Benefits of Their Knowledge

2. Individuals who are trying to achieve things similar to what you want to achieve:

Name and Contact	Strengths/Benefits of Their Knowledge

(Continued)

(Continued)

3. Others who were in the industry or business profession you are looking to enter:

Name and Contact	Strengths/Benefits of Their Knowledge

4. Experts who write or produce books or media in your industry or specialty:

Name and Contact	Strengths/Benefits of Their Knowledge

5. Individuals who are in your trade, business, or professional organizations:

Name and Contact	Strengths/Benefits of Their Knowledge

6. Individuals who consult with others in your chosen industry/market:

Name and Contact	Strengths/Benefits of Their Knowledge

SOURCE: Adapted from Ivan R. Misner and Robert Davis, *Business by Referral: A Sure-Fire Way to Generate New Business* (Austin, TX: Bard Press, 1997).

Using Networks and Groups for Building Social Capital

Many types of organizations and network groups can be used to develop your own social capital. Based on your industry norms as well as your schedule, consider the following groups as a starting point to developing your network (Misner, 2002):

Broad-Based Cross-Discipline Networks

This first type of networking group brings together individuals representing many professions.

Usually, there are no restrictions on who can join or the actual number of individuals from each type of profession. Many meetings and events may be directed to discussions involving local business or community affairs events or legislation that may have an impact on the surrounding businesses (e.g., chambers of commerce). Entrepreneurs can build their social capital by coming in contact with a diversity and breadth of business people who may be encountering similar business problems and opportunities (Misner, 2002).

Industry- or Market-Specific Network Groups

In industry-specific network groups, entrepreneurs from one particular type of industry or specialty may organize for the purpose of exchanging information and referrals (Misner, 2002). Members tend to be from one specific type of industry, including banking and architecture. Often, their meetings may include opportunities to hear short presentations, to participate in seminars, or simply to create an event where all can openly network and exchange referral information. An example of this type of organization is The Commonwealth Institute (TCI), an organization that assists high-growth women entrepreneurs, CEO's, and senior corporate executives who may be in the critical stages of developing their firms; TCI provides the resources to grow their emerging businesses. TCI offers a peer support network and forums for women to exchange ideas, opportunities, and solutions to challenging business problems. Organizations might also be seen as professional associations, which have been called knowledge networks (Misner, 2002). During the interview provided at length earlier in this chapter, entrepreneur Julie LeMoine said,

> I am a member of TCI because of the stellar advisement I receive from the Emerging Company CEO forum steering committee and the astounding caliber of the TCI membership who are willing to reach out to each other as pioneering women in business leadership. Both the forums and the membership are supported with professionalism by TCI staff who set a tone of helping with excellence for the organization. The founders and the staff that run it were and are very committed to sharing knowledge and contacts to enable its women-in-positions-of-leadership members to grow as significantly as possible in all respects. It is by far the most effective organization I've ever joined in my 20-year career as a technology leader and business woman. Via the TCI, U C How Technologies and I have found corporate advisers, directors, partners, customers, and developed colleague friendships that will help me for years to come.

Strategic Reflection Point

Building Your Own Social Capital

1. Do you agree with the following quote by Baker (cited in Misner, 2002), "Studies show that lucky people increase their chances of being in the right place at the right time by building a 'spider web structure' of relationships that catch information?" Why or why not?

2. Within your area, what are all the different broad-based cross-discipline networks and industry-specific network groups? In what ways can you leverage the contacts and expertise within these groups to build your own social capital?

Summary of Chapter Objectives

1. Understand the benefits and outcomes of creating and sustaining strategic alliances
   - Resource dependency theory views the development of interfirm alliances as a means by which organizations can support and facilitate their business initiatives, capabilities, and resources.
   - Some benefits of alliances include advancement into new market segments, shorter product-development lead times, lower entry costs, and greater speed to entry, usually resulting in increased market shares.

2. Learn how to determine the best "fit" among partners and resources in your environment and industry in forming your strategic alliances
   - Begin by conducting a strategic analysis of the market sectors and target audiences that make the most sense for your business.
   - When looking for a partner, consider checking with professional and industry organizations, professional service providers such as accounting and law firms, and parallel businesses in your industry.

3. Understand the value of investing in the social capital that can drive your business
   - Social capital is the accumulation of resources developed through personal and professional networks. These resources include ideas, knowledge, information, opportunities, contacts, and referrals.
   - Structured networking programs can provide the "common terms, activities and outcomes" (or system) that lead to building substantial social capital for the people who use the program effectively.

4. Know the different types of networks and groups that you can use to build your social capital and the variety of networking strategies used by entrepreneurs
   - There are at least six types of business organizations to consider joining to develop your business through networking.

CASE 8.1   FOX Relocation Management Corp.: Building a Code of Ethics Within a Networked Community

Gretchen Fox smiled as she drove back to her office one afternoon in June 1999. She had just attended an awards banquet for the New England Women Business Owners Association, where she was named Business Woman of the Year.

As she drove, Fox reflected on all that had transpired in her career since she earned her MBA in 1987. She had started her business, FOX Relocation Management Corp., a year after graduation. Over the next 11 years, the business, which specialized in moving offices, branches, or entire companies to new locations, had grown from a one-person consultancy to a successful private company employing 40 people. Fox wholly owned the subchapter S corporation and had thus far avoided taking out loans to grow the company, other than the use of an occasional line of credit.

Fox had reason to feel that she had "made it." But she also felt that she could not simply sit back and savor her success. Her business continued to have opportunities for growth. For Fox, change was not only inevitable, it was preferable. As she explained, "The real joy for me comes from founding and growing a business. We are a growing company, and we need sparks of excitement that come from change, from going to the next level. Opening new offices, going national or international, expanding the services we offer, going public—all these things would give us as a company more reasons to be proud. People here are invested in the future. We can't get to the future by standing still."

This growth showed the business was prospering, but it also posed urgent problems. For the first time, Fox had been forced to add another layer of management to her organization. Fox wasn't sure that the compensation and incentive plans currently in place were appropriate for this new layer. She also worried that more hierarchy would ruin the carefully constructed culture of independent thinking at her company.

Fox had built her business by maintaining close contact with both employees and clients. Her vivacious personality, intelligence, and "can do" attitude set the tone for her company. Fox's personal touch was one of the major motivators for her staff and one of the selling points for the company's services. The central question in Fox's mind was how to grow the business without losing the hands-on style that had made the company successful.

As Fox explained, "So much of what we do and who we are is attributable to our small size. We are more like a family than a company. We've always been fairly informal with our employees. Conventional wisdom would say that now we are getting too big to do business that way any more. We have put some formal procedures in place, but will they be enough as we move forward?"

An Easy Way to Start a Consulting Company

For Gretchen Fox, running a relocation company was a perfect fit. She had moved several times throughout the United States and internationally with her late husband, who was an officer in the U.S. Air Force. In 1983, she settled in the Boston area. She earned her MBA part-time while holding down a job and raising two children. Throughout the 1980s, she held administrative management positions at a variety of Boston law and consulting firms. As it happened, a common denominator of all her jobs was moving the office. As Fox recalled, "All the firms I worked for made major moves, and I ended up managing them. I became something of an expert at it. I preferred the project management aspect of moving rather than the day-to-day maintenance tasks."

In August 1987, at the end of the third year of her part-time MBA program, Fox was ready for a change. She felt restless at her job and wanted to try her hand at an entrepreneurial venture. Fox had become increasingly impatient with the rigid hierarchies she saw in the legal firms where she worked. She felt it took too long to make decisions and that they promoted a lack of accountability.

Fox explained, "One reason I really don't like hierarchies is their lack of immediate decision making. One example that had serious repercussions was when I worked at a law firm and we had a bad snow storm. I wanted to send people home early, but my boss had to go to his boss and on up the chain. By the time I got out of there, I ended up with a seven-hour drive home.

"The other part of it for me is that I don't automatically respect someone with a title or position, I'm more interested in a meritocracy. That's personal bias, I suppose. The law firms couldn't give underlings decision-making authority because they weren't lawyers. Conversely, I remember a time I was lugging huge water bottles to the cooler, and the big, strapping, male lawyers walked right by me; not one stopped to help. Being a partner took precedence over being a person. Those kinds of separations don't make for a cohesive team. I wanted to create a place where I didn't have to live by those rules anymore."

She felt she could be successful if she put all her experience with corporate relocation to work in a consulting business. Fox, however, was not sure how to get started—would companies actually pay her to be a "move expert"? In 1988, she had the answer to her question. An office manager from a large Boston law firm called Fox to see if she'd be interested in organizing their upcoming move. The call came about from a networking group that Fox had started while she was working for a law firm in Washington, D.C.

Fox explained the connections that led to her first consulting job: "I was working for the D.C. satellite office of a large Boston law firm. There was one other Boston firm that also had a satellite office, so I started a lunch group that brought together managers from both companies. I felt as though we probably dealt with

similar issues and could benefit from sharing experiences. I got to know the office manager of the other firm pretty well. A couple of years later, after I'd moved back to Boston, the office manager from the Boston firm happened to be talking to my friend from D.C. She was looking for someone to manage her move, and my friend immediately recommended me.

"I interviewed for the job along with about eight other people. The hiring manager told me later that even though he'd interviewed people with a lot more experience—one was a very senior architect—he said my interpersonal skills were so strong that they decided to offer the job to me."

The company offered Fox a full-time one-year contract to move its 950-member workforce, giving her the choice of being on payroll or acting as an independent contractor. As Fox recalled, "There I was—wondering how to start consulting, and this job dropped in my lap. I decided to go in as an independent contractor. I remember thinking—what easier way to start a consulting company? Of course, I didn't think then of what being a consultant meant. Later, I realized that in addition to delivering services, I would have to send out invoices, set up a bookkeeping system, and find more clients."

Fox set up shop in her Lexington home and worked independently on small projects until 1992, when she accepted a large job at Harvard Business School that eventually developed into a two-year commitment. She hired several temporary employees to help coordinate the move, but she realized in August 1992 that she would need permanent help. Fox hired Lori Coletti, a facility management specialist from a large telecommunications company. Coletti had a degree in interior design and experience with business furnishings that complemented Fox's business degree and relocation skills. Although Fox was happy to gain an employee with Coletti's background, hiring a full-time employee was unsettling.

As Fox explained, "Hiring Lori, my first permanent employee, was the first big milestone for the business. It was the hardest thing I have ever had to do. I was suddenly responsible for someone else—for her family—for her livelihood. It was a combination of worrying about not having enough work for her and having to pay her even if the work wasn't coming in. We sort of got around that. We negotiated an hourly wage, figuring that if I didn't need 40 hours per week consistently, I wouldn't have to pay for it. But in reality, Lori ended up working 50 hours a week from the start, and that has never really changed. She is still here—and is vice president of the company."

A Loose Collection of Consultants

In the fall of 1992, when a large regional bank hired Fox to move its Massachusetts headquarters, Fox hired two more employees. From September 1992 through May 1993, FOX Relocation moved 1,500 people for the bank. From that time on, Fox continued to augment the bank's project management staff, managing various aspects of employee relocation on a permanent basis.

By 1994, the company had seven hourly employees. The base of operations was still Fox's home, although most of the work was done on-site at client facilities. One long-time employee, Jane Menton, described the start-up phase: "I started working for Gretchen in 1992. At the time, FOX Relocation wasn't so much a company as a loose collection of consultants. She had one employee—Lori. Mostly, though, Gretchen would hire consultants to get the jobs done. Eventually, she hired me as the second employee.

"It was interesting working out of someone's house. I feel fortunate to have started that way because I was able to work directly with Gretchen. I got to really understand what she expected and how she worked with clients. At the time, she was a project manager running projects instead of the more administrative role she plays now as president of the company. I enjoyed those early days. I felt we were all learning at the same time."

The energy of starting something new and operating on a shoestring was exciting, but Fox felt the need to become established in a Boston location closer to her client base. "People were trying to do business out of phone booths," she recalled. "It was time we moved downtown."

In October 1994, the company's five employees were working with two large clients and managing four smaller projects. Fox decided to sublease space from a Boston real estate management firm. For $500 a month, Fox and her employees shared a small office and had use of the real estate firm's equipment and conference room. Fox felt that this arrangement was a good way to test the waters without incurring significant financial risk. It wasn't long, however, before the company outgrew the space. "We were getting in the way. We were using the conference room more than the company we were subleasing from," Fox explained.

By December 1995, FOX Relocation had doubled in size, with enough work to keep 10 full-time employees busy. The company moved to 2,200 square feet of space on the 11th floor of a downtown Boston office building. Six months later, another 2,200 square feet of office space was added.

Fox explained the financial risk the company took that year: "Instead of paying $6,000 a year on rent, we were now paying more than 10 times that amount. It was daunting. But the up side was that our business was expanding as well. By the end of 1996, we had over 20 employees. We had doubled in size in two years."

Relocation Consultants: A Niche Within the Facility Management Industry

Before 1980, the term *move consultants* was not in corporate America's vocabulary. Most—if not all—moves were performed by employees. Office managers in small to medium-sized firms, and facility management teams in large firms typically had the dubious honor of managing and executing a move. In the

1980s, however, as the tidal wave of downsizing swept away administrative personnel and departments, corporate executives found that there was no one left with the expertise and the time to plan a large move. The facility management outsourcing industry gave birth to a small subset of firms that chose to specialize in the high-stress world of corporate relocations.

Another trend in facilities management, called *workforce churn,* also fueled the growth of relocation consultants. *Churn* was the term used to describe the continual movement of employees as a result of expansion, downsizing, redeployment, or a project-oriented workforce. *The Boston Globe* reported in 1998 that the average churn rate (the percentage of employees who took part in some type of organizational move) was 44 percent nationwide, with the Boston area's rate much higher, at 60 to 70 percent (Valigra, 1998). As one facility management industry magazine wrote:

> American businesses are changing at an ever-increasing rate. Churn rates of 55 to 60 percent are now common compared to 25 to 30 percent just a few years ago. And churn rates of 100 percent are no longer shocking. A Texas computer manufacturer reports moving more than 12,000 people in one city over a one-year period to accommodate a one-third growth in employment and a 100 percent churn rate. An energy company moves more than 800 people, 40 percent of its employees, over a four-month period. (Fischer, 1998, p. 1)

The reasons for the high churn rates were increases in industry consolidations and corporate mergers and the rapid expansion of high-tech firms that used fluid teams to perform projects. As the article described:

> It's not unusual for companies to form teams involving up to 300 people, and then as the project nears completion, ramp-down to 20 people. This trend is particularly

prevalent among software and computer manufacturers. . . . About 15 percent of this activity involves moves into new facilities, consuming more than $10 billion each year in goods and services to do so. (Fischer, 1998, p. 1)

In addition to offering an experienced, cost-efficient team to manage moves, relocation consultants also took the heat of a stressful move off an employee or department. Since two thirds of employees in charge of a move are either fired or quit soon after the move, hiring a move consultant saved companies the cost of hiring and training new personnel (Valigra, 1998). Fox pointed out that consultants were, for the most part, protected from office politics and made space assignments and other decisions objectively.

The FOX Way

Throughout the early 1990s, Fox experienced growth in number and scope of assignments. She continued to hire project managers in response to the increasing demands of both new and existing clients. In 1995, Fox promoted Lori, her first employee and right arm, to the position of vice president. This marked a departure from Fox's "loose collection of consultants" and the installation of a rudimentary hierarchy. The bulk of the staff, the project managers, remained on the same level.

The company prided itself on its lack of formal titles and status symbols. As Fox explained, "We are not departmentalized. I didn't set up the company to operate that way. I didn't personally do all that well in hierarchical organizations that typically operated under the more traditional business model. I didn't like it, and I chose not to subject other people to it.

"That's not to say we don't have *any* hierarchy or that we have a totally flat organization. Of course, we do have some hierarchy—we have hierarchy of experience. We have some people who have been in this business for 25 years, and some who have been in it for one. The one with 25 years of experience is much more likely to be managing a project than the person with little experience. But we don't use titles, except for Lori and myself. It's not something that's needed internally.

"Despite the lack of titles, it was always clear to the client who to contact if there was a problem or issue. In the beginning, they always talked to me; then after I made Lori vice president, she talked to her clients, and I kept mine. There was perhaps more internal than external confusion."

Although most of the staff at FOX Relocation were female, Fox asserted that she didn't set out to build an all-female company. The fact was the overwhelming majority of applicants happened to be female. Fox believed the reason for this was that the work lent itself to a traditionally female approach to tasks and problem solving. As she explained, "The way we work is very hands-on. Of course, not all relocation companies work this way. One of our competitors is almost entirely male, and they don't offer the same level of hands-on attention to detail that we do. It's really a different business model.

"We are widely known for our incredible ability to coordinate and manage all the details of a move. One of our employees said to me at lunch the other day that a lot of what we do is handholding and giving pats on the back. And that really is important. People are traumatized by moves. Even if they are moving to a different floor in the same building, there is something very unsettling about it. We help communicate with people and listen to their concerns. At the same time, we handle a zillion details, from selecting voice/data networks to making sure there are coat hangers in every closet."

Employees at FOX Relocation expressed a strong sense of shared values and prided themselves on their customer-service orientation. As Project Manager Robin Dorogusker explained, "At FOX, we have a style of working that is tightly focused on customer service. We want the customer to be happy, and we want to do a good job. Everyone here is willing to get down and dirty

and do whatever it takes to get the job done—whether it's designing office space or crawling around on the floor looking for phone jacks."

The culture at FOX Relocation was expressed in its code of ethics and mission statement, written in the spring of 1997:

Code of Ethics

- We are a community and our clients are part of that community.
- We treat our employees and clients with utmost respect.
- We seek continuous improvement.
- We have as much fun as our work allows.

Mission Statement

Our mission is to provide a full range of corporate real estate program and project management services in a way that supports our clients' culture and fulfills their unique needs so as to ensure that the clients' business operations and revenue stream are not disrupted.

The culture at Fox was communicated to new employees in a variety of ways. One employee told of how, the first day on the job, they were added to the company-wide email distribution list. Here is one of the first e-mails:

As you all know, our good friend Bob will be retiring this Spring. The good news is that he has already sold his house. The bad news is that he has to be out of it by the week of January 12—yikes!

We are looking for volunteers to help pack his (4,400sf!) house on the following dates:
Saturday 1/3/03
Saturday 1/10/03
Sunday 1/11/03

Any and all help will be appreciated. Bob will offer snacks, beverages, and even a little pool playing during the breaks! Also—who knows what he will decide not to take? There may be a few cool items to raffle off to helpers! In any case, we will make it fun.

Please understand that this is not a FOX project (not billable) . . . it is merely helping out a fellow FOX (builds good karma)! Please let me know if you are able to help on any of these dates. I will be happy to provide directions as well as coordinating any carpooling if necessary.

Thanks!

Ginny

Workflow at FOX Relocation

Client projects at FOX Relocation generally fell into two categories: one-time moves and ongoing facility management. FOX Relocation employees were primarily coordinators. They did not actually pick up and move boxes; rather, they set schedules and coordinated the moving company's activities with the activities of other subcontractors such as security, electricians, and environmental systems. One-time moves involved anything from a small group relocating to another floor to 2,500 employees moving to a new building over the course of a single weekend. Teams were formed for each job and were disbanded when a job was completed.

The on-going facility work usually entailed at least two people working full-time, or nearly full-time, on-site at a client's facility. Ongoing work included: space planning; inventorying, refurbishment, or procurement of furniture and art; coordinating new construction and building maintenance; and moving and installing technology. Employees at FOX either worked for several clients and projects at once or were stationed full-time on-site as part of the client's facility management team. Clients included Harvard University Law School, Fleet Bank, BankBoston, and Bell Atlantic.

Fox and Coletti conducted most of the company's marketing, which took the form of networking, nurturing client relationships, following leads, and soliciting the occasional write-up in the local press media. Approximately 30 percent of new jobs came from repeat customers, and most new clients came to FOX Relocation through word of mouth. Once a new client or job was identified, Fox or Coletti wrote proposals and conducted negotiations.

Coletti maintained a two-month workflow projection based on current jobs and what she and Fox judged to be "in the pipeline." Jobs were assigned to project managers based on their availability and expertise. Employee preferences were taken into account whenever possible. Generally, jobs were given to teams of two or three people. Although one person usually functioned as the primary client contact and maintained a budget and schedule for the project, that person did not have authority over others in the team and did not act as team leader. When the job was completed, members of the team moved on to form new teams around a new project. In large or complex moves, the teams were bigger, and Fox or Coletti appointed a team leader to manage the overall move.

Fox explained the fluid nature of the project manager roles: "People are given projects based mainly on availability. They could be managing a large project this month and put on another project that someone else is running next month. So a person is not always in charge, nor is he or she always in the position of underling. This structure really makes a difference to how people see their roles."

As Robin Dorogusker explained, "We don't have politics at FOX. People don't have to vie for position. There's no real hierarchy. People aren't trying to get to the next level, because there is no next level. So there isn't a sense of competition— just a feeling that we want to do a good job on our projects. We enjoy each other's successes and help out from job to job. There is a lot of camaraderie."

Since most clients wanted to minimize the downtime associated with relocation, the actual moving was done over a short and convenient period of time—usually at night or over a weekend. The team in charge of the move often needed more people to get the job completed on schedule. In particularly large or complex moves, the entire company could be mobilized. As Project Manager Jane Menton explained, "We think of ourselves as a team—one that needs to work together. Everyone is very good about that. Because even if you're on a two-person team, you may have a large move, and you'll need extra help. I've never seen an instance when someone's needed help and no one has come forward. Sure, there are lots of times when you don't know what people are working on, but there are also the times when everyone—even Gretchen—will pitch in and help with a move. One great example of that was the Suffolk County Courthouse. We had to conduct a huge records inventory for that move. Everyone in the company had to contribute to get it done, and they were all willing to help."

Human Resources

New employees came to FOX Relocation almost exclusively through word of mouth. Even in the low unemployment job market of the late 1990s, the company had never needed to place a help-wanted advertisement. The company received several unsolicited resumes almost every week. Fox and Coletti conducted interviews on an ongoing basis. Most of the resumes came from people with art, architecture, interior design, space planning, or facility management backgrounds. Many had experience as project managers for larger companies. Some FOX Relocation employees had previously been downsized as their corporations outsourced their facility management divisions. Fox felt that despite the word-of-mouth method of hiring, she was as or more diverse in her hiring practices than most companies in her industry.

Project Manager Steven Smith recalled why he was attracted to FOX Relocation: "I wanted to work for a small company. I like to keep a balance between my work life and personal life and be able, for the most part, to maintain a 40-hour work week. I talked to some people who work for big companies, and they had war stories about how many hours they put in. One of the benefits of working at FOX Relocation is that Gretchen and Lori recognize that people have a life outside the office and empower us to manage our own workload and hours."

In the early years of the company, all employees interviewed and approved each new hire. Because the company was so small, Fox wanted to ensure that personalities meshed and that every employee understood and fit into the culture. Project Manager Larry Ellsworth, who was stationed full-time at a client site, described a typical FOX Relocation employee: "We are generally people who can fit in with other people. I like fitting in—I like understanding my client's needs, understanding their organization, and becoming part of it. I keep a reasonable distance while actively taking part in the job and acting in my client's interest. I think most of us here at FOX have that ability. We're chameleons. We can pick up the color of our surrounding environment. It helps to get the job done when you are able to think the way your client thinks."

As the company grew, it was no longer feasible for all employees to be involved in hiring decisions. Instead, new hires met with an ad hoc committee of veteran employees. Jane Menton described the hiring process and what she looked for in an applicant: "Nervous people don't do well here. This is a high stress job. We are usually the last people brought in—after the architect, the builders, and so on. We are also the last people standing there after the move is completed, and we end up taking responsibility for decisions we didn't make. It's also our job to stay on a bit after the move to make sure everyone is settled. Sometimes, this takes a lot of diplomacy. Lots of people hate their job or hate their company, and the way they express that is to say 'I hate my chair.' People will try to gain control over whatever they can. So we change the chair, the employees are happy, and the project is a success.

"Employees here also need to be comfortable with the lack of formal structure. People come from all kinds of backgrounds. Some, who've come from large organizations with a lot more structure, have a hard time adjusting to the flexibility we have at FOX. We have to work odd hours. We don't have defined roles. And we don't get a lot of formal feedback."

Other than annual reviews conducted by either Fox or Coletti, employees were given feedback and direction on a situational basis. Project managers had considerable autonomy over their projects. Menton explained the review process, "There is a form Gretchen uses for employee reviews, but she just uses it as a guide. I haven't seen her actually fill it out. We are not managed very closely at all. Basically, Gretchen and Lori look at whether we bring our projects in on budget and on time. At the beginning of a job, they give us a not-to-exceed price based on a scope of work, and then it is up to us to manage the job. We occasionally get feedback from clients through letters or telephone calls. Most times, we will ask the client if we can use them as a reference. We get a lot of our jobs through word of mouth, so it's important to have a good ongoing relationship with our clients."

Steven Smith described his feelings about the way employees were managed: "One thing I like more than anything else about this job is that, as far as the client is concerned, I *am* FOX Relocation. Lori, my boss—who I immediately report to—does not check in with us on a regular basis. We manage ourselves, and we represent our own company. I think it's great that I'm a reflection of our company. I've never fully had that feeling before in any other job. It's very satisfying. I have a feeling of ownership without all the liability that true ownership would bring."

However, Smith, also saw drawbacks to the lack of formal structure: "I have three people on my team. We are stationed full-time at one of our large corporate clients. I am considered the senior person of that team; there is also another project manager and what I'd call a junior person on the team. To the client, I am considered the team leader, but at FOX, we're all considered to be on the same level. That's where I think there is something lacking in the organization. There is some lack of clarity on our part; our internal roles don't always correspond with our external roles. Most people here seem comfortable with this ambiguity, so I have not made an issue of it."

As one would expect in a service business, payroll and related expenses comprised the largest percentage of expenses.[1] All the project managers at FOX Relocation had the choice of being paid on an hourly or salaried basis. Hourly wages and salaries were negotiated individually, with the applicant naming a preferred rate, which Fox compared to other employees in the company with similar experience. Occasionally, Fox researched architectural and design firm employee pay rates. However, Fox was more concerned with maintaining internal wage parity than comparing with other firms. Most employees chose to be paid hourly. As Coletti explained, "In the early days of the company, people were paid hourly because we weren't sure we could guarantee full-time employment. It was fine with the other employees and me—we didn't need the guarantee of a 40-hour salary. Now, paying hourly wages serves as a motivator for people. It's similar to being on a sales force. The employees have some control over how much they make because, in most situations, they can set their schedules.

"We certainly don't want people working significantly more than 40 hours per week on a regular basis. People know, however, that if they do need to put in that kind of time, they will be paid for it. In certain cases, individuals who are paid hourly make out better on an annual basis than those same individuals would have on salary, so I encourage some people to opt for hourly pay. A few of the people who started out as salaried have eventually asked to go hourly; I have never seen anyone go the other way."

Growing Pains

As the company grew, one way that Fox kept abreast of employee attitudes and morale was to conduct a workplace satisfaction survey. Fox explained the differences in responses over the last several years: "Every year, I've sent out a survey to people asking: 'What three things do you value in your workplace that you do have here?' and 'What three things do you value that you don't have here?' At first, the answer to the second question was health and dental benefits. So we added that. Then the answers were more in the vein of profit sharing and 401 K plans, so we added that. Now we have what I consider a generous and complete benefits package. In every year we have had the 401K plan, we have added the maximum amount. Most employees were matched 100 percent.

"The profit sharing plan was simple. All employees, excepting me, took an equal share in profits of the company, after an amount was set aside for future growth. I found that satisfaction in incentive plans fell along gender lines. The males seemed to want more to strive for, that they needed a goal. I disagree with that. When one big accounting firm was falling apart, the chairman went to the board to ask for more money, arguing that he needed more pay to get quality work. I have to ask: What are you paying them for now? I don't really believe in incentive pay. I don't think getting more money at the end of the year makes one person work harder than another.

"In 1998, 100 percent of the respondents said [what] they valued most about FOX was the flexibility and number two was the teamwork aspect. One thing they would like to see added now is the ability to have a greater role in firm management."

One FOX employee, Steven Smith, described how he saw incentives at FOX: "You have to find a way to continually challenge yourself. One thing

I did, after I'd been at one site for a number of years, was to move around a lot. I went to nine different clients last year. That was a big change. I find it a great challenge to be given autonomy and then to meet and exceed client expectations. Salary is just not discussed here. It is a closely guarded secret. No one knows what another person makes. Hourly pay [encourages] me to work longer hours, if I need to. I don't abuse it, but it does compensate me for when I'm working a lot."

In 1997 and 1998, many of FOX Relocation's bank clients experienced mergers, leading the company to double in size from 20 to 40 employees to meet their clients' relocation needs. Up until this point, the company had enjoyed steady, manageable expansion. Robin Dorogusker explained the impact of this growth spurt: "There was a rough period when we were growing rapidly. It was very difficult. We had some growing pains. We just weren't prepared for the pace at which we grew. We went to 40 employees before we had the infrastructure or the technology to support them. So many people were getting hired so quickly.

"People felt they were thrown into the lion's den without any training. We didn't have time to train, and we weren't able to communicate with each other. It's hard working in an organization with 38 people when you don't know who some of the new people are.

By 1998, Fox realized that the company needed to change the way it trained new employees, Dorogusker said: "It became clear that we could no longer train people just by osmosis. We had to institute a more formal training program, which is basically a mentoring system. New people, regardless of how much work experience they have, are partnered with someone more senior on projects until such time as they can go out on their own. There is no rule as to how long the mentoring will last—it depends on the person."

Dorogusker agreed that the worst of the transition times seemed past: "As things slowed down a little, we started making time for meetings, and Gretchen and Lori have made an effort to get people to know each other. They tried to shift around the teams to allow people to work with others they hadn't gotten to know yet. Gretchen started picking names out of a hat and having those people go to lunch with each other. Through all of this rapid growth, Gretchen and Lori have tried to keep up the family atmosphere. For example, they are very tolerant of people's personal lives. Some bring their children to the office now and then. Gretchen and Lori try to understand what is going on with everyone and how their personal lives may or may not interfere with their work."

In late 1997, Fox felt the time had come to replace the company's outdated equipment and secondhand office furniture. She established an employee committee to redesign the office layout, purchase new furniture, and research computer networks. The committee came up with a "partial hoteling" solution, where employees, such as Coletti, Fox, and the administrative personnel had permanent desks and offices. The rest of the space was assigned and reassigned based on how much time each employee spent at the office. Employees who were based in the office but were often at client sites had a desk and file cabinet. The employees who were stationed full-time on client sites had temporary use of desks; drafting tables, and phones when they visited the office. The new office furniture the committee chose was designed to be lightweight and flexible to allow for easy movement as employee needs changed.

In 1998, the company completed the installation of a computer network, and in 1999, it was in the process of designing a Web site. The network made it much easier for Fox to communicate to employees and for employees to communicate with each other. Employees were also given cell phones and beepers, and the company maintained an updated list of all phone, beeper numbers and employee e-mail addresses to make it easier for employees to keep in touch with the company.

Another way Fox communicated with her growing workforce was a two-hour bi-weekly staff luncheon. All employees attended the meetings—even those stationed off-site. At the meetings, people had a chance to apprise others of particular issues or staffing needs they may have on a project. The company also invited vendors or other experts to give presentations as a way to keep staff up to date on industry issues and new products. The company always paid for lunch, and each meeting concluded with a cake and celebration of staff birthdays and distribution of paychecks.

Growth at FOX Relocation was not only measured in the increased number of client projects and employees. The company was also expanding its capabilities. New employees brought with them a range of skills that FOX Relocation added to its capacities. In 1994, the company acquired a small interior design firm that had expertise in computer-aided design and computer-aided facilities management. FOX Relocation also developed expertise in art collection management. In addition, the company was handling bigger and more complex moving projects that required larger teams of people and a more formal hierarchy to execute.

Dorogusker described the team put in place to conduct the Federal Courthouse move: "The project was different in that it was much more massive than anything I had experienced before. It was the first time we designated an actual team leader, feeling that one point person would be most efficient. I was the project leader, and I had all the direct client contact. I directed three project managers who worked with the individual courts. I had to keep the project managers focused, maintain the schedules and budgets, and keep a view of the big picture.

"It was difficult at first. We had never worked in that kind of a structured team. It caused some tension because previously we'd been equals. But we talked it out and came to an understanding that our roles had to be different for this project.

In the end, we learned that sometimes we need that kind of structure to get the job done."

For Fox, growth also meant she was forced to step away from project management and the day-to-day oversight of her company. She refocused her role on marketing and public relations. As the company grew, Coletti shouldered more and more of the daily responsibility of running the company and supervising employees. As Dorogusker described, "Gretchen and Lori play different roles. Gretchen has become a personality—winning the award and being written about in the paper and that kind of thing. She is now more externally focused and involved in the marketing of the company.

"Lori is more hands-on. She keeps tabs on staffing and the status of projects. Lori also works with us and is connected to us on a more regular basis. Right now, I report to Lori. I used to work with Gretchen, and I'm fortunate in that respect. Most people here have not worked with Gretchen directly on a project."

As Coletti and Fox's roles evolved, some employees expressed a sense of ambiguity concerning reporting relationships and authority. As Larry Ellsworth said, "It's a little hard to say exactly what the reporting structure is here. Clearly, Gretchen is the president of the company. I think about her as the overall strategic 'big picture' person. Lori I think of more as the general manager/operations director. But I don't feel I have to go to only one of them about a specific problem. They are more like twin managers."

Coletti described the way she saw the reporting process: "Some employees will come to me, while others go to Gretchen. There is some ambiguity about who makes certain decisions. Sometimes, an employee will e-mail both of us with a question. It gets a little sticky when we come back with different answers, but we work it out."

The Future

As Fox sat at her desk, looking out over Boston's teeming business district, she felt satisfied that she had built a reputable company, had a great team of people who were happy to work for her, and had a client base that would continue to expand. She knew that some key questions had to be answered to meet the future proactively. In what direction should she take the company? What will be the impact of growing from 50 to 100 people? Fox was faced taking out a loan to pay off 50 percent of the $300,000 furniture and construction cost for the new space. She had never taken out a loan before.

SOURCE: This case was written by Cynthia Ingols, associate professor of management, Simmons College. Reprinted with permission.

Discussion Questions

1. What would be the impact of such a move? How much longer could she pay people on an hourly basis? She was sure that soon, she would have to move to a conventional salary model. How would that impact her incentive structure?

2. As Fox became more focused externally, how should she change her role and what should that new role be? Are isolated tensions and ambiguities indicative of systemic problems that could be exacerbated as the company grows?

3. Can FOX Relocation maintain its culture, structure, and ability to respond quickly and effectively to client needs throughout this period of rapid growth?

CASE 8.2 Laura McCann and Zweave: Building and Maintaining Social Capital

Laura McCann started her software company, Zweave, in 2000. She had successfully built an apparel manufacturing business but had no knowledge or connections in the software or consulting industry. Until she started Zweave, her contacts had been primarily in the apparel manufacturing industry: retailers, factories, designers, and mills. However, in 1994, a close friend, also an entrepreneur, introduced her to the Young Entrepreneur's Organization (YEO). McCann says, "I joined this organization and experienced a tenfold increase in my social capital.

"Initially I was a member and attended a monthly educational event in my local chapter. I also participated in a monthly 'forum meeting' which consisted of six to eight other young CEOs or founders sharing their challenges with each other. This meeting format provided a much needed support system of like-minded people. Once a year, I would attend a conference that would bring together 300 to 500 people over three days."

YEO provided a tremendous network for McCann with her peers across dozens of industries. "Once I discovered the power of this network, I also realized the best way to tap into it: volunteering to be on the local board. Within six months of joining the local New York board, I became its president. Within the year of my term, we doubled our membership and were recognized by the international board. I was invited to join the international board and participated in several roles over a two-year period. This led me to invitations from corporate boards as well. I went from being a local member to a highly visible player within the organization. I even received an invitation to speak on a panel at a conference in New Orleans in 1999 where I met my current business partner, David Buck, a fellow member from the Boston chapter."

Buck was a technology and consulting veteran with a successful technology company and exactly the kind of experience Zweave needed.

"Because of YEO, our mutual connections and the credibility I had within the organization, David, who had recently sold his business and was making investments in start-up technology companies, looked at my business plan. Although I had no technology background, he recognized that I had built something from nothing and had the drive to do it again. As a fellow entrepreneur, he understood that was key. The other factor he liked was the focus of our software and the size of the market we wanted to play in.

"David and I had another thing in common. We had both graduated from a three-year executive management class called the Birthing of Giants. This curriculum was designed to stretch the minds of leading entrepreneurs and was offered through a joint collaboration of MIT, INC magazine, and YEO. I had graduated one year after David, and this shared worldview and training brought us together with a common personal vision: We could change the way we grew a business, the rules of the market, and we could win big."

Buck and McCann have remained partners for more than five years as their business has grown, evolved, and changed. They have received six research and development grants from the Small Business Innovation Research (SBIR) program. McCann says, "I still continue to leverage my social capital every day." Zweave's key team members were all discovered through a series of introductions and are still attracting talent each and every day by staying connected with their networks and friends. "Whereas 10 years ago, when I started my first business at the age of 28, I could barely fill a Rolodex," McCann says, "today almost anyone I want to meet is only a few degrees of separation away."

McCann cites several ways entrepreneurs can start to build their own social capital networks. "I remember the first time I had ever heard of networking. I had read a book by Harvey McKay, a well-known author and motivational speaker, and was attending one of his seminars. At the end of the evening, he invited everyone to collect at least 10 business cards from people in the room. Today I have my own personal philosophy on networking, which I see as the entrepreneur's most important asset. My network is a living-breathing ecosystem. It requires food, water, light, and tender loving care."

Data. McCann attributes her healthy network to contact management software, the right PDA and mobile phone. "I update my data with Web-based programs like Plaxo. Using Web-based networking sites like LinkedIn and Guru.com, I keep my profile out there where people can see me and what I am up to. I join groups and organizations and access their membership lists and introduce myself. Business cards are kept in plastic envelopes and organized by months, and all important contacts are immediately put in the database. I shuffle the cards every quarter and remind myself of people I met and stay in touch, you just never know."

Get out. "I make it a point to attend as many conferences, breakfasts, and events as I can in my industry. I also attend at least five events a year that are not in my industry to keep me in the know about other trends and extend my reach. I try to have at least two lunch appointments a week specifically to network."

Random acts of kindness. "I help two people connect a day. No matter how busy I am, if someone asks me to connect him or her, I do. This is networking karma at its best. I tell everyone I meet I can connect them. Over the years, I have built a reputation as someone who delivers. When I need help, I have many people I can call on."

Be polite. "When I meet someone I want to invite into my close network I contact him or her within days of meeting them so they remember me. I always say thank you, nice to meet you, stay in touch. Usually, e-mail does the job, but I often use personal thank you notes when it really matters."

Events. "I bring everyone together at least once a year by hosting a party or event. Social currency is important when doing business. People want to know you are someone they should know and keep in touch with."

Invest in yourself. "Every year, I take a seminar or course. My favorites have been: The Strategic Coach, Landmark Education, The Birthing of Giants, and Leadership America. I join several organizations that have ties to the communities I want to play in."

Mapping. "I map my relationships. Take a big piece of paper, and write down a goal or idea. Then create groupings of people that could help you with that idea. For example, I was working on writing a book and my community included publishers, agents, mentors, people to interview, and friends who may know people to interview. In some of my groups, I had actual contacts whereas in others I had none. This is when the fun starts. Through a series of e-mails, calls, and social gatherings I share what I need. Within two months, I had filled in my community chart and was able to find an agent, people to interview, and had the support of my entire community."

Touch, move, and inspire. "It all starts with you. If you share yourself, your needs, and your dreams with people, they will support you. If you support them in making their dreams come true, too, everyone wins. I always remember it is my job to make a difference in how my contacts experience me as a professional and that they consider me an asset. I don't complain, gossip, or tell stories. I present myself as confident, capable, sincere, and caring. When the business is gone, what will remain is me and the people I know and their opinions of me."

SOURCE: Interview by Jill Kickul. Printed with permission.

Discussion Questions

1. How did McCann go about forming strategic alliances for her business idea?

2. What is social capital, and how did it help drive McCann's new venture?

3. What types of network groups did McCann use to build her social capital?

Note

1. Since FOX Relocation is a privately held company, no financial statements were available for publication.

References

Brush, C. G. (1996). Cooperative strategies in non-high-tech new ventures: An explanatory study. *Entrepreneurship: Theory and Practice, 21*(2), 37–54.

Doz, Y. L., & Hamel, G. (1998). *Alliance advantage: The art of creating value through partnering.* Cambridge, MA: Harvard Business School Press.

Fischer, G. (1998, March). Four elements of a successful move. *Buildings*, p. 1.

Gomes-Casseres, B. (1994, July–August). Group versus group: How alliance networks compete. *Harvard Business Review 72*(4), 62–74.

Granovetter, M. S. (1983). The strength of weak ties: A network theory revisited. *Sociological Theory, 1,* 203–233.

Harbison, J., & Pekar, P. (1998). *Smart alliances: A practical guide to repeatable success.* San Francisco: Jossey-Bass Business and Management Series.

Holmund, M., & Kock, S. (1996). Relationship marketing: The importance of customer-perceived service quality in retail banking. *Service Industries Journal, 16*(3), 287–304.

Jarratt, D. G. (1998). A strategic classification of business alliances: A qualitative perspective built from a study of small and medium-sized enterprises. *Qualitative Market Research, 1*(1), 39–49.

Kickul, J., & Gundry, L. K. (2000, Spring). Transforming the entrepreneurial landscape: Strategic innovations in Internet firms. *New England Journal of Entrepreneurship*, pp. 23–31.

Koza, M. P., & Lewin, A. Y. (1998). The co-evolution of strategic alliances. *Organization Science, 9,* 255–264.

Larson, A. (1991). Partner networks: Leveraging ties to improve entrepreneurial performance. *Business Venturing, 6*(3), 173–188.

Liljander, V., & Strandvik, T. (1993). Estimating zones of tolerance on the antecedents of service quality. *International Journal of Service Industry Management, 4*(2), 6–28.

Maynard, R. (1996). Striking the right match. *Nation's Business, 84*(5), 18–20+.

Miles, G., Preece, S., & Baetz, M. (1999). Dangers of dependence: The impact of strategic alliance use by small technology-based firms. *Journal of Small Business Management, 37*(2), 20–29.

Misner, I. (2002). Want to join a networking group? With six types to choose from, narrowing the field will help you find the groups that are best for your business. *Entrepreneur.* Retrieved December 11, 2005, from http://www.entrepreneur.com/article/0,4621,305516,00.html

Misner, I. (2004). Investing in your social capital: It pays to take advantage of knowledge and relationships when building your business—and your bottom line. *Entrepreneur.* Retrieved December 11, 2005, from http://www.entrepreneur.com/article/ 0,4621,316822,00.html

Morgan, R. M., & Hunt, S. D. (1994). The commitment-trust theory of relationship marketing. *Journal of Marketing, 58*(3), 20–38.

Nahapiet, J., & Ghoshal, S. (1998). Social capital, intellectual capital, and organizational advantage. *Academy of Management Review, 23*(2), 242–266.

Pfeffer, J., & Salancik, G. R. (1978). *The external control of organizations.* New York: Harper & Row.

Valigra, L. (1998, November 25). Helping firms on the move, *Boston Globe,* p. D4.

Varadarajan, P. R., & Cunningham, M. (1995). Strategic alliances: A synthesis of conceptual foundations. *Journal of the Academy of Marketing Science, 23*(4), 282–296.

PART III

Entrepreneurial Strategies for Sustaining Growth in the Established Venture

Innovative Strategies for Entrepreneurial Growth

The challenge isn't to keep your eye on big competitors. It's to pay attention to the innovators.

—Dave Duffield, Peoplesoft

Sometimes when you innovate, you make mistakes. It is best to admit them quickly, and get on with improving your other innovations.

—Steve Jobs, Apple CEO and founder

Always remember that someone, somewhere is making a product that will make your product obsolete.

—Georges Doriot, pioneer of Venture Capital

Objectives:

1. Understand the four perspectives on strategy for innovation and how an organization's strategic scope and capabilities determine the appropriate innovation strategy

2. Learn strategic approaches to future expansion of the new venture

3. Recognize the five innovation mistakes of individuals and organizations

4. Develop a portfolio of initiatives

5. Learn how to maintain an innovation-friendly environment in the established venture

Strategy in Action

Innovation Made E-Z—Annette Ricci and Reel E-Z Display, Inc.

Reel E-Z Display, Inc., located in Lake Forest, Illinois, was founded in 2003 based on a breakthrough idea. Annette Ricci, the owner and CEO of Reel E-Z Display, Inc., also owns and operates Design & Deliver, Inc. (D&D), which custom-designs, manufactures, and imports a wide variety of products. D&D developed the Reel E-Z Display system in response to a request from an ad agency that produced signage for a large retail drugstore chain in the United States. Later, D&D worked directly with this retailer to develop a solution to put up and take down in-store signage. This patented, retractable sign-hanging system allows signage that is hung from a ceiling to be accessed from the ground for easy sign changes.

The company currently produces three versions of the sign-hanging system, as well as several accessories, which are manufactured in China. Other products are in development. After patenting the sign-hanging system, Ricci created Reel E-Z Display, Inc., to sell the product in the larger display industry marketplace, which has more than $10 billion in annual sales. Based on research into the display industry, she discovered that the system could fill a void and had the potential to revolutionize the industry.

Reel E-Z Display is a unique sign-hanging system that attaches to the ceiling so signs and banners can be suspended in what is often unused retail space. Once the system is mounted in place, signs can be hung and changed from the ground using a lightweight pole.

The Reel E-Z system represents a major breakthrough in the display industry. Most in-store signage is currently hung and changed using a primitive process that involves climbing a ladder and using an assortment of clips and string. Two people are required to complete the process, which is time consuming and labor intensive. In addition, the safety challenges often affect compliance.

Reel E-Z addresses these issues and offers new possibilities as well. With this system, safety problems are eliminated, and both time and labor are significantly reduced. Easy compliance increases the likelihood that products will be supported with advertising signage, which can boost revenues by 67 percent. In addition, access to "air space" and easy sign-hanging makes it possible for retailers to lease the space and generate new revenues.

In March of 2003, Reel E-Z Display exhibited at its first tradeshow, GlobalShop. The response far exceeded Ricci's expectations, and that year, the company was recognized with a "Design of the Times Gold" award by *POP Times*, a Hoyt Publishing company. The company finalized its initial sale to the largest U.S. drugstore chain in September 2003 and received its first international sales to Mexico and Canada (in 2003) and Australia (in 2004).

The current marketing strategy is multifaceted and includes direct exposure through tradeshows, special promotions and pricing, Web site presence, advertising, and public relations. Annette Ricci applies her unique design creativity not only to new products but to the ways in which her company's products are marketed. Reel E-Z Display, Inc., uses innovative promotional mailings to set its products apart. For example, the company mailed potential clients a universal remote control with an insert that described the end user's ability to be "in control" of in-store signage by using Reel E-Z's new product. This successful promotion was aimed at getting the attention of buyers at large companies. It gave Reel E-Z direct contact with decision makers who are normally difficult to connect with and generated interest.

(Continued)

(Continued)

Ricci has assessed potential risks, both internally and externally. She identifies the major risks as competing innovations that would be brought to the marketplace by a large established company with resources, and the long sales cycle, including an extensive product evaluation process. Ricci regularly researches her competitors and has sought patents to safeguard her proprietary system. She has built a strong team that closely monitors her overseas manufacturing operations and sees the search for new manufacturing sources as ongoing. This allows Reel E-Z to maintain competitive with both its product offerings and its pricing. In 2004, Reel E-Z sales increased four-fold over its 2003 sales. More than 120 companies in the United States and abroad are testing and evaluating the product. These prospective customers include major retailers, who own hundreds to thousands of retail locations (requiring multiple signs in each) and major brand companies that are interested in promoting their products both domestically and internationally.

Ricci's seemingly simple solution to a basic industry problem is a great example of innovation in practice. Reel E-Z's innovative success was recognized in March of 2005, when the company received the INNOVATE Illinois award for the manufacturing sector. INNOVATE Illinois recognizes some of the most innovative and high-growth small companies in the 10-county region of Illinois. Annette Ricci has led her company to extraordinary success; it is a model of innovation in business.

Strategies for Innovation: Incremental to Revolutionary Perspectives

One of the myths of innovation is that valuable innovations are always revolutionary. In fact, most entrepreneurship and innovation is derived from incremental or evolutionary changes. The advantages and structural requirements for four distinct innovation strategies are described in this section (Hickman & Raia, 2002).

1. Improving Core Business

This strategy involves the development of incremental improvements to core products and services that can rapidly developed and inexpensively implemented.

Key strengths: Fast execution and cost efficiency as "new and improved" ideas are added to the offerings of the company; these changes often are not on radar screens of competitors.

Key weaknesses: Potentially inadequate responsiveness to market and competitor changes.

Structural requirements: This strategy requires innovation supports in the organization that encourage these types of improvements.

Examples: Microsoft Windows XP, Ford Thunderbird.

2. Exploiting Strategic Advantages

This strategy moves the firm's innovation focus beyond its current strategic scope. This enables the firm to leverage a unique brand and expand to reach a broader range of customers.

Key strengths: Involves a relatively low-risk investment for potential high return; strategic value/cost leverage.

Key weaknesses: This type of innovation could be easily duplicated by competitors.

Structural requirements: Use of external resources such as consultants, researchers, and advertising agencies.

Examples: Coleman (introduction of portable grill); Subway (introduction of partnership with American Heart Association); Frito-Lay (introduction of Natural line of organic snacks without preservatives).

3. Developing New Capabilities

This strategy involves developing or acquiring new technologies, competencies, services, and businesses to better serve the current strategic scope.

Key strengths: Builds and sustains long-term customer advantage and loyalty.

Key weaknesses: High investment cost and execution time.

Structural requirements: This strategy demands an organization that is highly fluid and flexible, including the use of joint ventures, strategic alliances, and licensing and franchising.

Examples: AOL-Time Warner, Sam's Club On-line Auction.

4. Creating Revolutionary Change

This strategy involves transcending the firm's current product and service lines to achieve fundamental changes to the strategic scope. Using this strategy, the firm envisions new business models, new markets, and new industries.

Key strengths: First mover advantage, ground-breaking position.

Key weaknesses: Lack of urgency may exist; high risk of imminent failure.

Structural requirements: Virtual teams and alliances.

Examples: Nokia, Starbucks, Amazon.com, and eBay.

Figure 9.1 presents these four innovation perspectives.

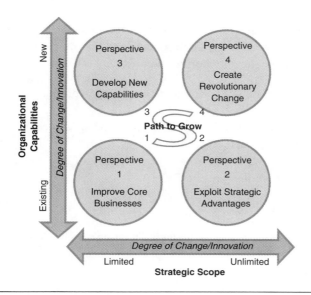

Figure 9.1   Four Innovation Perspectives

SOURCE: From Hickman, C., & Raia, C. (2002). Incubating innovation, *Journal of Business Strategy,* *23*(3), 14–18. Republished with permission from Emerald Group Publishing Limited.

Strategy in Action

Constant Compliance, Inc. (2Ci)

Charles (Chuck) Stack, MPH, knows firsthand the trials and tribulations of the entrepreneurial life. He has seen the business world both as an employee and employer. Stack started out as a premed student and ended up with a master's degree in public health because he wanted to take advantage of the enormous business opportunities being created in the emerging field of environmental technologies for public health protection. He formed his first company while in graduate school and developed an innovative technology that generates energy from waste materials, for which he was eventually awarded a patent. As a graduate student, he initiated an academic collaboration with another university, where he recruited his first employee, Prasad Kodukula, who was pursuing his Ph.D. in environmental engineering at that time. Stack sold his company a few years later and worked for others for a while before forming another company. In the meantime, Kodukula also worked for corporate America for a few years and started his own company. During these years, although Stack and Kodukula worked independently, they collaborated on projects in the United States and overseas. In 2001, Stack overcame a personal and professional challenge by undergoing brain surgery to cure his disabling epilepsy. Subsequently, Stack and Kodukula merged their respective businesses to form Constant Compliance, Inc. (2Ci), which was recognized in 2005 as the most innovative small business in the environmental sector by the state of Illinois.

2Ci develops technologies for public health, environmental protection, and homeland security applications. Industry, government, and agriculture operations use their innovative products and services to protect people from poison and pollution. The business model is based on development and commercialization of innovative environmental and homeland security technologies to address today's market needs. To commercialize their products, 2Ci partners with leading companies in the industry through licenses, strategic partnerships, and service agreements. These partners build, sell, and install 2Ci technologies for the ultimate end users. 2Ci's core competence lies in identifying and developing new innovations and providing follow-on support services to these partners and the end users of the technologies.

2Ci is constantly developing new and innovative products, and the company's current portfolio includes two classes of technologies: monitoring and treatment. The former class includes:

- AquaCoil: An early warning biosensor system to detect poison in drinking water supplies, beverages, and food (patent pending)
- BioCoil: An early warning biosensor system to detect toxic substances of concern in municipal and industrial wastewaters (patented)
- SCADAR®: A computer system that predicts and responds to industrial process malfunctions to prevent catastrophic events (patented)

The treatment technologies are:

- OmniFloat: Methane-producing anaerobic biological treatment technology for industrial wastewaters (patented)
- MPR: Integrated anaerobic-aerobic biological treatment technology for industrial wastewaters (patents in preparation)

The company is currently focusing on marketing AquaCoil and BioCoil, both of which are based on the same biosensor platform. This platform has been proven effective by a full-scale BioCoil system installation at a large sewage treatment facility. AquaCoil, a sister product, however, needs to be tested for drinking water, beverage, and food toxicity detection. There is a great need for such early warning systems in view of the potential terrorist threats today. The market for AquaCoil includes public drinking water systems, military installations, public venues (e.g., sports stadiums), and food and beverage industries. The first segment that the company plans to penetrate is the drinking water systems. 2Ci reports that based on the most recent U.S. Census Data (2003), there are 161,000 total drinking water systems in the United States, of which 367 serve communities of 100,000 people or more.

The BioCoil market is municipal sewage treatment plants and biological systems treating wastewater from a variety of industries including food processors, refineries, chemical plants, pulp and paper mills, and others. According to a U.S. Senate report, there are 16,000 municipal sewage treatment facilities, about 1 percent of which treat 100 million gallons/day or more. This is the segment 2Ci intends to pursue initially before addressing the industrial sector.

Whereas SCADAR technology is still under development, 2Ci has installed several full-scale OmniFloat and MPR systems. SCADAR monitors the performance of water and wastewater treatment processes and sends instantaneous alarms to the appropriate personnel in case of severe process failures and other emergencies. It uses artificial intelligence to predict such events and sends out early warnings, so that the authorities can take proper action to prevent major public health catastrophes. OmniFloat and MPR processes generate sustainable energy from industrial and agricultural wastes. These technologies are particularly attractive because of today's rising oil prices. They can also be used to obtain credits for greenhouse gases under the Kyoto protocol.

Stack and Kodukula have identified risks and developed mitigation strategies for their business. They do not see significant technology risks because their technologies have been proven at full scale or at least prototype level. However, they are cognizant of the market risks, which they are mitigating with aggressive licensing and sales and new product development. The company is minimizing the overall business risk particularly through its diversified portfolio of technologies, numerous licensees, and continuous refinement of its innovations.

In March of 2005, 2Ci was named the winner of the INNOVATE Illinois Challenge, which recognizes some of the most innovative and high-growth small companies in the 10-county region of Illinois. Constant Compliance Inc. received this accolade and was named the most innovative small business in the environmental sector. It was recognized for its innovative biosensor platform designed to detect toxic materials in drinking water, beverages, food, and wastewater.

What are the next steps for 2Ci? The company is in the process of testing AquaCoil for different applications. Within the next year, the company hopes to receive enough investment to fully develop and market the products in its current portfolio. Furthermore, 2Ci has several other innovative ideas in its R&D pipeline, which it will explore over the next few years. 2Ci's goal is to be the leading environmental technology development company in the United States.

Speaking of Strategy

Technology for a Better World—Improving Life Through Innovation

When the Millennium Technology Prize Committee met to find the first-ever winner, they had many prominent and distinguished names to choose from. However, their decision wasn't a difficult one. The inventor of the World Wide Web made a remarkable technological contribution that has greatly improved people's quality of life. The world's most valuable prize for technological innovation, the Millennium Technology Prize was awarded to Tim Berners-Lee by Tarja Halonen, President of the Republic of Finland, on June 14, 2004. The prize is a biennial award for an outstanding innovation that directly promotes people's quality of life, is based on humanitarian values and encourages sustainable economic development globally. Several fields are eligible for recognition, including Energy and the Environment, Information and Communication, New Materials and Processes, and Health Care and Life Sciences. The prize is awarded by the Finnish Technology Award Foundation, with financial support from both the public and private sectors.

British scientist Tim Berners-Lee got his first technical inspiration from his parents who built one of the first commercial computers in Britain. He attended Queen's College at Oxford University where he made his first computer with a soldering iron, TTL gates, an M6800 processor and an old television. Some years later he worked at the computing services section of CERN, the world's largest particle physics laboratory. It was there Berners-Lee came up with the idea of the World Wide Web. Various internets had already been in existence since 1969. However, there were no browsers, no hypertext markup language (HTML), no uniform resource locators (URLs), and, of course, no WWW addresses.

"It was not just a matter of inventing HTML, which is very simple and trivial," explains Berners-Lee, "it was a question of getting everyone to use the same HTML. The Web only works when you have standards."

One of Berners-Lee's most important ideas for the new Web was to keep it royalty-free. He and his Belgian colleague, Robert Cailliau, insisted on license-free technology. Berners-Lee believes that, had there been fees for HTML, others would have invented different webs and none of them would have got enough users to reach the critical mass to be viable for a World Wide Web.

In 1989, Berners-Lee started a global hypertext project that would later be known as the World Wide Web. The first Web program was publicly accessible on the Internet by 1991. It started out with ten hits a day, and grew to 100, then to 1,000, 10,000, 100,000, and so on at about a factor of ten every year. Berners-Lee calls it, "an explosion, but a very steady explosion." He compares the growth of the Web to launching a bobsleigh.

"First the team puts their weight behind it and they push. Nothing happens at first but eventually the sleigh starts to move slowly. Then it goes faster and faster until the sleigh reaches a point when the team must jump in or they won't be able to steer and it would go off the track. If we hadn't formed the World Wide Web Consortium in 1994 to oversee standards, then the whole thing would have gone off the track, too," says Berners-Lee, who is currently the director of the consortium.

We Aren't Done Yet

Berners-Lee says winning the Millennium Technology Prize, which included one million euro prize money, was a "very nice surprise." However, he cautions that there is still much to do.

"We must not rest on our laurels and celebrate as if the work on the Web were done. There is a need for international collaboration and many pieces are still missing. The Web was originally designed to be a very powerful tool which would operate across international boundaries, and people are impressed by what it can do. But do you find families in the Middle East or Africa putting up web logs or websites which people in other countries can browse? The web must be more accessible outside the developed world. After health care, clean water and energy, people should have access to information and be able to contribute their own knowledge."

SOURCE: From Snyder, R., The Web is a social creation in *Views on Finnish Technology*, copyright © 2005. Reprinted with permission of Tekes National Technology Agency, Finland.

Strategic Thinking: Ideas for Future Expansion[1]

There are many possible alternatives a new venture can implement to expand its portfolio of product and service offerings (Dundon & Pattakos, 2003):

- Bundling with other products or services, such as offering airfare, hotel, and care rental packages
- Adding a service to the product, such as free ski wax with purchase of new skis.
- Selling more to your current customers by offering promotions or volume discounts for a limited time or by promoting frequent purchases via a loyalty campaign
- Reminding current customers by advertising specific benefits of the products or services of which customers may be unaware
- Finding a new distribution channel, such as eBay or Amazon.com
- Creating a new occasion; for example, Hallmark is famous for promoting new holidays to encourage higher sales; cereal manufacturers encourage consumers to eat cereal as a snack in addition to breakfast
- Offering various price points, as hotels do with standard and deluxe suites
- Developing line extensions; Disney is a master at expanding the use of its movie properties to toys, clothing, and books
- Introducing new levels of service, such as American Express does with its card programs or as dry cleaning stores do with rush or regular service
- Expanding by offering new services; restaurants are expanding into the rental market where they are offering to rent their premises for cooking lessons, cooking parties, and even executive team training courses where team members can learn to break down their communication barriers by learning to cook together
- Developing new products in the same category
- Developing new products in a new category; for products and services operating in so-called "mature categories," it is wise to expand the definition of the category by combining one category with another by creating an entirely new category
- Finding new customers through a new distribution channel, such as Avon and Tupperware successfully did
- Finding new customers in new geographic zones

- Redefining the target market, attracting new customers groups, such as teens or families; for example, Tilley, the Canadian hat manufacturer, expanded its target market by supplying hats for soldiers who were serving in the U.S. Army's Desert Storm mission.
- Repositioning the product or service from a niche to a mainstream category to attract a larger customer base
- Cross-selling your products to new customers who are already your customers; for example, financial institutions are learning to sell their loan services to those customers who are holding savings accounts at the same branch
- Removing barriers to your current products or services; find out what the barriers to using your product or service have been
- Selling your knowledge to others outside of your industry sector; for example, Second City, well known for SCTV and comedy shows, has expanded its portfolio by offering its knowledge through improvisation training courses targeted to business people who want to improve their presentation and communication skills

The Five Innovation Mistakes

As has been seen throughout this text, entrepreneurs and entrepreneurial firms include some of the most creative individuals and teams in the population. That is why it is often surprising to see these same people finding themselves and their organizations in innovation ruts—wheels madly turning but getting nowhere. We start by introducing some of the pitfalls that can occur that lead to slipping off the innovative edge. While the demands of short-term analysis and rigorous expectations sometimes lead people to make the following mistakes, the key is to avoid making them repeatedly and thus turning a once-innovative organization into a stagnant environment in which risk and the generation of new ideas are avoided at all costs. Here are the five most common mistakes regarding creativity and innovation in organizations (Prather & Gundry, 1995):

1. Identifying the Wrong Problem

The most important thing to consider when deciding what to work on, is to question whether it is *really* the correct underlying problem or opportunity. Often, it is only the symptoms of a problem that are observable, and so we go to work on those. Like peeling back layers of an onion, it is critical to be sure the organization understands the root cause of the problem *before* it develop (and implements) solutions. Otherwise, the solutions will be tacked on to the wrong problem, and it may not be apparent immediately. Always question a problem: Are you sure this is what is actually wrong? Could it be something else you haven't yet considered?

2. Judging Ideas or Solutions Too Quickly

At many organizational meetings, an interesting phenomenon occurs: Someone shares a new idea or a possible solution, and within seconds, one or more other people come up with the reasons why it won't work. These reactions are known as *killer phrases* because they kill the flow of innovative thinking. Many of these have been recorded in history as ill-fated predictions.

In 1898, Charles Duell, then commissioner of the U. S. Patent Office, wanted to close the office. Why? Because he felt that everything that could be invented had already been invented! When PCs were developed, some executives doubted whether anyone would ever have use for one at home. In 1963, a group of four musicians sat on the floor of Decca Records waiting to audition. A vice president at the recording company came out of his office, looked at the guys, and said with a shrug, "Groups with guitars are out." And so the Beatles stood up and left Decca Records! As we read these infamous killer phrases and roll our eyes at how short-sighted these individuals were, here is what we must remember:

What assumptions or predictions are you making about your industry, market, or business that will elicit the same reaction 20 years from now—or even a year from now?

The Innovator's Toolkit: Challenging Your Assumptions for Breakthrough Thinking

It is usually the experts and experienced people among us (including ourselves!) who are the first ones to shoot down an idea or a possibility that challenges what we know already. After all, you already know all there is to know about this business, don't you? One of the best ways to open yourself up to new ideas and opportunities that can revive and stimulate your business (or a specific product or service that is growing stale) is to challenge your assumptions.

Step 1: Write down three assumptions you ordinarily make about your business or about a specific client, product, or service.

a. _____

b. _____

c. _____

Step 2: Now challenge each assumption by stating its opposite or by assuming the negative.

a. _____

b. _____

c. _____

Step 3: Write down potential advantages that could come from your challenges to these assumptions.

a. _____

b. _____

c. _____

(Continued)

(Continued)

Step 4: After studying the challenged assumptions and ideas in Steps 2 and 3, write down any suggestions you could use to discover a new business opportunity or solve a business problem.

_____

_____

_____

_____

_____

3. Stopping With the First Good Idea

The first idea you or your team thinks of is probably the easiest to get. It rarely is the best idea you can generate. Linus Pauling, the only person to be awarded two unshared Nobel Prizes for chemistry (1954) and for peace (1962), said that if you want to get a good idea, get lots of ideas. Thus, the argument for quantity of ideas is just as important as that of evaluating and determining the best idea (Chapter 3). One way to push yourself and your management team to keep searching for ideas is to ask the following question:

What good idea did we not think of because we stopped with this one?

This usually provides the motivation to keep generating more ideas.

4. Failing to Get Sponsorship

Even if the idea for innovation originates with the founder or management team, it still needs to be articulated to the stakeholders whose support is needed for the innovation to be successful. Realize that not everyone internal or external to the firm might understand the idea or see its relevance to or impact on the firm's strategy. They might lack the necessary information and knowledge to help implement the idea, so it is critical to share this information. Commitment and sponsorship, whether from individuals inside or outside the organization, usually is strengthened by involvement. Build the support you need from the ground up when innovating.

5. Obeying Rules That Don't Exist

One reason it is important to challenge the assumptions you hold about your new venture is that often (unintentionally), the founder and key members continue to operate under the "rules" that governed the industry and market at the time of start-up. Of course, they probably recognize market shifts and changing preferences, but they remain stuck in obsolete organizations that resist change.

Failures and Foibles

Developing a Portfolio of Initiatives

When Neil Franklin began offering round-the-clock telephone customer service in 1998, customers loved it. The offering fit the strategic direction Franklin had in mind for Dataworkforce, his Dallas-based telecommunications-engineer staffing agency, so he invested in a phone system to route after-hours calls to his 10 employees' home and mobile phones. Dataworkforce has grown to nearly 50 employees and continues to explore ways to improve its service. Twenty-four-hour phone service has stayed, but other trials have not. One failure was developing individual Web sites for each customer. "We took it too far and spent $30,000, then abandoned it," Franklin recalls. A try at globally extending the brand by advertising in major world cities was also dropped. "It worked pretty well," Franklin says, "until you added up the cost."

Franklin's efforts are similar to an approach called "portfolio of initiatives" strategy. The idea, according to Lowell Bryan, a principal in McKinsey & Co., the New York City consulting firm that developed it, is to always have a number of efforts underway to offer new products and services, attack new markets or otherwise implement strategies, and to actively manage these experiments so you don't miss an opportunity or over-commit to an unproven idea.

The portfolio of initiatives approach addresses a weakness of conventional business plans—that they make assumptions about uncertain future developments, such as market and technological trends, customer responses, sales and competitor reactions. Bryan compares the portfolio of initiatives strategy to the ship convoys used in World War II to get supplies across oceans. By assembling groups of military and transport vessels and sending them in a mutually supportive group, planners could rely on at least some reaching their destination. In the same way, entrepreneurs with a portfolio of initiatives can expect some of them to pan out.

Three steps define the portfolio of initiatives approach. First, you search for initiatives in which you have or can readily acquire a familiarity advantage—meaning you know more than competitors about a business. You can gain familiarity advantage using low-cost pilot programs and experiments, or by partnering with more knowledgeable allies. Avoid businesses in which you can't acquire a familiarity advantage, Bryan says.

After you identify familiarity-advantaged initiatives, begin investing in them using a disciplined, dynamic management approach. Pay attention to how initiatives relate to each other. They should be diverse enough that the failure of one won't endanger the others, but should also all fit into your overall strategic direction. Investments, represented by product development efforts, pilot programs, market tests and the like, should start small and increase only as they prove themselves. Avoid over-investing before initiatives have proved themselves. The third step is to pull the plug on initiatives that aren't working out, and step up investment in others. A portfolio of initiatives will work in any size company. Franklin pursues 20 to 30 at any time, knowing 90 percent won't pan out. "The main idea is to keep those initiatives running," he says. "If you don't, you're slowing down."

Maintaining an Innovation-Friendly Environment in the Established Venture

The work environment is symbolic of the venture's philosophy and approach to innovation and change. Increasingly, organizations need every member to be on the lookout for trends and shifts in the marketplace. If only the entrepreneur or the management team search for new opportunities, the venture will find it nearly impossible to survive, let alone grow. So how do entrepreneurs create an environment that encourages the continual flow of ideas and embraces change? In addition to the importance of honest and frequent communication, several elements can be built into the organization that instill the culture of innovation:

- Provide as much information as possible to employees. Knowledge stimulates creativity, and people cannot solve problems they don't know exist. Tell employees and team members about problems; don't try to solve everything yourself.

- Give employees permission to say "yes" to customers, suppliers, and so on, and make sure they have the resources they need to do so.

- Encourage experimentation. Reward nice tries instead of focusing only on mistakes. Make heroes out of the people who solve a problem in a different way, so others get the courage to emulate them.

- Encourage employees to improve one thing every day. Set up a suggestion system that collects ideas and solutions; provides feedback to everyone who contributes an idea, explaining whether or not it will be used and why; and rewards participation through recognition by the management team.

- Visit customers' organizations as well as other companies (even ones outside your industry). Have a "Share One Idea" day after these visits to discuss and potentially incorporate what you have observed at these other firms.

- Allow people to decorate their own work areas. Seemingly minor changes like this send the message that you want people to think and behave at work much as they do with family and friends: comfortably, openly, and productively. Cultures in which employees are rewarded for "face time" and other political behavior often implode: Employees use most of their creativity to figure out how to work the political system and look good compared to others. Successful entrepreneurial firms need and desire every member's creative contributions to keep the firm on the innovative edge of the industry and marketplace.

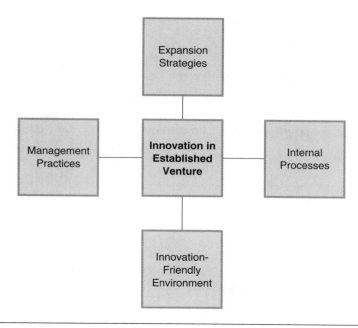

Figure 9.2   Innovation in the Established Venture

Research in Practice: Benchmarking Best Innovation Practices

New products and services fail at an alarming rate. Statistics show that only 10 percent of all new concepts become commercial successes. Only 25 percent of new development projects are successful. The odds of failure are high, and the stakes are huge for ventures that allocate resources to innovation. Why do some ventures achieve greater success in new product or service development than others? In a study of 103 business units in organizations, researchers identified the practices and approaches that separated the best from the worst performers and found the following three were the most important:

- The presence of a culture and climate within the business that supports innovation
- The role of senior management: their behavior and degree of commitment
- The nature of project teams and how they are organized.

Looking at the role of climate in explaining new product development success, the results below show the percentage of businesses with each element of a positive climate for innovation. W = worst performers; B = best performers.

Climate supports entrepreneurship and innovation:

   W = 7.7%   B = 62.1%

Product champions are recognized/rewarded:

   W = 0.0%   B = 58.6%

New product development team rewards/recognition for projects:

W = 7.7%   B = 55.2%

Employees understand new product development process ideas-to-launch:

W = 7.7%   B = 41.4%

Open communication among employees across functions/locations:

W = 34.6%   B = 72.4%

Business climate is not risk averse: invest in venture projects:
W = 3.8%   B = 32.1%

No punishment for product failure:

W = 42.3%   B = 55.2%

SOURCE: R. Cooper, S. J. Edgett, & E. J. Kleinschmidt, "Benchmarking Best NPD Practices," *Research Technology Management* 47, no. 1 (2004): 31–43.

Strategic Reflection Point

Expand Your Boundaries

Most of us look to our existing categories of products (or services or programs) as the first source for finding innovative ideas. We typically look at what we're already doing and then twist it a bit to make it just a little different. We might even look at similar companies or organizations in our market and copy some of the ideas they have already implemented.

Why not expand our boundaries and look beyond the walls of our categories to find innovative ideas? Look for ideas in neighboring countries to find ideas to extend the appeal of your current products or services, attract new user groups, cut costs, and work more effectively with suppliers.

Secondly, look beyond the borders of the current definition of your product, service or program to find ideas in "neighboring categories." For example, if you are looking for new ideas to market soft drinks, look at the beer, coffee, tea and snack markets. If you are looking for new ideas for your bookstore, look for ideas in the education and training market, in the card and gift store market, and in the restaurant market. They are all related in some way to your challenge. Expanding your boundaries will give you fresh, new ideas that you can bring to your category.

SOURCE: Dundon, E., & Pattakos, A. (2003). *Seeds of Innovation: Insights Journal* 1:91. Used with permission.

Summary of Chapter Objectives

1. Understand the four perspectives on strategy for innovation and how an organization's strategic scope and capabilities determine the appropriate innovation strategy
   - Improving Core Business: This strategy involves the development of incremental improvements to core products and services that can be rapidly developed and inexpensively implemented.
   - Exploiting Strategic Advantages: This strategy moves the firm's innovation focus beyond its current strategic scope. This enables the firm to leverage a unique brand and expand to reach a broader range of customers.
   - Developing New Capabilities: This strategy involves developing or acquiring new technologies, competencies, services, and businesses to better serve the current strategic scope.
   - Creating Revolutionary Change: This strategy involves transcending the firm's current product and service lines to achieve fundamental changes to the strategic scope. Using this strategy, the firm envisions new business models, new markets, and new industries.

2. Learn strategic approaches to future expansion of the new venture
   - There are many alternative growth extending strategies to implement, including the bundling of products and services, developing line extensions, and developing new products in a new category.

3. Recognize the five innovation mistakes of individuals and organizations
   - Identifying the problem incorrectly.
   - Judging ideas or solutions too quickly.
   - Stopping with the first good idea.
   - Failing to get sponsorship.
   - Obeying rules that don't exist.

4. Develop a portfolio of initiatives
   - First, search for initiatives in which you have or can readily acquire a familiarity advantage. Create a diverse set of initiatives in which the firm can invest. Some are likely to become successful.

5. Learn how to maintain an innovation-friendly environment in the established venture, including these recommendations:
   - Provide ample information to employees.
   - Allow room for experimentation.
   - Encourage employees to improve one thing every day.

CASE 9.1   Netflix

People thought this idea was crazy that consumers would rent movies through the mail . . . but it was precisely because it was a contrarian idea that enabled us to get ahead of our competitors.

—Reed Hastings, CEO, Netflix[2]

When traditional movie rental companies were trying to win customers by building more rental stores on every corner, Netflix saw an opportunity. The founder and CEO, Reed Hastings, reversed age-old assumptions about movie rental and created a business specifically for the Internet. Netflix has changed movie-watching behavior. Not only is the subscriber base growing at a rate of greater than 50 percent per year, but subscribers say they rent twice as many movies per month as they did prior to joining the service ("Fact sheet," 2005). But with competitive giants such as Blockbuster entering the market, will Netflix be able to survive? Hastings claims the answer is a resounding yes, saying "No one should doubt our resolve to maintain our leadership in a market we invented" ("Netflix profit," 2005, p. 8).

Netflix Overview

Netflix is an on-line movie rental service that provides DVD rental without due dates or late fees. Subscribers pay a monthly flat fee to rent as many movies as they wish, with a set number of movies out at a time. The movies are mailed directly to the customer's home with a prepaid envelope for returning each movie. As soon as Netflix receives a movie from the customer, it sends out another movie.

Nearly 90 percent of Netflix subscribers receive their DVDs in one business day ("About Netflix," 2005). This is quite a feat, considering the company ships an average of more than 4 million DVDs each week ("Fact sheet," 2005). With

more than 40,000 titles and more than 25 million DVDs total ("Fact sheet," 2005), it's no wonder the subscriber base is growing at a rate of greater than 50 percent each year (*Netflix passes*, 2005). A typical neighborhood video store has fewer than 3,000 titles ("Fact sheet," 2005).

Company Background

Netflix was founded in 1997 and launched its on-line movie rental service in 1999 with a single distribution center, in San Francisco, California ("Management," 2005). Today, Netflix is the world's largest on-line movie rental service with more than 3 million subscribers and 30 distribution centers across the United States (*Netflix passes*, 2005). The company grew at a rapid pace, reaching 1 million subscribers by February 2003, 2 million subscribers in May 2004, and 3 million subscribers by March 2005 (*Netflix passes*, 2005).

When the dot-com collapse forced most on-line companies out of the market, Netflix stayed the course and pushed forward with its on-line only business model. The company also continued to deliver on its promises to its subscribers. The strategy worked, and the company began making in money in 2002, also the year of its stock market debut. Today, Netflix employs more than 1,000 people at the corporate headquarters and shipping centers ("Fact sheet," 2005) and expects to generate more than $700 million in revenues in 2005 ("Management," 2005).

Industry Overview

The U.S. movie rental market is estimated at about $5.5 billion, of which on-line movie rentals make up about 10 percent (Gomes, 2005). For Netflix, this is only the beginning. The on-line movie market is estimated to grow to 6.6 million customers by 2008 (Williamson, 2004). In fact, 5 percent of U.S. households are expected to subscribe to an on-line movie service by 2006, growing the subscriber base to 5 million members and about $1 billion in revenue (Williamson, 2004).

Netflix Business Model

The Netflix business model not only supports the business but also represents a competitive advantage. This business was created specifically for the Internet, as opposed to Blockbuster and other bricks-and-mortar retailers that have extended their business models to include an on-line presence.

Second, the business model is straightforward. The service offers only DVD rental, so it did not have to endure a costly transition from VCR to DVD format as some of the traditional players in the movie rental industry did. In fact, Netflix's timing was critical to its success— the company entered the market at the very beginning of the DVD trend.

Since the Web site is the company's primary interaction with its customers and prospects, Netflix has invested the majority of its resources in keeping the Web site innovative. Hastings says, "If we differentiate the Web site well enough, with rating histories and other features consumers want, that's our strategic leverage" (Rivlin, 2005, p. G1). The Web site has achieved this by offering unique titles, as well as collaborative filtering technology.

Netflix has also been able to compete with the bigger retailers because of its fast turnaround time. With nearly 90 percent of its subscribers receiving delivery of their DVDs in one business day, there is little lag time ("About Netflix," 2005). The additional distribution centers have helped to shorten this time frame as the company has grown.

Netflix focuses on customer service, convenience, and selection as important influencing factors of its brand (Sacks, 2004). The company continues to expand its Web site services by listening to its customers. In December 2005, it rolled out Netflix Friends, a recommendation service that creates a social network for groups of friends to rate movies and share movie suggestions with individuals in their social network (Terdiman, 2004).

Holding Its Own Against the Competition

Netflix faces steep competition in the movie rental market from services of all sizes. Blockbuster created an on-line video rental service in 2004 to compete with Netflix and recently merged its stores with its on-line operations. In addition, it is expanding its on-line inventory to 30,000 (from 25,000) and offering a lower price than Netflix. Blockbuster also offers video games in its stores in addition to movies, and these account for a good part of rentals; they are not yet offered on-line (Nishi, 2005).

Amazon.com, although not yet a player in the American market, is likely to be a formidable competitor to Netflix because of its large existing customer base. The company has already launched a service in the United Kingdom, which some analysts suggest may be a test for a rollout into the U.S. market (Rivlin, 2005).

Wal-Mart was the first large retailer to enter the on-line movie market in 2003. It operated 14 distribution centers for its on-line DVD rental service (Rivlin, 2005). The ongoing price war between Blockbuster and Netflix, coupled with a weak on-line business model, led Wal-Mart to end its on-line rental service offering in May 2005. The company turned its subscribers (about 300,000) over to Netflix (McWilliams & Wingfield, 2005).

Another potential threat to the on-line movie rental business as a whole is the increasing interest in video-on-demand. Netflix recently announced a partnership with TiVo to deliver movies directly to customer's televisions through the TiVo service. The two companies will work together to develop technology and to work with Hollywood studios to obtain rights to content for digital distribution (*Netflix and TiVo*, 2004). There are, however, several issues to be worked out around ownership rights for making newly released movies available for customer viewing using such services (Whitney, 2004). At this point, Netflix doesn't think video-on-demand technology will take hold and cause a decline in DVD orders for quite some time (*Netflix profit*, 2005). Based on this prediction, it plans to keep its business model the same for now.

The Future of Netflix

So what will keep Netflix viable in the years to come? First of all, customers love the service. Few customers are canceling. In fact, the customer churn rate fell to 4.4 percent in January 2005, the lowest level in Netflix history (*Netflix profit*, 2005). Second, for the bricks-and-mortar companies that have entered the market, such as Blockbuster, it is not yet certain if their business models are strong enough to sustain on-line competition long-term, as evidenced by Wal-Mart's recent collapse. Hastings doesn't mind

the debate over his company's future success. To him, "To be doubted and successful is particularly satisfying" (Rivlin, 2005, p. G1).

SOURCE: This case was written by Laurel Ofstein, DePaul University.

Discussion Questions

1. What types of core innovations as well as practices have allowed Netflix to sustain its business model and market advantage?

2. What recommendations would you make to Netflix's entrepreneurial team to further expand its offerings?

3. How can the entrepreneurial team challenge some of the assumptions about the business and its customers for breakthrough thinking? Consider using the steps outlined in the Innovator's Toolkit.

CASE 9.2   Neeta Narula and Ebony Department Stores: Continuing Entrepreneurship in an Indian Family Business

It was Monday morning, February 16, 2004, as Neeta Narula, the managing director of the Ebony retail chain, scanned the latest stack of reports on the stores' recent business performance (see Exhibit 1 and organization chart in Exhibit 2). The Darshan Singh (DS) Group, Ebony's parent company, had set 2003 as a year of consolidation. Opening only one new store (in Faridabad) and closing another in Chennai, the company operated eight Ebony stores—all in the northern region of India (see map in Exhibit 3). Ebony had concluded fiscal year 2003 with a 15 percent growth in revenue and positive

profitability. H. S. Kohli, the CEO of Ebony, walked in, saying excitedly, "I believe these are harbingers that Ebony is on the right track. We should be well-poised to implement our growth plan to launch 20 new stores by the end of 2007."

Kohli laid out aggressive plans for Ebony's future national expansion. First, Kohli planned to strengthen Ebony's leadership position within Northern India by expanding into west Delhi, Gurgaon, Jaipur, Kanpur, Lucknow, Allahabad, Dehradun, and Varanasi. "We will also be evaluating new business models like joint ventures, franchisees, and mergers and acquisitions for a comprehensive regional presence" ("Ebony to Take," 2004). At an estimated cost of 1,500 million rupees,[3] the plan called for developing clusters of stores in both metropolitan areas and small (B-class) towns in south, central, and western India, with a focus on upgrading employees' skills and the retail infrastructure and standardizing processes. The new plan also called for 12 large-format stores, all situated in malls. Kohli observed, "Retailing is seeing a transition from high-street expansion to mall development. This is an encouraging trend as taking space in malls on lease would cost around one third of what we would pay in locations like Linking Road in Mumba" ("Ebony to Take," 2004).

Before assuming his present position as CEO in 2003, Kohli had been the chief operating officer of Ebony. He was very familiar with the retailing powerhouses—Shoppers' Stop, for example—that had mushroomed in large metropolitan areas, such as Delhi, Mumbai, Chennai, and Bangalore—the Category A markets. "I joined the Darshan Singh Group in 1980," Neeta remembered Kohli telling her, "and I have seen many changes in the retail landscape over the past 20 years. Probably the biggest changes occurred as a result of the economic reforms in 1991. Prior to then, retailing in India was largely unorganized . . . 12 million retail outlets—far more than in the United States—but nearly all of them were corner stores that were managed without any professional inputs.

"But," he had continued, "when the government eased the restrictions on the imports of branded as well as mass-produced international products into India, the large middle class began to adopt consumer-oriented values, seeking world-class shopping experiences. They wanted a wide range of merchandise, exclusive "shop-in-shop" (boutique) counters of international brands, and top customer service. This prompted a number of start-ups that used Western-style department store, supermarket, and discount store formats, including Ebony." Inspired by K. Raheja, the family group that pioneered the department store format in India with Shoppers'

Stop, the DS Group opened its first Ebony store in South Extension, Delhi, in 1994.

Ebony was a brainchild of Harpinder Singh Narula—chairman of the DS Group and the younger son of the group's founder—Darshan Singh Narula. In 1996, Birinder Singh Narula—Neeta's husband and the son of Harpinder's elder brother—took the challenge of growing Ebony. She [Neeta] recalled Birinder telling her in 1996, "After learning the ropes of retailing in the UK, I noticed that we were doing things in a very disorganized way in our Indian operations. And, unfortunately, we were very complacent about it. We did not get into the IT [information technology] side at all . . . everything was done manually. The picture of what Ebony stores should look like, and how they could become a chain, started emerging in my mind." And Birinder had just decided to lead the group's operations overseas, and she was at the helm of Ebony as the managing director.

Neeta was 35 years old and a mother of two children—Birneet (11 years) and Anadita (5 years). She had told Kohli, "In ten years from now, I would like to see Ebony become a leading national retail chain with 10 billion rupees turnover." She had noted, "My strength lies in managing the core team of professionals." She also continued, "I strive to gain family satisfaction through right blending of professional commitments and family happiness."

Kohli recognized many Indian family business groups, such as the DS Group, were no longer fiefdoms. As second and later generations entered the family groups and sought new growth opportunities, well-educated, nonfamily members—professional managers—were often brought in to expand a company's skills and resources. "At first," Kohli had told her that he felt "the family was slow to accept me. But over time, I proved my loyalty and gained their confidence. I believe that is why Birinder appointed me as Ebony's CEO. I hope I can retain their confidence . . . but I do sometimes wonder if passing of senior leadership into the hands of someone who is not part of the Narula family will make a difference."

History of the DS Group

In 1947, at the time of India's independence and partition, Darshan Singh Narula and his family arrived in India as refugees from Pakistan. Settling in Delhi, Darshan Singh launched a construction company—DS Construction—building roads and other infrastructure projects through contracts from the defense forces. As the years passed, Darshan Singh expanded operations into Libya (1960s), with his younger son, Harpinder Singh, taking over the Libyan operations in 1975.

"But," Harpinder noted, "both construction and Libya were tough business domains. Since I didn't want to put all the eggs in the same basket, I decided to spread out and chart some new areas and frontiers. I moved to the UK and set up the group headquarters in London. We chose Great Britain simply because of our comfort with that place. It was—and still is—an international focal hub, and language is a great advantage that we have. Great Britain has a big Indian diaspora. So, we knew something about it." In 1994, DS Group founded the "Elegant English" chain of boutique hotels (www.eeh.co.uk) in central London through acquisitions, and it set bold plans for its growth.

"Overall," said Harpinder, "the international growth of DS Group was a slow and steady process, with the Narula family working on it in a very focused manner." Although he was only in his early 50s, Harpinder, as the group president, focused on setting the overall direction. Putting a great emphasis on building competencies for managing in diverse work cultures, Harpinder observed, "I am very adaptable. I am a bottom-line person. Currently, I work in four different business cultures—in Gulf countries, Britain, America, and India. I even change my accent accordingly."

Harpinder attributed his success to his ability to identify the right personnel and delegate work to them. He noted, "Most of the people who work with me have been home grown, and I can rely on them, which is why I can take five weeks off and not be worried about things going wrong." Yet, even while on vacations, Harpinder always carried his laptop and mobile phone with him to keep in touch with his business. He clarified, "I spend my time working on business strategies and so have to delegate work to others. Business is a passion for me, not a compulsion."

Harpinder was a father of three sons, all of whom were studying. He had told his three sons, "You will not inherit any wealth if you don't learn to earn." While giving a $2 million luxury yacht as a gift to his wife, Surina, Harpinder made sure that his sons always traveled in economy class. Harpinder explained his philosophy: "I never think of anything as a problem; there are always opportunities. Some you can cash in quickly, but others are latent. There is nothing like a problem . . . But I am a very sure-footed animal and hedge my bets. I delegate powers. I adopt a project, devote six or seven months to it, and then move on to the next. I don't borrow easily" (Mitra, 2000).

Ebony Department Store

"Despite these successes," continued Harpinder, "the biggest dream shared by all the members of the Narula family was to raise the profile of DS Group in India. We saw the Raheja family's success with Shopper's Stop and believed that we could do the same. Our families shared the same community (Rahejas), and like us, they also began in the construction business. So we opened Ebony, our first department store, in Delhi with over 20,000 square feet of shopping area. Our vision was to provide a truly international shopping experience to Indian customers . . . the store offered shoppers a wide range of products in a comfortable, luxurious ambiance. While Ebony generated positive cash flows in its very first year, it was not entirely profitable because the cash flows were not sufficient to cover the imputed rent of the land and building.

"Unfortunately," Harpinder continued, "my father, Darshan Singh, passed away in 1996. When Birinder learned of his death, he returned to India and decided to lead the Group's operations in India. Birinder told me that my father was very dear to him; in fact, that about three days prior to his demise, my father had asked Birinder to return to India . . . he said my father had a very strong wish for him to come back and meet him. And so, Birinder came home saying, 'Somewhere I felt that I just had to come back and start my journey again in India. India is where you belong, you are Indian yourselves, you also feel you must do something.'"

"At the time," continued Harpinder, "I considered joining the Group's newly developing diversification into the U.S., but then decided to instead focus on taking Ebony forward to actualize the family's big India dream. The more I thought about it, the more I was convinced about the immense potential for organized retailing in India. By late 1997, I drew up the business plan for Ebony's expansion and started studying the local market."

The Organized Retail Landscape in India

Even before the 1991 economic reforms, there were national factory outlets such as Raymond and localized chains such as Nalli's in Tamil Nadu, Nilgiri's and Spencer's in the south, Akbarally's in Mumbai, and Snowhite and Delhi Cloth Mills (DCM) in Delhi. Yet, it was only after 1991 that Western-style organized retailing, based on a professional service-oriented platform to provide a holistic shopping experience, became a reality. The liberalization eased the restrictions on imports of branded as well as mass-produced international products into India and inspired a number of start-ups using Western-style department store, supermarket, and discount store formats. However, many folded up even before they could be launched, many others struggled and exhausted their capital in search of a viable business model, and still others were still evolving.

Nevertheless, in the late 1990s, India's retail sector had an estimated value of 4,000 billion rupees. The sector was highly fragmented and unorganized, with nearly 12 million retail outlets. The organized sector was estimated to be worth anywhere between 50 billion and 200 billion rupees (Singh, 2000).

Most departmental stores were seeking to compete on a platform of "international shopping experience" that combined convenience, quality, variety, and price worthiness, making it a lifestyle statement. The stores targeted affluent consumers looking for a good time and indulged them with food and entertainment. They strived to enhance the "shopping experience through innovative retail formats, or by clubbing fun with shopping" ("The Great," 2004). Birinder, however, felt that, "With several big names racing to the modern retail market . . . a shakeout was bound to happen in the retail chain industry as well because a whole lot of players enter this field without doing the necessary background work."

NANZ—India's first supermarket chain based on the international model—was a case in point. Launched in 1994 with a high-profile campaign as India's first modern supermarket chain, NANZ was a joint venture of Goetze (India), NANZ (Germany), and Marsh (United States). NANZ incurred losses averaging 2 million rupees a year and was eventually forced to shut down operations in January 2001. India's leading retail consultant, KSA Technopack, concluded that NANZ reflected not a "consumer failure but a management failure . . . NANZ was doomed right from the beginning. There wasn't any business model in place, the promoters didn't work out capitalization properly and back-end operations were never strengthened" ("The Great," 2004).

Meanwhile, other modern retail outlets mushroomed in large metropolitan cities, particularly Delhi, Mumbai, Chennai, and Bangalore—Category A markets—where consumers were believed to be most open to the platforms of an international shopping experience. Offering a combination of fun and food with shopping, the branded one-stop shops were a novelty for the average Indian consumer. They were also perceived to offer higher price tags.

Ebony's Business Strategy: Charting a Distinctive Course

Given its enterprising culture, DS Group had its eyes on the emerging opportunities in North India. "North Indians are so different from South Indians," observed Harpinder. "A South Indian works within the given guidelines. He is content with his work and the money he gets. On the other hand, a North Indian is outgoing and enterprising. He cannot be restricted. He always looks for greener pastures. That is perhaps one reason why software and other multinationals head for South India" (Sandhu, 1999).

"Birinder, my nephew, developed DS Group's plan for Ebony as a modern department store in Delhi," continued Harpinder. "He was convinced about the immense potential for organized retailing in India. He planted the seed of the idea that we should grow this business. He felt strongly that this was a good line and should not be just one store, maybe because of his exposure abroad. The time Birinder spent in the UK, learning the ropes of retailing and working in stores to get a feel for both the front-end and back-end of operations, helped him to gain a better sense of the difference between the retailing in the UK and retailing in India. That is when he began to form ideas about how DS Group could further develop the Indian operations."

Birinder's plan, developed in 1998, called for Ebony to become a national level chain by the end of 2001 and a viable and acknowledged leader in the Indian retail market. The plan was based on three major elements: (1) value-driven proposition, (2) small town strategy, and (3) cluster format approach. However, the first step of the strategy was to revamp and modernize the systems based on information technology [IT]. Advanced IT tools facilitated better logistics and inventory management and generated lower operational costs. Birinder recalled, "I had already started building the team in 1997–1998

for putting in the IT side. The Delhi South Extension store started with a very basic fox-pro system in 1994. I forced them to move into a Windows system, though it required designing our own Windows platform system. Though our new system did not have all the features we desired, it gave us the information we needed. In fact, we were the first store to adopt the bar code system in North India. As I built the team, the inputs encouraged us to experiment a bit more. We put the first Sensormatic electronic article surveillance system in department stores in North. The expansion then started anew."

Value-Driven Brand Proposition

Despite rapid growth, a shopping mall culture was not very common in the Indian consumer market. Therefore, a core aspect of the strategy was to define Ebony as a "good-value-for-the-money" brand, with a scalable proposition. Unlike most other department stores, DS Group felt that it should not define Ebony's target customer to be a high-end consumer. Rather, Ebony should offer options for the middle class, particularly if it wanted to become a flagship brand for the DS Group's strategy in India. Consequently, the company decided that it would "provide customers [with] a fabulous shopping experience which is quality merchandise at a reasonable price, a comfortable luxurious ambience, backed by international service." Noting that it would be operating in a buyers' market in which customers were discerning and savvy, it vowed not to "showcase anything that carries an outlandish price tag" (Chakravarty, 2000).

Harpinder observed, "The strategy behind Ebony has been to provide quality goods for the price-conscious bourgeois class." He continued, "The new Indian wants the ambience, the location, and all the trimmings but does not want to pay a penny more." Ebony began importing a good portion of its merchandise on its own and later started an in-house line. "By importing the products ourselves, we have ruled out the payments made to middlemen, pricing our products at least 15 to 20 percent lower than normal rates." Another aspect of Ebony's strategy was Harpinder's belief that Indians do not shop for leisure. He felt that the concept of shopping being a family outing like going to the movies was an incorrect picture. Instead, he reflected, "the biggest commodity is time, and people here don't want to waste time while shopping" (Deshpande, 2000).

Small Town Strategy

Recognizing the crowding in the Category A markets, Birinder believed that the smaller so-called "B-towns," with populations ranging from 1 to 2 million people, were ready for the Ebony-type concept. While the affluent segment of customers in Delhi and other large metros had an option to experience international shopping by going abroad, the people in smaller towns, or mini-metros, had fewer opportunities to travel overseas and so would have a greater desire for international shopping experiences. Birinder had also found newly published information that discredited the assumption that the purchasing power of the B-class towns was low. In fact, Birinder learned that many industrial families and families with large agrarian holdings lived in these B-class towns and that they often traveled to larger cities, such as Delhi and Mumbai, just for shopping.

Moreover, DS Group felt that it already had some knowledge of the consumers from the smaller towns. Birinder reflected, "We have relatives in most of these places. We would sit down and talk with them for hours to find out what traffic was like coming into the stores, what the people were like, and what they thought about a concept like Ebony. Finally, there was the gut feeling . . . and we finally said we just have to do it."

DS Group estimated the target segment in B-class towns to be 20 to 25 percent of the total population, which it felt was sufficient to sustain a store. According to Birinder, these towns were evolving rapidly due to media exposure and the increase in disposable income, and people were willing to pay for the convenience, variety, and availability in the modern retail format. Moreover, there was little competition in B-class towns, so Birinder reasoned it could attain a first-to-market advantage. In addition, the low costs of real estate in these towns would lower the overhead.

Cluster Format Approach

To further ensure the viability of the small town strategy accessible to the middle class, DS Group devised a unique cluster format approach with each cluster covering a major metropolitan area, satellite towns (suburbs), and nearby B-class towns. Within each cluster, a flagship store would be launched with branches nearby, so as to achieve both wider coverage and economies of scale, with a common advertising strategy geared toward the region's unique characteristics. A single regional warehouse would manage the entire supply chain and logistics.

The company planned to invest 1,500 million rupees over a three-year period, from 1999 to 2001, for its expansion from one store (city) to 13 stores (cities), to achieve a sales base of 3,000 million rupees in 2002. Rather than leasing, it planned to purchase properties outright, using internally generated funds. Birinder elaborated, "In India, the retailing is not really of the three-figure markup yet, as seen in the UK. We have 25 to 35 percent margins, and if the biggest component—real estate—is going to make it unviable, then the business is a non-starter."

DS Group decided to put the cluster approach into action first in the national capital region in Northern India, starting with Delhi and Chandigarh, and extend into Ludhiana, Lucknow and Jaipur. Harpinder observed, "We want to shed the image of being focused on the northern part of the country." He added, "There will be no room left for the small general store or corner store, unless it is a boutique," and he expected DS Group to be "ahead to capture the retail market" (Vidyasagar, 1999). Therefore, after the Northern India cluster, DS Group planned to develop a Western India cluster, starting with Mumbai, Pune, Ahmedabad, and Indore. Eastern India was perceived to be least developed in terms of consumer attitudes toward modern retailing; here, DS Group expected to focus on metro Kolkata first. Finally, the company would seek to expand into Southern India, where many modern retail outlets were being set up building on the dynamism from the IT revolution.

Implementing the Plan

According to Birinder, implementing Ebony's plan proved to be quite challenging. The target customers had mistaken perceptions about the value because the other players in the department store segment were focused on premium foreign products and high-income customers. "While the small town customers were fascinated by the international shopping experience, they were intimidated by the modern looks of the store," said Birinder. "Also, the anticipated efficiencies from the cluster format strategy proved to be limited, as the company strived to be more flexible and adaptive to the local needs for being close to the customer in the small towns. Moreover, outside of the North India region, the company could not find a viable and cost-effective deal for launching its cluster flagship store."

Supply Chain Management

One of the rationales for the small town strategy was the potential synergy in marketing, sourcing, logistics, and inventory management arising out of the integration of the flagship store in a metro area with the smaller cities. DS Group, however, quickly realized that the differences in local needs limited the efficiency benefits of complete supply chain integration, and it therefore began emphasizing the lead-time benefits of separate warehouses and local shelf management, giving each store the flexibility to order replenishments, subject to a 12-week

initial inventory. For instance, the company found that it "would not stock very many saris in a place like Ludhiana" (Bose, 2003), where the women preferred salwar suits, but would do so in Noida (Uttar Pradesh), bordering Delhi.

Real Estate Model

In smaller towns, DS Group adapted its retail outlet size, using smaller 10,000 to 15,000 square feet models, compared to 30,000 square feet models for the larger towns. Ebony achieved square feet sales of 5,000 rupees per year, which was less than the 8,000 rupees of Shopper's Stop but was still viable because the real estate costs in the smaller towns were less than half of that in the larger towns.

To execute its cluster format approach in North India, in 1998, DS Group acquired new land to build second and third Ebony stores in Chandigarh (May 1999) and Noida (August 1999), respectively. It aspired to build North India's largest shopping store at Chandigarh. However, Chandigarh was the home of the failed NANZ store, which became a negative factor for DS Group. Birinder noted, "The moment we gave the first ad, people said it would be just another NANZ. The core business people said that it's a wonderful concept for Delhi, but you should take another look at it for Chandigarh."

Managing Growth

After what was viewed as a successful launch in Chandigarh in October 2000, DS Group decided to open much larger stores in Ludhiana (Punjab) and Rajouri Garden (Delhi), in time for the local festive season at the start of the winter. Commenting on these new openings, Birinder remarked, "The first thing that strikes you when you go abroad is their large and grand department stores. This is what I have always wanted to establish in India. I am glad that I am well on my way to fulfilling my dream of setting up a chain of quality department stores in all major cities of India" (Prashar, 2000).

However, the property prices in most major cities of India had reached extremely high levels, and the company recognized a need for greater flexibility in its initial plan to consider only the outright purchase of properties. In October 2000, Harpinder noted that the company would consider the option of leasing the land as well. While expressing concern about the high rent in the retail chain industry, he indicated an interest in evolving innovative schemes like mini-malls with an anchor shop. In this scheme, Ebony, as the anchor shop, would rent more than 25 percent of space in the mini-mall, thereby securing concessions from the developer (Ghosh, 2000).

The opportunity to open the sixth store in Northern India cluster emerged in early 2001, when a client in Jalandhar (Punjab), attracted by Ebony's strong brand, expressed interest in bringing the store to his city, and offered his property for rent. The size of the property, at 10,000 square feet, was just right for the small city. However, DS Group found the location of the property to be only average, as it was far away from the central market.[4] The customer recognized the reluctance of DS Group and offered his property for a percentage share of revenues instead. DS Group agreed to this proposal because it minimized the overhead that would need to be covered. The store was launched and became profitable quite quickly, making "more profits than the Delhi stores" and at the same time allowing the "collaborator to earn more than he would get on a standard rent." Birinder observed that this performance was an eye opener for the company and underlined that Ebony had now created a niche as a "destination point" in the North.

On the whole, by early 2001, the company appeared to have perfected its strategic business model. Of the six Ebony stores, four had already broken even. The company reported a break-even time of between 12 and 18 months, or at least two seasons, with an investment of 80 to 100 million rupees in a standard 40,000 square-feet Ebony store in metro areas and a smaller investment in smaller towns.

At the same time, the company was finding it difficult to find viable deals for opening new stores. It had to back out of advanced negotiations for renting property in Kolkata to create a flagship store in the Eastern region. The ongoing negotiations for renting property in Mumbai for a flagship store in the Western region also failed. Given this turn of the events, the company decided to revise its strategic plan, and to first focus on South India. Birinder observed, "Our mind was focused on cluster management; we had wanted to build up a cluster North, and now we are trying to build South as a cluster. Mumbai (in Western India) had to be on our map, but we assessed which is the better cluster to go for. South had big metros as Chennai, but Cochins and Coimbatores also had large opportunities."

DS Group planned to invest 500 million rupees in six to ten stores in South India, across cities such as Chennai, Bangalore, Hyderabad, Kochi, and Coimbatore, by end 2002 ("Chennai To Be," 2001). Given the presence of a large number of modern retail outlets in South India, the region was increasingly being described as the "mecca of retailing." Birinder observed, "South India is far ahead in the retail formats and, importantly, the customer's acceptance of such formats. They just walk in very easily and are easy about it. They won't shy away as the customers do in the North, where we are still the fanciest thing in the region."

In October 2001, Ebony opened its flagship store in South India in Chennai (Tamil Nadu), along with an entire office "with buyers and category managers to oversee five to six stores." The Chennai store, spread across 40,000 square feet, was largest in the city, with six floors. To give a sense of being more than a complete department store, it adopted a shop-in-shop format and formed alliances with several leading companies. Some prominent alliances included Chennai-based appliance retailer Vivek's, which rented a space at Ebony for selling kitchen gadgets; Bata for selling footwear; Sify for offering an Internet café; Airtel for selling cellphones;

and Musicworld for selling music. Moreover, the space was also leased to Ebony's concept bookstore, Wordsworth, which formed an alliance with Qwiky's Coffee Pub for a browsing-and-coffee place in the store.

Yet, the awareness about the Ebony brand was very low in Chennai. In a prelaunch dipstick survey, only 3 percent of the target customers in Chennai were aware of Ebony retail brand. After the launch, 28 percent of the target market was found to be aware ("Ebony Scouting," 2002). The company faced a tough time in trying to create a loyal base of customers in a market already dominated by four big players—LifeStyle, Globus, Shoppers' Stop, and Westside—besides several smaller players. DS Group expected that it would take about two years to break even at the Chennai store. The average number of people visiting its Chennai store was only 1,000 on weekdays and 2,000 during the weekends.

Organizational Effectiveness

Until 2000 to 2001, Ebony generated positive cash flows overall, although these did not fully cover the cost of the property. However, by 2001 to 2002, Ebony had become a profitable business, with a profit of 10 million rupees on a sales base of 654 million rupees. Furthermore, by 2002, Ebony had emerged as the largest retail chain in Northern India. DS Group consolidated this position by opening its seventh Northern Indian store at Amritsar, the fourth in the state of Punjab, in October 2002. The eighth store was opened at Faridabad, the fourth in the national capital region, in January 2003. In total, the company had invested 450 million rupees in opening nine Ebony stores since its inception in 1994 (Bhushan, 2004), less than one third of the 1,500 million rupees it had planned to invest in 13 stores in 1998.

The year 2002 was a watershed in other ways as well. When the store in Amritsar was being built as part of a then under-construction mall, Birinder visited the place for a market survey. He "overheard a person saying that the Ebony Mall was coming up," although the mall was not named the Ebony Mall and Ebony was just one tenant. The incident at Amritsar indicated to Birinder that people of the town were proud that Ebony had arrived in their city. "Though [because of their lower incomes] they themselves may not even be consumers of Ebony, for them, it's a big thing as a status symbol of the city. Now those people could tell any visitor to their city that 'my B grade town has something international.'"

Birinder was proud that Ebony has begun making such an effect in small towns. He recalled that soon after Ebony got successfully established in Chandigarh, many other organized businesses, including Wills Sports, Reebok, and Nike, also entered the city. "This is wonderful because with our vision, we have that extra responsibility of creating something. For every new business, it becomes very easy because of prior acceptability of the concept."

Moving on to the Next Frontier

In January 2004, Birinder decided to shift his focus to Libya to oversee the DS Group's construction business, DS Constructions. The DS Group was expecting a surge in international competition in Libya because of the Libyan government's promise in December 2003 to dismantle its weapons of mass destruction and to end its support of terrorists.

Meanwhile, as of the end of 2003, less than one third of the funds that had been allocated for Ebony's start-up had been invested. Ebony was still a Northern India player, with presence only in national capital region and the state of Punjab. DS Group had set 2003 as a year of consolidation and opened only one store (in Faridabad in February 2003). As part of its consolidation strategy, in late 2003, the Chennai store was closed, leaving the company with only eight Ebony stores—all in the northern region.

Yet, Ebony had achieved a 15 percent overall revenue growth and positive profitability. While the retail business of Ebony was now consolidating, DS Group was eyeing other growth opportunities after enjoying a substantial jump in its worldwide revenues in 2003 to 2004. (See Exhibit 4.)

As Neeta reflected on Ebony's growth, she wondered how long it might be before the DS Group's vision for Ebony would be realized. Was DS Group's business model the right one to make Ebony a nationally successful and leading brand? Moreover, she wondered, how will she continue the tradition of successful entrepreneurship of DS Group, a tradition that started with Darshan Singh and has been continued by Harpinder Singh and her husband, Birinder Singh? What role might H. S. Kohli, a professional manager, be able to play in this regard? Would Kohli be committed to the highly conservative family philosophy of internally financed growth and close family control? And most significant, how would he perceive reporting to a woman managing director, who also happened to be much younger than him? (See Exhibit 5 for Neeta's personality profile.)

SOURCE: This case was written by Vipin Gupta, Simmons College; Nancy Levenburg, Grand Valley State University; and Pankaj Saran, EMPI Business School, Delhi. Used with permission.

Exhibit 1   Actual Versus Target Revenues

Year	Actual Revenues	Target Revenues (Jan. 2001)
2001–2002	Rs. 654 m	Rs. 1,000 m
2002–2003	Rs. 698 m	Rs. 2,000 m
2003–2004	Rs. 812 m	Rs. 3,000 m
2007–2008	N/A	Rs. 5,000 m

SOURCE: Company records.

Exhibit 2   Evolution of Ebony's Organization Chart

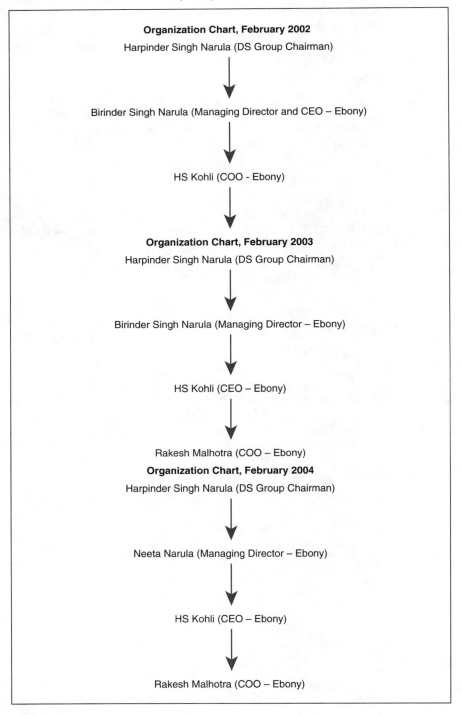

SOURCE: Company records.

Exhibit 3   Map of India (States and Their Capitals)

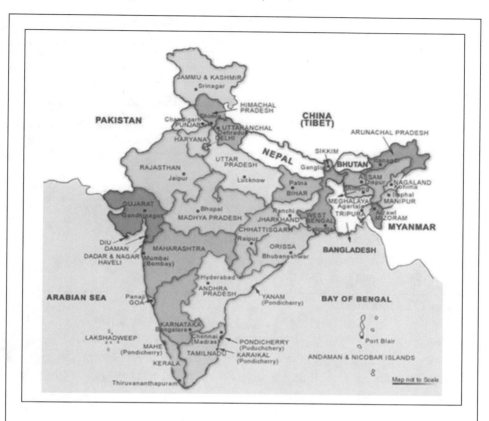

States and Cities Mentioned in the Case

Northern India
Punjab: Chandigarh, Jalandhar,
   Ludhiana, Amritsar
Uttar Pradesh: Noida, Kanpur, Lucknow,
   Varanasi, Allahabad
Uttaranchal: Dehradun
Haryana: Gurgaon, Faridabad
Rajasthan: Jaipur
Delhi
	Western India
	Maharashtra: Mumbai (Bombay), Pune
	Gujarat: Ahmedabad
	Madhya Pradesh: Indore

Southern India *Tamil Nadu:* Chennai (Madras) *Kerala:* Kochi, Coimbatore *Karnataka:* Bangalore	*Eastern India* *West Bengal:* Kolkata (Calcutta)

Exhibit 4   Revenues of the DS Group and Ebony Retail Holdings, 1999–2004

Fiscal (Apr–Mar)	DS Group	Ebony Retail Holdings
1999–2000	Rs. 15.1 b	Rs. 220 m
2000–2001	Rs. 17.1 b	Rs. 560 m
2001–2002	Rs. 19.1 b	Rs. 654 m
2002–2003	Rs. 21.8 b	Rs. 698 m
2003–2004	Rs. 27.5 b	Rs. 812 m

SOURCE: Media releases.

Exhibit 5   Neeta Narula's Personality Profile

People I admire most:

	Indian	Foreigner
Style Icon	Amitabh Bachchan	Tom Cruise
Business Person	Kumarmanglam Birla	Bill Gates
Person living full life	DS Narula	Madonna

My favorites:

Hobbies: Designing, cooking, traveling, listening to music

Pastime: Interior designing

Sport: Tennis

Holiday destination in India: Goa

Holiday destination abroad: Paris

SOURCE: Images Retail. (2004, April). "Neeta Narula—CEO Interviews."

Notes

1. Dundon, E., & Pattakos, A. (2003). Seeds of Innovation. *Insights Journal* 1:91. Used with permission.
2. Quoted in Gary Rivlin, "Does the Kid Stay in the Picture?" *The New York Times*, February 22, 2005, New York edition, p. G1.
3. 1US$ was approximately equal to 45 rupees during the early 2000s.
4. Less than 1 percent of the population owned an automobile; therefore, lacking an efficient connection through public transport system, a rapid growth of suburban shopping centers was not possible.

References

About Netflix. Retrieved March 28, 2005, from http://www.netflix.com/PressRoom?id= 1005&hnjr=3

Bhushan R. (2004, February 13). Change in Ebony's top management. *Hindu Business Line.*

Bose, S. (2003, February 11). Ebony's ivory-tower strategy. *Business Standard.*

Chakravarty, C. (2000, July 24). Ebony chalks out Rs. 140 Cr. expansion. *The Economic Times.*

Chennai to be Ebony's first southern stop (in its plan to set up 6–10 stores). (2001, April 21). *India Business Insight.*

Deshpande, V. (2000, November 2). The best only for his country. *The Indian Express.*

Dundon, E., & Pattakos, A. (2003). Seeds of innovation. *Insights Journal, 1,* 45, 81, 99.

Ebony scouting for sites in Bangalore, Hyderabad. (2002, September). *Images Retail.*

Ebony to take up space in malls, develop clusters. (2004, June 7). *Financial Express.*

Fact sheet. Retrieved March 28, 2005, from http://www.netflix.com/PressRoom? id=5206&hnjr=3

Ghosh, J. (2000, October 28). `One store a month' is the new Ebony slogan. *Times of India.*

Gomes, L. (2005, January 31). Web allows fans to see wide variety of movies that were hard to get. *The Wall Street Journal,* p. B1.

The great Indian middle class goes . . . shopping. Retrieved October 2, 2004, from http://www3.estart.com/india/finance/shopping.html

Hickman, C., & Raia, C. (2002). Incubating innovation. *Journal of Business Strategy, 23*(3), 14–18.

Management. Retrieved March 28, 2005, from http://www.netflix.com/PressRoom?id= 1006&hnjr=3

McWilliams, G., & Wingfield, N. (2005, May 20). Wal-Mart to end movie rentals via the Internet; retailer will turn over subscriber list to Netflix; Blockbuster steps up fight. *The Wall Street Journal,* p. B2.

Mitra, K. (2000, July 1). I am a very sure-footed animal, *The Economic Times.*

Netflix and TiVo announce a joint development agreement. (2004, September 30). Retrieved from http://www.netflix.com/PressRoom?id=5261

Netflix passes 3 million subscribers. (2005, March 28). Retrieved from http://www.netflix.com/PressRoom?id=5278

Netflix profit surges despite challenges. (2005, January 25). *Chicago Tribune,* p. 8.

Nishi, D. (2005, January 15). Competition heats up for mail-order movies; Current leaders see challenge from Wal-Mart, Amazon ahead. *Chicago Tribune,* p. 3.

Prashar, A. S. (2000, October 11). Shopping mall culture alien to India. *Tribune News Service.*

Prather, C. W., & Gundry, L. K. (1995). *Blueprints for innovation.* New York: American Management Association.

Rivlin, G. (2005, February 22). Does the kid stay in the picture? *New York Times,* p. G1.

Sacks, D. (2004, August). Netflix: Project a new experience. *Fast Company, 85,* 39–44.

Sandhu, N. (1999, September 6). The British have left us with file raj. *Tribune News Service.*

Singh, G. D. (2000, December 12). Shoppers won't stop. *NewsInsight.*

Terdiman, D. (2004, December 30). What are good friends for? Perhaps for recommending DVD's. *New York Times,* p. G5.

Vidyasagar, N. (1999, September 1). DS group to expand Ebony retail chain. *Times of India.*

Whitney, D. (2004, October 11). TiVo, Netflix ready movies-on-demand. *TelevisionWeek,* pp. 4, 32.

Williamson, R. (2004, August). Blockbuster breaks into net rental arena. *Adweek, 45*(32), p. 10.

CHAPTER 10

Strategies for the Growing Venture

*Mergers, Acquisitions,
Franchising, and Exit Strategies*

*The greater danger for most of us lies not in setting our aim too high
and falling short, but in setting our aim low and achieving our mark.*

—Michelangelo

Objectives:

1. Understand the advantages and disadvantages of choosing a merger or acquisition growth strategy

2. Learn practices for increasing the likelihood of merger or acquisition success

3. Learn about franchising as a growth strategy and how to determine if an organization is ready to franchise

4. Consider the importance of exit strategies to strategic planning

5. Evaluate different exit strategies and options available when the time comes to leave or modify your business

6. Scan diverse business valuation methods used to determine the value of your business

Speaking of Strategy

Carolyn Sanchez Crozier: CS&C-Julex Learning

CS&C-Julex Learning, Inc., was established in 1988 as a consulting firm specializing in education and technology. The firm provides innovative programs and services to enhance learning in education, business, and government on a local and national level. Caroline Sanchez Crozier, founder, CEO, and president, directs the company's business development and strategic relationships. Ms. Crozier is recognized as a leading visionary in the field of learning technologies and has a strong commitment to quality, community service, and excellence in education. Ms. Crozier has received numerous local and national awards, including the prestigious Small Business Person of the Year Award from the U.S. Small Business Administration in 1993. She participated in the Leadership Illinois Class of 2003 and is a member of the League of United Latin American Citizens (LULAC) and National Education Commission, board member of Hispanic Civic Committee of Chicago and the Women's Business Development Center; and a trustee of Dominican University.

Besides running her business, Ms. Crozier contributes much of her time and expertise to support technological and educational initiatives in Chicago. In 1998, she initiated a model for a new master of arts in teaching and technology for bilingual teachers of Dominican University. In 1999, Ms. Crozier established a tutoring model to support struggling readers, a model that uses a research-based curriculum and software. As a result of the program's success, CS&C has been approved as an SES Tutoring Provider under the federal No Child Left Behind Act, which funds private afterschool tutoring for K–12 education nationwide.

At the age of eight, Carolyn Sanchez emigrated from Mexico with her family, and she has been a Chicago area resident for more than 30 years. She was the first in her family to graduate from college in the United States, receiving a bachelor's degree from Dominican University in 1979, and she later became a CPA. Before becoming an entrepreneur, Ms. Crozier held various financial positions in major corporations including Premark, McDonald's Corporation, Continental Bank, and Deloitte & Touche. She formed CS&C in 1988 as a technology and education firm with her family and grew the company from one person to 20 people within five years.

CS&C's core competencies include supplemental reading resources (K–Adult), assessments, instructional software, professional development consultation, cognitive development software, bilingual/ESL programs (Spanish–English), professional development instructional materials, tutoring services, and training and technical services. CS&C's extensive client list includes: Apple, Dallas Independent School District, Illinois State Board of Education, U.S. Department of Labor, Chicago Public Schools, City Colleges of Chicago, City of Chicago, Oracle, and Unisys.

We spoke to Carolyn Sanchez Crozier about her business growth strategy:

What has helped you grow your business successfully?

CSC: What hasn't!

Your business did grow very large very quickly, so what were some things that helped you in growing it?

CSC: I think having the vision to move forward and to respond to the never-ending changes and sticking to that. Along the way I've tried different things, but ultimately having a focus where you can make it, where you're uniquely positioned—your competitive advantage [is the key]. Over the years, we've added different experience, different resources, [and] I think we have a unique position in this marketplace. So, I guess I would say vision and being visionary about putting all those pieces together is where we come in and have something unique to offer.

And the other, I have to say, is relationships. You can have the best program, and I would say there's never one, there are multiple [programs] out there, and there are other great programs, but what makes a difference is the relationships that you build and the trust that you establish with people around you.

So, one is finding something unique where you can position and have an advantage in terms of the programs and services [and] in terms of effectiveness. And the other is the relationships that you've established and continue to establish—where it's a personal connection where they're not just buying your program, but they're putting their faith in you and what you can deliver based on what you offered. So it really comes down to a personal commitment that you make. That is something that I lay out right up front with the people that hire me, or boards that I'm on.

The vision, the relationships, and being very passionate about seeing it through—the implementation is the key and building a team that helps you. Because you can have the vision, you can have the relationships, but if you're not going to have the resources to see it through, with people who have multiple strengths that complement yours, then you're not going to succeed.

What is the key piece of advice you would give to other entrepreneurs who are trying to manage growth?

CSC: That's a tough one! Be very honest with yourself about your capacity.

Because people tend to take on too much too fast?

CSC: Yes, because if you grow too big, it may turn around and haunt you. It's better to do it slow and not get the profits and revenue that you want, but in the end, you will have more stability and greater success. Again, it's your capacity: You'll be able to perform and meet the right expectations when you know what you truly have to deliver.

SOURCE: Interview conducted by Laurel Ofstein, December 21, 2004. Printed with permission.

Mergers and Acquisitions: Growth Strategies of Promise and Peril

As new ventures continue to grow, their founders find themselves in the position of having to make key decisions regarding how the firm will grow. This chapter reviews the key external growth strategies of mergers, acquisitions, and franchising. In the last decade in the United States, several factors have propelled consolidations among companies: a strong economy in the 1990s producing considerable investment capital, high levels of liquidity, and a variety of strategic imperatives, including heightened international competition, regulatory changes, an explosion of technologies, and a host of perceived synergies (Tetenbaum, 1999). For example, the dot-com bust of the early 2000s, falling commodity prices in the oil industry, excess capacity in the automobile industry, unsettling technological changes in the banking and telecommunications industries, and soaring costs of research in the pharmaceuticals industry have all led to a search for a silver bullet that, today, most often takes the form of a merger or acquisition. Mergers, acquisitions, and strategic alliances are an increasingly attractive alternative for many entrepreneurs who select these external strategies for growth.

Despite the volume of activity, research unequivocally indicates that 60 percent to 80 percent of all mergers are financial failures when measured by the ability of the new companies to outperform the stock market or deliver profit increases. Mark Sirower, a professor at the Stern School at New York University and author of *The Synergy Trap,* found two thirds of the 168 deals he analyzed, deals that occurred between 1979 and 1990, destroyed value for shareholders. Looking specifically at the shares of stock in 100 large companies that made major acquisitions between 1994 and 1997, Sirower found that, on average, the acquirer's stock trailed the S&P 500 by 8.6 percent one year after the deal was announced. Not only did 60 of these stocks underperform the market, but 32 posted negative returns, with prices below their level five days before the merger became public.

Despite overwhelming evidence that mergers fail to deliver anywhere near promised payoffs, companies in every industry continue to see mergers and acquisitions as the answer to their problems. Daimler-Benz recently acquired Chrysler for $40 billion, and Nissan, Volvo, and other auto companies are looking for partners, despite negative examples in the industry. Saab has been a consistent money-loser since General Motors acquired half-interest in the firm, and Jaguar cost Ford Company $5 billion before it turned profitable. Chrysler bought, then sold Lamborghini and Maserati in quick succession. The increase in mergers and acquisitions, curious in light of their extraordinarily high failure rate, can be explained by their potential to cut costs and to improve efficiency, both of which are irresistible to organizations. Buyers optimistically eye the major savings they believe can be taken from newly combined companies, and they anticipate some form of value creation or renewal or strategic and operational advantages neither company could achieve on its own (Tetenbaum, 1999).

Factors That Affect Merger Success: Strategic Intent and Organizational Alignment

Strategic intent is primarily concerned with performance and is at the heart of the potential for value creation between firms. The term describes how potential merger partners augment or complement each other's strategy and thereby make identifiable contributions to the financial and nonfinancial goals of the combined firm. Realizing strategic intent requires successfully sharing or exchanging those critical skills and resources that form the foundation for value creation (Pablo & Javidan, 2002). Similar questions that are asked in forming an alliance (as discussed in Chapter 8) should be considered when looking at the overall intentions and strategy of merging two firms.

The second major requirement for success is the effectiveness of organizational alignment between partners to ensure cooperation through attention to culture and organizational processes of decision making, communication, and trust building. Organizational alignment is primarily concerned with relationship management. That is, what type of experience has the entrepreneur or entrepreneurial team had in other mergers? What role did the entrepreneur or entrepreneurial team play in implementing the necessary changes to implement the merger? How effective were their processes in merging the diversity of roles or positions and cultures (Pablo & Javidan, 2002)?

Seven Practices for Integrating People and Cultures for Mergers and Acquisitions

Tetenbaum (1999) has identified seven practices that are critical to the successful integration of merged and acquired organizations. These practices reflect the importance of organizational culture as a major factor determining merger and acquisition success.

1. *Provide input into go-no go decision.* A key indicator of the significance that a company attaches to integration and to the human side of the endeavor is whether the top human resources (HR) officer is a member of the senior management team and a contributor to the business planning process. In contrast to organizations that underestimate the role of culture and that manage their integration accidentally, those bent on success will place transition issues and culture center stage, even before a letter of intent is offered. A successful merger requires an assessment of the fit between the two organizations and a judgment as to whether they can readily be joined. Gaining the desired synergies from the merger or acquisition requires intensive planning and data collection, particularly with regard to culture, throughout the process. The knowledge gained in a culture due-diligence audit can contribute not only to the decision about whether to proceed but to planning for the eventual integration, including anticipating potential problems if the union goes forward. Some of the questions the audit would address are listed in Table 10.1.

This audit is not meant to squelch the deal, but rather to discover likely trouble spots and to have a plan to manage the differences. To the degree that these questions can be answered early in the process, the acquiring company gains an advantage by having a clear idea from the outset of how it will integrate the two organizations. If not, what changes will be necessary? What performance barriers exist? How might they be removed? At what cost?

2. *Build organizational capability.* Organizational capability means having the right people in the right position to effectively perform the tasks that are needed to achieve the organization's goals. Retention is at the core of the effort when it comes to mergers and acquisitions. In today's information age, with knowledge workers a company's greatest asset, the primary goal of many mergers is to acquire not only a product or a process but the intellectual capital behind them. Research shows that when no coordinated retention actions are taken, 47 percent of all senior managers in an acquired firm leave within the first year of the acquisition, 72 percent within the first three years.

3. *Strategically align and implement appropriate systems and procedures.* Another major function of the integration team is to ensure that the systems and procedures

Table 10.1   Merger and Acquisition Audit

- What does the acquired company value?
- What does it stand for?
- What should one look for to see what it's about?
- Who are the company's heroes and heroines?
- What are its mottos and slogans?
- What gets celebrated?
- What gets rewarded?
- How is leadership expressed?
- How does the company handle conflict?
- How does it handle decision making?
- How do people communicate there?
- What are interactions like?
- What are the staff's perceptions, attitudes, expectations, needs?
- How is work monitored?
- How are people held accountable?

to be implemented are in keeping with the strategic intent of the merger or acquisition. For example, to acquire an entrepreneurial firm whose success is rooted in employee autonomy, risk taking, and creativity and to encase it in bureaucratic structures, procedures, and policies is to lose the very value for which the new company was acquired.

4. *Manage the culture.* The integration team must both identify a culture (i.e., values, norms, beliefs, behaviors) that supports the organization's strategic goals and inculcate that culture throughout the joined companies. The first phase, identifying an appropriate culture to support the business goals, is surprisingly difficult and time consuming. It is assumed that every company is clear about its goals and the environment needed to support those goals. In reality, few organizations pay sufficient attention to establishing the connection between the two. Too often, companies identify five or more positive-sounding values (e.g., customer service, respect for the individual, innovation, diversity, teamwork) that bear no relationship to the work of the organization. In such companies, the employees ridicule the plaques that adorn the offices and corridors proclaiming a list of "values we live by." They know full well that words are merely platitudes. Implementing a meaningful value system is a critical charge of the integration team.

5. *Manage the postmerger drift by managing the transition quickly.* Employees experiencing a merger are expected to absorb a monumental change while

simultaneously continuing to maintain a high level of productivity. The viability of the consolidation, in fact, presupposes a motivated workforce committed to making the merger work. But research shows a company can expect a 25 percent to 50 percent drop in productivity when going through a large-scale change. In the case of consolidation, this time period has been referred to as *postmerger drift*. The greatest lull is in the first few months, and it can take one or two years to recover. When a merger or acquisition is announced, people expect change and are relatively receptive to it. When it does not occur, they become preoccupied with security issues, with the result that productivity, customer service, and innovation deteriorate, draining value from the acquisition. There are so many questions to be answered, decisions to be made, changes to be effected—all of which take time and consume people's attention—that the acquirer can easily become immersed in internal issues without realizing it. This is what happened at Silicon Graphics, which was at the top of its industry when it acquired Cray Research. It became so focused on the integration process, it failed to keep an eye on its competitor, Sun Microsystems, which leapfrogged ahead of it during that time. Similarly, Boeing had a disappointing 1998, reporting its first loss in 50 years and writing off $4 billion, partly because it was distracted by implementing its merger with McDonnell Douglas.

6. *Manage the information flow.* Involving HR professionals early in the M&A (merger and acquisition) process is more likely to lead to success, according to a study conducted by Towers-Perrin (Schmidt, 2001). While planning their M&A strategies, many companies fail to anticipate the obstacles that can occur. As one electronics executive who participated in the study stated, "When it comes to people issues, most mergers and acquisitions are incredibly poorly planned by the chief executives" (Schmidt, 2001, p. 104). HR professionals can be strategic partners, contributing several key capabilities, according to the study. These include: the ability to evaluate another company quickly; M&A literacy and integration know-how; advice regarding employee sensitivities and attitudes; skills for motivating and retaining critically needed talent; and the ability to plan and lead complex integration projects (Schmidt, 2001).

7. *Build a standardized integration plan.* Integration plans are a key factor in achieving the desired synergies in a union, thereby gaining competitive advantage. As such, integration should not be left to chance; it must be planned. Companies whose growth strategy is founded on mergers and acquisitions are experienced deal makers and have developed procedures within their organization to streamline the process: What functions must be involved, how and when they should be involved, which people are responsible for due diligence, and which for planning and implementation. These companies document the process through a series of checklists that serve as reminders of tasks to be done, deadlines, and people responsible. This helps to ensure consistency among the different mergers and acquisitions handled throughout the company.

Cisco Systems is such a company, having a standard business process in place for acquisitions. At Cisco, as many as 60 people from various functional areas are dedicated to the task of acquiring and integrating companies. Going through the acquisition process repeatedly not only improves it every time, it also allows the company to move very quickly so it can manage 10 to 12 acquisitions a year. Cisco's top deal maker, Mike Volpi, has supervised 29 acquisitions and more than 40 equity investments (LaBarre, 1999). Mergers and acquisitions are on the rise, with the size and scope of deals escalating. Company executives seek to reduce annual expenses while creating ever more powerful operating and strategic synergies. Nevertheless, as consolidations have increased in volume, so too have the failures. Observations by knowledgeable business journalists as well as findings produced by empirical researchers attribute the failures primarily to nonintegrated, incompatible cultures resulting in lost value and unattained synergies.

Entrepreneurs need to appreciate that it is people who create much of the value and who are ultimately behind achieving the desired synergies. The savviest deal financial experts can negotiate and the most rigorous legal contract corporate lawyers can draw up will not guarantee success if the people in the two companies fail to unite behind the strategic goals underlying the consolidation. This realization should lead corporate senior leaders to:

- Redress the imbalance in import and resources awarded to deal making versus integration; concentrate on the marriage, not merely the wedding. Make HR and the integration team members equal partners with finance and legal staff in the go/no go decision as well as throughout the process. Provide any and all resources needed to accomplish a complete and appropriate culture integration.
- Select the best people for the integration team and a top performer as the team's leader, then assign them to the organization's efforts on a full-time basis.
- Keep everyone's focus on managing people's performance to minimize postmerger drift and maximize attention and efforts toward achieving strategic goals.

Unless organizations recognize the importance of the human component, its acquisitions will be forever doomed to failure. However, if senior leaders keep these few "shoulds" in mind, they stand a good chance of beating the odds in the merger and acquisitions sweepstakes (Tetenbaum, 1999).

Establishing a Transition Team for Mergers

Experts recommend that firms develop some form of transition structure when joining forces in a merger, acquisition, or alliance. Marks and Mirvis (2000) recommend that this temporary structure should last three to six months, but it can extend up to a year to provide for coordination and support during implementation of change. Driving a combination along a successful course requires an effective structure, able leadership, and systematic work processes to guide analyses and generate progress. This means molding individual contributors into transition teams and helping them handle the many operational and political factors that can otherwise transform good ideas into bad practice.

According to the researchers, a transition structure serves practical purposes in joining previously independent organizations into one. First, it creates a venue wherein the two sides can study and test how to put themselves together. In many combinations, executives have not fully identified possible synergies and pitfalls in premerger dealings, and they need an organized way to catch up and gain momentum after the combination receives legal approval. Even if they have done their homework, nuances and details remain that require close attention from those who are nearest to the action. We term this the knowledge building work of the transition organization.

Second, there is the matter of relationship building. In a transition structure, several layers of management, as well as professionals and sometimes frontline personnel, get the chance to think and work with their counterparts from the other organization. Here is where differences in style and culture come to light and can be worked on through substantive effort as opposed to, say, show-and-tell sessions or management proclamation. Nothing shatters stereotypes or supersedes differences more effectively than sharing a common problem and needing to arrive at an agreeable solution. Furthermore, building trust is integral to developing knowledge. Until the two sides get to know and trust one another, they will not reveal the details—and particularly the weak points—of how they do their respective business.

Early in the integration, it is critical that the entrepreneurial team do the following (Marks & Mirvis, 2002):

- Define combination goals, principles, and the desired end state
- Give transition planning task forces guidance for making recommendations on the alignment of people, structure, and processes
- Clarify the critical success factors for the merger
- Define the decision-making criteria through which integration recommendations will be evaluated
- Review and evaluate task force recommendations regarding their adherence to the critical success factors and their ability to achieve the strategic vision of the combination
- Identify gaps and opportunities not covered in task force recommendations and recommend actions

Later, as plans are being implemented and the two companies integrate, the steering committee should take on more of a change management role:

- Coordinate all major change efforts via a coherent, prioritized, and understandable plan
- Anticipate the impact of change and address inconsistencies between the espoused operating principles and actual management of change
- Define, promote, and support necessary changes in behaviors and mind-sets to successfully realize the postcombination organization
- Be role models on how to work together for the good of the organization
- Identify means by which to measure and monitor the progress of the transition

Review Questions

1. What are some requirements for a successful merger?

2. What methods can companies use to integrate people and culture for mergers?

3. Name some common pitfalls experienced during mergers.

4. What actions should a transition team take to ensure a successful merger?

Franchising: Growth Through Systems Creation

Franchising is a system of distribution in which the entrepreneur (the franchisor) enters into a contractual relationship with a local business owner or distribution partner (the franchisee) to handle specific products and services under mutually agreed-upon conditions. Franchise agreements include several elements:

- Franchise fee: a one-time upfront fee the franchisee pays to join the system
- Start-up costs: costs for the building (if applicable), leasehold arrangements, inventory, deposits, and so on
- Royalty fee: an ongoing continuous service fee, typically a percentage of gross revenues that the franchisee must pay the franchisor
- Advertising fee: An ongoing payment to national or local advertising fund for the system; the franchisee must pay the franchisor

The first franchisor was Isaac Singer of Singer Sewing Machines. Ace Hardware and Walgreens began franchising in the 1930s. Today, there are several thousand franchisors. Here are some recent statistics about the impact on franchising on the economies of the United States and Canada.

Franchising in the United States[1]

- In 2006, most analysts estimated that franchising companies and their franchisees accounted for $1 trillion in annual U.S. retail sales.
- The estimated number of franchised locations in the United States is more than 320,000 in 75 industries.
- Franchising is said to account for more than 40 percent of all U.S. retail sales.
- Industry analysts estimate that franchising employs more than 8 million people in the United States.
- A new franchise outlet opens somewhere in the United States every eight minutes.
- About 1 out of every 12 U.S. retail business establishments is a franchised business.

Franchising in Canada[2]

- About 1,800 franchise systems currently operate in Canada, representing about 75,000 outlets, 67,000 of which are franchisee-owned.

- The franchise industry has grown 20 percent since 1993.
- A new franchise opens in Canada every 90 minutes, 365 days of the year.
- Average annual franchise sales growth during the last few years has exceeded 10 percent compared to 7.4 percent growth in the Gross National Product.
- It's a multibillion dollar industry in Canada, with more than 48 cents out of every retail dollar spent going to a franchised outlet.
- Franchising created more than 155 new Canadian jobs each and every day throughout 1997.
- About 92 percent of franchise operations survive after the first five years, compared with only 23 percent of independent businesses.

Franchising's Benefits

- Exclusive, protected geographic territories
- Extensive training provided through the franchisor in all necessary areas including, operations, sales, technical, management, and product knowledge
- Proven systems, processes, and supplier relationships available for immediate set-up
- Advertising and promotion programs developed professionally for a large network of outlets, thereby reducing individual costs while increasing buying leverage and consumer reach
- Less risk, lower capital requirements, and reduced chance of failure

There are two general types of franchises:

1. *Product or trade name:* The most popular type of franchise, in which the franchisee enters into an exclusive arrangement with the franchisor to distribute and sell specific products or services or to be allowed to conduct business under the trade name.

2. *Business format:* An exclusive arrangement that centers around specific policies and procedures—a turnkey model for doing business.

There are several legal considerations for franchisors and franchisees. The sale of a franchise is regulated like the sale of a security. The Federal Trade Commission (FTC) requires that a franchisor must provide all prospective franchisees with documentation. These include the Offering Circular or Prospectus, which details fees, obligations, initial expenses, and financing arrangements, among other specific requirements; the Franchise Agreement, which is the actual document the business owner (franchisee) will sign, and three to five years of audited financial statements on the parent company. There is a 10-day waiting period designed to give the prospective franchise owner enough time to read the disclosure documents and make an informed decision.

Once a franchisor has generated a basic idea for a franchise (a quick print service, film development, fast-food provision, etc.), a pilot needs to be established by way of developing and testing the product/service itself, operational marketing strategies, staffing procedures, pricing policies, and so on. Every small business start-up plan inevitably requires considerable modification during its initial months of operation. The process of franchise system development should then, ideally, continue with the establishment of a second outlet in an alternative location as a test of ability to replicate the initial success with different staff, clientele, premises, lines of supply, and so on. There will, inevitably, be a steep learning curve here, and human and intellectual capital is vital in formulating a viable franchising strategy (Stanworth & Stanworth, 2004).

The Innovator's Toolkit: Assessing Franchise Readiness

Are you ready to franchise? The following quiz was developed by Francorp, a leader in the franchise consulting industry, which has been established for more than 25 years.

1. Do you have a profitable operating prototype?
   o Yes
   o No

2. How many units do you have in operation?
   o 1 Location
   o 2 Locations
   o 3 Locations
   o 4 Locations
   o 5 Locations
   o 5 or More Locations
   o No Locations opened

3. How long has your business been in operation?
   o Not in operation yet
   o Less than 6 months
   o 1 Year
   o 2 Years
   o 3 Years
   o 4+ Years

4. To what degree is your business distinctive from its competitors?
   o Not very distinctive
   o Somewhat distinctive
   o Very distinctive
   o Unique

5. How much would it cost to open one of your locations, not including franchise fees?
   o $400,000 or more
   o $200,000 to $399,000
   o $100,000 to $199,000
   o $50,000 to $99,000
   o Less than $50,000

6. The market for your business or service is:
   o Local
   o Regional
   o National
   o International

7. Competition for the products or services you sell is:
   o High
   o Moderate
   o Minimal

8. How systemized is the business?
   o Very little
   o Some basic policies and/or handbooks
   o Very well documented
   o Computerized

9. How long would it take you to teach
    someone how to operate your business?
    o   Special certification needed first
    o   2–6 months
    o   1–2 months
    o   1–3 weeks
    o   Less than 1 week

10. How do your business's sales compare to
    those of other businesses in your industry?
    o   Much lower
    o   Somewhat lower
    o   About the same
    o   Somewhat higher
    o   Much higher

SOURCE: http://www.francorp.com. Used with permission.

Review Questions

1. Name some elements included in a franchise agreement.

2. Discuss the benefits of franchising a business.

3. Why is a pilot important for a franchise?

Exit Strategies for the Entrepreneurial Firm

Although entrepreneurs may continually look for ways to grow and develop their businesses, unforeseen personal circumstances could lead to the need to change organizational leadership or quickly sell or dispose of a business. Changes in the market could lead to an unexpected acquisition possibility or, conversely, the need to close your doors. Although almost every entrepreneur speaks of the way that their ventures have continued to surprise them, focusing on potential exit strategies from the beginning can ensure that entrepreneurs are equipped to face these unexpected changes. In addition, continual consideration of the exit strategy focuses overall business strategy, leading the entrepreneur to make more appropriate decisions and giving him or her more control over the destiny of the business.

Risk of Not Considering the Graceful Exit

Over the life cycle of the business, entrepreneurs may not consider exit strategies for many reasons. These include thinking that the value of the business will increase. This leads the entrepreneur to believe that exit strategies currently available will not be appropriate for the future development of the business. Another factor coloring consideration of exit strategies is the emotional attachment of entrepreneurs to their ventures. The overwhelming consideration of what they will do with their time and energy beyond the venture may dissuade some entrepreneurs from considering life beyond the venture. In addition, many entrepreneurs do not continually consider exit strategies across the lifecycle of their ventures because of success. When a venture is highly profitable, a resulting mentality of "success in perpetuity" can develop. This leads entrepreneurs to get caught up in sustaining their venture "as is," without considering the long-term development of the business, changing market conditions, and their own role within the venture.

Failures and Foibles

ProjectMine

ProjectMine was a dot-com founded in Austin, Texas, by Christian Erickson in 1999. The company used a business model similar to eBay, but instead of auctioning off goods, the site would be a kind of yellow pages for services. After using a service found on ProjectMine, customers could post comments and give ratings about the service providers.

"We figured there were so many students in Austin, and they all needed to make some extra money," says the 34-year-old Mr. Erickson. However in the end only a few hundred customers tried the service. Erickson and his partners had sunk $15,000 in venture-capital funding and $45,000 of their own money into the business. They employed seven employees and had an office but couldn't raise funds to market their business.

"We'd put so much sweat equity into the business," says Mr. Erickson. "Equally upsetting was the pride side of things. You want to be the next Jeff Bezos. You want to be the next Internet kid. . . . It got to the point where the burn rate was just too high. And our commitment level had changed, too." At this point, the founders started to consider an exit strategy and, specifically, how to sell their business or some of their assets to larger companies. However, at that point, they discovered, "it was us and another thousand companies doing the same thing. All the headlines in Austin at that time were, 'Another dot-com folds.'" They shut the site down in mid-2001. There is some good news from this story, however—Erickson is now educating students about entrepreneurship in his new venture, Biz4Kids.

SOURCE: Based on Andrew Blackman, "Small Business (A Special Report); Know When to Give Up," *The Wall Street Journal* (Eastern edition), May 9, 2005, p. R9.

Linking the Exit Strategy to Overall Business Strategy

Failure to consider "what comes next" can be a highly risky strategy. Thinking that the business valuation will increase down the road, at which point you will consider an exit strategy, can result in missed business opportunities to sell while the business is in a positive position. In addition, it handicaps the entrepreneur's strategy. As the entrepreneur focuses on the venture's future, planning may be incomplete because of the lack of an end goal for the business. This can result in poor allocation of resources, poor decision making, and ultimately reduced profitability of the business. Emotional attachment to the venture presents an additional risk. Without continuing to keep an exit strategy in mind, the entrepreneur can develop a dependency on the venture which will blind them to opportunities to take advantage of the venture's position in the market and its attractiveness as an acquisition. A warped sense of success can also pose a dramatic risk for the entrepreneur. A profitable business can begin to decline when management believes its success is sustainable without further adaptation, change, or development. This decline, due to forces outside of the entrepreneur's control, will ultimately result in closure or reduced value of the business to potential acquirers.

The most important reason to know what you want to get out of the business in the future is that it will help inform and design your strategy accordingly today. Take, for example, the owner of an independent pet care store. If she determines her overall business goal in starting her venture is to sell to a larger pet care store, she will design her business in a way to make it attractive to outside buyers. If she determined that her strategy is to create a large chain of pet care stores, she will pursue a strategy of growth and expansion to attract additional investors with the ultimate goal of an initial public offering (IPO). Finally, if her goal is to maintain the business as a lifestyle business, she will keep her strategy focused on the maintenance and profitability of her single store. Each of these exit strategies will result in a different overall strategy for her business, impacting not only her planning but the way she carries out her day-to-day business activities.

Benefits and Challenges of Exit Strategies

While the appropriate exit strategy is unique to the characteristics of both the business and the market, there are general strategies that each entrepreneur should consider when designing a business. These include:

1. Selling the business (including a management buyout or a leveraged buyout)

2. Passing the business on to family

3. Dissolving the business

4. Going public (IPO)

Inherent in consideration of each option are several potential risks and challenges that must be explored.

Selling the Business

Selling the business is a great way for the entrepreneur to move on to another venture and make some money at the same time. Advantages to selling include avoiding risk of operating the business in slow economy, not to mention the probable financial reward for the entrepreneur. Entrepreneurial firms must consider if they are able to actually face pressure to grow from outside competition with their current resources and financing. Additional benefits from selling include the potential for the entrepreneur to stay on with the company on the entrepreneur's terms (Neuborne & Perton, 2000).

Strategy in Action

Christini Technologies, Inc.

Steve Christini had devised an ingenious design for a two-wheel-drive bicycle—the biking equivalent of a sport-utility vehicle—while he was still a mechanical engineering student at Villanova University in 1994. Two years later, he started his own mountain bike company, Christini Technologies Inc.

To build his company, Christini says, "we pulled a lot of all-nighters. I was sleeping on the office floor, running power tools without sleeping for three days." After patenting his own design, he built prototypes and began distributing bikes through a larger company. Bikers and manufacturers started to pay attention to his design, however, Christini had to make a choice: Should he seek additional financing to make the bikes himself or find a buyer for his company?

In 2000, he decided to sell to Derby Cycling Corp. Christini says, "People don't realize how difficult it is to make it on your own as a manufacturing company." However, selling did not mean the end of Christini's role in the company. He was now able to produce a lot more bikes, at a lower price than he could have on his own, through deciding to work in a small manufacturing unit of the company. "Instead of spending half my day on the phone with investment people, I can focus on what I do best, which is the design and marketing of products."

SOURCE: Based on Ellen Neuborne and Marc Perton, "Selling Out, Staying On," *Businessweek Online*, November 6, 2000. Retrieved February 15, 2006, from http://www.businessweek.com/2000/00_45/b3706051.htm

Entrepreneurs can sell their businesses through a management buyout or a leveraged buyout. A management buyout allows the members of the management team an opportunity to have their own stake in the business. The managers may need to seek outside funding to finance their share, however, their history and institutional knowledge remain intact as the organization moves forward. From the entrepreneur's perspective, one of the benefits is to receive the monies for the time and efforts of developing a financially stable and profitable business. The structure of the buyout may vary depending on the entrepreneur's goals and aspirations; in certain situations, the entrepreneur may remain as a consultant to the business and serve on the board of directors.

Another form of buyout is the leveraged buyout. This buyout allows an investor to obtain a majority of the firm's equity, which is financed through the use of borrowed money or debt. Most of the funding can usually come in the form of public or privately placed bonds.

Passing the Business on to Family

The Family Business Institute (2005) reports that currently, there are 24.2 million family businesses in the United States, accounting for 89 percent of the business tax returns. About 62 percent of the workforce (82 million people) are currently employed by family enterprises. Some of the most successful businesses in the United States are family run, including Wal-Mart, Home Depot, Heinz, Rubbermaid, and Black & Decker.

More than 30 percent of family-owned businesses survive into the second generation, and 12 percent are still viable into the third generation. Despite this success, only about 3 percent of all family businesses operate into the fourth generation and beyond (The Family Business Institute, 2005).

For many entrepreneurs, passing their business on to family members is an attractive and potentially successful exit strategy. However, despite the desire to "keep it all in the family," the intersection of family and business can pose challenges for the venture. A 2004 study titled "How Do Family Ownership, Control, and Management Affect Firm Value?" by Raphael Amit of the Wharton School and Belen Villalonga of the Harvard Business School found that family-owned corporations perform better than nonfamily firms when the founder serves as the CEO of the family firm or as its chairman, with a hired CEO. However, when a descendant serves as the CEO of a family-run company—even if the founder remains chairman—the firm's market value declines.

Key factors that have been identified as contributing to the successful transition of businesses between family members include preparation of the succeeding family members, positive family relationships, and preparation and attention to succession planning (Morris, Williams, & Nel, 1996). Within successful transitions, heirs are most likely to have spent time working in the business from the lowest levels and have worked in a variety of positions within the company.

Dissolving the Business

Dissolving the business is the most obvious way to actually exit a venture, however, it is likely to be the least profitable. Essential to this exit strategy is making sure that legal filings and tax issues have been attended to in order to officially close down operations.

Going Public

An IPO is defined as the company's first sale of stock to the public. Because most small businesses are privately held, it is not possible for the public to have equity stakes in their ownership. An IPO allows the public to become owners of the company. This exit strategy is particularly appealing when the company is at a point when growth is a necessity and large amounts of financing are needed to fuel this expansion.

Strategic Reflection Point

Understanding the IPO Process

When deciding to pursue an IPO, the company will take the following steps:

1. *Gather an IPO team.* This team includes a lead investment bank, an accountant and a law firm.
2. *Conduct an "all hands meeting."* In conjunction with management, this group will plan a timetable for going public.
3. *Produce a preliminary prospectus.* A preliminary prospectus will be developed for potential investors.
4. *File with the Securities and Exchange Commission.* An S-1 registration statement filed with the Securities and Exchange Commission includes a description of the company's business, the names and addresses of the key company officers (with salary and a five-year business history on each), the amount of stock that each of the key officers owns, the company's capitalization, a description of how the proceeds from the offering will be used, any legal proceedings that the company is involved in, and a description of a company's target market, competitors, and growth strategy.
5. *Quiet period.* This period lasts until 25 days after the stock has been issued. During this time, only the preliminary prospectus can be distributed, and management is on the road to meet with prospective investors.
6. *Final registration with the SEC:* This final registration includes the final prospectus. During this time, underwriters are allocating the IPO to clients.
7. *Finding a price:* The night before the IPO is issued, the final price is set. Management meets with investment backers to choose final offering price and size. Price is based on expected demand for the deal and other market conditions. The underwriters make a profit from the difference between the selling price from the company to the underwriter and what the underwriter is able to sell shares for on the market.
8. *The lock-up period:* Company insiders are unable to sell or trade their shares for 180 days following the IPO.

SOURCE: Adapted from "IPO Process" from Fraudbureau.com.

For the emerging venture, benefits of an IPO include a new source of financing. If the business wants to grow and has been unable to do so because of constrained financial resources, an IPO creates a new source of funding to support expansion. Mergers and acquisition are also a possibility later because of the ability to use equity as part of the deal. Moreover, an IPO creates greater *liquid security.* This means that the company will now have additional resources that it can use to increase its capacity, such as funding for employee stock ownership programs to keep and attract talented employees.

Drawbacks about the IPO include the large expense to execute a successful offering. Legal fees, government fees, and underwriting fees have a steep cost for any venture. In addition, companies pursuing and achieving an IPO will also face increased scrutiny now that they are public, and they will have to prepare and make transparent information about the company on a more regular basis than when the company was privately held. An IPO can also be challenging for the entrepreneur because of the new dilution of ownership. When equity is issued, stockholders are given voting rights within the company. Although it is likely that the entrepreneur will maintain large holdings of the company, the challenge of balancing the demands of public ownership and increased transparency require new businesses practices for the newly public venture.

Although an IPO is the ultimate dream for many entrepreneurs, as it represents the key to new funding sources to fuel expansion and growth, a company can consider other alternatives when an IPO does not seem to be an appropriate strategy. These alternatives include increasing debt and forming partnerships to benefit from sources of R&D instead of having to finance themselves alone. A company should also consider slower growth. When an IPO doesn't make sense for a company, this may be a sign that fast growth is not the best strategy and that the venture should realign its strategy to a slower growth model.

Many of the benefits, challenges, and considerations of various exit strategies are summarized in Table 10.2.

Table 10.2   Benefits, Challenges, and Considerations of Exit Strategies

Exit Strategy	Benefits	Challenges	Considerations
Selling the business	• Strong option during economic downturn	• Time period • Negotiating value • Employee well-being • Integrity of brand/idea	• Company valuation • Motivation for selling • Who would be interested?
Passing the business on to family member	• High potential to maintain integrity of business • High potential for continued involvement as desired	• Family might not be interested • Potentially damaging for relationships outside of the business	• Stability of family • Formality of succession planning • Current state of familial relationship • Interest level within the family
Dissolving the business	• Enables entrepreneur to move on to new ventures	• Least financially lucrative exit strategy	• Are debts settled? • Are legal protocols being followed?
Initial Public Offering	• Source of financing • Exit route for management • Create liquid security • Prestige	• Expensive process • Subject to careful scrutiny • Dilution of ownership • Pressure to meet earnings per share • Additional responsibility to shareholders	• Is it time to grow? • What are other options for financing growth besides IPO? • Are resources (management time and money) available?

Review Questions

1. Why is it important to focus on exit strategies from the very beginning?
2. What exit strategies are available to a business owner?
3. Discuss the benefits, challenges, and considerations for each exit strategy.

Research in Practice:	The Status of Women in Corporate Governance in High-Growth, High-Potential Firms

Surveys of the largest U.S. corporations routinely demonstrate that the role of women in corporate governance is acutely limited. The most recent data available shows that women represented just 16 percent of corporate executive officers among all Fortune 500 companies in 2002, compared to 9 percent in 1995 (Catalyst, 2002). Although this represents an absolute increase from prior decades, women in the United States in 2002 still held less than 3 percent of the most senior corporate executive positions and represented less than 6 percent of top corporate earners, including less than 1 percent of CEO and board chair positions.

In this research, we examine how high-growth entrepreneurial sectors of the economy in the United States compare to this standard, including a specific look at high-technology industries. We posit that high-demand labor markets, enhanced higher education of women, and dynamic industry and firm conditions may result in greater participation of women executives in firms moving toward major corporate status through IPO.

Conceptual Grounding

The underlying concept of "entrepreneurship as opportunity" is considered here as we examine how the role and rank of women in senior management vary between the Fortune 500 and high-growth, high-potential firms. High-potential firms may relax or resist employment conditions extant in traditional corporate America (Becker & Huselid, 1998; Crane, 2004; King, 2001; Resnick-West & Von Glinow, 1990); younger firms may focus more on competency building to win financial backing (Zacharakis & Meyer, 2000); high compensation levels resulting from demand conditions could entice more women to accept the maniac pace of the high-growth firm work style; younger, more dynamic firms and industries may be less rigid and more open to the untraditional (Abernathy & Utterback, 1988; Fligstein, 1991).

This optimism about the potential for women's advancement must be tempered by recognition of other forces likely at work to depress women's participation in the high-growth, high-potential environment. For example, a liability of newness may lead firms to emulate the practices and policies they see in their aspirants and companies; firms may abandon more idiosyncratic practices in favor of those believed to send specific signals to tradition-bound investors (Certo, 2003) as their potential to grow is acknowledged; and the work style of the high-growth environment may be untenable for many women, regardless of compensation level.

Therefore, theoretical tension exists, which makes it difficult to predict with a high degree of confidence women's participation rates and roles in the governance of high-technology, high-growth, high-potential firms relative to the Fortune 500. Core concepts of entrepreneurship are at odds: Liability of newness, at its core an argument for institutionalism in dynamic environments, stands at odds with entrepreneurialism, a working promise of opportunity for new thinking and practice.

Method

A random stratified sampling technique was used to select 100 firms from the population of the 569 firms listed on the Fortune 500 in 1998 and 1999 and 100 IPO firms from the population of 713 firms completing

IPOs in 1998 and 1999. Each group was further delineated to include 50 firms in technology-intensive industry sectors and 50 firms in other industry sectors. Our data source on the IPO firms was the public company mandated filings to the SEC, including the S-1, 10-K/KA, and DEF14A. Data on Fortune 500 firms came from 10-K/KA and DEF 14A SEC filings.

To determine women's participation in governance, we considered the percentage of female CEOs, senior executive officers, executive officers, board chairs, board members, and employee board members relative to total numbers and the percentage of firms, by sector, with any woman, by role. We also examined the authority hierarchy of the roles CEO, executive officer, and senior executive officer as well as board chair, employee board member, and board member. Finally, we compared the ratio of female to all executive officers and female to all board directors on chronological age of the individuals.

Findings

Our study results show few significant differences between women's participation in firms undergoing IPO versus the Fortune 500. Several of the findings directly contradict our hypotheses, with lower rates of women as board directors and a greater likelihood of the executive team being composed exclusively of men in high-growth, high-potential firms. Women are not present in the top leadership spots of CEO and board chair in either sector, and within high-growth firms, they are significantly less likely to be found on the boards of venture capital-backed companies.

Implications

Our ultimate objective in this and related projects is to understand: Is entrepreneurship changing the landscape of corporate life in America? In other words, as firms grow, do they become more conservative, leading to the low participation rates of women in leadership we now see in the Fortune 500? Or, has the most recent entrepreneurial wave changed how women participate, leading us to expect a different context and engagement level for women as firm founders and executive leaders in corporate life over the next 25 years? The results of this study say that corporate America provides more leadership opportunities for women and that there is no push along the start-up path pipeline. The results deserve further investigation.

The research shows that the most likely place to find a woman successfully climbing the corporate ladder is in a large, well-established, non-technology intensive firm, although even here participation rates were low: about 10 to 20 percent compared to men. For working women interested in exercising leadership, these findings inform career decisions including where to invest labor and how to think about employment choices by economic sector. Women seriously interested in exercising governance authority may then want to consider the business start-up option.

At the practice level, we believe these findings challenge graduate business education programs to examine how they educate women in terms of the impact of gender on business success. We believe a commitment to fair treatment of women has led programs to misjudge or undervalue the necessity of teaching women how to succeed despite poor odds. Real or perceived deficiencies and problems that are gender related can potentially be addressed through self-reflection, education, mentoring, impression management, or other activities and training. Women and their career mentors (e.g., men or women supervisors, faculty, and career counselors) can assess the gap between women's skills and knowledge and the requirements of leadership under working world conditions. In IPO situations, the interdependent intraorganizational networks of firms may be especially important, and women may lack the practice, signaling profile, reputation, knowledge, or some other attribute deemed important by the environment in which they hope to succeed.

SOURCE: By Teresa Nelson, Suffolk University, Boston; Laurie Levesque, Suffolk University, Boston. Printed with permission.

Valuation of the Business

When considering each potential exit strategy, the question arises: What is the company worth? Determining valuation of a business is a challenging process because of the great number of valuation methods available. In addition, valuation must combine the past financial information of the company or "hard data," its intangible assets, and projections of financial success (Fiduccia, 2001).

Common distinctions among valuation methods cite the following three general categories of valuations (Sonnhalter, 2005):

1. Market approach

2. Income approach

3. Asset approach

The market approach focuses on calculating the value of the company based on similar competitors in the marketplace. This approach will result in different calculations depending on suggested competition. Usually, a multiple will be used to value another company. This same multiple will then be used for the venture in question. When compared with public companies, however, private ventures will be valued at a lower level because of their lack of liquidity (Fiduccia, 2001). However, there are challenges to this popular method of valuation because it assumes that all companies are the same and also will depend on buyer competition (Linnert & Skowronski, 2005). If there is not a movement toward acquisition in a specific industry, the market approach would result in an estimation dependent not on the company's value but on how the buyer market is impacted.

The income approach looks specifically at the company's ability to generate income and usually results in the highest valuation of the company. This means an analyst will focus on future cash flow of the company, based on current financials. Usually, this is determined by discounting a company's future income or cash flow at an assumed opportunity cost of capital (Fiduccia, 2001) called *net present value.* Variations on the income approach include the following formulas:

- Gross Sales 1: 40 percent times gross sales
- Gross Sales 2: 75 percent times gross sales
- Future Earnings 1 (three years using historical growth rate): Discounted rate of 15 percent for manufacturing and 30 percent for retail, service, and wholesale. Uses a multiple of 10 times net earnings.
- Future Earnings 2 (three years using historical growth rate): Discounted rate of 20 percent for manufacturing, 40 percent for retail, service, and wholesale. Uses a multiple of 10 times net earnings.
- Earnings Before Interest and Taxes 1: EBIT at a multiple of five.
- Earnings Before Interest and Taxes 2: EBIT at a multiple of 10.
- Current Net Earnings at a Multiple of Five 1: A discount rate of 20 percent for manufacturing and 30 percent for retail, service, and wholesale.

- Current Earnings at a Multiple of Five 2: A discount rate of 20 percent for manufacturing and 40 percent for retail, service, and wholesale.
- Discretionary Cash Flow (return to owners) 1: At a multiple of five.
- Discretionary Cash Flow (return to owners) 2: At a multiple of 10.

The third approach, the asset approach, focuses on the assets of the company minus its liabilities. The idea of *adjusted book value* is a variation of this idea because it actually uses the fair market value of assets and liabilities rather than the book value. Another way to use the asset approach is to consider liquidation value. This is the value of the company if all of its assets are liquidated and its debts are repaid. Small entrepreneurial firms, however, can suffer under this valuation method due to the fact that assets may not possess large asset bases (Pricer & Johnson, 1997).

For smaller entrepreneurial firms, research indicates that a variation of the asset approach is the most accurate valuation method (Pricer & Johnson, 1997). This calculation is called the Corporate Investment Business Brokers method, pioneered by Corporate Investment Business Brokers, a firm that matches buyers and sellers of businesses. This calculation is equal to the book value of assets except inventory; plus inventory at cost; plus earnings before interest and tax; plus owners' compensation. Owners' compensation includes salary, health and life insurance premiums, rent payments paid on housing, and depreciation (Pricer & Johnson, 1997).

Review Question

1. Explain each of the three general approaches to valuation.

Summary of Chapter Objectives

1. Understand the advantages and disadvantages of choosing a merger or acquisition growth strategy
   - Advantages include the potential to cut costs and improve efficiencies, value creation or renewal, and strategic operational advantages that neither company could achieve on its own.
   - Disadvantages include financial failure, based on the ability to outperform the stock market or deliver profit increases. Mergers and acquisitions can even destroy value for shareholders.

2. Learn practices for increasing the likelihood of merger or acquisition success
   - Organizational alignment between partners is required to ensure cooperation through attention to culture and organizational processes of decision making, communication, and trust building. Organizational alignment is primarily concerned with relationship management.
   - There are seven practices for integrating people and cultures for mergers and acquisitions, including managing the information flow, building a standardized integration team, and selecting the best people for the integration team.

3. Learn about franchising as a growth strategy and how to determine if an organization is ready to franchise
    - Franchising is a system of distribution in which the entrepreneur (the franchisor) enters into a contractual relationship with a local business owner or distribution partner (the franchisee) to handle specific products and services under mutually agreed-upon conditions.
    - Several benefits and risks are associated with franchising. Consider the value of a pilot when formulating your growth strategy.

4. Consider the importance of exit strategies to strategic planning
    - Entering into business without an exit strategy can lead to problems and loss of business value.
    - Entrepreneurs should carefully consider their own connection and rationale for the business before planning toward an exit strategy.
    - Entrepreneurs should envision an exit strategy from the founding of the company.

5. Evaluate different exit strategies and options available when the time comes to leave or modify your business
    - Different exit strategies have different challenges and benefits depending on the business and the market.
    - Selling the business is a strong exit strategy in a poor economy.
    - An IPO provides opportunity for business growth.
    - Folding the business is the least profitable exit strategy.

6. Scan diverse business valuation methods used to determine the value of your business
    - Business valuation methods are varied and depend on the purpose of the valuation.
    - Market-based valuations focus on the value of the company compared to competitors in the marketplace.
    - Income-based valuation focuses on the company's financial statements and estimated future values.
    - Asset-based valuation is determined by the company's assets and liabilities. Variations on this valuation calculate values based on market rates rather than book rates of assets and liabilities.

CASE 10.1   Noodles & Co., Franchising for Growth

With an uncomplicated menu of carbohydrate-packed comfort food-noodles, whether Italian penne pastas, Japanese pan noodles, Wisconsin macaroni and cheese or pad Thai—the simply named Noodles & Co. is an unlikely choice for a red-hot restaurant chain.

But the Boulder Colo.–based eatery, which tripled its revenue in three years, is streaking its way to the top of industry hot lists. Its graced the Inc. 500 four years running, was named Hot Concept and Top 50 Quick Casual Concept by Nation's Restaurant News and Entrepreneur of the Year by Ernst & Young, among other plaudits. Having made it through the nationwide noodle-no vote—its sales climbed 34% to $91 million last year during the anti-carb craze—the 107-unit chain across 10 states has begun an aggressive bid for wider consumer appeal with a new president, new board members, a new store design and new advertising.

The 10-year-old company has snared Kevin Reddy, chief operating officer from fast-casual darling Chipotle, as its president-chief operating officer to serve as the operational yin to the brand yang of Aaron Kennedy, founder and CEO. "Kevin has an incredible track record in driving same-store sales," said Mr. Kennedy. Mr. Reddy will also join the privately held company's board of directors as the fourth addition in a year following Betsy McLaughlin, CEO of Hot Topic; Deborah Smith Hart, former chief financial officer of Chili's parent Brinker International; and private-equity guru Scott Hedrick, who also is on the board of Office Depot and Hot Topic.

Mr. Reddy "was part of putting the team together that we have today," said Steve Ells, founder and CEO of Chipotle. "Noodles is lucky to have him on their team now."

Mr. Reddy will spend the next several weeks getting familiar with Noodles operations after many years of being a regular customer. "There's a buzz in this building and excitement in the restaurants that reminds me of Chipotle in many respects, yet it's uniquely different," he said. "It has the ability to be relevant to customers at a variety of levels from quick casual to casual dining to fine dining. What makes it special is it's more sophisticated against its typical competitors."

Since the late '90s, the East-meets-West chain's growth strategy has been to saturate the American heartland. From its first store in Denver's upscale Cherry Creek neighborhood, it has spread to each coast through a dual target of wealthy urban locales and college towns where worldly, health-conscious consumers tend to root. With its diverse menu, it is equally appealing to young moms and kids as it is college students.

The average store brings in $1.1 million per year in sales, but Mr. Kennedy wants to see that number grow to $1.5 million. To get there, the marketer must grow traffic and the average check, which stands now about $7, and grow to 500 restaurants over the next decade. "Its success depends on how much better they can make their unit economics," said Malcolm Knapp, president of Malcolm M. Knapp restaurant consultant. Noodles would be "much more robust at $1.5 million [per store] because something that may have worked economically five years ago is now marginal and real estate is getting expensive and that changes your returns."

155 Restaurants

Two years ago the company began franchising stores and will add 15 to 20 company-owned stores and 10 to 15 franchised stores this year. In all, 155 restaurants have been committed via franchise agreements, many with owner/operators of Wendy's, Taco Bell, Burger King and Krispy Kreme.

Noodles is "proving that it has legs," said Tom Miner, principal at consultant Technomic, noting that the key is enough variety "so the whole family wants to go," and to go frequently.

Considering its whole concept relies on one main ingredient, Noodles' menu has evolved into many variants. First launched in October 1995, its offerings began with dishes made of noodles with Asian and Mediterranean flavors. It later added salads, sautéed and grilled meats and recently added a Noodle-less menu of meat-based sautéed dishes to appeal to heartier appetites. On Jan. 1 Noodles added a Whole-Grain Tuscan Fettuccine made with a fiber-packed 100% whole-wheat noodle.

First inspired by its 40-year-old CEO's frequent meals at Asian noodle shops when he was a brand manager at Pepsi, Mr. Kennedy didn't design the concept to fit into a segment. "I designed it from a customer perspective," he said, noting he relies heavily on "mother-in-law" research. "There's a tremendous amount of intuition in it." As a result, the mishmash of items that get put on the menu don't fit the typical fast-casual menu. "Even restaurant analysts have struggled with where Noodles & Co. fits."

Technomic has lumped the chain with Asian quick-casual brands such as Mama Fu's Asian House, Chin's Asia Fresh, Pei Wei Asian Diner and Pick Up Stix. That Asian noodle segment is small but growing quickly. Asian/noodle chains account for 5%, or $325 million, of the $6.5 billion quick-casual category, according to Technomic, with a combined three-year annual growth rate of 25%.

Its more direct rivals are a sub-segment of emerging brands, Nothing But Noodles and Wild Noodles, considered "global" noodle chains for their wider ethnic palettes. To further differentiate itself from the Asian noodle shops, Noodles & Co. has redesigned its store concept and is preparing to break fresh advertising. "Only 30% of our sales are Asian food," said Mr. Kennedy.

Changing Tack

It's also expanding its traditional out-of-home advertising, with radio, promotion and a Web component, while changing creative tack. The print and outdoor effort, shot by photographer Erik Almas, is aimed at bringing the brand's attributes of colorful, fresh and comfortable to life, through scenes of a Tuscan farmer tending his field, a quirky car with a large noodle bowl on top to promote takeout and a man breathing fire after eating a spicy dish. Sukle Advertising & Design, Denver, handles.

Noodles & Co.'s original out-of-home ads were built on "noodle doodles," which has since evolved from stark white and yellow creative to include color and more texture. "We've moved away from the noodle doodle to something that elevates the brand and give customers a more direct sense of where the food comes from," said Rich Miller, VP-marketing. This year, the marketer is also adding a seasonal-menu program starting with fresh asparagus for spring and supported by a whimsical marketing campaign that includes the chain's first contest, the Asparagus Queen contest.

Marketing spending is about 3% of sales and will include radio for the first time this year, along with a revamped Web site to build a better platform for relationship marketing. Mr. Miller is reviewing interactive agencies now and expects to soon assign the work. He declined to disclose the contenders.

Store Design

Store design, too, is changing. To-go service will have a dedicated door, seating, counter and parking to help drive takeout sales from one-third to half of total revenue. In addition to brighter colors, American B-side pop and European-inspired music, there is more diverse seating with single bar stools, u-shaped booths for families and a massive community table.

But the biggest change will be in the show kitchen where customers can watch the sauté action. "The show kitchen really demonstrates to people that the food is made for them, made to order," said Mr. Kennedy. "As they absorb that intuitively and think 'maybe I could have them hold the mushrooms or add more broccoli,' that allows mass customization."

Some observers muse that the chain is dressing up for sale. While Noodles & Co., which has 300 shareholders, acts like a public company and is "keeping its options open" for possible sale or public offering, "we do not have any imminent plans to become a public company," said Mr. Kennedy.

SOURCE: MacArthur, K. (2005). Upstart looks to borrow Chipotle's special sauce. *Advertising Age,* *76(15).* April 11: 18–20. Reprinted with permission.

Discussion Questions

1. Describe the path to growth that Noodles & Co. has followed since its launch in 1995.

2. What strengths does Kevin Reddy bring to the company? How might his experience at Chipotle influence his approach to growth at Noodles & Co.?

3. What opportunities and challenges might there be for Noodles & Co. as it attempts to meet its growth goals?

4. Why was franchising a suitable growth strategy for the company?

CASE 10.2   The Lizard King of SoBe Beverages

NEJE [New England Journal of Entrepreneurship]: John Bello, aka the "Lizard King," has been lionized in the business press as having been the brilliant entrepreneur who started a beverage company from scratch in early 1995 with his partner, Tom Schwalm, and then sold the product line to PepsiCo seven years later for a reported $375 million. What many people do not know is how close Bello came to failing with his SoBe line of innovative drinks. The following is an interview with Bello, conducted by the *New England Journal of Entrepreneurship.*

NEJE: Your great success must make you a very sought after speaker in MBA programs across the country.

Bello: It's true. I travel extensively talking to high school, college, and business school students— anyone who will listen—whenever I can about what it takes to be an entrepreneur. I have fun with MBA students, whom I tease. I tell them, "You aren't likely to be entrepreneurs or else you

wouldn't be here. You'd be out starting your own businesses and making money for yourselves." That really gets to them. Shakes them up.

NEJE: However, isn't it true, John, that an MBA degree can help entrepreneurs as much as it can those headed for corporate careers?

Bello: Perhaps, but I believe entrepreneurship cannot be taught, and at best, most universities just teach analytics. They don't teach how to overcome the inbred scourge to successful enterprise: Fear of failure. The worry about financial and job security paralyzes a lot of people from pursuing their dreams.

NEJE: What about business skills you can learn in college and then in graduate school?

Bello: Certainly, business school programs impart important skills, such as how to conduct market research or how to analyze a balance sheet, but the really successful entrepreneur needs to have an intimate knowledge and awareness of the product and the market. Passion is the key driver. Do it, move it, make it happen. You can't sit your way to success. You need to talk to the trade and interact with consumers. Salesmanship. That's the stuff you don't get in an MBA program. I have an MBA from Tuck at Dartmouth. Good time, good people, and good analytic education. But, what I learned about process and marketing, I learned at General Foods and in the street. At some point, you have to decide whether you have the intestinal fortitude, perseverance, and smarts to put together a successful venture. With entrepreneurs, it is deeds, not dialogue.

NEJE: Did you know right after grad school you wanted to be an entrepreneur?

Bello: I had a sense from the start that I didn't fit into the corporate mold. Or at least, I knew myself enough to know that I was a better leader than a follower. In the Navy as an officer, I did well but it wasn't easy. I had trouble following orders that were "busy work." In Vietnam, that changed. My job was clear and my CO let me do my thing with my team. We were successful doing things almost "by the book." The book, to me, is for nonthinkers. I guess I've always been an iconoclast. Basically, if I am motivated and have an objective I believe in, I'll show up with the goods. The lesson here is have a love and passion for what you do. Most people in this world settle for security and what's in front of them. Circumstances sometime dictate that, but in America, you can be whatever you want to be.

Back to Vietnam, I was put in charge of, among other things, a small "store" on the Mekong Delta that supported PBR's-an Apocalypse Now reality show. At 25, I had control of 60 men and was responsible for the care and feeding of 24 riverboats but the fun job was the base store. With the help of my troops, we turned that tiny shaving cream and cigarette store into a multimillion-dollar operation. We had generals showing up in their helicopters ready to buy television sets, cameras, stereo equipment, and tapes of Iron Butterfly, Steppenwolf, and CCR at great prices. And the profits paid for base welfare and recreation. It was an experience.

NEJE: So from Vietnam you came back to the States and tried your hand at entrepreneurship here?

Bello: No, I ran a Navy exchange at Moffett Field, California, and upon leaving the Navy, earned an MBA from Tuck. After graduating as an Edward Tuck Scholar, I went into corporate life with General Foods, then PepsiCo, and finally the National Football League. I did well because of performance but didn't pay attention to the politics. I wasn't good at that game but I was good at making money for other people. Besides, I found that process was usually an end, and not a means, and that careers were built on both process and politics. That wasn't me.

A lot of people argue about whether entrepreneurs are "made" or "born." I think that people are action-oriented or not. And either you are a risk-taker or rule-maker rather than a "by-the-book" type. Rules in marketing, to me, are guidelines. You simply cannot teach that to people.

I also believe that no matter how good you are, there are many things in a corporate environment that are beyond your control. I tell people in my talks that typically, they will all be fired sooner or later and they better be prepared. I did an outstanding job at NFL Properties, building the company into a $250 million business and creating the template as to how sports marketing was done. When the new commissioner came in, he wanted his own team and I was forced out. It was time to leave. Change is good. But you better plan for the eventuality. It happens to virtually everyone.

NEJE: It sounds like you got fired somewhere along the line.

Bello: Not fired, exactly, but I saw the handwriting on the wall after almost 15 years working in the NFL's Licensing and Properties Division. I knew I had to leave. It was a shock to me; it was 1993 and I was 47 years old but I had run my course at the NFL. I took a year off —wondering what to do next when a buddy called me from Arizona Beverages and asked me to join them in restructuring the brand to make it more attractive as a take-over target. I only lasted four, or maybe five, months as a consultant. It was tough because they didn't like my ideas and I firmly believed I could do a better job than they were doing. We really clashed. I came back East thinking that maybe my time with Arizona was well spent because I was intrigued with the opportunities in the beverage industry.

NEJE: The beverage category is so saturated. Why did you think you could make a difference?

Bello: Call it ego, or maybe it was intuition or stupidity, but I saw how California Coolers had made it big, then Clearly Canadian, and then Arizona Teas. I felt there was still plenty of room left for a more relevant lifestyle brand.

So, in December 1994, I decided to start a beverage company with a partner, Tom Schwalm, who had 24 years of beverage experience and a big checkbook. We sought outside investors but put in plenty of our own money to start the business. It took a year to develop the concept of "South Beach" drinks. No income, no support system. I wanted to introduce a beverage built on lifestyle. That's so important these days. Consumers are advertised to death; they're bored with most of the new products that try to get their attention, and so these products fail. I wanted to develop something special for the marketplace, something that could generate a lot of "buzz" and word of mouth advertising, more credible and a lot less costly.

We traveled down to South Beach, Florida, to get a sense of the hot, hip, and trendy lifestyle for which SoBe was known. While there, we saw lots of lizards around the city, including a fresco lizard on the Abbey hotel that became our new product icon. We thought we were on to something so we decided to call our product "South Beach," and we created a glass bottle design that incorporated a lizard on it.

We had our brand name and we had the packaging. Now we had to develop innovative flavors and a strong product benefit for our consumers. We worked with flavor and bottling companies to see what strategic alliances we could form with them. It wasn't easy. It is a cut-throat business but all is fair in the marketing wars—threats, law suits, intimidation, lack of funding, everything is against you. You have to believe in yourself and persevere. However, there was no way we were going to be pushed around. We eventually found companies who were willing to work with us and launched the brand in December 1995.

NEJE: You were on your way.

Bello: Or so we thought. Just three months into the venture, by February 1996, we knew we had some significant problems. There were production problems. We were having trouble getting enough distribution and our investors were balking at putting in more money. We had already spent $2 million and they weren't about to fork over more cash. Consumers liked some of what we had done, but that wasn't enough to break through.

At that point, some entrepreneurs would have called it quits and given up. Or some might have insisted they had the right mix and gone off a cliff holding fast to their original concept. I knew we had problems and we had to face reality. Either we'd change our thinking or fail. We started over—mortgaged our homes, shortened the name of the product from "South Beach" to "SoBe," altered the labeling to add two lizards in a "yin and yang" relationship (that was my daughter's suggestion, by the way), and changed the product's formulation.

We walked away from a "me-too" iced tea, to a line of healthy refreshment beverages, capitalizing on an emerging interest in energy and health drinks. Health was a cultural shift by the mid-1990s, so instead of just a "fun" drink, we decided to change our positioning and produce a drink that contained herbs and vitamins. Elements such as ginseng, ginkgo biloba, and echinacea that were said to have therapeutic benefits on the mind, body, and spirit were added to our formulation. We thought our audience would quickly recognize the value of drinking a refreshing beverage that was also good for them.

When reevaluating our marketing options, I happened to pick up an issue of Shape magazine that had an article on how yohimbe, arginine, and carnitine could spice up your sex life. This led to our Energy drink that then led to Power, Wisdom, Drive, and Eros. You get the picture. Applying them to our different flavor and herb combinations offered us the marketing opportunity to make a strong product-benefit story.

NEJE: How long did it take for you to re-create yourselves?

Bello: Nine months. Nine harrowing and very tense months. However by November 1996 we were finally ready to relaunch the brand. We decided on a strong flavor profile, a new graphic look, and a font we took from the movie *Braveheart*. It just seemed to fit with the image we were trying to create.

We went to the bottlers and produced 25,000 cases of the product. Our distributor hit the market in New Hampshire and the SoBe concept exploded. The product flew off the shelves. I mean, it just blew out everyone's expectations about what the product would do.

We went to the InterBev Trade Show soon after and a Snapple distributor discovered us and offered to help us expand the line. Word was getting around the country that we had a winner and everyone wanted to get in on the action. I knew the more publicity we got, the better we could launch SoBe, so I became the "Lizard King" and worked the public relations angle every chance I could.

We did everything we could think of to create a "buzz" factor. We used a fleet of decorated "Lizard Love Buses" to sample the product and create an image for SoBe that soon everyone was trying to copy. The buzz got louder and louder and the trade listened. We expanded distribution rapidly, spending more money than we had, but "carpe diem." We sampled like everywhere. We, my team including me, went into every retail outlet we could find to talk to the owners and get them to take on our line. If we met resistance, we would give them a couple of free cases, tell them to stock the product in the refrigerated case area, and see what happened. We would not take "no" for an answer. There was always a way to get to "yes" and that's what we needed. Lots of "yeses."

We sought out hip, cool athletes to spread the word about the brand and join "Team Lizard." John Daly, the golfer, and Bode Miller, the ski jumper, were brought on board to help us tell our story. A lot of folks thought we were wrong to turn to John Daly because of some of his past personal problems, but he was really fantastic for us. John was very effective.

NEJE: Smooth sailing from that point on?

Bello: I only wish. We just couldn't make enough of the product from March to May 1997. I was on the road constantly selling the concept while Tom was trying to hire professional operational and logistics people. It was chaotic. Keeping up with orders was a nightmare.

We were selling health and energy and that combination was a winner. We had a product with no preservatives and no phosphates. We were different. Different with our packaging, different with our formulation, our brand name, heck even our bottle top was different because we put funny sayings on each one; people even started to collect the bottle tops to show their friends.

NEJE: Besides having to catch up with demand, what other problems did you have?

Bello: Legal. We got sued by Arizona Teas in 1997 and 1998 for allegedly infringing on their packaging and bottling design. That distracted us but we eventually won the lawsuits.

NEJE: When did you know you had "arrived"?

Bello: Easy. Beverage companies started to mimic us. Wannabes. Lots of them. They were coming out with "me too" products that ripped off our concept.

NEJE: What did you do about it?

Bello: We kept innovating, being the best, working, and selling. We owned the concept, and in life, if you are not the "lizard," you are the loser. America is a good place for winners. It's a free country and our competition was entitled to try to catch up to us. That's why we had to stay nimble and never take anything for granted. That's the big difference between a large corporation and a start-up like we were. Innovate or die.

We had to stay one step ahead of everyone else. It's really all about leadership. To inspire our sales force, I had to be in the trenches with them. They had to take their inspiration from me. They saw how I never took "no" for an answer. I'd fly off any time, to any place, for any reason that could take our brand further. There were no limits. Growth, in terms of sales and distribution outlets, was my driving force. We had a lot of sales contests with "Lizard Leaders" winning great awards. We also had our "Lizard Laggards"; those folks either turned things around or they were dropped. Be good or be gone.

I made sure to listen to people everywhere I went. Wholesalers, retailers, our salespeople, customers, you name it. I listened, and I listened hard. I never felt I had all the answers. There were always bright, insightful people along the way who added enormously to our success. You just have to know how to listen.

NEJE: Why sell out to PepsiCo? Why not continue to ride the wave?

Bello: There were a couple of reasons. First, as an independent beverage company, it's hard to keep growing without the marketing muscle of a large corporation. We had gone as far and as fast as I thought we could go without someone like Pepsi behind us.

Second, we wanted to take our chips off the table. We had worked exhaustively for five, six years, once we reformulated the brand, and we were tired. It was time to rest up some and enjoy being rich.

NEJE: Your busy offices here in Norwalk, Connecticut, suggest you haven't retired.

Bello: No, I ain't done yet. Only now it's a hobby. I am working on a new food line that we are going to call the "Firefighter" brand with colleagues from my NFL and SoBe days. As a social venture, it will benefit Firefighters. Think of chili, snack chips, coffee, and maybe even a "Firefighter" line of clothing. There's also a beverage line being developed, someone else is working on that as an independent company.

After 9/11, I was inspired by the heroism of New York's firefighters. I've always admired Paul Newman, who has developed some very good consumer products; then his company donates the profits to charity. That's sort of what we're going to do. We're going to donate 25 percent of our net profits to firefighter causes. We've got national, as well as some local, firefighter associations already lined up behind us. The products will be "hazardous material free." No high fructose, transfats, fewer calories, and generally better-for-you fun food. We are working with a firefighter to be one of our chefs.

NEJE: You're only 58 years old so I know you have lots of energy left, but why take on the strain of launching another product nationwide? Why not something less ambitious?

Bello: Because I don't want to say someday I "could have, would have, should have" done this or that. Life is good and it is as good as you want to make it. It's about making a little money and having lots of fun. Any one can do it. Being involved in new product development, working with wonderful people, and seeing my concepts succeed in the marketplace makes me smile. I started off, like so many Americans, in a small town (Plainville, Connecticut). I'm proud of what we did in Vietnam, at the NFL, with SoBe, and I'm ready to follow that up with something exciting, new, and different.

SOURCE: This case was written by Laurence Weinstein, Sacred Heart University. It was originally published in the *New England Journal of Entrepreneurship, 7*(1) Spring, 2004: 7–10. Used with permission.

Discussion Questions

1. What problems and symptoms did Bello experience in growing the business of SoBe beverages?

2. What personal and educational experiences have prepared Bello and given him his entrepreneurial background?

3. What innovative techniques and solutions did he use to "re-create" SoBe?

4. What additional recommendations would you make to the firm in creating further "buzz" around SoBe beverages?

Notes

1. Source: http://www.francorp.com/why/who.html
2. Source: http://www.newbusinesscentre.com/franbiz.html

References

Abernathy, W., & Utterback, J. (1988). Patterns of industrial innovation. In M. Tushman & W. Moore (Eds.), *Readings in the management of innovation.* (pp. 55–78) New York: Harper Business.

Amit, R., & Villalonga, B. (2004). How do family ownership, control, and management affect firm value? *Knowledge@Wharton.* Retrieved February 25, 2006, from http://knowledge .wharton.upenn.edu/index.cfm?fa=viewPaper&id=1295

Becker, B., & Huselid, M. (1998). High-performance work systems and firm performance: A synthesis of research and managerial implications. In G. Fends (Ed.), *Research in personnel and human resource management* (Vol. 16, pp. 53–101). Greenwich, CT: JAI Press.

Catalyst. (2002). *Census of women corporate officers and top earners.* New York: Author.

Certo, S. T. (2003). Influencing initial public offering investors with prestige: Signaling with board structures. *Academy of Management Review, 28,* 432–446.

Crane, J. (2004, March 28). Path from lab to boardroom open to women who take steps. *Boston Globe,* p. G6–G7.

The Family Business Institute. (2005). *Fact and figures.* Retrieved May 27, 2005, from http://www.familybusinessinstitute.com/index.php?customernumber=215456546224 &pr=Facts_And_Figures&=SID

Fiduccia, B. (2001, December). Whether you're selling your business. *Entrepreneur's Start-Ups Magazine.* Retrieved May 28, 2005, from http://www.entrepreneur.com/mag/article/ 0,1539,295301,00.html

Fligstein, N. (1991). The structural transformation of American industry. In W. Powell & P. DiMaggio (Eds.), *The new institutionalism in organizational analysis* (pp. 311–336). Chicago: University of Chicago Press.

King, J. (2001). More women in top spot than ever before. *Corporate Legal Times, 11*(117), 10–12.

LaBarre, P. (1999, January). What's new, what's not. *FastCompany, issue 21,* p. 73.

Linnert, P., & Skowronski, D. (2005). Don't sell yourself short. *Rough Notes, 148*(4), 26–29.

Marks, M. L., & Mirvis, P. H. (2000). Managing mergers, acquisitions, and alliances: Creating an effective transition structure. *Organizational Dynamics, 28*(3), 35–47.

Morris, M, Williams, R., & Nel, D. (1996). Factors influencing family business succession. *International Journal of Entrepreneurial Behaviour & Research, 2*(3), 68.

Neuborne E., & Perton, M. (2000, November 6). Selling out, staying on. *Businessweek Online.* Retrieved February 15, 2006, from http://www.businessweek.com/2000/00_45/ b3706051.htm.

Pablo, A. L., & Javidan, M. (2002). Thinking of a merger? Do you know their risk propensity profile? *Organizational Dynamics, 30*(3), 206–222.

Pennington, A. Y. (2005, June). Exhale. *Entrepreneur,* p. 86.

Pricer, R., & Johnson A. (1997). The accuracy of valuation methods in predicting the selling price of small firms. *Journal of Small Business Management, 35*(4), 24.

Resnick-West, S., & Von Glinow, M. A. (1990). Beyond the clash: Managing high technology professionals. In M. Von Glinow, & S. Mohrman (Eds.), *Managing complexity in high technology organizations* (pp. 237–254). New York: Oxford University Press.

Schmidt, J. A. (2001). The correct spelling of M&A begins with HR. *HR Magazine, 46*(6), 102–108.

Sirower, M. (1997). *The synergy trap.* New York: The Free Press.

Sonnhalter, A. (2005). Valuing your business. *Industrial Distribution, 94*(3), 60.

Stanworth, J., & Stanworth, C. (2004). Franchising as a small business growth strategy: A resource-based view of organizational development. *International Small Business Journal, 22*(6), 539–559.

Tetenbaum, T. J. (1999). Beating the odds of merger & acquisition failure: Seven key practices that improve the chance for expected integration and synergies. *Organizational Dynamics, 28*(2), 22–36.

Zacharakis, A., & Meyer, G. (2000). The potential of actuarial decision models: Can they improve venture capital investment decisions? *Journal of Business Venturing, 15,* 323–346.

CHAPTER 11

Beyond the Strategic Entrepreneurial Model

Learning From Failure

Nobody talks of entrepreneurship as survival, but that's exactly what it is and what nurtures creative thinking.

— Anita Roddick, Founder, The Body Shop International

My first six years in the business were hopeless. There are a lot of times when you sit and you say "Why am I doing this? I'll never make it. It's just not going to happen. I should go out and get a real job, and try to survive."

— George Lucas, film producer

If you let failure bother you, you'll never succeed. Don't fear failure. Learn from it.

— John Peterman, chairman and CEO of J. Peterman Co.

Objectives:

1. Understand the other side of success: rapid growth

2. Learn some of the solutions for problems during rapid growth

3. Know the warning signs of failure and what key areas of the business can be monitored

4. Learn what the remedies and solutions are for your entrepreneurial venture that can be implemented to avoid failure

5. Gain a final perspective on failure from hearing about the latest research and comments from entrepreneurs who have failed but later succeeded

Speaking of Strategy

An Interview With Addie Swartz, CEO of B*tween Productions, Inc.

Addie Swartz is the principal creator and CEO of B*tween Productions, Inc. Addie has previously worked at Walt Disney, Lotus Development, and Reebok. In 1992, she founded BrightIdeas, which sold children's educational software to parents and teachers. BrightIdeas was acquired by Addison Wesley in 1996. As a woman entrepreneur, Addie has been featured in the *Wall Street Journal, Inc. Magazine, Working Woman Magazine, Child Magazine*, and *Working Mother Magazine* and has appeared on *Good Morning America* and MSNBC. Addie graduated from Stanford University and got her MBA from Northwestern University's Kellogg School. Addie lives in Boston with her husband and two "tween-age" girls, ages 10 and 14. She is committed to make a real difference for girls and provide them with healthier role models and more positive messages as they approach adolescence.

One of the opening quotes is from Anita Roddick, who says, "Nobody talks of entrepreneurship as survival, but that's exactly what it is and what nurtures creative thinking." Do you agree and see any similarities on how you view your entrepreneurial career?

Swartz: By definition, entrepreneurs have extremely limited resources. And necessity breeds creativity. The $5 million ad campaign is not open to you, so you use the $50,000 guerilla marketing campaign instead. In many cases, the latter can be much more fresh and effective. In both of my two companies, resource constraints have bred an amazing amount of resourcefulness. That has led to more focused initiatives and successful results.

Many say that entrepreneurship can't be taught. What hard lessons have you learned in the start-up process of your various ventures?

Swartz: A good entrepreneur has to be good at a lot of things, some of which can be taught, some of which are innate.

1. Raising money—which means creating and selling a vision of what a company can be (can be learned if one is passionate about project).

2. Managing a lot of balls at the same time (hard to teach).

3. Never giving up, no matter what (hard to teach, goes to the psyche).

4. Persevering (same as above).

5. Continuing to analyze what's been created to understand what's working, what isn't, and how to respond to ever-changing environments (teachable).

6. Instinctually knowing what projects/activities to spend time and resources on and what ones not to.

7. Being focused and not being focused at the same time (comes with the job—on-the-job experience).

On that same note, what hard lessons have you learned in the growth and maturity of those businesses?
Swartz:

1. Listen to everyone—good ideas can come from anyone.

2. You need to give your people room to build out the vision.

3. Don't underestimate the fresh perspective that can be brought in by outsiders.

4. Patience patience patience. Often things just take a bit longer than you anticipate. When it seems that nothing's going on, the phone doesn't ring, etc. . . . , it's just momentary. Results will come and come on strong when you least expect it.

5. It takes different skill sets at different times in the company's development to build a successful enterprise. Skills needed to start something from scratch are different than those that are needed to grow a business.

6. It almost always takes longer to raise money than you thought it was going to; so it's imperative to be stingy with your capital.

As an entrepreneur, how do you view failure? Any early lessons that made you more resilient?
Swartz: Failure is one of the most valuable teachers. I've learned as much from things that haven't worked as from roaring successes. The key is to separate out emotion and clearly distill the learning.

What triggered/motivated you to launch Beacon Street Girls? How has the business evolved in the last three years?
Swartz: I first recognized my two daughters being bombarded by media messages and images that were inappropriate, oversexualized, and preyed upon their self-esteem. As an entrepreneur, I wondered if something could be created that was fun and contemporary and could offer healthier role models—could help girls feel better about themselves, and do so in an entertaining way. And that is what I set out to do with the Beacon Street Girls—to build a place that uses the power of character and story to reach out to girls and help build their self-esteem.

SOURCE: Interview with Addie Swartz by Jill Kickul.

The Other Side of Success: Rapid Growth[1]

As firms grow rapidly, it is possible that the very growth that propelled the new venture to success can begin to cover up weak management, poor planning, or wasted resources. Rapid growth can also dilute effective leadership and can cause the venture to stray away from its goals and objectives. Furthermore, rapid growth can lead to stress and burnout, where the management team no longer has the energy or capability to focus on key strategic needs.

Entrepreneurs who have experienced failure, the downside of rapid growth, have learned at least three important lessons:

1. *Capital management:* The need for greater initial capitalization. It is easy to underproject the financing needed for expansion, and as the firm grows, there is insufficient capital at critical junctures.

2. *Market monitoring:* The need for more, and better, market research. Ironically, as successful new ventures grow, entrepreneurs or members of the management team may come to believe that success will be continual, and whatever the firm launches is likely to reach predicted margins. In fact, markets change continually. If the firm loses touch with shifting market needs, or if it relies on outdated market research (or insufficient market research), the results can be disastrous.

3. *Innovation:* The need for skills in operating an innovative enterprise. As we have seen, some firms lack the innovative skills to embrace change successfully. Throughout this book, we have introduced methods entrepreneurs can use to approach problems and opportunities more innovatively. If entrepreneurs continue to approach situations as they have done in the past, they will never be able to position their organizations as leaders. It is also increasingly likely that the company's performance will decline. Innovation is key to survival.

Solutions for Problems During Rapid Growth[2]

Ironically, fast growth is often the cause of many businesses' inability to succeed. In a situation of rapid growth, the entrepreneur must be prepared to create an organization that can adapt to changes in real time. No matter how quickly the organization grows, if it is not flexible to respond to these types of changes, failure is a strong possibility. In her article, "Rapid Growth and High Performance: The Entrepeneur's 'Impossible Dream?'" Charlene L. Nicholls-Nixon outlines the structural and human areas that business owners need to monitor and consciously shape to prepare the enterprise to capitalize on any initial successes.

Minding the Vision

No matter how an entrepreneur structures the enterprise, it is important to keep the core values as the guiding structural force. Nicholls-Nixon points to the essential development of "deep structure" as the foundation for business development. Deep structure is defined as "a simple set of shared rules that define the firm's business logic, or reason for being, and its basic principles of organization." If deep structure is developed in an organization, the vision of the organization, not policies and procedures, become the guiding force for business decisions. The point is to avoid bureaucracy and to create an institution where all the parts are focused on the same goal. By creating a structure that is not tied to processes, the organization will be poised to capitalize on its strengths and redeploy its assets in a faster, more relevant way.

Communicating Information

Accessing and monitoring meaningful information is crucial to an organization's ability to make sound decisions. It is important for a business to track its growth, the bottom line, and the competitive environment. Although information always exists in an organization, the key is to structure the flow of information to capture it quickly and share it with employees so that all people in the organization can be effective decision makers.

Building Relationships

Strong relationships are important not only within an organization but also between the entrepreneur and staff and key people and organizations that are external to the firm. To maintain the internal relationships, it is important to provide for a balance between work and family life. Employees who have this balance are much more likely to be effective contributors to the organization. External relationships provide an objective resource for problem solving and allow for even faster information sharing.

Managing and Monitoring Politics

Although politics are often unavoidable in any organization, maintaining a constructive, trusting environment is crucial to the structural, informational, and relational goals. Negative behavior can undermine any positive improvements the business is trying to develop.

Setting Direction

Because entrepreneurs are so involved with every detail of their business development, once the business is self-sustaining, it is difficult to step back and take a hands-off leadership role. However, at this phase, it is crucial that the entrepreneur redirect his or her efforts from handling day-to-day tasks to developing a sustainable business organization. The adaptable organization needs a unifying vision to govern its structure, to create information sharing, and to empower employees to make smart decisions. The entrepreneur's next steps should focus on these leadership areas and allow the organization to govern itself.

Review Questions

1. Are the above techniques only applicable in periods of growth?
2. How might creating a "deep structure" in an organization stimulate growth?

Dimension	What Entrepreneurs Can Do
Minding the vision	Focus on strategy and goals, not process Find ways to support and encourage experimentation Give decision-making authority and autonomy
Communicating information	Create an open book culture, sharing key performance metrics Use your communication and information systems to establish and develop competence (not as a control vehicle) Allow and create opportunities for informal communication among employees
Building relationships	Use cross-functional groups Support work-life integration Allow for a sense of fun and enjoyment in the firm
Managing and monitoring politics	Create and establish norms of what is acceptable behavior and performance Look for ways to select new employees based on an even balance of mind-set and values as well as skills and experience Give fair and meaningful opportunities for employees to develop and advance in the organization
Setting direction	Use your power to mediate, not dictate Know that change and chaos are part of the entrepreneurial journey and find ways to embrace them

SOURCE: Adapted from Charlene Nicholls-Nixon, "Rapid Growth and High Performance: The Entrepreneur's 'Impossible Dream?'" *Academy of Management Executives* 19, no. 1(2005): 77–89.

Entrepreneurs and Failure: The Warning Signs

Performing consistent business-plan diagnosis is important for the development of new ventures, however, it is sometimes difficult to self-evaluate. Entrepreneurs frequently rely on external cues as warning signs that their business is not heading in the right direction. To avoid the common pitfalls that lead to the failure of many businesses, entrepreneurs should ask themselves a series of diagnostic questions at the launching phase of their venture to probe the degree to which their venture is vulnerable in its strategic foundations. The Innovator's Toolkit lists the types of questions.

The Innovator's Toolkit: Problem-Solving Checklist

- Does/did your business prepare a written sales forecast?
- Does/did your business prepare a written forecast of cash requirements for at least 12 months into the future?

- Does/did your business prepare a written pro forma capital expenditure forecast?
- Does/did your business use its plans to satisfy information requests from sources of capital and/or creditors?

Employee Development

- Does/did your business prepare a written staffing forecast?
- Did your business have problems in defining or anticipating products that customers would buy in sufficient quantities that an attractive return would be provided to the investors in the business?
- Does/did your business incorporate major goals and objectives spelled out in its plans into its employee performance appraisal system?

Customer Relationship Management

- Do your customers recommend your business to their peers?
- Are you attracting your target customer?
- Are you incorporating customer feedback into your business development?

Monitoring Goals

- Does/did your business analyze its competition and prepare a written identification of strategies and measurable goals that extend/extended three or more years into the future?
- Does/did your business monitor its progress compared to its plans no less often than monthly?
- Did your business have problems in actually producing and selling the defined products at the costs anticipated?
- Does/did your business use its plans for public relations purposes by giving them to customers, prospects, employment candidates, or others not specifically requesting them?

Additional Red Flags

Some red flags that may be symptoms of problems in some of the critical business development areas listed in the Toolkit are illustrated in the following table. If entrepreneurs are experiencing any of these warning signs, it is critical that they reevaluate the current situation using the questions in the Toolkit as a guide to discovering the source of the problem. Entrepreneurs need to develop efficient, flexible, and sustainable solutions to business problems on a constant basis.

Along with these symptoms, research conducted by the Price Group has found the following characteristics among failed businesses:[3]

- About 75 percent of the firms did not use financial data or information or failed to determine weaknesses/shortfalls or to make changes in their business planning.
- Almost 30 percent were not able to show their monthly financial reports (an increase of 50 percent from previous research analyzed five years ago).
- In terms of organizational structure, only 52 percent had a formal one, and of that percentage, 80 percent did not actually implement the structure.

Entrepreneurial Strategy and Planning	Symptoms
Resource management	• Management of finances becomes lax • Directors can't document or explain major transactions • Customers are given large discounts to enhance payments because of poor cash flow • Contracts are accepted at below standard amounts to generate cash • Materials are inadequate to meet orders • Payroll taxes are not paid • Suppliers demand payment in cash
Employee development	• Key personnel leave company
Customer relationship management	• Customer complaints increase
Monitoring goals	• Costs are uncontrollable • Public recognition of business has not grown • Product lines are not selling • Management discussions on business development do not exist

- About 87 percent believed that they had identified their customer markets, but only 13 percent actually implemented a formal marketing plan. About 87 percent had no marketing strategy at all in the beginning.
- Within the firms, communication problems were present for 79 percent of the companies (a red flag in terms of productivity).
- Although they knew they needed to adapt to changes within their markets and industries, only 59 percent actually had an implementation plan and strategy to confront these changes.

Strategy in Action

Is Your Business in Trouble?

Have you ever had this nightmare? A growing company begins to achieve, and even exceed, its projected growth plans. It moves into new offices, recruits new employees, increases management salaries and benefits, hires a team of outside advisors and begins plans for acquisitions and, eventually, a public offering. The founding entrepreneur has built a successful company but has also overshot his experience and capabilities. Ego and bullheadedness prevent the CEO from accepting the fact that a professional management team needs to be appointed.

A culture of growth at any price begins to build within the company. Most of the staff ride an emotional roller coaster that goes from excitement and fear to blind trust. Cash-flow shortages are subtle at first, but with each new month of growth, expenses begin to exceed revenues.

In addition to neglecting the bottom line, the company is getting so caught up in its own buzz that it is not paying sufficient attention to aggressive steps being taken by competitors or to changes in the marketplace that are affecting its industry.

Something like that has been happening in the waking world. Rapid growth of the Internet-driven economy in the late 1990s, followed by a harsh dose of reality in 2000, led to high-profile bankruptcies at companies that were previously regarded as industry pioneers and leaders, but whose management teams failed to manage and adapt. According to recent studies published by Webmergers.com, over 300 dot-com and high-tech companies have failed since 1999, leaving thousands of employees without jobs and many holding shares without value. Some of these troubled companies filed for formal bankruptcy, others shut down informally and some were sold to third parties at a very deep discount.

What to Watch

In today's competitive and rapidly changing marketplace, entrepreneurs need to prevent trouble before it starts. Here's a basic list of management goals for keeping a business on track.

- Anticipate financial problems.
- Monitor the company's business plan and business model to ensure that growth and profitability targets are met.
- Manage the costs and risks associated with economic problems.
- Keep a close watch on business trends that may require your business to change strategic direction.
- Understand the methods and alternatives available for resolving financial problems.

Symptoms of Distress

Many struggling companies had misguided business strategies, misjudged their markets, relied too heavily on a given customer, allowed their technologies to become obsolete, suffered from embarrassing accounting irregularities, or simply grew too fast. Some purchased competitors nationwide, paying too much and acquiring targets too quickly, which did not allow time for integration of the companies and prevented post-acquisition operating efficiencies from being achieved. Otherwise healthy companies were forced to file for bankruptcy to contend with the devastating costs of product liability and class-action lawsuits. The cost of defending against legal attack can be very significant and can drastically dilute what would otherwise be healthy earnings.

Most business problems are caused by repeated financial, legal, operational and strategic mistakes, or miscalculations that went largely undetected by management over a long period of time. Some of the more obvious "symptoms," indicating that a company is heading down the wrong course, include:

- persistent operating losses
- the departure of several key employees
- the loss of more than 5 percent market share per quarter in two consecutive quarters

(Continued)

(Continued)

- recurring cash flow shortages
- a general loss of morale and enthusiasm among employees at all levels.

Distressed companies often share common traits: an inability to service debt, a decline in profits and margins, inefficiency in management structure or delivery of services. It is also often difficult to convince management of the actual steps necessary to cure the problem(s). In my experience, most entrepreneurs believe that "more is better" and that selling more or doing more can solve problems. More often, it can't.

Costs of Distress

A company's financial distress also affects its employees, customers, stockholders, creditors, and suppliers. For example, customers and vendors often attempt to avoid dealing with a troubled company, which is likely to further damage its financial performance and ability to raise capital. Vendors, to the extent that they are willing to sell to a distressed business at all, may demand unreasonable sales terms in order to protect their risk. Key employees, fearful for their jobs, may flee to a more stable competitor, taking their enthusiasm, ideas and expertise with them. And turnover makes it even more difficult to attract and retain skilled personnel whom the company may desperately need in order to stay alive.

Stockholders often dispose of an ailing company's securities, driving down the market price per share. Creditors will accelerate obligations so as to protect against the risk of default. During this difficult period, it is also likely that inventory is becoming obsolete, buildings and machinery are deteriorating and equipment is not being maintained because the company lacks the resources to commit to servicing or replacing worn parts. Finally, competitors are likely to become more aggressive, taking advantage of the window of opportunity created by your financial distress.

Remedies for Sore Spots

If your growing company is heading downhill toward disaster, try to take action in these "red flag" areas.

- *Strengthen the management team.* A company's risk of business failure is greatly increased when it depends on an overly centralized management team made up of the original founders. Long-term health lies in the founders' ability to recruit and retain qualified personnel who are capable of taking and guiding the business to its next phase of growth.
- *Keep up with technology.* Operating in a marketplace where rapidly changing technology could render your products and services suddenly obsolete greatly increases your chances of business failure. As a result, management must stay abreast of technological developments, attempt to establish product diversification and ensure adequate capitalization for ongoing research and modernization of equipment.

- *Diversify customers, suppliers, lenders and contracts.* Many rapid-growth companies rely on a single critical customer, source of supply or special relationship with a lender or investor. But if you want to grow your business even more, you can't be a hostage to any third party who cannot be completely controlled. What if the key customer is lost to a competitor? Worse yet, if the customer is aware of the company's dependence, how many demands will you have to grant out of a need to preserve the account? Similarly, excessive dependence on particular patents, licenses, concessions and related contractual advantages, which may expire or be terminated, significantly boosts your risk of business failure. You can mitigate the risk of dependence on a third party by diversifying product lines, geographic trading areas, targeted markets and distribution channels.

- *Rethink funding for specific projects.* You can't take advantage of market opportunities if you lack the capital necessary to complete the project. For example, manufacturing a new product is a waste of time and resources if no capital is available for bringing it to market. It might make more sense to sell or license the technology to another company, then use the proceeds or royalties to exploit an existing product or service.

- *Upgrade information and monitoring systems.* You need to be aware of competition, internal costs and budgets, changes in the economic and political environment, inventory controls, management problems and internal conflicts, cash flow and sales growth. If your company gets this information in an organized, timely and accessible fashion, it will be easier to make informed, day-to-day decisions or meaningful, long-term strategic plans.

- *Get rid of the deadwood.* In my experience, most fast-growth companies have some unproductive personnel, operating division or asset that's putting a strain on the overall profitability of the business—slowing down performance or bleeding precious cash. Especially dangerous are projects or people kept on for paternalistic or egotistical reasons. Also, obsolete or idle equipment, unused real estate and unnecessary employee benefits (like the company car, boat, condominium or plane) should all be candidates for elimination when cash is at a premium.

- *Clean up your accounts receivable.* Even with a tremendous increase in sales, you may have a management problem with receivables. Customers must be carefully monitored. Don't provide further goods or services when overdue accounts reach certain levels. As soon as a customer shows signs of difficulty in paying, obtain collateral to secure the obligation. Use collection agencies and attorneys for larger, problematic accounts. If cash flow becomes a real problem, consider discounting the accounts receivable at a commercial bank, obtaining the services of a factoring company or obtaining credit insurance to protect against excessive bad-debt losses.

Take these steps before your company shows the first sign of trouble. Then, if something happens that's beyond your control, you'll be better placed to keep the situation from getting worse and start remedial action to put it right.

SOURCE: Is Your Business in Trouble? By Andrew Sherman, Partner, Dickstein Shapiro Morin & Oshinsky LLP (June 25, 2001) http://eventuring.kauffman.org/eShip/appmanager/eVenturing/eVenturingDesktop?_nfpb=true&_pageLabel=eShip_articleDetail&_nfls=false&id=Entrepreneurship/Resource/Resource_307.htm&_fromSearch=true&_nfls=false Used with permission.

Research in Practice: Entrepreneurial Failures—A Research Overview

Statistical data have indicated a high mortality rate for newly founded and entrepreneurial firms. New firms fail at an alarming rate, and that failure is a norm, rather than exception (Dean, Turner, & Bamford, 1997). However, current entrepreneurship research has largely focused on successful ventures, and little is known about why ventures fail and how they fail.

What Do We Mean by Entrepreneurial Failures?

In studies of entrepreneurship and small business failure, researchers have mainly used four different definitions. The first one is *discontinuance criterion.* The discontinuance or exit includes every change in ownership and closure for any reasons, which is referred to as discontinuance of ownership (Baum & Mezias, 1992; Mitchell, 1994). However, not all closure is financially related, and a venture closure could be a deliberate process that reflects a voluntary proactive decision to exit by entrepreneurs as a part of a venture's intended exit strategy.

The second definition of entrepreneurial failure is the *bankruptcy criterion.* Business failures occur when a firm is deemed to be legally bankrupt or has ceased operation with resulting losses to creditors (Perry, 2001). This definition may exclude those businesses that do not declare bankruptcy, yet barely break even and provide no reasonable income for the owner or fair return to the investors. It also excludes businesses that ceased operation with substantial losses to owners but not to creditors.

The third definition is the *loss cutting criterion.* Failed firms are those that are disposed of with a loss to avoid further losses (Ulmer & Nelson, 1947). Not every venture that an entrepreneur would describe as failed necessarily ends in bankruptcy. A venture may be terminated to avoid or limit losses because deteriorating financial performance is anticipated. This closure is viewed as an intentional choice of discontinuing operation of a venture. However, many businesses that are still in operation may be regarded as failure, if they are not earning a rate of return that is commensurate with the firms' opportunity costs of capital.

The fourth definition of entrepreneurial failure is the *earning criterion.* A firm is viewed as failed if the firm is not earning an adequate return—a rate of return on invested capital that is significantly and continually below prevailing rates on similar investments (Altman, 1968; Cochran, 1981).

What Do We Know About the Factors Leading to a Venture's Failure?

Studies have examined entrepreneurial failure as a result of the following four groups of factors.

1. *Individual characteristics—the entrepreneurs.* Most researchers in the field have learned that the founder is the key to venture survival and failure. Studies have investigated the effects of the founder's education, working experience, industry-specific experience, and family (e.g., Bates, 1990a, 1990b). This stream of research is mostly built on human capital theory (Becker, 1975) and in general argues that when the founder is endowed with high human capital, the chances for entrepreneurial failure decrease. Deficiency in human capital makes new firms vulnerable. Presumably, the more specific the human capital to the nature of the business start-up, the lower the likelihood of entrepreneurial failure.

2. *Resources, strategies, and other organizational attributes—the firms.* First, firm age and liability of newness have an impact; organizational ecologists have elaborated on age-dependent organizational mortality, showing that young and new organizations have a higher risk of failure than older organizations (Singh, Tucker, & House, 1986). Second, the theory of firm size and liability of smallness suggests that dissolution rates decline

with greater size. The argument has been that a large pool of resources at the time of founding enables a new firm to weather the critical start-up period and also raise additional capital. Size may also lead to additional cost savings because of economies of scale or economies of scope. Third, founding strategies are classified as generalist (r-strategists) and specialist (k-strategists), and these are considered to be another factor related to venture failures (Hannan & Freeman, 1977). The generalists offer a wide array of products or services aiming at a broad range of customers, whereas the specialists focus on a niche market to avoid direct competition with large and more established firms. Because of the liability of newness and smallness, new ventures are limited in their capability to compete on the basis of price. Therefore, targeting a narrow market segment and serving customers through differentiated products or services would decrease the odds for entrepreneurial failure (Romanelli, 1989).

Another dimension of founding strategies is market aggressiveness, which is defined as "the depth and rapidity of resource-acquiring activities in either broad or narrow market domains" (Romanelli, 1989, p. 374). It is generally expected that aggressive firms will have a higher likelihood of surviving their early years than efficient firms (Romanelli, 1989). Fourth, management incompetence and inexperience still remain the major causes of business failure. As a consequence of those weaknesses, management fails to access or prepare information to assist in decision making, to change product designs, and to recognize shifts in consumer's preference.

Finally, a firm's failure has been attributed to poor economic performance—survival of the fittest. Penrose (1952) succinctly summarized the relationship between economic performance and survival in that "positive profits can be treated as the criterion of natural selection—the firms that make profits are selected or 'adopted' by the environment, others are rejected and disappear" (p. 810).

3. *Environmental conditions—the contexts.* In the strategy area, there has been a long-standing debate about the relative importance of environmental determinism and managerial choice as explanations of organizational survival and failure (e.g., Rumelt, 1991). Intuitively, attractive industries (i.e., growing industries) should make survival easier, and therefore, businesses in those areas should have low failure rates. Brittain and Freeman (1980) referred to these conditions as the excess carrying capacity of an environment. Researchers have related demand conditions of an industry to the odds of survivals. Romanelli's (1989) empirical study of 108 start-ups in the personal computer industry found that environmental conditions (demand and competition) and founding strategies (breadth and aggressiveness) jointly affect survival. In addition, competitive concentration—calculated in terms of such factors as percentage of sales, plant capacity, and whether distribution channels are controlled by the largest four or eight competitors—is related to a firm's ability to acquire or increase control of available resources in the industry. Thus, increasing competitive concentration should indicate increased difficulties for young and small firms in acquiring resources and subsequently lead to high failure rates.

4. *Events for failure—the processes.* In their study of the failure of large corporations, Hambrick and D'Aveni (1988) found that the process of failure was a protracted downward spiral. Research by Venkataraman, Van de Ven, Buckeye, and Hudson (1990) shifts the focus of failure research from the question of why to how— how the process of failure unfolds. In their case studies of 10 educational software start-ups, the authors found that new and small firms engage in transactions with others. Because of their liabilities of newness and smallness, entrepreneurs often use these transactions as collateral to attract valuable customers and resources. The leveraged strategy makes the set of transactions of the firm tightly coupled. When one transaction within the set fails, the set collapses, leading to the failure of the firm.

Challenges Facing Entrepreneurial Failure Research

Entrepreneurial failure research is currently confronted by theoretical and methodological challenges. From a theoretical standpoint, there seems to lack of a general consensus about what constitutes entrepreneurial failure. A variety of definitions leads to various measures and data collection methods, which lead to confounding conclusions. In addition, many studies of entrepreneurial failures have examined failure from a unique theoretical angle, such as strategy, organizational behavior, organizational ecology, economics, or finance. Scant attention has been given to the interplay between variables. An integrative model that links multiple theoretical frameworks is notably missing. Entrepreneurial failure is a complex and multidimensional phenomenon, and it is highly plausible that the impact of one variable (e.g., founding strategy) on entrepreneurial failure may depend on another variable (e.g., competitive conditions). Finally, whereas a significant amount of attention has been given to the question of why—the factors (i.e., the entrepreneur, the venture, and the context) that may contribute to entrepreneurial failure—a paucity of research has been devoted to process-based research that addresses the issue of how—the process by which failure unfolds. In this regard, case-based research method is particularly relevant.

From a methodological standpoint, it is difficult to locate ventures that failed because of poor performance. Homogenous samples are hard to come by. Also, entrepreneurs are reticent about failure. Those who do agree to participate find it difficult to identify the reasons for venture failure, especially when the failure took place in the past. Therefore, they may have a hard time understanding and articulating causations. In addition, as attribution theory suggests, entrepreneurs are more likely to attribute failure to external causes than to internal ones. Another major caveat related to the research design of many entrepreneurial failure studies is that they fail to take the temporal issue into consideration. Theoretically, there should be a time gap between predictors of venture failure and the actual failure, and data collection and modeling should reflect the time gap.

SOURCE: Jianwen Liao, associate professor of management, Department of Management and Marketing, Northeastern Illinois University. Used with permission.

Speaking of Strategy

Yomega and the Yo-Yo With a Brain

Joyce Amaral began her career at Parker Brothers, perhaps most famous for its Monopoly board game and now a subsidiary of Hasbro. Joyce didn't know it then, but working at Parker Brothers turned out to be the beginning of a major turning point in her career as a marketer.

While at Parker Brothers, she met a young man who had invented and patented an automatically returning yo-yo. The design incorporated a centrifugal clutch, which opens on the down swing, enabling long smooth spins. When the spin cycle slows, the yo-yo returns automatically, turning even a novice player into a pro!

Joyce introduced the young man to her brothers, and in 1984, Yomega Corporation and the Yo-Yo with a BRAIN were born. Sales rose exponentially in the late 1990s, with distribution in the United States, parts of Europe, Australia, Israel, and Japan. While still maintaining ownership in the business, Joyce retired from her position as vice president of marketing and sales in 1998 to pursue other goals. She discusses the key business skill that enables the entrepreneur to come back from failure:

"I would say failure was not an option for us. Sheer tenacity and a supreme belief in the worth of the product and business. But beyond that, I must say that my brother Len is gifted with extraordinary powers of problem solving. He recounted a story about how he solved the massive problem of the first manufacture of yo-yos. The whole design was faulty, but we didn't know it until we manufactured and paid for 10,000 pieces. The original axles were hammered into the plastic (they had a knurled end that was suppose to grab), and they would eventually fall apart.

"Remember, yo-yos are meant to withstand a fair amount of abuse; kids inadvertently hit the floor/cement in their quest to make the yo-yo sleep. In addition, the clear lens caps that were glued on the yo-halves were also falling off. What a mess! Anyway, my brother would talk to various people who might know how to solve the lens cap adherence problem, and someone mentioned a possible solution—sonic welding, which basically is process by which the vibration of the lens against the ridge of the yo half will create a fusion; the plastic melts where the sonic welder is placed.

"So, both brothers met with the manufacturer of these sonic welders, and we bought one that was customized to do the job. That problem was solved. By sheer luck, as my brothers were meeting with this company, another rep was making a sales call. He gave my brother a handful of varying sizes of this thing called a helicoil, with no thought as to how it might be used. But, Len's mind, which was hyperactively thinking of possible solutions to the problem of the axles falling out, started to think about how this helicoil (little brass nuts so to speak that could be insert molded into each half, creating something that the axles could now screw into), and with trial and experimentation, Lenny invented a much stronger design that was now "modular" and another marketing advantage.

I liken the whole process to having a baby. When something is wrong with your baby, you will go to the end of the Earth to find a solution. Len would eat, sleep, and breathe the problem until a solution was found. My brother likes to use the metaphor of the perfect storm. The three of us had unique skills and personality traits that together, took a concept and turned it into a wonderful success.

Review Questions

1. One of the most difficult periods for an entrepreneur is the transition from a business-starter to a business leader. This requires almost a fundamental shift in behavior that is critical to the success of the organization. What techniques or management practices can entrepreneurs adapt to help with this transition?

2. What entrepreneurial qualities did the owners of Yomega Corporation demonstrate that enabled them to overcome obstacles in their product development?

3. What if the Yo-Yo with a BRAIN product failed? What other opportunities or strengths might the owners have capitalized on? What type of future venture could they pursue, taking into account all the lessons learned?

Failures and Foibles

What-If, Inc., Versus Get-It-Right, Co.

What follows are two stories of fictional companies, showing the differences between a company environment that encourages exploration and risk-taking and one that is more concerned with getting it right.

What-If, Inc.

At What If, Inc., people can play with possibilities. They are experimenting with what can be, and they do not get bogged down by expectations and having to get things exactly right at the start. They are in a learning mode every day, applying what they know to see what they can create. Mistakes are considered options that did not work the way expected. But everyone is well aware of the 3M glue that did not work as expected and became the famous "post-it" note glue. The world is their oyster, and they are not sure what will come out of their experiments, but that is OK because every experiment leads to more learning and more inquiry. What-if, Inc. employees believe in exploration and know that experimentation gives them permission and space to try new things and have a "let's see" mentality. They know in what direction they are headed and have freedom to sail the best course to get there.

Get-It-Right, Co.

Down the road at Get-It-Right, Co., there are experts working to get it right. They know everything about their jobs, and they are considered gurus. They have the answers, and they have a reputation to protect. At Get-It-Right, people know there are two approaches to everything: right and wrong. If they get it wrong, there are dire consequences. They feel the "tyranny of the OR"[4]—having to choose between two things you are not sure of and making one right. Everything is yes or no/black or white—no room for gray or play here. Mistakes are wrong and bad; hopefully buried not to be found. Thus, mistakes are never discussed or used as the valuable learning that they are. At Get-It-Right, Co., people are stressed out. In fact, during the Y2K conversion, a department head was heard saying to the project team leader, "If you mess this conversion up, it's your job." The threat affected the entire department's activities, and many decided to leave Get-It-Right, Co. Having to get it right the first time has them afraid to take any risks, thus censoring all kinds of possibilities right out of the running. They are given directions and are expected to execute flawlessly.

SOURCE: L. Gundry and L. LaMantia, *Breakthrough Teams for Breakneck Times: Unlocking the Genius of Creative Collaboration* (New York: Dearborn Books, 2001).

Strategic Reflection Point

Look Who Failed

What 7-year-old future entrepreneur blew the wallpaper off his parents' kitchen wall with his first prototype?

One day in 1884, seven-year-old Joshua Lionel Cowen attached a small steam engine to a wooden locomotive he had carved. Moments later, the precocious youngster watched in amazement as the world's first Lionel train exploded, taking most of the kitchen wallpaper with it and earning the boy a good paddling from his father, a New York City businessman. The locomotive incident was one of the several ill-fated experiments conducted by Joshua Cowen (born Cohen), a small dark-haired boy who was fascinated with mechanical devices of all kinds.

Another of young Cowen's inventions, "the electric flowerpot," resulted in an even more ironic twist. The gadget consisted of a thin tube with a battery fitted into one end and a small light bulb in the other. When attached to a flowerpot, the tube illuminated the plant inside. Cowen sold the rights to his invention to a restaurateur named Conrad Hubert, who tried marketing it as a decorative object. After failing to generate much interest in the unusual flowerpot, Hubert decided to detach the tubes and sell them on their own illuminatory merit. Calling his revised product the Eveready Flashlight, he became a millionaire.

Joshua Cowen's early mechanical genius was what got his famous model train business started. But it was his talent for marketing in his middle years that built the Lionel name into a national institution.

After serving in the confederate army, what unsuccessful Atlanta pharmacist created something "refreshing and delicious"?

John Pemberton served as a major in the confederate army during the Civil War. After the war, he settled in Atlanta and began a pharmacy. Though he was qualified, Pemberton experimented too much to be a successful pharmacist.

Pemberton began concentrating on developing a soft drink. After much trial and error, he created a syrup (which would serve as the drink's primary flavor) on May 8, 1886. The syrup was added to carbonated water to form the drink, which was christened "Coca-Cola" by Pemberton's partner.

In 1886, thirteen drinks a day were being sold in the Atlanta drug stores. A century later, production would reach a billion gallons a year. Pemberton, however, sold all rights to the formula in 1888 for $2,300.00. He died shortly after.

Coca-Cola was bottled by another young entrepreneur in 1894. John Biedenharn was the son of a candy merchant, who sold Coca-Cola syrup to drug stores for use at their soda fountains, along with bottled carbonated water. John combined the two and began the Coca-Cola dynasty as we know it today.

What highly successful entrepreneur poured $200 million into an unsuccessful attempt to thwart the fax machine?

The story of Federal Express is well known. Conceived by Fred Smith for a term paper at Harvard, the idea survived a war before being implemented in 1973. By advancing the seemingly outrageous notion of overnight delivery, Smith redesigned the way and the time frame in which American businesses sent packages. However, Smith did not live happily ever after.

With the package delivery business in his pocket, Smith attempted to thwart the fax machine with his version of "same day mail." Zap Mail cost Smith's company almost $200 million before it was ultimately abandoned.

What female entrepreneur made a splash after deserting an unsuccessful restaurant-hotel venture?

(Continued)

(Continued)

From traveling around the world, Anita Roddick got the idea for a lucrative business project. During her lengthy vacation, she learned how women in other societies cleansed and moisturized their skin and hair, and thought that products made from their natural recipes might also have considerable appeal in her native England.

However, Roddick did not pursue the idea immediately. She and her husband Gordon first bought an old Victorian house and converted it into a hotel, and subsequently bought a restaurant. They worked extremely hard, but didn't seem to be getting anywhere. It was only then that Anita told her husband about her natural products idea, and he agreed that she should give it a try. They sold the restaurant and put a friend in charge of the hotel. Anita got a modest loan from the bank and found a small shop in Brighton, England.

"The Body Shop," says Anita, "fosters a spirit of experimentation and a creative climate in which we produce new products out of old ingredients. We are not afraid to reach into the past, or look at the practices of other cultures, in order to improve what we have here and now—and in the future. The past is our prologue."

What fashion entrepreneur survived a failed singing career?

Gabrielle Chanel, orphaned at an early age, was raised by nuns. Gabrielle wanted to be a singer. She debuted in a concert cafe. Each of the two songs Gabrielle sang contained the word Coco. The name, which was given to her by the audience, stuck for more than eighty years. Her singing career, however, did not. Coco's voice was limited and work did not come easily. After her short attempt at a singing career, Coco Chanel quit performing to begin work as a hat maker.

Coco Chanel went from designing hats to designing daring new fashions for the women of the 1920s. Her rebellious styles liberated women from the past and became the symbol of modernity.

In 1921, Chanel introduced her first fragrance, Chanel No. 5. She continued to lead the fashion world until her death in 1971.

SOURCE: "Entrepreneurship Failure Quiz," Ball State University, http://www.bsu.edu/web/entrepreneurship/pages/failure.htm Reprinted with permission.

Learning From Failure

Those who never made a mistake never tried anything new.

—Albert Einstein

Many successful entrepreneurs have failed in initial attempts at building and growing a business. The key is to take the lessons learned from failure and apply these to the next endeavor. Through each phase of business development, failure is always a possibility. Even as entrepreneurs plan and develop their business strategically, there is always an element of risk. If there were no risks, there might be no entrepreneurs. Risk is the element that makes starting a business exciting and challenging. As entrepreneurs, it is important to embrace the risk, fears, and doubts and know that by taking the initial leap of faith, you have come very far. Failing is acceptable; not learning from failure is not acceptable. All great entrepreneurs have failed at something, but what makes them great is their ability to stick to their vision and adapt to a changing environment. As entrepreneurs, it is important that you plan for failure and build measures into your business plan that will enable you to monitor your success. However, sometimes, the best innovations come out of defeat. The only true failures are the ones that don't get up and try again. Entrepreneurship is a journey of learning, practice, evaluation, and resilience.

Summary of Chapter Objectives

1. Understand the other side of success: Rapid growth
   - Entrepreneurs who have experienced failure, the downside of rapid growth, have learned at least three important lessons and areas that need improvement including:
   - Capital management
   - Market monitoring
   - Innovation

2. Learn some of the solutions for problems during rapid growth
   - These include the structural and human areas that entrepreneurs need to monitor and consciously shape to prepare the enterprise to capitalize on any initial successes, including the areas of:
   - Minding the vision
   - Communicating information
   - Building relationships
   - Managing and monitoring politics
   - Setting direction

3. Know the warning signs of failure and what key areas of the business can be monitored, such as:
   - Resource management
   - Employee development
   - Customer relationship management
   - Monitoring goals as well as additional red flags and symptoms

4. Learn what the remedies and solutions are for your entrepreneurial venture that can be implemented to avoid failure
   - Some of these remedies include strengthening the management team; keeping up with technology; diversifying customers, suppliers, lenders, and contracts; rethinking funding for specific projects; and upgrading information and monitoring systems.

5. Gain a final perspective on failure from hearing about the latest research and comments from entrepreneurs who have failed but later succeeded

CASE 11.1   Ken and Michael Xie, Fortinet, Inc.

While viruses and spyware can mean disaster for the common computer user, they can signify unlimited profits and potential for tech companies that have made network security their specialty, like Sunnyvale, California-based, Fortinet, Inc. Fortinet's innovative products, such as the FortiGate series of ASIC-accelerated anti-virus firewalls, have won the company awards and have secured Fortinet's place on the Hot 100 list.

But profits and accolades don't come without hard work and risk. Brothers Ken and Michael Xie, 42 and 36, respectively, founded Fortinet in 2000 knowing the key to success in their competitive market was having superior products. Devoting two years to R&D, their goal was to produce a technology that would be effective in both securing network content and allowing consumers to use the Internet safely and without delays. Once they launched their initial FortiGate products in May 2002, they concentrated on building channel networks, securing financing and expanding product lines. Fortinet has grown rapidly, due in part to the $93 million in venture capital it's received along the way. With 2005 projected sales of $100 million, the company has become a global village of 550 employees with offices in Asia, Canada and Europe as well as the United States. And while fast growth has its challenges, such as staffing adequately to keep up with demand and constantly advancing their technology, the Xies

haven't skipped a beat. The strength of the team has proved invaluable, as has Ken's previous experience as founder and CEO of NetScreen, which internet infrastructure solutions provider Juniper Networks bought for $4 billion in 2004. What contributed to Fortinet's success? "Hiring a strong group of talented employees who brought and applied direct industry experience and relationships," says Ken.

Fortinet has made itself right at home in the fast lane. A 2003 IDC study found that Fortinet held 29.5 percent of the unified threat management security market and was growing strong. And Ken says going public is in the company's future. Meanwhile, the brothers remain focused on innovation in the areas of web content filtering, spyware and anti-spam technology. Says Ken, "Going forward, the internet is changing so fast that we have to stay very close to the customer and all the new technology."

SOURCE: From Wilson, S., "Fortinet, Inc.," in *Entrepreneur*, June 2005. Reprinted with permission of Entrepreneur Magazine.

Discussion Questions

1. What steps did Ken and Michael Xie take to reduce the risk of failure?

2. How did Fortinet, Inc., manage their rapid growth?

CASE 11.2   The Bay House Cafe: Against All Odds

Dudley-Anne Thomson is the current manager of the Bay House Cafe, located 10 kilometers from Westport, South Island, New Zealand. She rents the space from Brian Finlayson and Michael

Varekam, who both started the Bay House Cafe eight years ago and then moved on to open restaurants in Sydney, Australia. All three entrepreneurs were interviewed in this article.

New England Journal of Entrepreneurship (NEJE): Brian, the Bay House is located five hours driving time from Christchurch, the only major city on the South Island. The west coast of the South Island has a grand total of only 35,000 residents from Karamea in the north to Te Ann in the south. Many of the hundreds of kilometers of coastline are desolate. How did you pick this location?

Brian: I'm from the area originally, and I always thought the town of Westport, even with just 6,000 residents, could use an upscale cafe. We get an awful lot of tourists coming through from October through March when it's our summer, and I counted on that business as well. We typically closed the restaurant from April to September because we needed a chance to rest from a hectic summer season and to review our menu, promotional efforts, and past business strategies to plan on what we wanted to change.

The veranda we are sitting on and the inside dining area were added on to my batch (beach home) when Michael and I decided to start the cafe. I bought the batch 25 but decided only fairly recently to open up an upscale restaurant. It seemed like we could make a go of it.

Michael: The location, while away from the town, is spectacular. We are right across from a surfing beach, and the sunsets are a great selling point. Across the bay, we have a view of the Seal Colony where tourists by the hundreds walk every day to see the fur seals and their pups lying on the rocks. Can you think of a more beautiful place to eat a gourmet meal while looking out at the Tasman Sea?

NEJE: However, you have to admit, it must have been tough to attract enough business at first to make a go of it.

Brian: Actually, the tough part was working with the local town council to give us the necessary permits to open the cafe. It took six months to convince them to give us the go-ahead.

Michael: Everyone in town knew Brian, but they didn't know me. Outsiders, people who have not grown up in this area, are considered with great suspicion until the local townspeople feel they can trust you. If you're local, the council will bend the rules and even change the laws to help you out. However, I didn't have that advantage and the council, at first, interpreted the local ordinances in ways that were meant to stymie us.

Brian: The legal part took half a year of wrangling, but it took only three months to convert the front part of the batch into a restaurant and then add the deck. Once the Department of Conservation, which owned the land around the restaurant, gave us the final approval to proceed, we moved rapidly to start the cafe.

NEJE: It's one thing to get all the local town council approvals and convert the batch into a cafe, quite another to generate a positive cash flow.

Brian: That's true, but enough locals knew me from when I managed a restaurant in Westport called "Mandala's" to follow us out here. I also spent two years managing a bar/cafe in town called "Diego's." Originally, I had apprenticed as a pastry chef, then moved on to main courses, then eventually to managing the whole operation. I was ready to open up the "Bay House," and there was a built-in following.

Michael: In fact, there were so many people who wanted to come to the cafe, we were booked solid for three months and even had to turn people away.

NEJE: It sounds like you started making money right away.

Michael: Actually, everything cost us so much more than we had anticipated that we worked like dogs just to pay off the $40,000 (New Zealand) we needed to borrow to construct the dining area. The second year of business we broke even and had all our debts paid off.

Our location has superb views, but the downside was we were on a dirt road with no electricity and no local water, at least not enough to operate a cafe. We faced a lot of up-front expenses before we even served our first meal.

Brian: We probably would have achieved break-even sooner, but we underpriced ourselves in the marketplace. We weren't charging enough for our lunches and dinners. Breakfast seemed okay, but we were not making sufficient margin on the other meals. We had put together a business plan, this is something I learned how to do because I worked for a U.S. firm as a product manager for several years; but we made some costly errors in the beginning.

NEJE: How long did you own and manage the cafe?

Michael: Five years, and we became enormously successful at it. However, I'm from Sydney and I missed the city. I convinced Brian to lease out the restaurant, keep the batch, and move to Sydney. Brian agreed, and we opened up the "Chocolate Dog Cafe" in the Rocks Section of the city.

NEJE: After struggling to establish the Bay House Cafe, you left it to start another venture? Why not just ride your first success and coast for awhile?

Brian: We wanted to challenge ourselves and see if we could establish a successful restaurant in a large, cosmopolitan city like Sydney. "The Chocolate Dog" was open seven days a week. The cafe was well accepted by the locals as well as tourists, and we did extraordinarily well. I really like to create spaces where I can entertain people and see them enjoying themselves. The experience was very fulfilling. I loved it.

NEJE: And that's where Dudley-Anne comes in. You sold the business to her.

Michael: Hmmm . . . not exactly. I only wish we had.

Brian: What happened was we sold the cafe to an Australian entrepreneur who made all sorts of noises about all this experience he had and what he could do for the restaurant to expand it and to make it even more profitable. Turns out, he ran up debt all around Westport, never paid it off, and pretty much was an absentee owner from the get-go.

Michael: We knew we had a serious problem within 60 days of handing over the cafe to this guy. Our friends in town called and told us the food quality and service were going down rapidly. The fellow didn't seem to care about the cafe's image, nor return phone calls about when he was going to pay for the merchandise and services he had purchased.

Dudley-Anne: Now that's where I come into the picture. Mark, who at the time three years ago was my boyfriend and business partner, and I were looking to move to the Westport area. Mark, and I'd rather not provide his last name, grew up here and has close family ties around Westport. Neither of us knew much about the Bay House Cafe. I had grown up in Hastings on the North Island of New Zealand and hadn't traveled much in the South Island. I did have restaurant experience, and that's to the good; but Mark and I did not have a good enough credit rating to borrow the money to buy the Bay House. That's where our financial "angel" came in.

While in the North Island, Mark and I met an American fellow who so took to us that he promised to put up money for a business we might want to buy some day. Well, when we found out the Bay House was up for sale, we called him and told him we were ready to call him on his offer to back us. He was surprised at first that we were ready to take him up on his promise; but he followed through just as he said he would, and we bought the business.

Brian: We tried to talk Mark out of buying it, though, because we were ready to throw out the

Aussie chap since he wasn't paying the monthly rent to us. We never got a penny from that guy after he purchased the cafe. Nothing in three months. But Mark wouldn't listen to us and insisted on buying the business outright from the owner who charged him twice what he had paid us. What a waste of money.

Dudley-Anne: I didn't know anyone in town except Mark and his family; they lived around the Westport area so I just followed his lead. That proved to be unfortunate. At the beginning, Mark was the chef and I took care of the front operation. It took me two years just to get to know the local market enough to where I was sufficiently confident to start making changes.

But talk about surprises. We went into the cafe expecting to use the kitchen equipment only to find out that some new equipment included in the sale didn't belong to the seller. They were never paid off, and some people showed up ready to cart them away. It was a tough start.

NEJE: What changes did you make?

Dudley-Anne: For one, getting rid of the tour buses that would stop off, discharge dozens of passengers who would monopolize the cafe, order a soda and perhaps a scone, stay for an hour or two to fill out their postcards, and then move on. The buses were a nuisance, the margins on soda and scones low; and this discouraged local trade from coming out here.

We are not a tea cafe. We serve gourmet meals at competitive prices, but this means attracting a market that wants excellent food and service and a fairly quiet environment. The buses were ruining that.

Everyone in Westport thought I was crazy; but I had a long-term vision of the business and where I wanted to take it, and the tour buses did not fit into that vision. Mark and I tried to stay open during the winter months here, but after two years we gave up. We were serving too few meals and lost a lot of money because we

couldn't meet the overhead. Now, we close from May to August to replenish our energies, conduct needed maintenance, and get ready for the busy summer seasons.

NEJE: Did you also put together a business plan like Brian and Michael did?

Dudley-Anne: Yes, we did; but it was more to please our financial backer than to guide our everyday activities. Recently, though, we put together a new business plan because it was required by the government as part of our application to win one of the national "Tourism Awards" given out by the New Zealand Tourism Commission. Mark thought the effort wasn't worth it; but I was more sensitive to the marketing value of the award, and so I decided to go after it. We hired a consultant from Christchurch, and he guided us through the planning process.

To our great surprise, considering the commission representatives came to see the cafe during the winter months when we weren't serving meals, we won "Best Cafe" for our size for the west coast of the South Island out of 32 entrants. This award, and the other tourism awards we've won since, has given us much greater visibility than we ever had before. We are now attracting an international clientele.

NEJE: That must have convinced Mark you were right to invest the time and money to apply for the awards.

Dudley-Anne: No, Mark and I ended our personal relationship 18 months ago because we just didn't share the same vision for the cafe and for our personal lives. We continued to run the business for the next year together, but it became really hard. Mark didn't like sharing the kitchen operation with anyone else; but as we got busier and busier, he couldn't manage it all. We needed other chefs in the kitchen to handle the volume, but he kept worrying about spending more money on additional staff.

Mark saw his job as a "9-to-5" operation, and you can't do that when running a restaurant. It's flat-out 7 days a week, an 18-hours-a-day job. You can't avoid it if you want to be successful. He only wanted to cook at certain times of the day, and that really limited our menu.

Mark left the business for good about four months ago, and I must say, I couldn't have been more relieved. I am happier now than I've ever been; the business is completely mine to run, and I don't have to check in with him any more. No more hassles and fights about how the restaurant should operate. I love it!

The cafe now has more of a "lady's touch" to it and the restaurant is much more tidy and attractive than it used to be. I really look after the "front of the house," so to speak, and rearrange the lounge every other week to keep things looking new and different to our regular customers. They seem to appreciate that.

I've also increased the number of meals we can serve on any given night by making sure the tables turn at least twice; there's a 6 to 6:30 PM sitting and another one at 8:30 PM. If guests continue to linger at their tables past 8:30, we ask them to take their dessert and coffee to the lounge. That way we keep things moving. We just had the best Saturday night we've ever had this past weekend. The velocity of our business has picked up considerably.

NEJE: What market research have you conducted? Have you advertised regularly?

Dudley-Anne: We did conduct a survey of local motels about who their clientele was and we asked our diners how they had heard about us. We thought we should provide incentives to the moteliers to send their guests to us, but after a bit, we realized that the motels in the area were getting calls from customers who first made dinner reservations with us, then called around for a place to stay.

We did not advertise the first two years we were in business; we were depending on word-of-mouth. Now we advertise in local publications, and we're part of the "pure New Zealand" website. We also have our own website (dine@bayhousecafe.co.nz).

NEJE: Do you have trouble keeping staff?

Dudley-Anne: Not at all. We're all pretty close. Communication is key, and I ask my staff on a regular basis to "yarn it out"—to tell me what is bothering them, what concerns they have, and what suggestions they have to increase business. Listening is a skill that every small business owner should have.

NEJE: How long do you want to continue managing the Bay House?

Dudley-Anne: I've built it up through a ton of hard work, and now it's my baby. It's me. If I leave, what will happen to the Bay House and to my customers? As we've gotten more successful, I've left more and more of the day-to-day operations in the hands of the staff. That gives me more freedom to relax and not feel as much anxiety and tension as I used to. I can travel a bit more during the summer season and that's nice, too.

NEJE: What keeps you fellows in the restaurant business in Sydney?

Brian: Well, actually right now we're taking a breather. We've sold the "Chocolate Dog Cafe," and we're thinking about what to do next. For me, though, being in my own business means I don't have a boss looking over me. I like to take on the challenge of creating a new business from scratch and seeing if I can make a lot of folks happy by entertaining them and serving good food at the right price.

Michael: For me, I like seeing customers enjoy what I've been able to create. I love receiving compliments on what we've designed either from an original concept or from taking an existing business and moving it from "point A" to "point B." The fun is in the process. Once we achieve our goals, I'm ready to move on. I look forward to the next project and the next success. That's what keeps me motivated.

SOURCE: From Weinstein, L., "The Bay House Café: Against All Odds," in *New England Journal of Entrepreneurship* 6(2) Fall 2003: 15–18. Reprinted with permission.

Discussion Questions

1. What entrepreneurial characteristics do Michael and Brian possess? How about Dudley-Anne?

2. How could having a business plan at an earlier stage of the café have helped Michael and Brian avoid some of the challenges they faced?

3. How did the entrepreneurs learn from failure? Do you think the mistakes they made influenced the strategies they incorporated into the business?

4. In what ways does Dudley-Anne maintain an entrepreneurial edge with her growing business? What lessons could other entrepreneurs take from this company's story of founding, growth, and reinvention?

Notes

1. Adapted from Charlene Nicholls-Nixon, "Rapid Growth and High Performance: The Entrepreneur's 'Impossible Dream?'," *Academy of Management Executives* 19, no. 1(2005): 77–89.

2. Adapted from Charlene Nicholls-Nixon, "Rapid Growth and High Performance: The Entrepreneur's 'Impossible Dream?'," *Academy of Management Executives* 19, no. 1(2005): 77–89.

3. Adapted from Bette Price, "Fatal Flaws—Strategic Solutions," *Financial Services Advisor* 145, no. 1(January/February 2002): 14–16.

4. Concept described in J. C. Collins and J. I. Porras, *Built to Last: Successful Habits of Visionary Companies* (New York: Harperbusiness, 1997).

References

Altman, E. I. (1968). Financial ratios, discriminant analysis, and the prediction of corporate bankruptcy. *Journal of Finance, 4*, 589–609.

Bates, T. (1990a). Entrepreneurial human capital inputs and small business longevity. *Review of Economics and Statistics, 72*, 551–559.

Bates, T. (1990b). *Self-employment trends among Mexican Americans* (Discussion Paper No. 90–9, Center for Economic Studies). Washington, DC: U.S. Bureau of the Census.

Baum, J. A. C., & Mezias, S. J. (1992). Localized competition and organizational failure in the Manhattan hotel industry. *Administrative Science Quarterly, 37*, 580–604.

Becker, G. (1975). *Human capital* (2nd ed.). Chicago: University of Chicago Press.

Brittain, J. W., & Freeman, J. H. (1980). Organizational proliferation and density dependent selection. In J. R. Kimberly & R. H. Miles (Eds.), *The organizational life cycle* (pp. 291–338). San Francisco: Jossey-Bass.

Cochran, A. B. (1981). Small business mortality rates: A review of the literature. *Journal of Small Business Management, 19*(4), 50–59.

Dean, T., Turner, C. A., & Bamford, C. E. (1997). Impediments to imitation and rate of new firm failure. *Academy of Management Proceedings*, pp. 103–107.

Hambrick, D. C., & D'Aveni, R. A. (1988, March). Large corporate failures as downward spirals. *Administrative Science Quarterly, 33*(1), 1–23.

Hannan, M., & Freeman, J. (1977). The population ecology of organizations. *American Journal of Sociology, 82*, 929–964.

Mitchell, W. (1994). The dynamics of evolving markets: The effects of business sales and age on dissolutions and divestitures. *Administrative Science Quarterly, 39*, 575–602.

Penrose, E. (1952). Biological analogies in the theory of the firm. *American Economic Review, 42*, 804–819.

Perry, S. C. (2001). A comparison of failed and non-failed small businesses in the United States: Do men and women use different planning and decision making strategies. *Journal of Developmental Entrepreneurship, 7*(4), 415–428.

Romanelli, E. (1989). Environments and strategies of organization start-up: Effects of early survivals. *Administrative Science Quarterly, 34*, 369–387.

Rumelt, R. (1991). How much does industry matter? *Strategic Management Journal, 12*, 167–185.

Singh, J. V., Tucker, D. J., & House, R. (1986). Organizational legitimacy and the liability of newness. *Administrative Science Quarterly, 31*, 171–193.

Ulmer, K. J., & Nelson, A. (1947). Business turnover and causes of failure. *Survey of Current Business Research, 27*(4) (April) pp. 10–16.

Venkataraman, N., Van de Ven, A. H., Buckeye, J., & Hudson, R. (1990). Start-up in a turbulent environment: A process model of failure among firms with high customer dependence. *Journal of Business Venturing, 5*, 277–295.

Index

Page numbers in *italic* type refer to figures or tables.

F. H. Clothing Co., 39
Financial projections, for potential
    investors, 200
Financing, 172–230
    debt, 174–186
    due diligence checklist, 194
    equity, 174–176, 186–198
    estimating expenses, 90–96
    Failures and Foibles, 184
    failure to get, 199–200
    feasibility analysis
        concerning, 74–75
    sources, 180–183
    stages during business life cycle,
        177–178
Financing lease, 182
Finlayson, Brian, 380–384
Firing, 236, 371
First-mover advantage, 199
Flaherty, Therese, 184
Ford, Henry, II, 41–42
Ford Motor Company, 41–42, 142, 330
Fortinet, 380
Fox, Gretchen, 279–289
FOX Relocation Management, 279–289
Franchising, 336–339
    benefits of, 337
    Canada, 336–337
    case study, 351–353
    development of, 337–338
    early history, 336
    elements, 336
    legal issues, 337
    readiness, 338–339
    types, 337
    United States, 336
Francorp, 338
Franklin, Neil, 305
Freitas, Pushpika, 8–9
Friends
    financing from, 180
    ideas for new ventures from, 39

Gadia, Madhu, 127–128
Gates, Bill, 142
General Motors, 330
General partnerships, 248–249

Ghost Wings (magazine), 204–206
Global Positioning Systems (GPS), 44
Gohrs, Joe, 204
Going public with business, 343–345
Goldman Sachs, 172
Gomes-Casseres, Benjamin, 268
Goodnight, James, 97
Google, 107–108
Go-to-Market (GTM) strategy,
    141–146, *142–143*
Government-guaranteed loans, 183
Grant, James, 9
Grassroots Landscaping, 80–84
Grills, cooking, 44
Growth
    exit strategies, 339–346
    franchising, 336–339
    innovation, 294–324
    mergers and acquisitions,
        329–336
    rapid, 363–366
    valuation of business, 348–349
Gundry, Lisa, 14, 269
Gupta, Anand, 123
Gupta, Navita, 123

Haldiram, 118–126, 128
Halonen, Tarja, 300
Hamel, Gary, 273
Harbison, John R., 269
Harris Corporation, 116
Hart, Deborah Smith, 351
Hastings, Reed, 310, 312
Hedrick, Scott, 351
Heinz, 343
Hinson, Matthew, 55–57
Hiring, 236–237
Hispanics, 6
Hobbies, ideas for new
    ventures from, 38
Home Depot, 343
Hostile environments,
    market pioneering in, 141
Hubert, Conrad, 376–377
Hull House Settlement, Chicago, 9
Human resources, mergers and
    involvement of, 331, 333, 334

About the Authors

Lisa K. Gundry is Professor of Management in the Charles H. Kellstadt Graduate School of Business at DePaul University, where she teaches courses in Creativity in Business and Entrepreneurship Strategy. She is Director of the Leo V. Ryan Center for Creativity and Innovation at DePaul. The Ryan Center offers programs on creative discovery and business innovation to the academic, business, and nonprofit communities. The Ryan Center's Idea Clinic program was recognized by *Fortune Small Business* magazine as being one of the Top 10 innovative programs for business owners. She has also received the Innovation in Business Education Award by the AACSB's Mid-Continent East Association, and the DePaul University Excellence in Teaching Award.

Dr. Gundry has coauthored books, including *Breakthrough Teams for Breakneck Times: Unlocking the Genius of Creative Collaboration* (2001, with L. LaMantia), *Blueprints for Innovation* (1995, with C. W. Prather), and *Field Casework: Methods for Consulting to Small and Start-up Businesses* (Sage, 1996, with A. Buchko). She has published more than 40 articles and book chapters, some of which have appeared in *Journal of Business Venturing, Journal of Management, Journal of Business Ethics, Human Relations, Journal of Small Business Management, Journal of Enterprising Culture, Journal of Developmental Entrepreneurship*, and *Organizational Dynamics*. She conducts research on issues related to innovation in organizations, entrepreneurial growth strategies, and creativity in business. Her work has been featured in media such as *The Wall Street Journal, Newsweek, Business Week, Chicago Tribune, Crain's Chicago Business, NBC News*, and *ABC News*. She received her Ph.D. from Northwestern University.

Jill R. Kickul is the Richard A. Forsythe Endowed Chair in Entrepreneurship in the Thomas C. Page Center for Entrepreneurship at Miami University (Ohio) and Professor in the Management Department in the Richard T. Farmer School of Business. Prior to joining the faculty of Miami University, she was the Elizabeth J. McCandless Professor in Entrepreneurship at the Simmons School of Management. She has taught courses on Entrepreneurship Strategy, Entrepreneurship and New Venture Management, Management of Fast-Growing Firms, Strategic Analysis for Competing Globally, and Management Strategy. She has also taught entrepreneurship internationally for the Helsinki School of Economics and for the International

Bank of Asia (Hong Kong MBA Program), and she has delivered research seminars at the Stockholm School of Economics and the Jönköping International Business School.

Dr. Kickul's research interests include entrepreneurial intentions and behavior, strategic and innovation processes in start-up ventures, and, most recently, women in entrepreneurship. She was awarded the Cason Hall & Company Publishers Best Paper Award as well as the Coleman Foundation Best Empirical Paper and the John Jack Award for Entrepreneurship Education. She has many publications in entrepreneurship and management journals, including *Journal of Management, Journal of Small Business Management, Journal of Organizational Behavior, Frontiers of Entrepreneurship Research, International Journal of Entrepreneurship and Innovation, International Journal of Entrepreneurial Behavior and Research,* and *Academy of Management Learning and Education Journal.* Her work on entrepreneurship education development and curriculum design of the Simmons Post-MBA Certificate in Entrepreneurship has been nationally recognized and supported through the Coleman Foundation Entrepreneurship Excellence in Teaching Colleges Grant and has been named by *Fortune Small Business* as one of the Top 10 Innovative Programs in Entrepreneurship Education. She received her Ph.D. from Northern Illinois University.